An Anthology of Russian Literature

in the Soviet Period

from Gorki to Pasternak

BERNARD GUILBERT GUERNEY was born at the turn of the century in Nicolaiev, a naval town in the south of Russia. He came to the U.S.A. in 1905; and sold his first short story in 1917. In 1920, with the publication of Merejkowski's *Menace of the Mob,* he became a translator. Among his many translations (overwhelmingly from the Russian) are the *Christ and Antichrist* trilogy of Merejkowski, consisting of *Julian the Apostate, The Romance of Leonardo da Vinci* and *Peter and Alexei; The Gentleman from San Francisco and Other Stories* and *Elaghin Affair and Other Stories,* both by Bunin; Gogol's *Dead Souls* (a translation described by Vladimir Nabokov as "an extraordinarily fine piece of work"); Gorki's *Bystander;* Kuprin's *Yama* and "The Poems of Doctor Zhivago" (contained in *Doctor Zhivago,* by Pasternak). In addition to the present work (which is part of a projected four-part anthology) he has edited and translated *A Treasury of Russian Literature, The Portable Russian Reader* and *New Russian Stories.*

Mr. Guerney is also a bookseller, having founded, in 1922, the Blue Faun Bookshop, which he is still conducting in Greenwich Village.

An Anthology of
RUSSIAN LITERATURE
in the Soviet Period
from Gorki to Pasternak

edited and translated by

BERNARD   GUILBERT   GUERNEY

RANDOM HOUSE · NEW YORK

Random House IS THE PUBLISHER OF *The Modern Library*

BENNETT CERF · DONALD S. KLOPFER

Manufactured in the United States of America by H. Wolff

The Exhilarating Labors
Involved in This
Anthology
Are Dedicated with Love
by the
Anthologist
to

ELIZABETH GUERNEY

His
Severest Friend
and
Gentlest Critic

CONTENTS

FOREWORD

Literature must become Party literature. Down with non-Party literati, down with literary supermen!

N. LENIN

am afraid there will be no authentic literature among us until we cease to regard the Russian demos as a babe whose innocency must be safeguarded. I am afraid there will be no authentic literature among us until we cure ourselves of a certain new Catholicism which, even as the old, is apprehensive of every heretical work. But if this disease is incurable, I am afraid that Russian literature has but one future— its past.

E. ZAMIATIN

If we should eliminate Pilnyak, the Serapion Brethren, Mayakovsky and Yessenin, what will remain of a future proletarian literature except a few defaulted promissory notes?

L. TROTSKY

Because the literature this anthology deals with is still regarded as controversial I have striven to be as objective as possible; I have also tried to make the work representative, even to the extent of including a full-length novel, one of the glories of Soviet letters, despite its still being under interdict in its author's native land. Drama, however, had to be omitted, with regret, for a number of reasons, all of them cogent.

Poetry is represented—yet, admittedly, none of it is at all recent. This is due not to any political or ideological prejudice on my part but solely to the fact that Mayakovsky's complaint, "there just aren't any poets around," which may have been merely whimsical in 1924, is lamentably true today. Two of the many texts I have had to slog through in preparing this collection are *An Anthology of Russian Soviet Poesy, 1917-1957* and *Day of Poesy*, both issued in Moscow and dated 1957. If one omits the giants and genuine lyricists of the early days, and duplications and translations, one finds in these volumes 426 Workers of the Lyre, every last one branded on his or her rump with the seal of Soviet *kosheruth*, and 1343 selections, all bearing the Soviet imprimatur. An example or two, taken utterly at random, will, I think, convince the reader that in this instance I have been merciful to him and charitable to Soviet literature.

"The Song of the Commune," by V. V. Knyazev (b. 1887), consists of seven sestets, but only the haunting refrain, occurring four times, need be given:

> Communards never, never,
> > Never, never
> Shall be slaves!

"At the Partkom [Party Committee]," by S. P. Shchipachev (b. 1889), thrice awarded the Order of the Red Star and twice given the Stalin Prize, could hardly be improved in translation by adherence to the original rhyme scheme and meter:

You may have happend to sit in/ At a Partkom meeting for so long, friends,/ That when you take your jacket off at home/ You notice that even your underwear reeks of tobacco./ It has long been spring out of doors;/ The grass is spattered with rain;/ Yet in here the winter still holds sway./ But the Secretary yanked the window open—/ And branches rushed toward his hands,/ At his flushed face./ The drone of planes, the chattering of children./ A whiff of earth, as in a forest./ The ground is whitened by an apple-tree,/ And the years lying ahead are clear./ You cannot decide Party business/ Unless you can feel the spring.

The short story, however, is well represented here, since the Russians still are, despite all restrictions, superb story-tellers; nor is there any stint of humor, satire, folk wit. But (unless one counts the extremely puzzling bit at the very end of Block's "The 12") there is not a trace of mysticism: Soviet literature is still too vital for that.

The Great Revolution's only clean break with its literary past was the liquidation of three characters—two of them notorious featherbedders and a third one known as the Indecent Letter—from the Cyrillic alphabet. Practically every literary movement and school of czarist Russia had its continuum after the Revolution. One of the most important was Symbolism. All movements in the arts have the eternal novelty of sunrises and the tides, and I am certain that the reader is sufficiently acquainted with Pre-Raphaelitism and Aestheticism, with the French Romanticists, Symbolists, Decadents, Modernists, Parnassians (the Parnassians, above all!) to have but little difficulty in forming an idea of the *fin de siècle* growth of the Russian Symbolists (who were also called, in derision, Modernists and Decadents). But, although Symbolism in Russia was of Western origin, it took on a Slavic vigor that was all its own, shortly after its beginnings in the latter half of the 1890's. With undevastating originality the Symbolists proclaimed Symbolism a cult of beauty and themselves artists-for-art's-sake; they found literature was long on social preaching but short on craftsmanship, and its reformation on both counts was the avowed aim of the new movement.

Pasternak, who to this day is regarded as a Symbolist, flirted with them; Bunin, who kept aloof, called them sick children; Leo Tolstoi fulminated against them; Block was at first impatient with them and later upset by their mysticism. F. I. Tiutchev (1803-1873), A. A. Foeth (or Shenshin [1820-1892]) and C. Fofanov (1862-1911) were their precursors; N. Vilenkin ("N. Minsky" [1855-1937]) was their pioneer; D. Merezhkovsky (1866-1941) was their prophet and promulgator; V. Briussov (1873-1924) was their pontiff and Alexander Block their psyche. By 1905 the movement had become definitely known as Symbolism, had attained popularity and taken on something very like an aristocratic tinge; after 1905 it began toying with social problems and dabbling in politics, and by 1912 it had grown so very fusty that an anti-Symbolist movement sprang up called, tentatively, Adamism and then Acmeism (also promptly dubbed "a St. Petersburg disease"), under the leadership of the brilliant Nicholai S. Gumilev (1886-1921). The avowed aim of Acmeism was to rejuvenate doddering Symbolism by purging it of its mysticism, esotericism and sloppiness in craftsmanship. Symbolism still lingered on, but it was moribund and, in the early 1920's, its brilliance dimmed to the phosphorescence of a passé mackerel. Nevertheless, during its lifetime it had produced a considerable number of superb poets and an imposing amount of fine poetry, and had had a revivifying effect on Russian painting, music, theatre, as well as literature.

Russian Futurism also preceded the Revolution; the movement began in 1908 and was known definitely as Futurism by 1910. All arts must have their Wild Beasts (or, as in the case of Russian painting, their Barbarians) if they are not to turn into stagnant pools covered over with the green scum of academic smugness; at the same time one must remember Darwin's observation in speaking of insects: Specific differences in the species of large genera are often exceedingly small— and, one may add, very often practically their entire interest lies in their nomenclature. The only parallel to the multiplication-by-division of the Russian Futurists is that of the Old Believers (or Schismatics, or Sectarians). Some of the Futurist cliques, coteries, claques, ateliers and groups (large or splinter) were Cubists, Cubo-Futurists (which included Mayakovsky), Ego-Futurists (including the tinkling "Igor Severyanin" (I. Lotyrev [1887-1942]), Imagists (Yessenin's final affiliation, and in no way connected with the American movement), Expressionists, Free-Versists, Luminists, Cosmists, Bio-Cosmists, Neo-Classicists, Nothingists (or No-Matterists), Pfuists, the Jack of Diamonds and the Ass' Tail groups of Futurists in the visual arts, and a whole boiling of others.

Although admittedly deriving from the Italian movement, the Russian Futurists soon, in a very vigorously Slavic way, rejected the Italo-Futurists, and had as little use for

Marinetti as they had for Pushkin. The Symbolists were, of course, lingering on merely to save funeral expenses; literature was, naturally, stuffy as to content and sloppy as to form; it was, obviously, up to the Futurists to redeem matters. Mayakovsky advised poets to "spit on rhymes and arias, and the rose-bush, and all such melancrockery." All art movements groan, at first, under the mortmain of the classics—but the Futurists wanted to chuck the babies out with the bathwater. "We must jettison Pushkin, Dostoevsky and Tolstoi from the ship of modernity," Mayakovsky declared in 1912, in the famous manifesto, "A Slap in the Face of Public Taste," and again, in 1918: "The White Guard is handed over to the firing squad—why not Pushkin?" The game of trying to topple Pushkin had begun soon after his assassination-by-duel in 1837, and disparaging him was as good a gambit for the aspiring Russian poet as belittling Shakespeare still is for the budding British playwright. All these rodomontades did not deter Mayakovsky from writing a "Jubilee Song" in 1924, a long, whimsical and a somewhat pensive monologue in which he assures Alexander Sergheievich that he, Mayakovsky, is probably the only one who regrets that the older poet is not among the living.

In 1918-1920, because of hardships brought about by the war and the Revolution, the murmurous Moscow salons had been supplanted by boisterous basement bistros—Pegasus' Stable, the Poets' Cafe, the Stray Dog Club—and *conversazione*, jasmine tea and *madeleine* cakes were replaced by shenanigans, dried-carrot tea and donnybrooks. The Symbolists had set out to bait the Philistines; the Futurists wanted to shock the bourzhuis and did. They spat at their audiences and addressed them in unprintable terms; Mayakovsky recited in an orange jacket, without a tie but in an opera hat and with blue roses painted on his cheeks.

Briussov was considered their precursor, Bely was the patron, and Pasternak flirted with them, too. The Party had welcomed them, although not without reservations, as Singers of the Revolution, but in 1923, the year which may be considered the high-water mark of the movement, the tarnished tag of Futurism was exchanged for that of the Left Front of the Arts (LEF); Mayakovsky, dropping the role of ragshag, emerged as a giant. But from that point on, the movement met with hostility not only from the hard-shell Marxists but from Fellow Travelers,* who were beginning to resent the political pressures being put on literature.

In 1927 Mayakovsky had to change the name of his review to the *New LEF,* but this did not help a mite. The group that gathered around *The Thing*—a periodical started in 1922— who might be called Functionalists ("art must be functional, utilitarian"), and the Formalists, a coterie of scholars and critics, were adherents of the LEF; Constructivism, an off- shoot of Futurism, appeared in 1924, with a platform calling for art *loadified* with purposefulness and Socialism; there were only two Constructivists worth mentioning—(both of them poets who also had a way with prose): Ilya Selvinsky (b. 1894) and Vera Inber (b. 1892). But by 1930 Futurism with all its ramifications was as dead as decency, and since then there has been no new art movement or school of any sort in Russia. As for Mayakovsky, he would have emerged as "the greatest poet of the Soviet epoch," as Stalin called him, even if there had been no Futurism or luridly striped blazers, just as Gautier would have emerged as a great writer even if there had been no Romanticism or red embroidered waistcoats, or as Wilde would have emerged as a lord of lan- guage even if there had been no Aestheticism or knee breeches of gray velvet.

Proletarian literature, too, had really begun before 1908. Leo Tolstoi had given the accolade to the mouzhik as the supreme arbiter of all art; the Proletarian Writers, who were sworn foes of the LEF, nominated the proletarian as the sole

* The term, made current by Trotsky, did not for some years have the opprobrious connotation it eventually ac- quired, especially abroad. A Fellow Traveler, usually a non- proletarian, was simply not a joiner, feeling that he could be an artist without having the makings of a good Party mem- ber, in contradistinction to the professional proletarian who felt that his Party ticket automatically bestowed upon him the makings of an artist.

creator of all future Russian art (and of all Russian science as well). They carried the civil war over into literature, resorting to all means of coercion, from censorship to physical violence, in fighting all writers of aristocratic, intellectual or bourgeois origin.

The initial attempts at creating a strictly proletarian culture by persons of 100 percent proletarian origin were made through the Proletcults (Proletarian Cultural Educational Organizations), formed shortly before the Revolution. (There were, not unnaturally, temptingly plump subsidies from the new regime.) In 1920 the Proletcults were operating three hundred literary workshops with an enrollment of eighty-four thousand; by 1922 there were only twenty ateliers and, by 1924, only seven, with a membership of less than five hundred, and the idea of creating a new literature by shock-brigade methods was given up as utterly useless. In fact, the Soviets have not yet produced a single worth-while poet of proletarian origin. There were the Peasant Poets (reclassified in due time as the Koulak Poets), such as Yessenin and Kluyev; the intellectuals exceeded their quota of good poets, and the greatest poets of the Revolution, Block and Mayakovsky, were of the nobility, while still another, Ephim Pridvorov ("Demian Bedny—Demian the Poor" [1883-1935]), exceedingly popular and effective as a satirist and fabulist from 1917 to 1930, was the by-blow of a Grand Duke. And the only two authentic poets still surviving in Russia—Boris Pasternak and Anna Akhmatova—are anything but proletarians.

The Smithy, a Moscow proletarian clique that functioned outside the Proletcults, was formed in 1920; 1922 saw the formation, also in Moscow, of the October group, likewise proletarian but not Proletcult. The Mountain Pass clique, consisting of moderates, was an offshoot of the Smithy group, while the On Guardists, who were extremists, stemmed from the October set. All these proletarian outfits, while snarling at all non-proletarians, were also bickering among themselves, but by 1925 they combined into the Russian Association of Proletarian Pencraftsmen (the infamous RAPP), with the unspeakable Leopold Auerbach, the brother-in-law of Yagoda, the Chief of the Political Police, as its Grand Inquisitor.

In something like a decade and a half of their reign of terror these proletarian ideologues contrived to wreak greater harm upon Soviet literature than all the theologues of the Dark Ages had wrought upon the literatures of Europe in a millennium, and have left a methodology of criticism which is used in the Soviets to this day. The RAPP insisted that art must be made an integral part of the first Five Year Plan (1928); by 1932 the situation had become so bad that the government stepped in and dissolved the RAPP, which was succeeded by the Union of Soviet Writers, the avowed purpose of which was the creation of "artistic writing" to glorify the victories of socialism, expound the wisdom and heroism of the Party and (to echo Lenin) "portray Soviet Man and his moral qualities fully and with full force." *

And that is how, with the Party as midwife, Social Realism was born.

Since then the government has made the caponization of writers a delightful do-it-yourself project, and any Soviet writer who gets into ideological-theological difficulties can fully rely upon much the same sort of loyal support and staunch defense as that which a Hollywood script-writer, let us say, may expect and get from his colleagues in similar circumstances.

Still another school that had its beginnings even before World War I was Neo-Realism, which gained recognition between 1912 and 1917. The Neo-Realists could hardly be called trail blazers in their choice of backgrounds and characters: Alexei N. Tolstoi did not go over any provincial ground that Shchedrin-Saltykov had not covered before, and there is nothing startlingly new about Zamiatin's *Out in the Sticks* to those who remember Kuprin's *The Duel*, which likewise deals with garrison life in backwoods Russia. Mi-

---

* There was also the All-Union Association of Proletarian Pencraftsmen (VAPP), but the difference between the RAPP and the VAPP was every bit as great as the difference between Tweedledeesky and Tweedledumov.

chael M. Prishvin (b. 1873) all through czarism, through World War I, through the Revolution, the civil war and the Soviets, has clung to the hardly "Neo" theme of Nature. No, the main merit of these Realists (one must not omit mention of Alexei Chapyghin [1870-1937], Serghei Sergheiev-Tsensky [b. 1876], and Vyacheslav Shishkov [1873-1945]) lay in their striving to revivify their beloved speech. They did not disdain certain stylistic devices of the Symbolists, were not ashamed to follow Bely, and went as far as need be to bring about an Antaean contact of the Russian language with the soil of Mother Russia. In these efforts their undisputed leader was Alexei Remizov (b. 1876), who was as much of a refugee from Soviet reality as Greenevsky, and even more of a Puck in his private life.

There was one movement, however, which was unique in that it came into being and ran its entire course under the Soviets, and which, one is tempted to say, was of greater importance to Soviet literature than all the others combined: the Serapion Brethren, who took their name from the title of a story within a story by E. T. A. Hoffman. They had their very informal start in February, 1921, in starving, freezing, no-trolleys-running Petrograd, under the ægis of Gorki and the tutelage of Zamiatin; Yuri Tynyanov (1894-1943) also became a friend of theirs. Of these Brethren, V. Pozner was eighteen; Benjamin Kaverin (whose real name was Zilberg), and Leo Lunz, who signed the manifesto of the Brethren, were twenty; V. Shklovsky, E. Gruzdev (both critics), N. Tikhonov, V. Polonskaya (both poets, and the latter the only Sister), Vsevolod Ivanov (who opened up new and strange regions of Russia in his writings) and Michael Zoshchenko were in their mid-twenties or edging into their thirties; Constantin Fedin, who was to do so much for the Soviet novel, had reached thirty.

Their main interest lay in literary craftsmanship, in experimentation, in ingenuity and individuality of presentation. O. Henry was not foreign to them; they had a leaning toward the bizarre, the grotesque; if it had not been for the influence of their venturesomeness in satire, Valentin Kataev might never have written *The Embezzlers,* Ilf and Petrov might never have produced *Twelve Chairs* and *The Golden Calf*, and such strange plays as Michael Bulgakov's *Purple Island* and Mayakovsky's *Bedbug* might never have come into being. Nor were the Brethren initiators in satire alone: although they were all Fellow Travelers, it was they who brought to the fore and popularized the themes of the Revolution and the civil war, although they preferred to do so in their own fashion rather than to follow the dictates of the Party. And in revivifying and enriching Russian prose they did even more than the Neo-Realists, since the Brethren caught and transmitted not only mouzhik-talk but the speech of the city dweller as well. "We demand but one thing," they proclaimed in their manifesto, "that a work of art must be organic and that it live its own organic life."

Gorki has been likened to a bridge between the old Russian culture and the new; the Serapion Brethren have been likened to a ferry: "In those years," Olga Forsh has written, "having nailed themselves into a stout raft, they ferried over upon themselves across the river of the events of those years all that which mattered to the life of the arts. And, withal, they did this without the least pretension to being Argonauts." And, one may add, without insisting on feeding poor old Pushkin to the fishes. But, in the 1940's, they were most effectively silenced by literary theologians, their most grievous heresy being that of insisting upon art-for-art's-sake.

English is admittedly the supreme literary language, but Russian is the richest, raciest, and earthiest, and all Russian writers worth their salt have always sought to invigorate it with folk speech and new regionalisms; Count Leo Tolstoï did not hesitate, on occasion, to use four-letter words (in Russian, however, they run to three or five letters); the aristocratic Bunin was proud of giving unerringly the speech of any Russian social stratum; Shchedrin-Saltykov enriched it with his "Aesopic language" and Leskov with his trade and cant terms and marvelous puns and coinages. The Revolution opened up new and vast regions whose vernaculars enriched the language; industrialization has added innumerable technical and scientific terms as well as the argot of city workers; as a time of experimentation and innovation it encouraged novelty in stylistics. Block, the exquisite, achieved his "sound of a world crashing" in "The 12" through catchwords, slogans, topical slang, street talk, snatches of nonsensical street songs; Mayakovsky's deliberately outrageous rhymes and concertina lines (surpassing not only Ogden Nash's but those of Nash's master, W. S. Gilbert), his irregular rhythms and slang, can be, at will, either vastly funny or as crushing as a trip hammer; Zoshchenko's sketches were such favorites with the Soviet man in the street because he caught in them his own brash and broken accents. I regret if, in English, my reader (or even readers) should fail to share fully the Soviet reader's delight in the language of his authors, but I do hope that something of the stylistics will come over the hurdles of translation.

Naturally, it cannot be denied that there is also the prose (and verse) of the overwhelmingly predominant *halturniks*, teeming with folksyisms, peasantish passementerie and pseudo-pscientific gibberish, asperged with bureaucratic alphabet soup (but cooked after a Soviet recipe) and larded with much the same double talk one can hear in the towers of Madison Avenue or read in the columns of our political pontificators, the whole garnished with ideological gobbledegook. I have tried to be fair to one of the many literatures I love by not offering even one specimen; as for the reader, he will not miss it, since I have a very shrewd suspicion that the Russians themselves—sensible fellows!—never read it: except, perhaps, strictly for laughs.

Captain Marryat called the literary scene of his day a rat pit; Poe called his a prison house; Soviet literature, up to the 1940's, was a game of Russian roulette; from the 1940's to the present it has been a not too gentle literary version of musical chairs. "One recalls with considerable perturbation," Gorki wrote in 1929 in his defense of Pilnyak, "these small-town, burgherish, wolfish baitings of man as one sees how avidly and lecherously all throw themselves upon one individual so that, having annihilated him for having made a single misstep, they may take his place."

During its first four years Soviet literature was turbulent, tempestuous, but there was some possibility of self-expression. From 1921 to 1928, during what may be called the NEP (New Economic Policy) as applied to Workers in the Arts, there was a period of tolerance for writers and writing; this was followed by the Inquisition and Reign of Terror of the RAPP and VAPP, until the relaxation of 1934-36, after which there was another La Brea Tar Pit period until the easing up of pressures during 1942-45, since the writers were doing more than their bit for the war; this was succeeded by the particularly idiotic and vicious period of 1946-48, with its houndings, purges and accusations of such dread heresies as Pessimism, Decadence, Formalism and, worst of all, Rootless and Stateless Literary Vagabondage (or Cosmopolitanism), hurled at the literary protestants by the Soviet literary Holy Office.

There were signs of another literary amnesty after the death of Stalin, but the stagnancy of Soviet literature remained practically undisturbed until the *Doctor Zhivago* affair in 1958. Still, there are, as of the present writing, some encouraging straws in the wind: a novel exposing the machinations of the Soviet equivalent of the FBI has been published in Russia and is enjoying a wide and unhindered circulation there; not only has the interdict on Anna Akhmatova been lifted but a celebration was held in her honor; and the *Doctor Zhivago* episode is being pumiced over as a preliminary to restoring the author's union cards to him.

Zamiatin's *mot* about the future of Russia's literature may have been applicable at the time of its utterance, in 1921; but that literature has long since become Soviet literature and acquired a worth-while past of its own: four decades of it. And since good literature has appeared and is likely to appear throughout the world, despite all the efforts to interfere with its production, it would be astounding if good writing had not appeared and will not again appear in Soviet Russia, despite all the Party theologues and the self-caponizers among the Workers of the Pen themselves. This is not to deny, however, that no other literature in the world is as afflicted with *haltura** as Soviet literature, and that no other country offers such generous rewards to its *halturniks;* consequently no country has so vastly exceeded its quota of literary trimmers, getters-on, fat cats and trained seals, of writers who attend so many literary congresses, conventions, seminars, who deliver so many speeches, conduct so vast a correspondence, fill so many positions in the writing trades organizations, and do so very, very little writing. And no other land offers as deplorable an example of what can befall any literature when the critics thereof are taken seriously.

As for the future of Soviet literature (or rather its futures, for its clear and potable waters will keep welling up, no matter how much and how often ideological rubble is dumped in to stop up its stream) I, and a number of others whose percipience is much greater than mine, can see no reason for despair. One can feel far more despondent about the decay of the short story, say, everywhere except in Russia, and no anthologist need feel at all apprehensive about turning out anthology upon anthology of good and readable things by Soviet writers.

The availability of translations has been generally indicated in connection with the selections; but at this point it is both my duty and pleasure to recommend most earnestly the acquisition of the following (all, as of now, in print): Marc Slonim's *Modern Russian Literature from Chekhov to the Present* (Oxford University Press), not only for its sound, authoritative and admirably objective scholarship but for its good writing (by no means an ordinary combination), and *A Treasury of Russian Verse,* edited by Avrahm Yarmolinsky (Macmillan Company), for its rich representation of Soviet

---

* This most puissant word, which should by all means be taken over with all its derivations into English, is fully explained in connection with the selections by Ilf and Petrov; here it applies to the sort of writing which is laureled by funded prizes and canonized by being digested for periodicals of fantastically large circulation.

poets, good translations and excellent scholarship; it is immeasurably superior to all the other anthologies in its field. My previous anthologies are mentioned here not out of hucksterish impudicity but solely because they contain material either not easily available elsewhere or not available at all in English; the first and second deal with Soviet literature in part, the third consists entirely of Soviet material: *A Treasury of Russian Literature* (Vanguard Press), *The Portable Russian Reader* (Viking Press), and *New Russian Stories* (New Directions). I also commend, and that most warmly, Professor Gleb Struve's *Soviet Literature: 1917-1950* (University of Oklahoma Press)—but only to those who happen to share my taste for the macabre, the grand-guignolish. I strongly doubt if, in all the galactic range of literary scholarship, there is to be found a more delectably spine-tingling phantasmagoria.

No anthology is Athena, in full armor sprung, and no anthologist I know of has the brow of Jove. Still, one can be indifferent honest and acknowledge his indebtedness. I therefore extend earnest thanks to Professor Marc Slonim not only for the invaluable data in his *Modern Russian Literature*, to which I have so freely helped myself, but for certain vital first-hand information. The obtaining of many Soviet texts is often extremely difficult at present due to the idiocies and vandalism engendered by the Cold War, and my thanks go out to Morris Spiegel, a confrère of mine: had it not been for his skill in obtaining the unobtainable it would have been impossible to include some of the selections herein. In this connection I also voice my appreciation of two fellow bibliopoles who specialize in Russian books: A. Buschke and Gregory Rakovsky. And finally I express my gratitude to Dr. Janis E. Guerney, Professor Michael J. Fine and Bruce W. Guerney, M.A.: their scholarship, of a far more orthodox and disciplined order than mine, was, throughout the shaping-up of this book, most helpful and enspiriting.

As long as printing endures, editors will have to go on pointing out that limitations of space demand selectivity, while selectivity in its turn calls for sacrifices which, as often as not, grieve an editor far more than anybody else. Undoubtedly the names of many excluded authors will occur to the reader, but he may feel fairly certain that they were considered but found to be addicted to epics—and it was not quite practical to include any considerable number of novels of from 250,000 words to 500,000 words each in an anthology of only something like 200,000 words; or they may have proven far short of what they were drummed up to be, being quite as hollow as the instrument of their aggrandizement; or they may have had little if any regard for the not entirely unimportant factor of even ordinary readability. Extracted chapters are none too happy an expedient: extracts, snippets, Beauties of . . . , Flowers of . . . , Gems of . . . , and so forth pertain more to chrestomathies and tend toward a quantitative monotony, like that of the gambler's classical baggage of fifty-four pieces: a pair of socks and a pack of cards. Only one extract has been included, but it is an integer in itself. And there has been no abridgment whatsoever.

Still, no reader should ever underestimate the ignorance of any editor. I therefore once more reiterate what I have said so many times before: All corrections, criticisms and comments will be appreciated and carefully considered.

Nu ee vot!

BERNARD GUILBERT GUERNEY

At the Sign of the Blue Faun,
New York,
Summer of 1959.

An Anthology of Russian Literature
in the Soviet Period
from Gorki to Pasternak

Maxim GORKI

("Maxim the Bitter"—Alexei Maximovich PESHKOV
[1868-1936])

> *I made a solemn pledge to myself that,
> on growing up, I would help people
> and serve them honestly.*
>
> GORKI

Besides his stature as a giant of Russian literature, Gorki is of the utmost importance in that he formed something very like a living bridge between the culture of old Russia and that of Russia after the Revolution. He was the prime mover, the greatest force, in the preservation of the best elements of the older Russian literature and in the creation of the new.

The many literatures of the world are, of course, not altogether barren of authors who have merited, to varying extents, the title of world shakers. One cannot readily think, however, of any non-Russian writer whose sweep can quite compare with that of a great Russian writer who becomes also a man of action. Leo Tolstoi, whose renunciation of any remuneration for his writings benefited hardly anybody but the publishers, insisted on full royalties for *Resurrection* and, with the proceeds of this one book, transplanted several thousand of the czar-persecuted Spirit Wrestlers to Canada. But even the Grand Old Man was surpassed by Maxim the Bitter. An active, prison-sitting revolutionary from the 1890's on, he consistently financed Russian revolutionary movements through his fabulous earnings as a writer. "Tremendous" is the only word to describe the merely financial aid he extended when Messina was devastated by earthquake and tidal wave in

3

1908. And the number of writers alone, beginners or veterans, whom he helped throughout his career materially or professionally (or both) is incomputable.

After he had accepted the October Revolution (at first not without reservations), Gorki, who knew what hunger was, saw to it that writers and other intellectuals should not starve to death, by forming what may be roughly described as an early predecessor of our WPA program for the arts, supplementing out of his own pocket the funds issued by the struggling new regime. And since Russian writers have another quaint peculiarity, that of nonreticence in acknowledging aid, there is no lack of testimony. An émigré literary star of the first magnitude told the present writer in Paris how Alexei Maximovich set him to translating from the German so that he might have cold veal and hot tea during the indescribable hardships of 1917. "Toward the end of 1920 Gorki helped me to get to Leningrad," Vsevolod Ivanov has written of his beginnings. "He . . . saw to it that I was fed. . . ." The wife of Alexander Greenevsky called Gorki his "savior." In 1920 Greenevsky, hardly recovered from typhus, had only the granite streets of Leningrad for shelter and the sub-zero frost for sustenance. Gorki tracked him down and "did everything for him." He procured for the Russian Poe something that was then almost completely unobtainable, an Academic Food Card, and a room in the House of Arts: heated, well lighted—and with a table to write on, which overwhelmed poor Greenevsky most of all. And "he [Gorki] provided him with work. . . ."

Gorki's most important literary works after the Revolution were *The Artamonov Business, Egor Bulychev* (a play), and the *Klim Samghin* tetralogy;* in all of these he was still battling his sworn enemy, *meshchanstvo*—the deadliest of all the varieties of bourgeoisie. But his most important work for literature (and culture in general) in the post-Revolutionary period was in keeping the new broom from sweeping even the classics into limbo, in saving the older literati, scientists and

* All four volumes were translated into English, but have been long out of print.

intellectuals in general as a sort of leaven for the future, in fostering the younger aspirants of actual promise, whatever their arts might be, in ameliorating the hardships and oppressions of the scholars of his time and, above all, in valiantly contending against the cohorts of *halturniks* and trimmers who eventually succeeded in making Soviet literature the ersatz thing it is today.

He was a power in the land and a voice which was not only heard but heeded: the chief example of the Russian writer as Man of Action.

THE WAG

The small sandy shoal was a swatch of yellow satin tossed into the greenish water of the sea; spreading before it, to the south, was a shoreless, glassy-smooth expanse; spreading behind it was a streak of dazzling clear water; further back were the rather squat coppery knolls of the shore; the knolls were covered with miserable scrub consisting of some sort of nondescript twigs, while still further, among the incandescent dunes, were the dirty smudges of the fishery buildings.

The day was so bright that even from here, from the shoal, one could see over there, on the knolls, almost a mile away, the fish scales glistening in silvery sparks.

Everything was quiet, as after a great calamity—quiet and void.

Barinov, who hailed from Sergach, was sprawled out on the moist sand, languishing from the heat, his albinoid eyes shut; droningly, somnolently, he was sermonizing for my benefit: "In my meditations I have crossed all lands, have sailed across all the seas; in my meditations I have sampled all sins—"

I listened to him and did not believe a word he was saying. He was a timid fellow, behaving like a toady before others, and whenever he spoke to the clerk at the fishery his legs shook and his voice had a caressing squeal to it. This man was as lazy as a water buffalo, indefatigable in discoursing, and exceedingly hirsute: his flat snub-nosed face wore a woolen mask of sandy hue, tufts of rust-colored wool stuck out of flaring nostrils that looked exactly like those of a camel; the same sort of tufts stuck out of his ears; his bared chest, coppery from sunburn, was matted all over like a bear's; thick little clumps of bushy hair sprouted even over his knuckles. He had bandy legs, like a tailor's; his arms were as long and thick as his legs; most probably he would have found it very convenient to walk on all fours.

Yet this was an extremely good-natured, extremely placid beast; whenever his fellow workers gave him a beating for his laziness and remissness all he did was to beg them, without resentment and without complaint, as he rolled like a keg at their feet: "There, that'll do, fellows—that'll do! There, you've given me a drubbing—there, let it go at that, now!"

His bald head was tightly bound with something red; from a distance it looked as if he had been scalped.

"But in real life I'm a shallow man," he remarked, justly enough, uninterested in whether or not I was listening to him. "As shallow as a tambourine: if they strike me, I respond; if they don't, I'm silent."

He sounded as if he were delirious; I was half asleep. Over us was an exceedingly blue sky, around us was the greenish sea—as if the sky were below us as well as above. While we, upon the atlas swatch of the shoal, were suspended in a bottomless void, as if we were on a flying carpet.

The flying carpet was motionless, however. And, in one's soul as well, everything was motionless.

A little more than a mile ahead there was another shoal, much the same as ours; it would have been invisible within the mass of molten, incandescently sparkling glass, had it not been for a dark figure walking upon it, as if it were floating in the air. This was a third comrade of ours, some Oriental or other, either a Persian or an Armenian from Persia, by the name of Izet. He spoke almost no Russian but he understood excellently everything he was ordered to do— a most convenient fellow.

The three of us had been sent from the fishery to that

shoal to take off the gear that had been left there that morning, but Barinov and I had felt too lazy to go that far in the heat; we had laid ourselves down on the shoal nearer the shore while we ordered Izet to go after the gear; obedient as a placid horse, he had gone.

"I'm over forty-five," Barinov spoke on, as if in delirium, stretching himself. "I've seen such a great deal of all sorts of things, it would have been enough for a dozen men. But, should you ask me what it was all about—well, that's something I won't tell you. It's all a lot of goddamn nonsense. And yet you talk about the common people—"

There was nothing for the eye to rest on amid this coruscating void; the brain spread out in it as a tatter of white foam spreads out on the warm water of the sea. And there was nothing to think about.

Barinov? What he was saying I had already heard—from him and others. All these reflections on life serve merely to deaden it, bringing only vexation and despondence to one's heart.

If, shutting one's eyes, one were to lie thus without moving for several minutes, one would begin to feel in every muscle of one's body, at its every point, an unpleasant expansion, a thawing, and as if one were plunging into an abyss of fire. That, possibly, is how a small lump of hard dough feels when it is thrown into a caldron of heated water.

An old gull mewed abominably, puffing out her gray cheeks; two of her companions, also females, eyed her suspiciously and malevolently and, straightening their wings out with difficulty, slowly flew out to sea; their reflections dragged along the water like two swatches of silk. Yonder, suspended in the air over the water, stout roly-poly Izet was fossicking, nudging a barrel along toward the boat.

"There was a clerk in our village, now, by the name of Kolobashkin," Barinov was telling himself a story. "A good fellow, even though he was a hopeless drunkard. Well, now, he used to say: 'All people ought to live in the same way. You mouzhiks,' he used to say, 'ought to flog one another as often as possible. When you've done a thorough job of flogging one another you'll get to feeling ashamed before one another and start living together more friendly like. Everybody's got to live together at some point; let that point be even a feeling of shame, as long as you're unanimous about it. But when each grain is all on its own you won't cook any porridge.' Look over there, now—who's that coming?"

He was looking toward the shore, his shaggy paw up to his eyes. Someone was walking along the very edge of the water, waddling along, his feet extinguishing the sparks of fish scales.

"He's looking for a ford. Call out to him: he ought to head more to the right; there's a ridge there—"

I kept silent—I didn't feel like calling out. Barinov, too, kept silent. It was getting hotter and hotter; the warm air, laden with salt, was heavy and humid; it was hard to breathe. The salt was on one's lips; one wanted to drink, but the canteen with the fresh water was in the boat. Silvery herrings glinted in the sea, right near the shoal, looking like the reflections of wingless birds hovering in the air—one involuntarily glanced upward to where, amid the azure sultriness, the sun had come to a dead stop and was becoming molten.

The man hit upon the way to us: a mane of sand washed up by the spring storms. This mane had become curved into an S; its lower tip was the little island on which we were lying. At the lowest spot of the ridge the water would come up only to one's armpits.

"Not one of our men," Barinov remarked. I believed him: he had a seaman's eyesight.

The man entered the water and was slowly advancing, with elbows tilted up, getting in deeper with every step, his belly plowing comically through the water.

"A Persian," Barinov decided.

I saw above the water a dark clean-shaven face, a gray mustache clipped short, white teeth bared in a smile. There was a round felt hat that looked like a flowerpot on the man's head; he had his blue trousers slung over his shoulder. His jacket was also blue; the white shirt under it was open at the throat. The water shoaled: copper-colored legs, glistening in the sun, rose out of it.

"How you!" he called out, even at that distance, nodding his round head time and again.

"He's full of fun," Barinov remarked, smiling. "Persians are all like that; cheerful, kind-hearted, the whole lot of them. Rather foolish—more foolish than a baby. Nothing easier than fooling a Persian!"

The man came out on the shoal, put on his trousers, shoved his hat on the nape of his neck, revealing a forehead that was blue where it was shaven, and came toward us calling out in his broken speech: "How you! How you!"

He was spare, gaunt; his dark face was scrawled all over with minuscular wrinkles, in the midst of which gaily sparkled aureate pupils on bluish whites; the eyes were large, almond-shaped. He must have been very good-looking in his youth. Pliantly tucking his long legs under him he squatted deftly, and asked: "You got tabac?"

With that he took a redolent pouch and a black pipe out of the bosom of his shirt and held them out to Barinov. The latter benignly accepted the offering and, packing the pipe tight with the shredded, moist tobacco, began: "Why has Persian come here?"

The man glanced at the way Barinov was tamping down the tobacco with his thumb, smiled a little and took the pipe from him: "She no draw!"

He scraped out the dottle and, after filling the pipe anew, handed it back to Barinov: "Now she draw."

"Persian hired out for work?"

"Work," the newcomer nodded. "Will be work—*chik!*"

"Just as I told you—he likes his fun," said Barinov, smiling a little in his turn.

The Persian, for his part, looked out to sea where Izet was still fossicking about the boat and asked, extending his arm in that direction: "That one—who he?"

"One of yours—your own kind."

"Ours—" the Persian said, but one could not tell whether he was concurring or putting the question again.

"Izet, they call him."

The Persian shook his head sharply: "Him called Hassan."

"Well, have it your way."

"Him my fri-end."

"Your friend? I see."

Barinov was smoking earnestly and awkwardly, gulping whole clouds of smoke and letting them out in a long blue stream. The Persian, smiling, was watching him, humming an odd song very, very softly and for some reason clenching and unclenching his right hand. The silence all around us was becoming more and more intensified.

"A sweet tobacco, yet strong," Barinov muttered, looking at me with eyes that had grown heavy. "It went to my head, for sure—"

He fell on his back and closed his eyes.

For several minutes the Persian sat without stirring, as though he had fallen asleep, except that one caught the glint of small aureate sparks in his puckered eyes. Then he made a wry face, rubbed it hard with his hands and, having cupped them, looked at his palms just as if they were a book, moved his lips and rubbed his face anew.

And suddenly, throwing his head back until his Adam's apple was jutting, he sent up a howl, soft yet in a very high-pitched, almost feminine voice: *"Ai, yai, yai-ai-ee!"*

"My, something's sure got you," Barinov said somnolently, turning his back to the sun, while the Persian, hugging his knees, kept swaying and howling, filling the silence with his high-pitched wail.

Over there, on the other shoal, Izet, standing in water up to his knees, was launching the boat off the sand; when the Persian sent up his howl Izet swung his arm up and then, straightening, began looking in our direction from under his elbow.

The Persian nudged me with his shoulder.

"Him hear!" he said. And, baring his teeth in a grin, he added gaily: "Him will be *chik!*"

"What's this *chik?*"

"Like this," said the Persian, rolling up his eyes under his forehead and snorting like a horse.

This was funny.

Izet stood and looked for a while, shoved the boat off

leisurely and clambered into it over the stern; one could see how the boat began to rock on the smooth water that was indistinguishable from the air.

As for the Persian, he narrowed his eyes and struck up his yowling chant anew, ever so softly; he sang throatily, with unexpected tones that turned into squeals, oddly gulping down the sound, capriciously interrupting its indolent flow. This song aggravated still further the sultry oppressiveness of the vacuous day; hindering nothing, arousing nothing, the sounds and words (both alien to me) floated along like a school of small fish. By now it seemed as if the song had been long sounding amid the silence, as if it had always sounded in it; its melody was elusive and evaded the memory, refusing to submit to the efforts made to capture it. In the bleak void the boat moved jerkily, just like some ungainly fish with long, slender fins; Izet was barely rowing, raising and lowering the oars slowly.

"What are you singing—what are you singing about?" I asked the Persian when I had become fed up with his howling.

He immediately fell silent, bared his teeth in a grin and willingly began telling me: "Such a gay song; *tasnif,* we call him—*tasnif!*"

He ran out of words, however; shutting his eyes, he began swaying and vociferating again:

> *"Ai, yai, yai-ai-ee!*
> I must to go to Farsista-an—"

Breaking off his song, he winked to me and spoke: "Must to go, must not to go—who know? Allah know; leetle man no know! Young wooman stay home; took another husband, no took another husband—who know? Tell me, good djinn, which of my good friends my wife's new husband is? . . . That how *tasnif* song go. Shaitan, him have fun; leetle man, him cry—"

Barinov stirred and spoke up in a condemnatory tone: "All their songs are about wimmen; that's all they know, the dogs!"

But the Persian kept on talking, with a gay and lively glint

in his eyes, mixing words in a language I did not know with
words of broken Russian: "Must to go to Farsistan, must not
to go? Will be drinking wine, will be fooling fri-end and all
peoples—that how *tasnif* go! Leetle man home, him wise; on
road—him foolish!"

He broke into laughter, rubbing his hands hard, and suddenly, his face darkening, became plunged in thought as he
gazed stonily at the flashing mirror of the sea. I, too, became
thoughtful, arranging his amusing words into an unpretentious song:

> "Good works are what I fain would do,
> But I must away to Farsistan!
> Tell me, tell me, my good djinn,
> How much evil, how much rue
> Shaitan has in store for me?

> "I have a wife so fair, so young,
> Yet must I away to Farsistan!
> Tell me, tell me, my good djinn,
> With whom will my wife do me wrong—
> Though I love her dimpled knees?

> "Of true friends I count but two—
> Ah, I must away to Farsistan!
> Tell me, tell me, my good djinn,
> Which friend of mine will prove untrue—
> Though I miss them both so much?

> "Although I do not care to roam,
> Still must I away to Farsistan!
> Tell me, tell me, my good djinn,
> Had I not better stay at home,
> For I am a man of peace?

> "And yet it may be best of all
> If I go not to Farsistan
> And fool them one and all, good djinn,
> By drinking wine until I fall—
> Let Shaitan take my wife and friends!"

The boat moved close to our shoal; I could see the round red face of the grim Izet; he was sitting erect, rowing without bending his back. The Persian lithely got to his feet, groped in the bosom of his shirt and headed for the boat with a spring in his step.

"Well, we've got to get in the boat too and start out," said Barinov, stretching so hard that his tendons made a crackling noise. "However, let's wait a bit; give them a chance to talk awhile, friendly like—"

Izet jumped out of the boat into the water and started for the shore, stooping over, hiding his hands behind his back, while the Persian suddenly squatted on his heels. Thereupon Izet, halting for a second, adjusted his hat, ran the palm of his hand over his face and, mopping the sweat off it, in his turn bent his knees in a funny fashion.

"Hey, hey, you devils!" Barinov yelled out in fright, jumping to his feet, and hurriedly said to me: "They want to fight, the good-for-nothings! Hey, you—you mustn't! Why, they fight with knives!"

Yes: a long slender knife that looked like a live fish was flashing in the hand of each friend. Squatting on their heels, reminding one of black grouse on a drumming log, they were shifting from foot to foot, hopping about, while Barinov was looking around him, muttering in alarm: "Eh, what a pity there's no stick handy—ought to bash them over the head with a stick—"

Suddenly the Persian quickly thrust his whole body forward, while Izet let out a grunt, flung his arms wide and fell over on his back.

"Where you going? They'll slit your throat!" Barinov cried out as I ran toward the boat.

Standing on his knees the Persian was thrusting his knife into the sand with his left hand: he would thrust the knife in, draw it out and, after wiping the blade with the skirt of his jacket, thrust it in again.

"What have you done?" I asked him.

He answered, baring his teeth, stroking the knife with his fingers: "Me look for him long time, the dog."

Crimson streamlets of blood were running down his right hand from under the sleeve; the blood dripped in heavy drops onto the sand and disappeared, leaving rust-colored spots behind it.

Izet was lying on his back, his feet lowered into the water, his cheek pressed tight against the moist sand. His face had turned brown; the glazed eyes were staring intently at the unclenched hand he had flung out and at the knife lying near it. The fingers of the other hand had dug into the sand, while his lips were angrily pouting.

"Find him heart," the Persian winked at me. *"Chik!"*

Cautiously, sidling along, Barinov made his way to the boat, clambered into it and shouted to me: "Hell, let's go!"

When, after having shoved the boat off, I sat down at the oars, he began yelling as he shifted heavily to the stern: "Wait, you swine—we'll fix you right away, you villain—"

The Persian, standing on his knees, was gaily nodding to us and suddenly called out in a ringing voice: "Good-bye!"

He pulled the jacket off his shoulders, then his shirt, and exposed his long arm, which was red to the shoulder: it burst into a vivid glow in the sun, as if it had been forged out of some metal the color of blood.

And everything around was, anew, like a dream. . . .

1918

Alexander Alexandrovich BLOCK

[1880-1921]

> *Block will live as long as dreamers*
> *exist—and their tribe is immortal.*
>
> EUGENE ZAMIATIN

> *Block's poem, "The 12," will endure*
> *as the greatest phenomenon*
> *in Russian literature.*
> *. . . Pushkin was Russia's first love; after him*
> *she loved many, but Block she came to*
> *know during fearsome, fatal days, during*
> *her great ordeal by fire; when she could*
> *not love, she came to know and to love him.*
>
> ILYA ERENBURG

Alexander Block, aristocrat and intellectual, belongs in the same galaxy as Pushkin and Lermontov and, without need of abiding anybody's judgment, is the supreme Russian poet of this century; he may also be said to have personified the entire Symbolist movement. His first volume of poems was brought out in 1904; in 1906 Meyerhold produced his poetical play, *Show Booth*. In the revolutionary year of 1905 Block carried the Red flag at the head of a procession; in 1917 he was at the front; he took the October Revolution to his heart and bosom and remained true to it to his very end, even though that Revolution eyed him askance for what it regarded as deviations from its theology and metaphysics. And, to this day, he is the most popular modern poet in Russia. He died from a coronary complaint, aggravated by privations due to the blockade which Russia's erstwhile allies were maintaining against her. In "The 12," a comparatively

short poem which is said to have been written in a single
night, this magnificent poet has succeeded in doing what
many an excellent historian, after devoting a lifetime to turning out ponderous tome after ponderous tome, has failed to
do. He has epitomized a revolution. And, over and above
that, has also epitomized all Revolution as it always has been,
is, and will be. "The Scythians" is offered here not merely as
a barbaric but as a truly prophetic yawp sent over the roofs
of the non-Slavic world. Unfortunately, statesmen are little
(if at all) given to heeding either poets or prophets; the
reader, however, can judge after reading the quatrain next to
the last if the poet has in any detail exaggerated the actions,
just a historical second ago, of Germany which is, nevertheless, at present the coddled darling of all the non-Slavic
world; as for the Strontium-90-haunted future, the reader
is referred to the fourteenth quatrain. And to the sixteenth.

THE 12*

I

Black the night.
White the snow.
Blow, wind, blow—
You can't keep on your feet—hold tight!
Blow, wind, blow—
Over all of God's world go!

Watch the wind swirl
The white, fluffy snow.
Snow on top, thin ice below.

* From *A Treasury of Russian Literature* . . . Translated
. . . selected and edited . . . by Bernard Guilbert Guerney,
published (and copyright, 1943) by The Vanguard Press,
Inc., New York. The Editor hereby gratefully acknowledges
his indebtedness to The Vanguard Press, Inc., for permission
to include "The 12" in this Anthology.

Watch out—don't trip;
Better walk slow.
Ah, the poor fellow—he sure did slip!

From tower to tower
Stretches thick twine.
On this twine hangs a sign:
To the Ratifying Assembly—All Power!
A little crone, in despair, is groaning, keening—
She simply cannot grasp the placard's full meaning:
Where is the need of such a huge sign?
There's enough cloth in that canvas square
Many a good lad's boots for to line—
For our lads have no clothes and their feet are bare . . .

Like an old hen the crone
Surmounts a snowdrift both deep and wet:
"Oh, Mother of God, defend your own!
Oh, them Bolsheviks will be the death of me yet!"

The wind is most ornery!
The frost is as fierce.
The bourzhui on the corner, he
Turns his coat collar right up to his ears.

And who is this? Hair long, unsheared,
And he mumbles into his beard:
"The treacherous swine!
Russia is through!"
Some writing gent, with a high-class line,
Now up the flue.

And there, through snowdrifts slinking,
Goes a cassocked roly-poly:
Why so sad, so shrinking,
Comrade Holy?

Remember your old tricks?
How proudly you would stalk,
Your belly, outthrust, bore a crucifix
And shone on all the folk.

Two ladies meet and walk side by side;
The one in caracul voices her woes:
"We just cried *and* cried—"
She slips—*wham!* There she goes,
Stretched out from her head to her toes!
Upsy-daisy;
Lift her, now—go easy!

The wind is bracing,
And evil, and fine,
Under skirts racing,
Lashing at heads,
Bearing off, torn into shreds,
The huge canvas sign:
To the Ratifying Assembly—All Power!
And every word it spreads:

". . . We, too, had a parley . . .
. . . In that house, 'cross the way . . .
. . . And in conclusion
. . . Made a resolution:
Ten roubles for time, twenty-five for all night . . .
. . . No girl will take less; it wouldn't be right . . .
. . . C'mon, dearie, let's hit the hay . . ."

It's getting late.
The street is forsaken—
Save for a tramp
By the cold overtaken;
And the whistling wind will not abate.

"Hey, you poor scamp!
Come here, I say—
Let's kiss, old unshaven! . . ."

"Give me bread!"
"What comes after that, hey?
Git! On your way!"
Black, black the sky overhead.

Rancor, rancor to make one weep,
To make one's blood seethe in dismay,
Rancor sanctified, rancor black and deep . . .

Comrade, on this day
Vigil keep!

II

The wind roams free, the snowflakes flutter;
Twelve men are marching in the gutter.

Their rifle-straps are black, yet glow:
They shall have lights where'er they go!

Their caps are crumpled; they smoke, they gripe:
By rights their backs should bear the convict's stripe!

Liberty, Liberty—
Eh, eh, no crosses on 'em hang!

Bang—bang—bang!

Comrades, it's cold, cold as can be!

"Well, Vanka and Katka are hitting the booze—
She's got plenty of Kerenski bills in her shoes!"

"Vanka is rich now; he's rich—and how!"
"Vanka was one of us; he's a soldier lad now!"

"C'mon, Vanka, bourzhui, son-of-a-bitch!
Try my girl's kisses—ain't she a witch?"

Liberty, liberty!
Eh, eh, no crosses on 'em hang!

"So Katka is busy in Vanka's flat?
What's she so busy with—tell me, what?"

Bang—bang—bang!

They shall have lights where'er they go!
The rifles on their shoulders glow.

In revolution march abreast!
Your foe knows neither sleep nor rest!

Grip rifle, friend; don't show the white feather:
Let Holy Russia have it; fire all together—

At Russia stolid, unrefined,
With huts unfit for humankind,
With her big, broad, fat behind!

Eh, eh, no crosses on 'em hang!

III

So our lads laid down their tools,
The Red Army for to serve,
The Red Army for to serve—
And to die like fightin' fools!

Eh, the troubles we have borne!
Ain't we got fun?
A uniform all torn
And an Austrian gun!

To bring all bourzhuis to ruination
We'll fan a world-wide conflagration—
World conflagration, fed by blood.
Bless us, O Lord!

IV

Snowflakes swirl, runners skirl:
Vanka's out with his girl!
On the shafts small lanterns
Glow.
Eh, eh, let 'er go!

His army coat is a disgrace—
And what a silly-looking face!
He twirls, twirls his black mustache—
One more twirl, one more twirl,
Fooling with his Kitty girl.

Vanka—my, he's broad of shoulder!
Vanka—my, no man talks bolder!
Watch him hugging that fool girl,
Setting her head in a whirl!

She is lolling back in style
Giving him the pearly smile.

Oh, you Kitty, my sweet Kitty—
Your plump face is no end pretty!

V

"On your neck, my darling Kitty,
A knife scar has not yet healed;
Under your breasts, darling Kitty,
That fresh scratch can't be concealed!

"Eh, eh, dance and smile!
Your legs sure the eye beguile!

"What lace undies you wore—
Wear 'em, wear 'em, be in style!
For officers you played the whore—
Whore on, whore, on, for a while!

"Eh, eh, whore awhile—
Till you turn my heart to bile!

"There was that officer—recall?
He did not escape the knife. . . .
You got no memory at all?
I'll refresh it, you low-life!

"I'll give it a trial—
Just lie down with me awhile!

"Spats of suede you once was sporting;
You liked chocolates—and how!
With cadets you went cavorting—
With plain sojers cavort now!

"Eh, eh, sin awhile—
Then the soul won't feel so vile!"

VI

. . . Again the turnout onward dashes;
The driver yells, and flies, and lashes. . . .
"Hold on, hold on! Help me, Andrei!
And you, Pete, run behind the sleigh!"

Bang—bangety—bang—bang—bang—bang—bang!
The stirred up snow-motes in the cold air hang.

Driver—and Vanka—race the sleigh. . . .
"Fire one more shot! Now! That's the way!"

Bangety-bang! "Now you'll know
How with another's gal to go!"

.   .   .   .

"He's run away! Just wait, you trash—
Tomorrow I will cook your hash!"

But where is Kitty? Dead, dead, dead:
The bullet went right through her head.

"You glad now, Kitty?"—"Not a peep!
Lie in the snow, you carrion cheap!"

In revolution march abreast!
Your foe knows neither sleep nor rest!

VII

And again the twelve go marching,
Each with rifle slung in place;
The poor murderer alone
Tries to hide his guilty face.

He strides faster, ever faster—
He has not recovered yet;
Winds his muffler tighter, tighter—
If he only could forget. . . .

"Come on, friend, what's got you down?
You ain't your own self as yet!"
"Come on now, Pete, you old clown—
Is it Kitty you regret?"

"Oh, my friends, she was my steady;
Why, I loved that wench no end. . . .
Many nights, black nights and heady,
With that wench I used to spend!"

"For the deviltry alone
Gleaming in her eyes of fire,
For a mole that scarlet shone
When her body I'd admire—
Like a fool I've killed my own
Dearest one—my heart's desire!"

"Why, you bitch! So that's your worry!
What are you—a woman? Hey?
Want to spill your heart-throb story?
Well, not at *this* time of day!
We can't now play nursie with you—
Not in this earth-shaking year;
Greater burdens strain our sinew—
Think that over, comrade dear!"

Thereupon his restless pace
To his comrades' pace Pete slows—
And again lifts up his face,
Off his shoulders worry throws.

Eh, eh, no harm is done
Just to have a little fun!

Lock up every house door tight—
There'll be robberies tonight!

Open every cellar wide—
Tonight all the beggars ride!

VIII

Oh, the troubles we have borne!

What weariness weary,
Deathly, dreary!

How the time will pass, somehow
I will watch, I will watch. . . .

And for pastime head and brow
I will scratch, I will scratch. . . .

Some polly seeds to chew, now,
I will snatch, I will snatch. . . .

I will slit the throat, I vow,
Of some wretch, of some wretch. . . .

You'd better fly, you bourzhui crow!
I'll let your blood flow,
To avenge one I know—
Her brows like the sloe. . . .
Lo-rd—re-hest—the-so-houl—of—thi-his Tha-hy
    handmaiden!

What   w e a r i n e s s !

IX

The towers brood in the still night,
No more is heard the city's din;
Not a policeman is in sight—
"Lads, paint the town, though there's no gin!"

A bourzhui at a crossing, shrinking,
Tries hard to warm his nose and hands;
With tucked-in tail, famished, slinking,
A mangy hound beside him stands.

Starved like the dog, the bourzhui pale
Stands silent, like a question mark;
Like mongrel hound with tucked-in tail
The old world heels him in the dark.

X

"That is sure a growing blizzard—
What a blizzard, what a blizzard!
To see four steps off a wizard
Would be needed! Nasty as a buzzard's gizzard!"

The snow like a cyclone swirls,
The snow in upright pillars whirls.

"Holy Savior, how it's snowing!"
"Hey, Pete, watch out where you're going!
Did any golden altar screen
Save you from committing sin?
From the neck up you are dead—

Get some sense into your head!
Ain't your hands with dried blood gritty,
Just because you loved poor Kitty?"

"In Revolution march abreast!
Your foe is near—he knows no rest!"

Ahead, ahead, ahead—
   All ye who earn your bread!

XI

Unblessed, the twelve march steady,
Into the distance going;
For all things set and ready,
For nothing pity knowing.

Their rifles they all train
Upon their unseen foe,
At every blind lane
Where wind and blizzard blow,
And where their boots remain
Stuck in soft, drifted snow. . . .

    A flag—red—
    Makes eyes ache.

    Measured tread
    Makes earth quake.

    Hark! The dread
    Foe may wake. . . .

And the blizzard blinds their sight
    Day and night
    Endless, white. . . .

Ahead, ahead—
   All ye who earn your bread!

XII

. . . They march on with sovereign tread. . . .
"Who's that, now? Come on out!"

'Tis the wind, far off ahead,
Trying the red flag to rout. . . .

A deep snowdrift lies ahead:
"Who's in there? Hey, come on out!"
Just a hungry hound, half-dead,
Skulks behind them as they shout. . . .

"Mangy mutt, don't hang around—
Or you'll feel my bayonet!
The old world is a scabby hound—
Git! A beating's all you'll get!"

It still skulks, nor will give ground,
Tail tucked in and wolf fangs bare—
Hungry hound, mongrel hound!
"Hey there, answer! Who goes there?"

"That red flag—who waves it so?"
"It's so dark—can't see at all!"
"Who's that running? See him go,
Hiding behind every wall?"

"It's no use; come on out, friend—
I will get you, live or dead!"
"You'll fare poorly in the end,
For we'll fill you full of lead!"

Bang—bang—bang! And echo only
Mid the houses loudly rang,
While the blizzard, laughing snowily,
Pealed and shrieked and howled and sang.

> *Bang—bang—bang!*
> *Bang—bang—bang.* . . .

. . . Thus they their sovereign march pursue:
Behind them skulks the hound half-dead;
Ahead (with flag of sanguine hue)—

> Invisible within the storm,
> Immune from any bullet's harm,

Walking with laden step and gentle
In snowy, pearl-strewn mantle,

With small, white roses garlanded—
Jesus the Christ walks at their head.

January 1918

THE SCYTHIANS

> *Panmongolism! Though it sound queer,*
> *It falls like a caress upon my ear.*
>
> VLADIMIR SOLOVIEV

You come in millions. Our hosts darken earth.
Try us in combat—let us see who dies!
Yea, we are Scythians! Yea, Asia gave us birth—
Gave us our slanted and our greed-filled eyes!

Yours are the ages; an hour our lifetime spans.
Like clods that homage to their masters yield,
Between the Mongols and old Europa's clans
For long we served as but a battered shield.

For ages, ages, your ancient forges pounded
Louder than any avalanche's roar;
When Lisbon and Messina vanished, their fall sounded
Like a wild tale for children, and no more.

For centuries your eyes toward the East were turned,
While with our treasures you your coffers filled—
Yet, mocking us, you for the time yearned
When with your mortars we might all be killed.

The time has come. On wings misfortunes dart—
With every day our wrongs increase amain;
Yet there will come a day: your Paestums will depart
And not a trace of them will upon earth remain!

If you are wise, as Oedipus once was
(While yet your heart in a sweet torment shrinks
Ere your end comes), O Old World, pause
Before the ancient enigma of the Sphinx!

That Sphinx is Russia. Exulting, sorrowing,
Spurting black blood—her eyes still gaze and gaze
Upon your visage; those eyes are harrowing
In their great hatred, yet with love ablaze.

'Tis long since any of you loved, for you are cold;
You cannot love—your blood is not hot, like ours!
You have forgotten that the world can hold
A love that sears like flame and, like flame, devours.

We love all things: the fire of numbers chill,
The dower of all celestial visions seen;
We grasp all things: the Gallic wit and skill,
The somber genius of the Teutonic spleen.

We recall all: Parisian streets infernal,
And coolness of Venetian canals;
Fair, far-off lemon groves, in fragrant bloom and vernal,
And Cologne's massive, smoke-begrimed walls.

We love the flesh: its taste, its tones,
Its charnel odor, breathed through Death's jaws. . . .
Are we to blame if your fragile bones
Should crack beneath our heavy, gentle paws?

We have a way of breaking wildest steeds—
Though we may have to snap their spines in two;
And captive women, though sprung from fieriest breeds,
We also gentle and to our ways subdue.

Come ye to us! Let us in peace embrace
Before war's horror all mankind smothers;
Before it is too late your swords in sheaths replace—
Come, comrades! Let us all be brothers!

But if you will not, what have we to lose?
For we, like you, can stoop to perfidy!

For ages, ages will you reap the curses and abuse
Of your degenerate and sick posterity!

To seemly Europe we shall yield the path,
Scatter through forests, vanish without trace—
Then, in due time, will turn on you in wrath,
Showing our savage, our Asiatic face!

Go, all of you, to where the Urals to the skies aspire!
There we are clearing ground for the final fight
Between machines of steel, steel monsters that breathe fire,
And all the savage hordes of the Mongolian might!

But we ourselves henceforth are not your shield—
If there be war, we shall not enter it
But merely watch the raging battlefield,
With each eye narrowed to the narrowest slit!

We shall not stir when the ferocious Hun
Will burn your towns, strip your corpses nude,
Make of each church a stud or cattle run
And his white brothers broil alive for food. . . .

For the last time, Old World, think ere you cease!
Come to our feast as brethren; share our fire!
For the last time, to share our toil and peace
We summon you with our barbaric lyre!

January 30, 1918

Vladimir Vladimirovich
MAYAKOVSKY*

[1893-1930]

Block was the poet who created the Poem of the Great Russian Revolution: Mayakovsky was the Poet of the Great Russian Revolution. The Georgian city of Bagdadi, where he was born, is now called Mayakovsky.

He was active (at twelve) in the Revolution of 1905. From thirteen on he had to fend for himself; at fifteen he had to drop out of the *gymnasia* and was arrested for his part in running an underground press—his age got him a sentence of only eleven months, and this imprisonment gave him a chance to read and to begin writing; at sixteen he was arrested twice, but drew only six months; from his seventeenth year to his twenty-first he studied art; at nineteen (in 1912), together with other Cubo-Futurists (not to be confused with Ego- or other Futurists), he promulgated the famous (and notorious) Futurist Manifesto, *A Slap in the Face of Public Taste*. While it did not dispel all the miasmas pervading the poetical atmosphere it did decidedly jolt the Symbolists and their like, who by that time were definitely stuffed-shirt and old hat. It was also in 1912 that he made his debut in print.

Mayakovsky vigorously opposed World War I and with still greater vigor welcomed the Revolution of 1917 (one of his poems, prophesying its coming, missed the exact date by just a few months). He took part in the fighting, and in practically no time at all turned out at least three thousand different revolutionary posters and six thousand or more rhymed squibs on various revolutionary themes.

* A *mayak* is a *beacon.—Ed.-Trans.*

1930, the year Mayakovsky shot himself, was marked by a twenty-year jubilee of his artistic activity, as well as an exhibition of his work during that period, but what made his suicide still more shocking was his having condemned Yessenin's suicide: "In this life dying is not hard;/ To construct life is considerably harder."

As a master poet Mayakovsky was a Promethean innovator, and his unorthodox poetics is as effective as a sledge hammer. And, since he had very little use for poetic "melancrockery," satire, not unnaturally, is overwhelmingly preponderant in his poetry and drama. His popularity in the USSR, even today, is paralleled only by that of Block.

For a considerable number of reasons, all of them cogent, it was found feasible to show here only the consternation of this life-long foe of the bourgeoisie and its mores over the lusty second growth of the bourzhuis-ification of his beloved Russia, after thinking that process (today rapidly approaching its full bloom) had been destroyed root, stock and branch by his equally beloved Revolution; also, his cockiness as a citizen of his native land (surely, Americans should chuckle as appreciatively over this as the Russians do over Whitman when he so expertly makes the eagle scream); and, finally, his attitude (on the whole one of quite tolerant admiration) toward America, which he visited in 1925; this selection has the additional merit of demonstrating that Mayakovsky could be quite as much of a prophet as Block was.

TRASH

Glory, Glory, Glory to the heroes!!!
But, no doubt,
They
Have had their bellyful of glory-hash;
Today
Let us mere zeros

Talk about
Trash.

The storms of revolt are all dead as the Czar.
The Soviet whirlpools are covered with scum.
And there has peeped out
From behind the back of the USSR
The burgher's damned snout—
His day has come.

(Don't get me wrong, for I by no means
Am opposed in the least to burghers *en masse:*
In fact I am ready to chant hymns and paeans
To every gradation of that great class.)
From all the vast stretches of Russia's black loam
Soon as the Soviets were born they came on the run;
Quickly turning their coats they made Home Sweet Home
Of all institutions, missing nary a one.

By sitting five years with never a letup
They've grown corns hard as rocks on their rosy cans;
By peacefully sitting they've hatched out their plans,
And each one by now has a beautiful setup
Of comfy boodwars and right cosy dens.

And, as nightfall is nearing,
This turd or that,
From gallons of tea all in a sweat,
At his fatter half leering
As she runs through the scales on the grand pianner,
Will say: "Comrade Nadia! My dear little pet—
I'm due for a raise that'll put me up there,
In the high brackets;
I'll get me some clothes in the grand manner;
Real Norfolk jackets
Wide as the Pacific,
And me like a reef in 'em—simply terrific!"
Then Nadia pipes up, with a sweet girlish snigger:
"And get me a dress
With every last emblem—
Them emblems, I guess,

Are now strickly *de rigger;*
I'll have to assemble 'em
Right *here* and right *there;*
If the Hammer-and-Sickle don't cover her all
A girl just can't show her face anywhere!
Now, what shall I wear
To show off my figger
At tonight's
Revolutionary
Military
Soviet
Ball?"

Marx, he was peeping
From a dear little frame (still red, even though peeling)
Hung up on a wall;
On the latest *Izvestia*
A dear little kitten was sleeping;
Whilst near the dear little ceiling
A damn-fool canary,
Hog-fat and yellow,
Kept beeping and cheeping.

So Marx he kept peeping and peeping
At this and that *bestia*—
Then suddenly opened his mouth wide
And did he let out a bellow!
"The Philistines are taking us all for a ride—
They've got the Revolution all balled up in a tangle!
The bourzhuis and their ways are more rotting than caries;
More to be dreaded than even Wrangel.
Quick! Twist the damned neck of every bloody canary,
So's Communism won't get licked by canaries!"

1920-1921

LINES ON A SOVIET PASSPORT

Like a wolf
                I'd gnaw clean
                                all bureaucratism.
Before mandates
                I never
                                fall prone.
For all of me
                all papers
                                can go plumb to hell—
All, that is, but
                just one
                                that I own.

Down the long row
                        of cabins,
                                        or train seats,
An official moves
                with
                                due deference;
The passengers hand over
                                passports;
                                                I, too,
Hand over my
                purplish-red
                                reference.
Some passports
                evoke
                                the warmest of smiles,
Whilst others
                are treated with
                                chilliest scorn—
But there's always
                the deepest respect
                                        for the British

Lion-
    forenenst-
        Unicorn.

They'll always snub some
               good-natured
                    slob,
Or squelch some
          poor soul
              with a look;
Then,
      scraping and bowing,
               as if getting a tip,
They'll receive
          an American's
              book.

The way
        goats
           at billboards stare,
At passports from
              Poland
                they glare
With a policemanish
               pachydermal
                   ponderosity:
"Who ever heard of this
              geographical
                   monstrosity?"

Their cabbage heads pay
             little
               heed,
Show no interest
          and still less
              dismay
Over papers of
         Dane
           or of Swede,

Of Greek,
          or of Turk
                    or Malay.
But suddenly something
                    pains
                         the bureaucrat's puss,
Something
          bothers
                  the official gent:
He's got
          to pick up
                    from this Russ
His red-bound
                Soviet
                      document.

He picks it up like a
                    quilled
                           porcupine;
He picks it up like a
                    live
                       hand grenade;
He picks it up like a
                    fifteen-foot
                               rattler
Or a honed
          razor
               with a double-edged blade.
The porter looks willing
                       his tip
                              to forego—
He winks,
         lays a finger
                     alongside his nose;
But the
        dick in plain clothes,
                              he looks at the gendarme—
And the gendarme,
                  he looks at the
                                dick in plain clothes.

The whole gendarme
                    caste
                        would be glad to work over me;
To crucify me
            they'd be only
                        too tickled,
Because my Red passport
                    is Soviety,
                            Hammery;
Because it is Starred,
                because it is
                            Sickled.

Like a wolf
        I'd gnaw clean
                    all bureaucratism.
Before mandates
            I never
                fall prone.
For all of me
            all papers
                    can go plumb to hell—
All, that is, but
            just one
                that I own.

It is a manifest,
                you benighted
                            fellows,
Of a priceless
            cargo,
                marked by a Star;
Go on and read it!
                You're right to be
                            jealous:
I am a
    citizen
        of the USSR.

1929

AMERICANS WONDER

With devouring
        eyes
            behind tortoise-shell spectacles,
Standing on tiptoes
        on its shore,
            from afar,
America
    wonders,
        watches unblinking,
America
    measures
        the USSR.
What are
    these Russians?
            Of what rare breed?
Beavering,
    building,
        making and tilling,
They've struck on
    the notion
        of their Five-Year Plans—
But these
    in four years
        they are now fulfilling.
You can't
    approach them
        with an American yardstick;
Dollars (or roubles)
    they don't think
        the best pay;
With each bit
    of energy
        that is within them
They work
    the whole week now,
        without a rest day.

What are
        these Russians?
                        How were they tempered?
They are not driven
                by knout
                        or by stick—
Who, then, has
                impelled them
                        to labor so hard?
It's their own
                steel discipline
                        that makes them tick!
Misters,
        skill-buying
                to you is an old story—
It takes just
                a twist
                        of your puffy wrists;
Misters,
        you can't know
                the drive and the glory,
The roots of
                the zeal
                        of our Communists!
Bourzhuis,
        keep wondering,
                        but don't get hystericky;
Watch us work, live and play,
                        but
                                make no mistake:
Your fleet-footed,
                much advertised
                        'Meriky
We'll not only catch up with
                        but
                                will overtake.

1929

Serghei Alexandrovich YESSENIN

[1895-1925]

Yessenin was a peasant-nugget from Ryazan; he became prominent among the Imagists—a 1919 by-blow of the Futurists. As a poet he ranged, to borrow a critical *bon mot,* from cherub to hooligan; he claimed, in one poem: "Had I not been born a poet,/ For sure, I'd be swindler and thief," and, in another, described himself as a "Russian, scandalous poet." At any rate, there can be no more doubt about Yessenin's nationality, scandalousness and stature as a poet than there can be about Villon's.

But, whatever his not-undeserved popularity in Russia as a genuine though hardly self-disciplined poet, the Yessenin cult abroad was based on little more than a prurient interest in his affair with Isadora Duncan (who was accidentally strangled with a silk scarf), and such oddments as his travels (he visited the U.S.A.), his Hollywoodish good looks, certain traditionally titivating Parnassian gestures (Yessenin wrote his last poem in his blood), and his much criticized suicide (in a state of aberration and a Leningrad hotel room, by hanging himself with a valise strap), which act lent itself most handily to perversion into musk-scented propaganda against the then still-struggling Soviets.

In "Drove of Stallions" Yessenin is in his most characteristic vein. The present writer cannot help feeling that, as pure poetry, this poem (at least in the Russian) is of the same quality as "The Dalliance of the Eagles." Which, however, is not meant to imply the least Whitmanesque influence.

DROVE OF STALLIONS

Stallions in a drove on green hillocks graze;
Their nostrils blow aureate dust off the days.

From a high knoll into the blue-shimmering bay
Pitch-blackness plummets as their dark manes sway.

Their heads, aquiver, over still waters idle:
The crescent moon stalks them with silver bridle.

Snorting, they from their own shadows shy
And greet the new day with their manes tossed high.

The spring day peals above the equine ear
In welcome to the first flies of the year.

At evenfall, mid meadows, with tails switching
The stallions run, heels kicking high, ears twitching.

Ever more harsh the clangor that to their hooves is clinging
Now drowning in the air, now from the willows swinging.

And let a wave but reach out for a star—
The midges fleck the waters like ashes strewn far.

The sun has faded. Softly, drowsily
The drover's pipe sounds on the distant lea.

Forehead to forehead stands the drove and heeds
The tousled yokel's song upon his reeds.

Nuzzling the stallions, sportive, has the echo flown
To bear their pensive dreams to other leas unknown.

Loving each day of yours, and your nights' ebon hue,
I wrought, O native land of mine, this song for you.

1915

Alexei Nicholaievich TOLSTOI

[1882-1945]

Alexei Nicholaievich Tolstoi (himself a count before the Revolution) was related not only to Count Leo Nicholaievich Tolstoi but also to Count Alexis Constantinovich Tolstoi, the dramatist, poet and wit, while on his mother's side he was a direct descendant of Ivan Turgenev. But, avoiding the obvious expediency of a pen name, he persisted in writing under his own, and achieved both popularity and pre-eminence.

A 100 percent Slav in World War I, he was rabidly anti-Bolshevik in 1917, served as a propagandist for the White General Denikin, and in due course found his way to Paris. By 1921, however, he decided that Communism had come to stay in Russia and in 1923 returned to his native land, where he became a symbol, as it were, of the *rapprochement* between the old Russia and the new, and, after Gorki's death, the official dean of Soviet letters and a diplomatic and cultural ambassador of the new regime.

His first appearance in print was in 1908, with a volume of poems; his output is extensive and varied, ranging from a Russianized version of *Pinocchio* to such three-deckers as *The Road to Calvary* and *Peter the Great* (the third and final volume of which was published posthumously). Both trilogies are Soviet classics—*Peter the Great* is approaching the status of a world classic; both have appeared in English, but these out of print translations can be adequately described only in unprintable terms. As a historical novelist, Tolstoi's predilection was for parlous times; he was never afraid of being a storyteller; his many plays were good theatre. He was an innovator in science-fiction, a practically neglected field in Russian literature. His *Aelitta* would be merely amusing to the devotees of Edgar Rice Burroughs, since the hero is no swashbuckling John Carter but a New Soviet Man who is more intent on making Mars a really Red planet than carrying on with the chartreuse-skinned but comely Aelitta; however, *The Council of Five* and *The Hyperboloid of the Engineer Garin**** are in the true Verne-Wells vein, while the latter also leaves Oppenheim and Buchan far behind as masters of the novel of international intrigue. It is a pity, too, that neither *Black Gold*, a rather lurid thriller, nor *Ibicus*, that fascinating grotesque and satirical picaresque, is likely to be translated into English in the foreseeable future.

AMID THE SNOWS

In the night a man in a long overcoat of dogskin emerged on the crest of a snow-covered knoll, looked over the clear, steep slope flooded with moonlight, adjusted the rifle on his back and started at a fast run downward on his broad skis and was enveloped in the blizzard.

After him a second man emerged on the crest, and another, and another still, all of them in long belted overcoats. One after the other, leaning back, legs spread out, they flew downward, to where the blue shadows of the pines lay on the snow. They sped downward and vanished in the forest.

After a brief while a wolf came out on the same hill; the pack followed him. The wolf squatted. Some of the others lay down, placing their muzzles on their paws: they were listening, their eyes fixed on the point where, at the foot of the hill, two rows of frost-gripped rails glistened beyond the forest.

The wolves were sleek of pelt. They had been long following the tracks of the partisans. The partisans, traversing hillocks and forests, were penetrating deep into the rear of the

* Published in England (Methuen, 1934), in the Editor's translation, under the title of *The Death Box*, now a collectors' item.

retreating remnants of the ill-starred provisional ruler's troops. For thousands of miles around, the Siberian mouzhiks had risen in their homesteads and villages, had dashed off in pursuit of the ruler's countless treasures, now going off toward the east.

That same night, at no great distance from these localities, a freight train enveloped in smoke was crawling toward the east. Smoke and sparks were rising from each cattle car. Furnaces or braziers were going in some of the cars, and here and there there would be an actual bonfire on the floor of the car.

They were strange, the men sitting about the fires—soot-covered, with hungry frightening faces, in torn army overcoats, in sheepskin coats—some simply in countrywives' fur coats, their noses frostbitten, their feet wrapped in rags, in pieces of carpeting.

They stared at the fire, these men. All the jests had been told over and over long since—they were in no mood for jests. They were traveling for the third week, from Moscow itself, in pursuit of the treasure—that treasure, surrounded by the remnants of the ruler's troops, was receding ever further toward the east.

Suddenly chains thundered, buffers creaked, the cars stopped. Doors were flung wide open. Out with you!

They leapt out of the cars. Breath turned to billows of steam. One could not breathe, so bitter the frost. Seven rainbow rings around the moon. The charred uprights of the railway station stuck up out of the snow. The voices of the officers were hoarse as they called out their orders.

The fighters started off in a scattered cordon over the snowy plain, not knowing where they were heading—there was no end to it in sight. They went on, they lay down in a cordon. They got up, again plodded over the brittle, wavy snow, stumbling against the snowdrifts.

During that night several men had seen something of such a nature that later, when they had returned to their cattle cars after the battle, they could not tell their stories right away—it made their teeth chatter so. What they had seen was mouzhiks standing mother-naked on the plain, spaced about a hundred feet apart. The mouzhiks, to make them stand firmly, had had water poured over them, and each had his arm raised to point out the road. Folks were saying the ruler had placed a lot of such landmarks along the roads.

The battle that night had been a light one: the enemy wouldn't let them near, had disappeared. In the end they never did make out whom they had been fighting against: the ruler, the Czechs, the hetmans.

They sat down again in their cattle cars, riding on toward the east in pursuit of the treasure.

The treasure—six hundred thousand pounds of gold, avoirdupois—was crawling in twenty cars over the deserts of snow toward the east. The cars left a trail of blood. The train was making its way onward like a beast surrounded by wolfhounds.

Invisible, piercing rays emanated from this gold, lost amid the snows. It made heads spin; dispatches in code flew from land to land. Speeches about military expeditions to Moscow were delivered in sundry parliaments. Loans were arranged for the purchase of arms. Military forces were being equipped.

Six hundred thousand pounds of gold, avoirdupois, were moving toward the east, ever nearer, nearer to the open sea. One effort more and—so it seemed—the gold would be snatched out of the boundaries of mad Russia, and that would be the end of the crazy antics in the east.

But, tightly gripped as far as the very boundaries of what had been the Duchy of Grand Duke Ivan the Third, Great Russia was desperately battling on all four sides of her, struggling to get at bread, at the sea, at the gold.

That same night, at the conclusion of a conference, the provisional ruler's authorized representative in Paris descended into the enormous glass-roofed vestibule of the Russian embassy and, as he was pulling on his skin-tight gloves, was saying to the general who was the authorized representative of the Southern Army: "I assure you that we are liberals, that we are true republicans. After your report, General, our old men crawled under the table. What have you gone and done, Your Excellency?"

The general was staring with rancorous, turbid eyes at the other authorized representative—face rosy, beard well tended, eyes merry, a full-fleshed fellow, well grown and with a way of rocking on his heels. He seized the general's arm and, gurgling with laughter, drew him down the stairs.

"Your Excellency, the Frenchmen won't give four sous to back up your report. Why all these Hannibalic battles? We ought to march with banners unfurled; the populace will greet us in raptures, the Red troops will joyously come over to our side. . . . I assure you that the French have become fed up with military events; what they are thirsting for is the idealistic. That gold train, for instance—now *that* is something. Every day it is drawing nearer to Vladivostok—and every day the French are becoming more amenable to extending credit. Whereas all you have to offer are the same mountains of corpses. The ideal thing would be if you could manage to march up to Moscow without firing a shot."

"You're laughing, are you?" the general asked, looked at his feet, twitched his mustachios, put on his cheap derby and his spring overcoat and walked out. The February wind caught him up on the front steps, piercing him to the bone.

The provisional ruler's authorized agent jumped out of the taxi and, holding on to his velour hat, darted across the rain-lashed sidewalk; tossing his overcoat into the doorman's arms he asked: "Are they expecting me?" The doorman, attuned to an amatory adventure, answered: "Mademoiselle has just arrived." And the authorized agent went up to the second floor of the restaurant, feeling particularly buoyant because of his evening clothes, the music, the lights.

There was a fire in the fireplace of the private cabinet; one could smell the coals, and there was a hint of an elusive perfume, just a trifle on the bitter side. Mlle. Bouchard, in a skimpy black dress, the lower part of her face buried in a muff of cat fur, was perched on the divan. Standing by the fireplace was her brother, an extraordinarily respectable young man with a mustache. He bowed, without the least relaxation of his extremely serious air. Mlle. Bouchard, without removing the muff from her chin, held out her beautiful hand; her arms were bare.

The authorized representative sighed, kissed her fingers, seated himself on the divan, stretched his enormous legs toward the fire and smiled, exposing every tooth in his toothy mouth: "It's fine to be near a fire in weather such as this—"

Mlle. Bouchard's brother made a few weighty remarks concerning the Parisian climate, after which he praised the Russian climate, which he had read about.

The maître d'hôtel, followed by a waiter and the wine steward, brought in the food and wine. The maître d'hôtel examined the table hypercritically, adjusted the coals in the fireplace with the tip of his shoe and backed out of the room.

Mlle. Bouchard, a very young actress from the Theatre de Jimiez, placed her muff on the divan and bestowed a radiant smile on the Russian. She had a pretty little face—wide forehead, childlike eyes, snub nose, sharp chin. She drank and ate like a market porter. After the second course the brother of Mlle. Bouchard considered himself duty bound to tell several anecdotes he had garnered from the evening paper; Mademoiselle, flushed from the wine and the heat of the fireplace, was laughing for all she was worth.

The authorized representative had read those anecdotes himself that day, and although he was aware that the brother of Mlle. Bouchard was not her brother at all but most probably her lover, and that Mademoiselle had firmly resolved not to place her charms at the Russian's disposal on any other basis save that of contractual benefits for herself, he nevertheless was in a gay and carefree mood today.

Glancing occasionally at the rather bony back of Mlle. Bouchard, bare to the waist, at all the poverty-stricken ingenuities of her skimpy little dress, smiling from time to time, he kept reiterating to himself: "You little fool, you little fool—don't be afraid, I won't fool you; at any rate I'll feed you better than you're being fed now and not worse; we'll see about getting the better of your rickets, and when the people on your block find out about the gold train you'll be your block's most famous kitten—"

After the champagne, deep wrinkles appeared on the brow of the brother of Mlle. Bouchard and, with his eyes fixed on the snowy tablecloth, he said, in a rather stifled voice: "I do hope the bad news from the eastern front is without confirmation?"

"What news?"

"An hour ago the courier of our department showed me a radiogram—" He turned around to the fireplace and tossed the end of his cigarette into the flames. Mlle. Bouchard (and this was altogether strange and even eerie) glanced at the provisional ruler's representative with eyes that were no longer childlike but attentive, clever. Her little mouth was compressed in a hard line.

"The gold train of the provisional ruler—so the courier told me—has been seized by the Bolsheviks—"

"Bosh!" The Russian stood up and took three stumbling steps through the cabinet, his body seeming to fill the whole room. "Bosh—a Moscow provocation—"

"Ah! So much the better." Mlle. Bouchard's brother settled down to coffee and cognac. Mademoiselle picked up her muff and yawned into the cat fur. The authorized agent launched into a speech about the inevitable ruin of the Bolsheviks, about the imminent fraternal union of France and renascent Russia, but suddenly became conscious that he had forgotten half the French words. He scowled and took to poking the coals in the fireplace with the fire tongs. The supper was ruined.

On that same night, while the wolves were watching from the crest of the hill, the partisan skiers approached the road-bed. Some of them scattered among the tree trunks, others pulled axes out of their belts, and the axes began to ring, like glass on glass, against the frost-bound trees.

The summit of a pine that would have made a proud mast for a ship swayed against the sky, creaked, and crashed on the rails glistening under the moon.

The axe strokes rang. And suddenly a monstrous howl rent

the frosty night. The roadbed began to shake. Lone pines on the hillsides emerged in blood-red outlines. From around a turn, through a notch in the hills an enormous train appeared, drawn by two locomotives that were breathing heat; the cars and platforms were screened; the cannon mouths dully reflected the moonlight.

Blinding flames spurted. The snow-covered hills flared. Weapons roared choppily, machine guns beat a tattoo, rousing echoes.

The train ran full tilt against the felled trees and stopped.

The rifles of the partisans chirked from behind the pines. Some fell into the long sleep, blanketed in snowdrifts. Some ran toward the second turn of the rails and made their axes ring there.

And it was on this night also that an echelon detrained at a station amid shattered cars and dead horses, amid a thousand yelling Red Army men. Steam rose in billows from the men, from the caldrons of boiling water. The locomotives howled. The frost was cruel. Seven rainbows on the moon, which had risen high—very, very high. And, beyond a hill, there was the glow of a conflagration. The provisional ruler's stock piles were on fire, the men were saying.

The men were going off into the lunar mirage in cordons . . . in companies, battalions, regiments. A host of sleigh runners, screaking over the snow. Sleighs going off with machine guns and ordnance.

The frosty murk shudders from double blows. It's that train with the treasure trove of the provisional ruler, fallen into an ambush—so they're saying.

The train is being fired upon from all sides. From the woods and hills. The ways have been blocked. Rails are ripped up. They are unrelenting in their attack, the hungry, the tattered ones, clad in horse cloths, lengths of carpeting, in the fur coats of peasant women—the soot-covered men with frightful eyes.

On that night the treasure train shuddered amid the deserts of snow and started on its return trip, back toward the west.

The golden rays created a fantastic protuberance in the earth's atmosphere. Many heads began to turn vertiginously, becoming muddled. . . .

In a still more westerly direction there was one man who, on returning from the restaurant, spent all that night, until the very morning, sitting up in bed and rocking as if he were in the throes of toothache.

The putrid wind was noisy, rattling the iron shutters. Rain cascaded over the panes. Darkness covered the heart like a pall.

"Who could have conceived, who could have grasped," this man was thinking, "that my life could have tumbled apart like a house of cards from a single piece of news—nonsensical, I feel sure, and false. . . . Horrible! . . ."

1924

Isaac Immanuelovich BABEL

[1894-?]

Odessa is known as the Paris of Russia (although it might be much nearer the mark to liken it to Marseilles—it even boasts a famous staircase street that is twin to the Cannebière); Odessites are Russian Gascons who speak a patois all their own, consisting of exquisitely mangled Russian, and when Odessiennes (the most muliebrile of all the world's women) roll their *r*'s the sound is even more delectable than the summer-rain-patter-on-a-roof canorousness of their Spanish sisters.

When Babel wrote about Odessa, he did so as a native. Odessa Stories are a recognized and duly appreciated genre in Russian literature, but while they were little more than good-natured regional fun to such master humorists as Doroshevich, Averchenko or Valentin Kataev, or highly sentimental in an almost Dickensian fashion when done by Yushkevich, in Babel's hands they became supreme literature: droll (or sardonic), sentimental (and realistic), purely (or Baudelaireanly) lyrical. It has been repeatedly suggested that Chekhov and Maupassant were Babel's chosen masters; perhaps it would be better to say that Chekhov, Maupassant, Zola and Rabelais (if one may dream of such a collaboration) would not be ashamed of the least of Babel's Odessa Stories as their collective effort. And it was with one of these stories that Babel made his literary debut in 1915, with the encouragement of Gorki, in the latter's *Chronicle*.

During the civil war Babel was attached as a political commissar to Budenny's Red Cavalry (the "hetman of the mouzhiks" in "Aphonka Bida" is a self-portrait); the first of his unique and imperishable *Horse Army* pieces appeared in

1924. "Grotesque, sardonic, filled with wormwood poetry, delicate as a dandelion ball at dusk, brutal as dark-red hacked horseflesh, they remain unsurpassed to this day as a series of Goyaesques of revolution, internecine war—of all war." Upon their appearance in book form in 1927 Budenny was extremely enthusiastic about them; subsequently, however, when all sorts of heretical deviations from Communist theology were discovered in them, the commander of the Red Cavalry was just as extremely vehement in his denunciations: Babel was, apparently, more Vereshchagin than Meissonier in depicting war.

These *Horse Army* sketches, the Odessa Stories,* two plays (*Sunset,* 1928, and *Marie,* 1935), and *Benny Kriek* (1926, a screen dramatization of some of the Babel stories dealing with Benny the Yell, a semilegendary holdup-nik who became something very like an Odessa folk hero because of his leadership in resisting the pogroms and his efforts during World War I), constitute practically his whole output; "The Beginning," a short tribute to Gorki, published in an annual in 1938, marked the last appearance in Soviet letters of one whom Gorki had acclaimed a great Soviet writer. Yet, although he was duly drowned in the waters of the river Lethe by the official Soviet critics, it must be pointed out that "The Awakening" is included in a three-volume anthology of Soviet short story writers issued in Moscow in July, 1957, in a first printing of 75,000 copies.

In 1931 he was doing "Soviet literary work" in Paris; after traveling abroad he returned to Russia in 1934 and for a while managed a Caucasian stud farm; his love affair with the sister

---

* Only one collection (comparatively small) brought out in 1928, bears the specific title of *Odessa Stories*; but, with the definite exception of the *Horse Army* pieces, the majority of his writings belong to the Odessa Stories genre. Both groups are, at the present writing, available in *The Collected Tales of Isaac Babel,* edited by Walter Morison (Criterion Books, Inc., New York), a collection admirable for its completeness, containing not only all the stories published in the USSR but those few which had appeared only in French or had survived only in proofs.

of Yagoda, ex-chief of political police, executed in 1937, is said to have led to accusations of Trotskyism against Babel and, about 1938, to his disappearance—a disappearance as mysterious as that of Ambrose Bierce. At any rate, the end of Babel offers a lovely *bonne bouche* to the phantasmagoric school of the historians of Soviet literature: he died from (a) typhoid, (b) lead poison injected via the rifles of a firing squad; or (a) in a concentration camp, (b) in a prison labor camp, (c) abroad—in 1939 (or 1940).

APHONKA BIDA

We were fighting at Leshnuvo. The wall of the enemy's cavalry rose up everywhere. The mainspring of the intensified Polish strategy was uncoiling with a sinister twang. We were being subjected to a pincers movement. For the first time during the entire campaign we were experiencing upon our own hides the devilish sharpness of breakthroughs in the rear and of blows at our flanks—the pitiless bite of that very weapon which had served us for so long and with such good luck.

It was the infantry that was maintaining the front at Leshnuvo. The albinoid and unshod mouzhikhood of Volynak was milling about within the crookedly dug small trenches. These foot soldiers had been taken only the day before from their plows to form an infantry reserve for the Horse Army. The peasants had gone willingly enough; they fought with the greatest zeal—their peasant ferocity amazed even the veterans who had fought under Budenny. Their hatred of Polack landowners was made of material that was unprepossessing but of sturdy quality.

During the second stage of the war, when battle cries failed to impress the imaginations of the foe and cavalry attacks against the entrenched enemy became impossible, this home-grown infantry would have proved of the greatest benefit to the Horse Army. But our poverty got the upper hand of us:

the mouzhiks were issued one gun for every three men and
cartridges that were of the wrong caliber for their rifles. We
had to drop the scheme and send this militia, so authentically
the people's own, back to their homes.

Now let us turn to the Leshnuvo battles. The infantry dug
itself in two miles from the small town. A round-shouldered,
bespectacled young man with a sword dangling at his side
was pacing about at the front line. He had a discontented air
about him, and was hopping, sort of, as if his boots were
too tight for him. This hetman of the mouzhiks, elected
by them and by them beloved, was a Jew, a purblind Jewish
youth, with the puny and absorbed face of a Talmudist. In
battle he evinced a circumspect courage and a *sang-froid*
that was akin to the absent-mindedness of a dreamer.

It was the third hour of an expansive afternoon in July.
The iridescent gossamer of sultriness shimmered in the air. A
festal streak of uniforms, and of horses' manes interwoven
with ribbons, flashed beyond the knolls. The young man gave
a sign to alert his men. The mouzhiks, their bast sandals
flapping, ran to their places and picked their weapons up,
holding them at the ready. It turned out to be a false alarm,
however. The colorful squadrons emerging upon the Leshnuvo highway were those of Maslak. Their gaunt but spirited
steeds were going at a round clip. The impressive banners
upon gilt poles overloaded with velvet tassels swayed amid
fiery pillars of dust. The horsemen rode with majestic and
bold assurance. The shaggy infantry crawled out of its fox-
holes and, letting their jaws drop, gazed at the resilient pos-
turing of the now slowly flowing torrent.

At the head of the regiment, on a loose-legged pony of the
steppe breed, rode the brigade commander Maslak,* swollen
with tipsy blood and fat-bloated purulence. His belly was
lying, like a great tomcat, upon the silver-mounted pommel
of his saddle. On catching sight of the wretched infantry his

---

* Maslakov, Commander of the 1st Brigade, 4th Division,
an incorrigible Partisan, who shortly betrayed the Soviets.—
Author. A *maslok* (sic) is the cannon bone of a horse or
other hoofed quadruped.—*Ed.-Trans.*

face turned purple with suppressed laughter and he beckoned to Aphonka Bida, a platoon leader. This platoon leader bore the nickname of Mahno among us because of his resemblance to the celebrated hetman. They held a whispered consultation for a minute or so, this commander and Aphonka, then the latter turned around to the first commandant, leaned over and issued a low-voiced command: "On the reins!"

The Cossacks, platoon by platoon, changed over to a trot. They had warmed up their mounts and were making a dash for the trenches. The infantry, enjoying the spectacle, stared at them.

"Get set for fightin'!" Aphonka's dolorous and seemingly far-off voice sang out.

Maslak, loudly gasping, coughing, and having a good time, rode off to one side; the Cossacks threw themselves into the attack. The infantry, poor fellows, started running but it was too late. The Cossack lashes had already dusted their raggedy short coats. The horsemen were circling over the field and whirling their quirts with extraordinary artistry.

"What are you carrying on like that for?" I yelled at Aphonka.

"For laughs," he answered me, fidgeting in his saddle and trying to get at a lad who had hidden himself in some bushes. "For laughs!" he shouted, worrying the lad who was now out of his senses from fright.

The fun ended when Maslak, softened up by laughter, waved his pudgy hand with a regal air.

"Keep your wits about you, infantry!" Aphonka shouted and straightened his emaciated body. "Go and catch fleas, infantry—"

The Cossacks, laughing among themselves, were forming into ranks. There was nor hide nor hair to be seen of the infantry. The trenches were deserted, and only the stoop-shouldered Jew still stood at his former place, peering at the Cossacks point-blank and proudly through his spectacles.

The exchange of gunfire from the direction of Leshnuvo did not abate. The Polacks were encircling us. The individual figures of the mounted scouts could be distinguished through the binoculars. They came leaping out of the little town and then seemed to fall through the ground like so many roly-poly toys. Maslak drew up his squadron, disposing it on both sides of the highway. The glittering sky soared high over Leshnuvo, a sky ineffably void, as always in hours of danger. The Jew, with his head thrown back, was mournfully and piercingly blowing a metal whistle. And the infantry, that never-to-be-duplicated, bequirted infantry, was returning to its positions.

The bullets came flying thick in our direction. The brigade staff had gotten into the zone of machine-gun fire. We made a dash for a grove and started scrambling through the brush-wood to the right of the highway. The bullets were fussily grunting over our heads. When we had clambered out of the bushes the Cossacks were no longer in their former position. In accordance with the order of the division commander they were withdrawing in the direction of Brody [The Fords]. The mouzhiks alone were snarling back from their trenches with their guns, and Aphonka, who had fallen behind, was riding hard to catch up with his platoon.

He was riding at the very edge of the road, looking about him and sniffing the air. There was a momentary lull in the firing. The Cossack got it into his head to take advantage of the breathing spell and started off, careering at full speed. At that instant a bullet went through the neck of his horse. Aphonka rode on for a hundred or so paces further and at that point, in our ranks, the steed bent his forelegs sharply and slumped to the ground.

Aphonka carefully took out of its stirrup the leg that had been caught under the animal. He squatted and poked a coppery finger into the horse's wound. After that Bida straightened up and swept the glittering horizon with a harassed look.

"Farewell, Stepan," said he in a wooden voice, stepping back from the dying animal and bowing low before him. "How will I come back without thee to our peaceful Cossack village? Where am I to put the finely worked little saddle that was thine? Farewell, Stepan," he repeated in a stronger voice, gulped for air, squeaked like a caught mouse and sent up a howl. His choppy howling came to our ears and we saw Aphonka bowing and beating his forehead against the ground at each bow, like a hysterical countrywife in church. "No, I ain't goin' to give in to that bloody whore Fate," he began to scream, taking his hands away from his face, which had become deathlike. "No, I'm goin' to cut down them unspeakable Polack bastards without any mercy! I'll get at their heart's breath and their Mother-of-God blood. Before all Cossacks born and bred, my brethren dear, I make thee this vow, Stepan—"

Aphonka lay down, putting his face in the wound, and grew quiet and motionless. Fixing his glowing eye of deep violet hue upon his master, the steed listened to Aphonka's strained breathing. In a gentle coma he moved his drooping muzzle jerkily over the ground, and streams of blood, like twin ruby-colored breech bands, were running down his chest, paved with white muscles.

Aphonka lay there without stirring. Mincing on his thick legs, Maslak walked up to the animal, put his revolver in its ear and fired. Aphonka leapt up and turned his pock-marked horrible face on Maslak.

"Get your harness together, Athanassy," Maslak told him kindly. "Go to your unit—"

And we, on our hillock, saw Aphonka, bowed down under the weight of the saddle, with his face red and raw as hacked meat, infinitely lonely amid the dusty, blazing desert of the fields, meander off to his squadron.

Late in the evening I came upon him in our wagon train. He was sleeping on the cart that was the custodian of all his belongings—sabers, Norfolk jackets and gold coins with holes bored through them. The blood-clotted head of the platoon leader, its dead mouth twisted, was lolling as if crucified upon the hollow of his saddle. Lying alongside him was the harness of the slain horse, the quaint and fantastic caparisons of a Cossack's charger: pectorals with black tassels, pliant breechings and cruppers studded with colored stones, and a bridle stamped with silver.

Darkness was advancing upon us, growing steadily denser. The wagon train wound on its way, becoming more and more steep, over Brody ridge; unassuming little stars rolled over the milky ways of the sky, and distant villages were burning in

the cool profundity of the night. Orlov, second to the
squadron commander, and the long-mustachioed Bitzenko,
were also perched on Aphonka's cart and discussing Aphonka's misfortune.

"He brought that horse along all the way from home," said
the long-mustachioed Bitzenko. "Where's he goin' to find him
another horse like that?"

"A horse, now—he's your friend," Orlov responded.

"A horse, now—he's like a father to you," sighed Bitzenko,
"savin' your life times without end. Bida, he's done for without a horse—"

And, come morning, Bida vanished.

The battles at Brody began and ended. Overwhelming defeat changed to temporary victory; we lived through the re-
placement of the commander of our division; but still there
was no Aphonka. And only the sinister growling of the villages at the predatory marauding of Aphonka gave us any
indication of the thorny path he was pursuing.

"He's gettin' himself a horse," they said of the platoon
leader in our squadron, and during the unimaginable evenings
of our wanderings I heard not a few tales of this stolid,
ferocious quest.

Fighters from other units stumbled upon Aphonka scores
of miles from our positions. He lay in ambush for lagging
Polish cavalrymen or roved the forests seeking out the droves
of horses the peasants had hidden. He put whole villages to
the torch and shot the elders of Polish villages against a wall
for concealing horses. Echoes of this frenzied monomachy
came to our ears, echoes of the desperate and thievish as-
saults of the lone wolf against whole communities.

One more week passed. The latest bitter news of that week
disrupted our routine of stories concerning Aphonka's somber derring-do, and our Mahno began to be forgotten. Then
a rumor swept by that Galician peasants had cut his throat
somewhere in the woods. And on the day of our entrance
into Berstechko, Emilian Budiak, from the First Squadron,
had lost no time in going to the commander of our division to
ask him for Aphonka's saddle and his yellow saddlecloth.

Emilian was hankering to appear at review with a new saddle, only things didn't work out that way for him.

We entered Berstechko on August sixth. Moving at the head of our division were the Asiatic tunic and the red cossackeen of our new commander. Levka, that mad, low-down devil, was leading a brood mare behind the commander. A military march, fraught with a drawn-out threat, swept along the quaint and beggarly streets. Ancient blind alleys, a bedaubed forest of decrepit and convulsed crossbeams, were all over the little place. Its heartwood, eaten out by the ages, breathed sad corruption upon us. The smugglers and holier-than-thou's had hidden themselves in their roomy murky huts. Pan Liudomirski the bell ringer, in his green coat, was the only one to meet us near the Roman Catholic *costella*.

We crossed the river and plunged into the Borough of the Burghers. We were nearing the house of the Polish Roman Catholic priest when Aphonka rode out from behind a corner of the house, mounted on a stalwart bay stallion.

"Greetings," he uttered in his barking voice and, jostling the fighters aside, took his place in the ranks.

Maslak fixed his eyes on the colorless distance and got out hoarsely, without turning his head: "Where did you get that horse from?"

"It's me own," Aphonka answered, rolled himself a cigarette and, with a slight flicker of his tongue, glued it together.

The Cossacks rode up to him one by one and greeted him. Where one of his eyes had been, a monstrous rosy swelling gaped repulsively upon his face, which was now all angles.

And next morning Bida had himself a high time. In the *costella* he smashed up the shrine of St. Valentius and made a stab at playing the organ. He had on a jacket cut out of a blue rug, with a lily embroidered on the back, and his sweaty topknot was combed over his empty eye socket.

After dinner he saddled his steed and shot off his rifle into the shattered, paneless windows of the castle of the Counts Ratziborski. The Cossacks stood around him in a semicircle. They lifted up the stallion's tail, felt his legs and counted his teeth.

"A fine figger of a horse," pronounced Orlov, aide to the leader of the squadron.

"A likely horse," the walrus-mustached Bitzenko seconded him.

1924

THE AWAKENING

All the people in our circle—small-time middlemen, shop-keepers, clerks in banks and steamship offices—were teaching their children music. Our fathers, seeing no way out for themselves, had struck on the notion of a lottery. This lottery they founded on the bones of the little ones. Odessa was possessed by this madness more than other towns were and, true enough, for several decades running our town supplied the Wunderkinder for the concert platforms of the world. Mischa Elman, Zimbalist, Gabrilovitch—they all came from Odessa; Jascha Heifetz got his start among us.

When a boy turned four or five his mother would lead the tiny and puny creature to Mr. Zagursky. Zagursky ran a factory of Wunderkinder, a factory that turned out Jewish dwarfs in little lace collars and little pumps of patent leather. He sought them out in the lairs of Moldavanka, in the malodorous courtyards of the Old Market. Zagursky gave them the first impetus; later on the children were sent off to Professor Auer in St. Petersburg. Mighty harmony dwelt within the souls of these starvelings with their bloated livid heads. They became celebrated virtuosi. And so my father decided to catch up with them, even though I was overage for a Wunderkind—I was going on fourteen; in height and puniness, however, I might have passed for an eight-year-old. Which constituted the last hope.

I was led off to Zagursky. Because of his high regard for my grandfather he consented to take only one rouble for each lesson—a cheap enough rate. My grandfather, Leivi

Itzok, was the laughingstock of the town and, at the same time, its ornament. He walked about the streets in an opera hat and foot clouts and resolved points of doubt in the most obscure matters. They would ask him what a Gobelin was, why the Jacobins had betrayed Robespierre, how synthetic silk was prepared, what the Caesarian section was. My grandfather was able to answer all these questions. So, out of high regard for his learning and madness Zagursky took only one rouble a lesson from us. And it was also because he was afraid of Grandfather that he went to a lot of bother with me, since there was really nothing to bother with. The sounds slithered off my violin like metal shavings. These sounds grated on my own heart, yet my father would not give up. The talk at home was about nothing but Mischa Elman, who had been exempted from military service by the Czar himself. Zimbalist, according to information gathered by my father, had been presented to the King of England and had played at Buckingham Palace; the parents of Gabrilovitch had bought two mansions in St. Petersburg. These Wunderkinder had brought riches to their parents. My father might have reconciled himself to poverty, but fame was something he had to have.

"It is impossible," people who dined at his expense used to murmur in his ear, "it is impossible that the grandson of such a grandfather should fail—" However, my mind was on other things. During my violin exercises I would put the books of Turgenev or Dumas on the music stand and, as I scraped away, kept devouring page after page. In the daytime I told all sorts of cock-and-bull stories to the little boys in the neighborhood; at night I transferred these stories to paper. Writing was a hereditary compulsion in the family. Leivi Itzok, who had become touched in his old age, had been writing a novel all his life under the title of *The Man Without a Head*. I took after him.

Three times a week, loaded down with violin case and music, I used to plod to Witte Street (at one time called Gentry Street), to Zagursky's studio. There, lined along the wall awaiting their turns, hysterically fervent Jewish women sat hugging against their weak knees violins the dimensions of which exceeded those of the beings who were slated to play them in Buckingham Palace.

The door to the sanctum would open. Big-headed, freckled children with necks as slender as flower stalks and a hectic flush on their cheeks would come staggering out of Zagursky's study. The door would slam to after swallowing up the next dwarf. On the other side of the wall the teacher, sporting a Windsor tie, with curly red hair and legs more fluid than solid, was straining himself, chanting the notes and conducting. The director of this monstrous lottery was populating Moldavanka and the stygian dead ends of the Old Market with the specters of pizzicato and cantilena. Later on Professor Auer brought this sing-song to a diabolical brilliance.

I had no business among these sectarians. Much the same sort of dwarf as all of them, I nevertheless discerned a different admonition in the voice of my ancestors.

The first step came hard to me. One day I left the house laden like a beast of burden with violin case, violin, notes and twelve roubles—payment for a month's tuition. I was walking along Nezhinskaya Street and should have turned into Gentry Street to get to Zagursky's house; instead I went up Tiraspolskaya and found myself in the port. The hours supposed to be spent in learning the violin flew by in Practical Harbor. Thus did my liberation begin. Zagursky's reception room never saw me again. Matters of greater importance took up all my thoughts. Together with Nemanov, a classmate of mine, I took to haunting the steamer *Kensington*, visiting a certain old sailor by the name of Mr. Trottybairn. Nemanov was a year younger than I, but from the age of eight he had been carrying on the most intricate trading in the world. He was a genius in business and carried out whatever he promised to do. He is now a millionaire in New York, a director of the General Motors company, a firm which is just as tremendous as Ford. Nemanov dragged me along everywhere because I submitted to him in all things without offering a word of objection. He used to buy tobacco pipes from Mr. Trottybairn which were smuggled in. These pipes were turned out at Lincoln by a brother of the old sailor.

"Gentlemen," Mr. Trottybairn used to say to us, "mark my word: children must be made with one's own hands. Smoking a factory-made pipe is the same as putting an enema tube into your mouth. Do you know who Benvenuto Cellini was? There was a master! My brother in Lincoln could tell you about him. My brother doesn't stand in anybody's way. He is simply convinced that children must be made with one's own hands and not the hands of others. We cannot do otherwise than agree with him, gentlemen."

Nemanov sold Trottybairn's pipes to bank directors, foreign consuls, wealthy Greeks. He made 100 percent profit on them.

The pipes of the Lincoln master breathed poesy. A thought, a drop of eternity had been set within each one of them. A small yellow eye glinted in the mouthpiece of each; their cases were lined with satin. I tried to picture to myself how Matthew Trottybairn, the last of the master pipe makers, was living in old England as he resisted the course of things.

"We cannot do otherwise than agree, gentlemen, that children must be made with one's own hands."

The heavy waves near the sea wall removed me further and further from our house, permeated with the smell of onions and Jewish destiny. From Practical Harbor I migrated to the other side of the breakwater, where a small patch of sandy shoal was inhabited by urchins from Seafront Street. They did not bother putting on their pants from morning till night, diving under the wherries, stealing coconuts for their dinner, and biding their time till the watermelon-laden barges would come trailing one another from Kherson and Kamenka and they would have a chance to split some of these watermelons against the stanchions in the port.

To be able to swim became a dream of mine. It was shameful to confess to these bronzed urchins that I, who had been born in Odessa, had not seen the sea until I was ten and that at fourteen I still did not know how to swim.

How late it befell me to learn the things one had to know! In my childhood, nailed down to the Gemara, I had led the life of a sage; when I grew up I took to climbing trees.

The ability to swim proved beyond me. The hydrophobia

of all my ancestors—Spanish rabbis and Frankfort money-changers—kept dragging me to the bottom. The water would not bear me up. Covered with welts, bloated with briny water, I would return to shore, to my violin and notes. I was bound to the instruments of my crime and was dragging them with me. The struggle of the rabbis against the sea continued until such time as the water god of those places—Ephim Nikitich Smolich, a proofreader on the Odessa *News*—took pity on me. Pity for little Jewish boys dwelt within the athletic bosom of this man. He was supreme ruler over hordes of rachitic starvelings. Nikitich used to collect them from the bedbug-ridden hovels of Moldavanka, lead them to the sea, bury them in the sand, do gymnastics with them, dive with them, teach them songs and, as he broiled himself under the direct rays of the sun, would tell them stories about fishermen and animals. To grownups Nikitich explained that he was a natural philosopher. The Jewish children laughed so hard at Nikitich's stories that they rolled on the ground; they fawned and squealed like puppies. The sun spattered them with crawling freckles that were the color of lizards.

This old man watched my monomachy against the sea as a silent bystander. Perceiving that the fight was hopeless and that I would never learn how to swim, he included me among the number of the lodgers in his heart. All of it was here with us, that gay heart of his; it never put on airs, it was not tainted with greed and was not disquieted. With his coppery shoulders, the head of an aged gladiator and bronzed legs that were just the least bit bandy, he would lie in our midst beyond the breakwater as if he were the sovereign of those waters abounding in watermelon rinds and reeking of kerosene. I came to love this man as only a boy afflicted with hysteria and headaches can come to love an athlete. I would not leave his side and tried to be of service to him.

"Don't go at it so hard," he told me. "Strengthen your nerves. Swimming will come of itself. How can it be that the water won't bear you up—why shouldn't it?"

Noticing how I was drawn to him, Nikitich made an exception of me among all his disciples, inviting me to visit him in his clean, roomy garret carpeted with matting, showed me his dogs, his hedgehog, turtle and pigeons. In exchange for this largess I brought him a tragedy I had written recently.

"I just knew that you wrote a bit," said Nikitich. "You even have that look about you. More and more often your eyes don't watch anything in particular—"

He read my writings, shrugged, passed his hand over his short gray curls, paced about his garret a little.

"I would guess," he pronounced drawlingly, pausing after each word, "that the divine spark is in you—"

We went out into the street. The old man stopped, tapped his stick hard against the sidewalk and fixed me with his eyes.

"What do you lack? The fact that you're young is no calamity—that will pass with the years. . . . What you lack is a feeling for nature."

With his stick he pointed out a tree to me; it had a brownish trunk and a low crown.

"What tree is that?"

I did not know.

"What's growing on that bush?"

I did not know that either. We were walking through a small square on the Alexandrovsky Prospect. The old man kept pointing his stick at all the trees; he clutched my shoulder whenever birds happened to fly past and compelled me to listen to the individual voice of each.

"What bird is singing now?"

I could not tell him anything in answer. The names of trees and birds, their division into genera, where the birds were flying to, what direction the sun rose in, when the dew was heaviest—all these things were beyond my ken.

"And you have the audacity to write? A man who does not live in the midst of nature the way a stone or an animal lives won't write two worth-while lines in his whole lifetime. Your landscapes resemble descriptions of stage sets. What were your parents thinking about for fourteen years, may the Devil take me?"

What had my parents been thinking about? About protested promissory notes, about Mischa Elman's mansions. I did not say anything about this to Nikitich; I kept my mouth shut.

At home, during dinner, I did not touch my food. It stuck in my throat.

"A feeling for nature!" I kept thinking. "My God, why had no conception of that ever entered my head? Where can I find a man who will explain everything to me about the ways of birds and the names of trees? What do I know about them? I might be able to recognize lilacs—and even then only when they're in bloom. Lilacs—and acacias. De Ribas and Greek streets are lined with acacias—"

At dinner Father told a new story about Jascha Heifetz. Just before reaching Robinat's, Father had run into Mendelson, Jascha's uncle. The boy, it turned out, was getting eight hundred roubles for each appearance. Count that up—see how much that comes to if one gives fifteen concerts a month!

I did count it up: the result was twelve thousand a month. As I was doing the multiplication and carrying four, I happened to look out the window. In a gently billowing cape, with his tightly coiled, rusty-colored curls struggling out from under his soft hat, leaning upon a cane, Mr. Zagursky, my music teacher, was making stately progress through our small, concrete-paved courtyard. One could hardly say that he had been very prompt in discovering my truancy. By now more than three months had passed since my violin had foundered on the sands near the breakwater.

Zagursky was approaching our front door. I made a dash for the back entrance—and remembered it had been nailed up the evening before to keep burglars out. Whereupon I locked myself in the washroom. Within half an hour the whole family had gathered around my door. The women were weeping. One of my grandmothers was rubbing her fat shoulder against the door and going off into hysterical peals of sobbing. My father was silent. When he did break into speech he was quieter and more articulate than he had ever been in his whole life.

"I am an officer in the army," said my father. "I have an

estate. I go hunting. The mouzhiks pay me rent. I have placed my son in the Cadet Corps. There is no need for me to worry about my son—"

He fell silent. The women were breathing hard. Then a terrific blow crashed against the washroom door. My father was pounding against it with his whole body; he persisted in running full tilt against it.

"I am an officer in the army!" he was screaming. "I go hunting! I'll kill him—this is the end!"

The hook flew off the door; there was a bolt on the door— it was still holding by a single nail. The women were rolling on the floor, they were catching at my father's legs; out of his mind by now, he was struggling to get free. An old woman —my father's mother—came hurrying to find out what the hubbub was about.

"My child," she said to her son in Yiddish, "great is our grief. It has no bounds. The only thing lacking in our house is bloodshed. I do not want to see bloodshed in our house—"

My father broke into moans. I heard his steps receding. The bolt was hanging by its single nail.

I sat in my fortress till nightfall. When everybody had gone to bed my Aunt Bobka led me off to my grandmother's. The way there was a long one. The moonlight lay in a catalepsy upon unknown bushes, upon trees for which there were no names. . . . Some unseen bird in the distance emitted a whistle and became extinguished: it may have gone to sleep. . . . What bird was it? What did they call it? Is there any dewfall of evenings? Where is the constellation of Ursa Major located? Where does the sun rise? . . .

We were walking along Post Office Street. Aunt Bobka had a firm hold of my hand, so that I would not run away. She was right. Flight was what I had in mind.

1930

Boris Andreievich LAVRENEV

[1894—]

Officially tagged by the Soviet Literary Encyclopedia as a Fellow Traveler and Sentimental Romantic, Lavrenev, who had finished the law course at the University of Moscow, began writing before World War I—poetry, for the most part. He was mobilized into the army in 1915, and served in the Red Army from 1918 to 1921. In addition to fiction he has written successful dramas, but none have been produced outside of Russia. To quote further official estimates, he "is far from understanding the Party-nature of art" and, *horribile dictu,* "the superficial reader-interest lowers considerably the value of his works." As far as one can translate this from the *Halturish,* what this really means is that the wretch knows how to tell a good story.

FAST FREIGHT*

1

Hardly had the *Lizzie Waldon* dropped anchor in the middle of the roadstead at Constantinople and let down her rusty trap ladder, creaking at every joint, when a caïque rowed

* With the exception of certain geographical names, all proper names in this story are entirely fictitious. Any resemblance to the name (or names) of any person (or persons), living or dead, or to the name of any ship, is coincidental. *Ed.-Trans.*

up alongside. A Turkish postman, the greasy tassel of his fez dangling over his humped sweaty nose, went up the shaky steps and held out a cablegram.

Captain Timmons himself accepted it at the top landing of the trap ladder, quickly signed the receipt, thrust a piaster at the postman and headed for his cabin. There he leisurely rammed home a load of Navy Cut into his pipe, puffed a few mouthfuls of the pungent smoke and tore the narrow blue band that sealed the edges of the cablegram. The cablegram was from the shipowner in New Orleans. The shipowner informed the captain that the firm of Shelby, Shelly, Shelty & Co., which had chartered the *Lizzie Waldon*, was insisting the ship take on the freight at Odessa as quickly as possible and start on her return trip without delay, since there was an anticipation of a demand in the very near future for oil-cake fertilizer, which was the very thing for which the *Lizzie Waldon* had sailed to far-off Russia.

The captain shrugged, puffed out a particularly dense billow of smoke, shifted the pipe to the other corner of his mouth and let a protracted "God damn!" trickle through his compressed lips. He recalled that the shipowner, having begrudged the two cents extra on each ton of coal, had filled the bunkers with such street sweepings that in crossing the Atlantic *Lizzie* had barely crawled against the waves and winds and had had difficulty in keeping up the minimal pressure of steam. With things in such a state one could not depend on speed, but the order had been received, the captain had grown used to carrying out orders and, having rung for the steward, he ordered him to call O'Hiddy, the chief engineer.

A minute later a red head with a crew haircut thrust itself in the cabin doorway, looked the cabin and the captain over with eyes of cornflower blue and towed in a stoop-shouldered torso in a football sweater and nothing under that but swimming trunks.

"What's on your mind, Fred?" the head engineer asked in a lazy drawl. "This damned climate is killing me—I never crawl out of the tub. When we get back home I'm going to ask the owner to transfer me to some northern line." O'Hiddy hitched his trunks up over his sunken-in belly and added: "When you're unfortunate enough to get born in the Klondike and pass half your life in a fur sack it's tough to get used to this infernal temperature."

"I've got news that'll make you happy, if that's the case," said the captain. "I intended to stay here until Sunday, so's to give the crew a chance to send their money down the drain in the Galata dives and then touch up the tub's sides with paint before going to Odessa, but here's a cablegram from the owner. He's rushing me! That means we pull up anchor toward evening. Odessa isn't Alaska, but still it's cooler there."

"But why all this rush?" asked O'Hiddy, stuffing his pipe with the captain's tobacco.

"Shelby wants to get his oil cakes in as soon as possible. There's a demand for them on the market."

The engineer thoughtfully slapped his bare knee.

"But do you know, Fred, that you'll get stuck in Odessa, having your boilers cleaned?" he asked with apathetic malice.

For an instant the mask of indifference slipped from the face of Captain Timmons and was replaced by something that resembled interest. He took the pipe out of his mouth: "How come? We carried out a general cleaning during our previous trip. Why get in a mess when they're demanding that we hurry?"

O'Hiddy expectorated into the cuspidor and smirked: "A fellow might think the nurse hasn't taken you out of your diapers yet—that's how simple-minded the questions are that you let fall from your rosy lips. Did you see what we're using for coal?"

"I did," the captain answered drily.

"What are you asking for, then? A mixture of that grade you'll find only up the rectum of a cachalot. Because of the caked soot half the stacks don't draw any more. Without a thorough cleaning we'll never reach home—especially with a cargo."

"That's out of the question. We may lose the bonus. Get through with the fuss and bother as fast as you can. We can't lose a minute."

"I'll try. Luckily there's a Mr. Bikoff in Odessa. For money he'll do the impossible."

The captain contented himself with the answer, and again his facial muscles froze into calm indifference.

"Good! I'm depending on you. Only thing is, warn the crew they're to be at their posts by six this evening. If any man doesn't get here in time I'm not going to wait. Let him panhandle on the Galata until my return trip. We must be out in the Black Sea by sunset, before those damned Turks fire their signal gun. Otherwise we'll have to wait till the morning."

"Right!" answered the engineer. "Will do!"

2

The *Lizzie Waldon* passed through the narrow gates of the Bosporus at sunset, when the crests of the waves were giving off a sheen of rose-tinted gold, and, tacking about sharply, set a northward course.

Captain Timmons was standing on the bridge, his gold-braided blue cap down over his forehead and his hands thrust in his pockets.

Thousands of steamers pass over the sea lanes of the world at the hour when the waves give off a sheen of rose-tinted gold. Old freighters and transports, licked by the salty kisses of all the seas and oceans, fast liners and magnificent six-tiered transatlantic luxury colossi before the prows of which the water, crushed by their weight, steps to either side with grim rumblings. By sunlit or foggy day, and by night, under the twinkling traceries of starry nets, they traverse the seaways, peering into the universal darkness with the colored lights of their electric eyes.

They are moved and driven through the green sea troughs by the will of the banks, counting houses and maritime shipping companies, by the business-is-business will of capital, a cruel will which knows neither mercy nor delay.

Against the illusory azure of the sea's horizon spring up the mirages of fairy-tale lands. Awaiting in the fairy-tale lands are mountains of cargo which the banks and offices need. To the sound of curses and the whistling of lashes, yellow, brown, black slaves load into the reverberating iron bellies of the steamers materials and spices, cotton and ores, fruits and crude rubber, gotten, grown, gathered by just such other slaves as themselves, to much the same whistling of lashes. Amid the rumble of winches the hulls of the steamships settle into the glassy depths until the water covers their load lines.

Through fogs and waves, through networks of stars and the unleashed screaming of hurricanes the ships cautiously carry their burdens to distant ports so that there may be no cessation of that feverish, arid, mysterious work done to the clatter of adding machines, carried on behind plate-glass windows screened halfway up with curtains of green pongee, in offices located on streets rumbling with traffic. Behind those windows lies the kingdom of greed.

Electric bulbs suspended on cords send streams of dead, even light upon high counter-desks, upon bald skulls, upon earth-colored spectacled faces bent over huge ledgers and thick account books. The owners of these faces are just as tough and crisp as the paper of their account books, and when they move their lips one somehow thinks of the rustle of turning ledger pages. Long and short columns of figures grow on this paper. They direct the destinies of the cargoes carried by the ships, cargoes that are preserved in the matting enveloping the bales, a matting silky to the touch, the strange tantalizing aromas of fairy-tale lands that blossom beyond the mirages of azure horizons.

The breed of men in the banks and offices are unaware of these fragrances. The only aroma they know is that of crackling colorful bits of paper on which numerals, and short words in all of the world's tongues, dispose themselves in dreary designs.

The people of the banks and offices transmute the cargoes they have guided through the pages of their account books into colorful bits of paper and clinking disks of metal. They are in a hurry to consummate this magic transmutation, so that the figures which are chalked up on boards by the dispassionate hands of stockbrokers may remain at the reassuring level of prosperity.

And anew, submitting to the curt yapping orders of greed, the engines of the ships strain their muscles of steel, bend the greased knees and elbows of their levers; with redoubled force their smokestacks spew forth into the fresh sky over the ocean their poison-laden soot, their propellers rumble more rapidly and captains ask the men on watch more frequently for readings of the log.

The captains are experienced and level-headed, like Captain Timmons. They stand phlegmatically on their bridges, their blue gold-braided caps shoved down over their foreheads and their hands shoved into their pockets. Their narrowed eyes see a path stretching away between the gray tatters of sea foam, a path that is invisible to the eyes of other men.

The path between the flat green delta of New Orleans to the ocherous rocks of Odessa's littoral is clearly visible to Captain Timmons. And likewise clear to him is the path taken by the transmutation of his cargo into colorful bits of paper and bright disks of metal, a moiety of both going to pay for the services of the captain and the crew. The captain puts by the greater part of the colorful bits of paper that fall to his share, to safeguard his family against a rainy day. The sailors, who have nothing to put away, let their money go down the drain during their attacks of frenzied blues for the benefit of sundry port tavern keepers and pitiful painted tarts. The money, having performed its precharted course, returns to the banks, traverses the pages of account books and is transmuted into new cargoes.

The ships take these cargoes into their holds and again follow the sea paths, treacherous and quaggy, teeming with unforeseen contingencies and threatening both captain and crew with destruction and loss of earnings—the latter being more fearsome than destruction. That was why Captain Timmons came up on deck three times each night, wrapping himself in a short waterproof, and asked one of the watch for readings of the copper whirligig that was tinkling in a melancholy way over the great deep being churned into foam at the stern.

3

Squat houses of porous soot-covered stone had lodged themselves deep along the steep street on the other side of the railroad tracks that coiled like snakes under the wooden spans of a trestle. Day and night these houses were sprayed by the rumbling and soot of brick-red freight cars passing by in endless files to receive their loads from or to deliver them to the mooring places of limestone against which the turbidly green water dashed, lapping.

Peeling gilt letters over the doorway of one of these houses proclaimed it the office of P. K. Bykov—Steam Boilers Repaired and Cleaned.

Prov Kiriakovich Bykov himself was seated at his desk in the office. He attended personally to everything connected with his business, rarely stirring from the big chair in which he would sit enthroned from morning to night. He was all alone in the office, unless one took into account two portraits: one of Nicholas II, Emperor and Autocrat of All the Russias, and the other that of the great saint, Ioann of Kronstadt. There were two holes in the portrait of the autocrat. They had come into being two years before, when the armor-clad *Potemkin* and its mutinous crew had visited the port of Odessa. After a stay of forty-eight hours, inspiring unheard-of fear in the authorities and stirring a mighty flare-up of revolutionary fervor in the city, the armor-clad had left, going in a southerly direction. The satraps, on recovering from their panic, had flooded Odessa with the blood of the barricade fighters and the peaceful population, while the infuriated Black Hundreds had organized a bloody and bestial pogrom. It was then that the wreckers and drunken hoodlums had burst into Prov Kiriakovich's office and asked for the Czar's portrait so that they might tramp through the streets to their hearts' content under the aegis of the sovereign; the visage of the Czar was supposed to sanction the carnage and the looting.

Things turned out differently, however. The pogrom became so sweeping that it threatened to leap from the districts where the city's riffraff lived into the wealthier areas and to inundate the dwelling places of non-Jews also. The authorities, frightened for a second time, issued orders to put a stop to the pogrom through any measures whatsoever, and hardly had the frenzied horde left Bykov's office and turned the corner when three clanging metallic volleys resounded. Prov Kiriakovich had seen the pogromists, frightened out of their wits, dash past his windows, one of them flinging the portrait of the Czar on the cobblestones of the roadway.

When the dragoons had galloped past and everything had quieted down Prov Kiriakovich had crept like a badger out of its hole and carried the portrait back into the office. The broken glass had fallen out of the frame, and the autocrat himself had been disfigured by two bullets. One had torn off an ear, the other had gone up his nostril. Two unknown sharpshooters, gripped in the vise of discipline, had vented their rancor, as best they could, on the portrait of the Czar. Prov Kiriakovich had given an aggrieved sigh. It would be necessary to buy a new portrait, yet it was a pity to spend the money and, after a closer look, he decided that the damage could be mended. He did not bother at all with stopping up the hole in the nostril: after all, there is a hole at that very spot even in nature; as for the ear, he pasted it over with a bit of paper and blacked it over with a stub of pencil.

And that's how the Autocrat of All the Russias came to be hanging there, breathing in the office dust with one natural nostril. As for the urchins who worked for Bykov as boiler scrapers and who were forever milling about in the yard behind the office, they had peeped in through a window and disrespectfully dubbed the portrait Nicky the Torn Nostril.

Prov Kiriakovich's business was a big one and everybody in the port knew of it. Hundreds of ships came to Odessa from all sorts of queer lands, at all seasons of the year. Now and then one of them would have its name and the name of its home port lettered on its stern in a language that even Motka Hliup, a student of philology who had gone down in defeat before the demon rum and who in wintertime walked about in felt Tatar hats tied about his feet instead of boots— well, even this Motka Hliup was unable to read these names.

Ships follow the seaways for long periods and their smokestacks and boiler pipes get clogged up with carbon and soot. In order to keep going the ship has to attend to its stomach, it has to purge its metallic guts, must scrape off them all the caked refuse. There's no percentage in going into drydock over such a trifle; the cleaning is done while the ship rides at anchor—and that's when Prov Kiriakovich, Doctor of Engines, comes to the aid of ailing steamers.

For this sort of thing he has a whole regiment of urchins.

The narrow stacks become still narrower from the soot and incrustation; a full-grown man simply couldn't manage to go through them, whereas a lad still in his first decade is just what the doctor ordered. He slips like an eel into the affected pipe and crawls from one end of it to the other, no matter how narrow the passage, how suffocating it may be and how overpowering the stench of its incrusted soot, and with a steel scraper—and, if need be, even with a calking iron or chisel— knocks the thick coating of soot and incrustations off the metal.

Prov Kiriakovich assembles his troupe from the most beggarly hell holes of the city—from Peresyp, from the Mills (both Near and Far), from Moldavanka. Only there can you find anyone willing to go through hell for a fifteen-kopeck coin a day—with one's own keep.

Engineers of ailing ships of all nations come knocking at the door of Bykov's office. Bykov accepts the commissions, entering them in his hen tracks in a daybook. It's a strain for him to write—schooling had come hard to him. He breathes hard from the exertion as he pens the crabbed letters and smears the ink over the paper with his shaggy beard, like that of Dwarf Black Death in the fairy tale. And, having accepted the commission, he opens one of the ventilators in the window facing the yard and yells at the top of his lungs: "Senka, Mishka, Pashka, Alëshka! Get a move on, you bastards—get to work! Don't hang around! Look aaalive!"

4

O'Hiddy, in a brand-new pongee jacket and glistening orange oxfords, twirling a Malacca cane, descended from the boulevard where he had put away a mountain of ice cream,

went down the famous wide steps leading to the port and
ambled off over the filthy street with its windrows of coal
dust in the company of Leizer Zwiebel the commissionaire.
Leizer was known to every captain and engineer who had
called even once at the port of Odessa. He carried out every
possible sort of commission, from berthing the seagoing giants
ahead of their turns to furnishing sailors out for a good time
on terra firma with insouciant and unpretentious momentary
lady friends.

Leizer knew all languages to the extent needed by a commissionaire to enable him to fulfill the above-named duties.
He mangled all languages without mercy but managed to
make himself understood, and to seamen lost in the streets of
a strange city he was the saving clue of Ariadne that led them
out of the labyrinth. However, every now and then when
Leizer grew excited he would fire away in all the languages
at once, and at such times it was utterly impossible to understand him.

Right now Leizer was guiding O'Hiddy to Prov Kiriakovich's office. The engineer might have found the way there by
himself—this wasn't the first time in his wandering life that
he was polishing with his soles the blue lava sidewalks of
Odessa—but he would not have been able to negotiate with
Bykov all on his own. In English Prov Kiriakovich knew only
the sailors' cuss words; as for O'Hiddy, he could utter only
three phrases in Russian, all three as essential as bread and
all three exquisitely broken: *Zdrastei, Kak zhiviosh* and *Ti
krassivei devush'—ya liublieu tibe* ("How you," "How you
living," and "You booful gal—I loving you"). However, for
talking business that was rather insufficient.

Prov Kiriakovich stood up with dignity before the engineer
and extended his plump stubby-fingered hand covered with
fine black hair. O'Hiddy shook it energetically. Leizer hastily
and warily touched the tips of the Bykovian stubs.

"How are you getting on, Prov Kiriakovich?" he asked,
smiling the gentle, uneasy and cautious smile of an intimidated and harassed man.

"We manage to get along. And how are you, you Jerusalem
chicken?"

"Oi, what do you mean, 'chicken'? Was I a sure-enough chicken I'd be bringing home a grain or two a day and feeding my little ones. But I don't happen to be a chicken, and I'm actually ashamed to say what I am—" At this point he sniffed. "But now, maybe I'll make something today because, after all, I've brought you a client—and, oi, what a client, he should live long. So he'll give me something and then you, too, will give something to a poor Jew."

"What sort of work, now?" Bykov inquired, opening his order book.

"Oi, what a question! Work fit for a king, like from nothing. Mister must have his boilers cleaned in two days, because Mister has to rush back to his America, and he has freight that has to go fast, such as I shall never have."

"Two days? To have it done in two days he will have to pay accordingly," Bykov responded glumly.

"Well, am I saying anything? What does it mean to the Mister? For he's a little richer than old Leizer. He's willing to pay."

"Good thing he's willing. Tell him it'll cost him—" Bykov scratched his nose and named a staggering figure.

Zwiebel shuddered and turned pale.

"Oi, oi!" he got out in a whisper. "That figure is entirely too frightful. There, can I possibly say it out loud?"

"Well, if he don't want to pay it," Bykov answered without changing his tone, "he don't have to. Things are humming. There's enough clients to go around. If not him, then somebody else will turn up."

Leizer spread his hands and timidly stated the figure in English for the engineer's benefit. To his amazement O'Hiddy didn't as much as bat an eye and answered with a curt "Very well!" adding that if the work wasn't finished in forty-eight hours, 25 percent would be withheld from the moneys due to Bykov for each day of delay.

"It don't matter," said Bykov, entering the order. "They won't be keeping anything back; it'll be done on time, seeing as how it's me that's undertaking the job."

The engineer put the deposit on the desk, accepted a receipt and tossed a five-dollar bill to Zwiebel for his efforts.

Shaking Bykov's hand once more he left the office, leaving Zwiebel to settle the details.

Out on the sidewalk he paused, attracted by shouts and laughter.

Five soot-covered tattered urchins were playing hopscotch in the roadway, tossing the patsy and hopping about on one leg. O'Hiddy had never happened to see this game and was looking on with curiosity. One of the players, small and with unruly hair, hopped about more nimbly than all the others and was laughing boastfully, rejoicing over his skill. Having knocked the patsy out of its chalked square with a deft side-swipe of his foot he raised his head and caught sight of the engineer. The boy's lips stretched in a grin, exposing two sparkling rows of milk-white teeth. He dashed up to O'Hiddy, holding out a tiny paw that looked like a monkey's because of the soot on it, and started shouting, prancing in time to the words: "Capitain, capitain! *Giff me shilling eef you please* —may you turn to a hunk of cheese! *Good-bye! How you do?*"

O'Hiddy grinned. He had not understood the Russian words spliced on to the English, but he recalled other sassy imps just like this one on the levees of New Orleans and he felt the warm breath of wind from a land he knew; his hand crept of itself to his pocket and he put a shining dollar into the small hand held out to him. With the speed of lightning the coin vanished into the urchin's cheek; he turned a somersault, stood on his hands and, slapping one bare sole against the other, shouted: "Hip, hip, hurrah!"

O'Hiddy grinned still more kindly. He patted the cheek of the urchin, who was right side up once more, wondered at the boy's magnificent teeth, like those of some small beast of prey, and uttered two of the three phrases that always came to his rescue: *"Zdrastei, kak zhiviosh?"*

The brats neighed, while one of them, spitting, called out rapturously: "Listen to that, now! He knows how to talk our language, the dog face!"

O'Hiddy wanted to say something else, but the declaration of love to a pretty girl obviously did not suit the circumstances and he grunted helplessly. However, he was delivered from his awkward situation by the trumpeting voice of Bykov who was standing on the steps of his office: "Petka! Sanka! Kryssa! Get on the job!"

O'Hiddy tipped his hat courteously, bowed to the boys and set out for the waterfront.

5

Among the Bykovian boiler scrapers there was one whose fame had spread all over the Black Sea—eleven-year-old Mitka, nicknamed the Rat, the very one who had fished the fresh-minted dollar out of O'Hiddy's pocket and whose white-toothed smile the engineer had found so pleasing.

No one knew whence Mitka came, to whom he belonged, what his family name was. Prov Kiriakovich had picked him up under the railroad trestle one autumn night two years before, half dead and burning up with fever, and after seeing him through his illness and feeding him a bit had put him to work.

The other boys had families; they were the offspring of Odessa's poverty, of its stevedores and roustabouts; Mitka hadn't anybody in Odessa or for thousands of miles around. All interrogations had succeeded in eliciting only one detail from him: his *mamka* had worn a blue skirt. But there are very many blue skirts in this universe, and with a distinguishing characteristic like that Mitka's chances of finding the vanished *mamka* who had abandoned him in the port were sort of slim.

The money Prov Kiriakovich had expended on Mitka did not go to waste. He proved to be a gold hoard for the enterprise. The gaunt, slim body bent and wound itself into such coils as would have snapped the bones and muscles of a normal man. And, in Prov Kiriakovich's line, limberness was the chief requirement. Whenever the other lads had to throw in the sponge they would call in Mitka. He glided like a conger through the narrowest of pipes; he crawled into crannies so hidden and windings so tortuous that they could not be gotten at without taking the whole mechanism apart. On one occasion he contrived to crawl through the spiral suction pipe of a refrigerating machine which twisted in a

boalike spiral with a full turn every meter and a half. This
bit of magic made his name celebrated throughout the port,
and Bykov's competitors had more than once offered Mitka
double pay to entice such a wonder into their employ, but
Mitka, who could remember only the color of his *mamke's*
skirt, had a knightly code all his own. He contemptuously
sniffed through his pointed little nose, because of which,
together with his more than human limberness, he had received his nickname of Kryssa (or Rat), and answered sternly
and with temper, in the purest Odessian: "Meanin' I'm to act
worse'n any low-down crook to my boss? He give me food
and drink, and I'm supposed to shove a fig right up his nose?
I'm well enough off with him!"

Bykov's competitors cursed and cast off with empty holds.
There had even been an attempt to liquidate the Rat, and ten
or so of the boys had been talked into putting the kibosh on
Mitka, but the ganging-up had been noticed in time by some
seamen from the *Chihachev* and they succeeded in saving the
boy, who was all bloody.

Thus the Rat had stayed with Bykov, remaining loyal to his
first master, and Prov Kiriakovich who, for the least trans-
gressions, often sailed into his boys with the first thing that
came to hand and aimed at any opening he saw, never laid
a finger on Mitka. He did not refrain out of pity, however,
but for fear of injuring such a precious rarity.

And now, having received a rush order to clean the *Lizzie
Waldon's* boilers (a profitable, well-paid commission), he
decided to put Mitka on the job, knowing that he alone
would do the work of ten. Bykov issued scrapers, brushes,
calking irons and mallets to the boys and sent them off under
the escort of Leizer, who would have to show them where the
ship was moored.

O'Hiddy, upon coming aboard, reported at the captain's
cabin.

"It's a dirty shame!" he declared as he entered, mopping
his forehead. "This year even Odessa is no cooler than the
tropics. All the sap's been drained out of me. Let's have a sip
of your infernal cherry brandy."

"Go to it!" said Timmons, pouring out a tumbler for the other. "How's the boiler situation?"

"We've made an agreement. Mr. Bikoff undertakes to do the job in two days."

"All right! There's a new cablegram from the owner. The Shelby firm agrees to double the bonus if we shorten the return trip by two days more. You and I will be rich, Dicky. I'll be able to put something in the bank for the future of my youngsters."

The engineer drained his glass in one gulp: "That doesn't mean a thing to me. I have no youngsters. But I sympathize with you, Fred. I'm going to climb into my bathing suit now. Otherwise I'll get cooked like a lobster."

O'Hiddy left. Timmons walked over to his berth. Hanging on the wall above it was the photograph of a plump woman with magnificent hair; she had two very young children in her arms. The captain sighed, stretched himself out on the berth and dozed off.

6

O'Hiddy had just finished dousing himself when the door of his cabin was flung open by a stoker in frayed and oil-soaked overalls: "Sir, they've come aboard to clean the boilers."

"Let them go down to the stokehold. I'll be along right away."

He dried himself, pulled on his bathing trunks, hung up the towel and, crossing the deck to the engine-room hatchway, trotted down the metallically ringing trap ladder to the stokehold. The boys had put on sleeveless sacks of stiff tarpaulin to protect their bodies against scratches as they crawled through the pipes.

"They're going to start in right away," Leizer bowed politely to the engineer. "They're such nimble boys—you may set your mind at rest."

One of the urchins turned around on hearing Zwiebel's voice and even in the gloom of the stokehold the porcelain sheen of his teeth was dazzling. The engineer recognized the boy to whom he had given a dollar. He winked at him and said once more: *"Zdrastei! Kak zhiviosh?"*

"All Polly knows is to ask for a cracker!" Mitka smiled mockingly. "I told you I was doin' well. Don't you fret, Uncle dear—once we've taken on the job we'll clean her out! Well, fellows, let's go!"

He thrust calking iron and mallet into the outside pocket of his protective sack and once more gave the engineer a smile. Then he dived into a pipe head first. O'Hiddy watched as the remaining boiler scrapers vanished one by one into the pipes, then he turned to Zwiebel and amiably invited him to have some coffee. Appreciative of such courtesy, Zwiebel crept up the trap ladder after the engineer, lifting his feet high in their holey socks and clawing at the railings.

In the tidy small cabin of the American he had sweetened coffee and cakes, and even risked downing a glass of liqueur. No sooner had he finished this glass, however, than he had a fit of the blues. He recalled his miserable lair in Moldavanka where his perpetually hungry Rachel was sitting with their brood of nine. He also recalled that close by his lair was the police station of his precinct, and that there was a police inspector in that precinct house, and that every month he had to bring ten roubles to this police inspector, so that Mr. Police Inspector might feel well disposed toward Leizer. And that he had to bring five roubles a month to Mr. Lieutenant of Police, and three roubles a month to Mr. Patrolman on the Beat. And because of these thoughts Zwiebel became so depressed that, forgetting himself, he started telling the engineer about his troubles in broken English. The American listened politely but was, obviously, bored. Leizer, perceiving this, became confused and got up hurriedly to say good-bye.

At this point, however, the cabin door flew open and the same stoker as before appeared on the threshold: "I beg your pardon, sir, but you'd better come down at once."

"What for?" asked O'Hiddy with evident displeasure.

"A bit of trouble down there. One of the boys got himself stuck in a pipe and can't get out."

"What? Damn!" and he rushed out of the cabin.

In the stokehold he found the machinists, stokers and Bykov's boys all crowded in a close circle about the opening of one of the pipes.

"What's the matter?" O'Hiddy asked angrily. "Why the crowd? How did it happen?"

"The boy was already far in the pipe," the chief machinist answered soberly, "when he suddenly started yelling. We came on the run but couldn't make out what he was yelling about. Now he's crying. Looks like he's got stuck and can't go through."

"Oi, what is this?" cried out Leizer, who had scrambled down after O'Hiddy. "Tell me, boys—what is all this?"

"Mitka got caught in the pipe."

"He crawled in but he can't crawl out."

"He's bawling."

"Got to pull him out!"

The boiler scrapers were clamoring, each in a different voice.

Leizer thrust his head into the opening and, as his ears caught the low sobbing, asked in agitation: "Rat! Say, what's the meaning of all this? What's come over you, may all your livers dry up, that you're disgracing me and your master like that?"

The Rat's voice, interrupted by crying, came as a muffled echo from the pipe: "Can't understand it myself, Leizer Abramovich. Because I'm not to blame, I swear to God. I was crawling up this pipe like I always do, but right at this place my hand got twisted under my belly—can't pull it out, nohow! It hurts!" And Mitka again started crying.

"It got twisted!" Leizer wrung his hands. "Did you ever see such a thing? Why, how could your hand possibly get twisted when, after all, you're being paid not to get it twisted! Crawl out of there, may you lose your appetite, you crazy no good kid!"

Rustling and moans issued from the pipe, and a faint voice: "Oh, I can't! The bone will snap!"

Leizer began to twitch:

"Do you want to ruin me, you mangy good-for-nothing?"

he shouted into the pipe. "There, you'd better crawl out, or else I'll tell Prov Kiriakovich and he'll pull your ears off you!"

"I can't!"

"Eh? He can't! Did you ever hear of such a thing? Petka! Crawl into the pipe, grab a hold of his legs, and we'll be pulling you out together with him. There, crawl in, you loafer! Oi, woe is me with such children!"

Petka started crawling into the pipe.

"Hold him by the legs! Hold him fast as you can—don't let go!" Leizer was issuing commands. "Have you grabbed him? Well, boys, pull Petka by his feet. I want you should pull the Rat out at last, sure as I am alive!"

The urchins with much laughter seized Petka's dirty bare heels sticking out of the pipe and tugged. And suddenly Mitka's piercing, excruciating scream burst from the pipe: "Oh, boys, dear fellows, leave me be! It hurts me. . . . My hand—oh, oh, oh!"

The boiler scrapers in confusion let go of Petka's feet and glumly exchanged looks that were not at all childlike. Leizer paled.

"Don't upset yourself, Mr. Engineer," he began hurriedly. "This is nothing—these are just trifles. I'll bring Mr. Bykov right away; he'll drag him out in one little minute."

He made a dash for the trap ladder and ran up it with a rapidity which would have done credit to O'Hiddy himself.

The rest stood in silence about the wailing pipe.

"You've got to flood the pipe with lubricating oil," one of the machinists suggested. "It'll get slippery and then you can pull the young one out."

O'Hiddy bent over the opening of the pipe. He had been pained to learn that it was the white-toothed little devil who had instantly attracted his attention in the street who had gotten stuck in the pipe. He had a gnawing sensation at the pit of his stomach and, feeling a poignant desire to help in some way, he called out in a kindly voice: "Hello, baby!"— then, in his Russian: *"Zdrastei, kak zhiviosh?"*

The urchins snickered. The mournful answer, punctuated by weeping, reached him from the pipe: "Things are bad! My hand hurts just like it was broken—"

Without having understood anything, O'Hiddy became still more aggrieved and upset; he began pacing the cramped stokehold.

7

The treads of the trap ladder shook and reverberated under the weight of Prov Kiriakovich himself.

Without as much as glancing at O'Hiddy, Bykov immediately let out a low roar at the boys who, having quieted down, had gathered in a knot about the pipe Mitka was in.

"What's this? You going to take things easy? And who's going to do the work? Crawl inside them pipes, you dog leavings, or I'll knock all your blocks off!"

"The Rat got stuck, Prov Kiriakovich," Petka got out in a piteous squeak. Prov Kiriakovich's hand yanked at Petka's ear with feeling.

"What, you're going to give us a spiel, you snotnose? Anybody asking you? Stuck, is he? I'll show him what getting stuck means! Get into them pipes! Who's going to pay me if I don't get the work done in time—you? Ohh, you sons of bitches!"

The urchins scattered and disappeared inside the pipes.

Prov Kiriakovich walked with a heavy tread over to the ill-fated pipe.

"Mitka!" he called threateningly. "What are you up to, you good-for-nothing? What's the idea of playing dirty tricks? Get out of there this minute!"

"Prov Kiriakovich, dearest, my own, don't go getting angry at me. I'd be glad to get out myself but I just can't, I swear it on the true Cross. I've dislocated my hand altogether," Bykov caught a faint voice in answer, muffled by the metal. Bykov's face became suffused with blood.

"Don't you be putting on no act for me, you accursed devil! Crawl out of there or I'll bash your whole face in!"

Again there was weeping within the pipe.

"You'd better kill me—I can't bear to suffer any more. Oh, it hurts!"

Prov Kiriakovich scratched the nape of his neck.

"There, now! He must have got stuck there for sure, the puppy. Got to put a rope around his feet and pull him out."

Leizer warily approached Bykov from behind.

"What a misfortune, what a misfortune. . . . We've already tried—there's no pulling him out. That machinist gentleman says we ought to flood the pipe with lubricating oil—everything will get slippery then—"

"Scat, you sheeny!" Bykov cut him short. "I know that without you. Tell the limeys to bring the oil."

One of the stokers, a broad-shouldered Canadian with a knife scar across one cheek, brought a bucket of the thick oil. Prov Kiriakovich threw off his lustrine jacket and with a full sweep splashed the oil far up the pipe.

"Get me a mop!" he shouted to the frightened Leizer—then, snatching the mop from the hands of the stoker who had brought it, started shoving it into the pipe.

"Another bucket!"

A second bucketful of the greenish-black viscid mess was sent splashing into the pipe.

"Petka—crawl in there with a rope, you scum! Tie it around his feet—"

Petka started to crawl into the pipe. Tears and beads of sweat were coursing down his dirty cheeks. He was frightened and felt sorry for the Rat. In a short while he clambered out, all black and sticky from the oil.

"I've tied on the rope," he got out hoarsely, trying to spit out the oil.

Prov Kiriakovich wound the end of the rope about his hand, threw the rope over his shoulder and pulled. Desperate wailing issued from the pipe.

"Quiet!" Bykov became infuriated. "What a fine gentleman we have here! Bear it awhile—I'll pull you out right away."

He drew the rope taut once more—and a piercing cry of unbearable pain resounded through the stokehold. Before Prov Kiriakovich had time to draw the rope taut a third time O'Hiddy grabbed him by the shoulders and tossed him upon a heap of slag in a corner.

"Tell him I won't allow him to torture the lad!" he shouted to Leizer.

Bykov picked himself up, his face deep purple with rage.

"Hey, you! Tell this heathen from me if that's the case he can mess around here all by himself. And if he don't want to do that he'll have to break through the pipe."

Leizer, practically in a cataleptic state, interpreted. O'Hiddy tossed his head: "Very well! I'm going up to report to the captain."

He ran up the trap ladder and disappeared in the hatchway. Prov Kiriakovich wanted to have another try at the rope but the Canadian with the scar raised a threatening fist and Bykov made no further move.

O'Hiddy's head appeared in the hatchway: "Mr. Zwiebel, come on up and ask Mr. Bikoff to come along with you. The captain wants to have a talk with you."

Prov Kiriakovich spat, called on the Devil and started climbing.

Captain Timmons was standing at the hatchway and regarded Bykov with cold, narrowed eyes. He asked for an explanation of what had happened and, having heard Leizer's story to the end, said in an unhurried and bored voice: "I cannot allow the pipe to be broken without the consent of the owners of the cargo and the shipowner. I shall send a special cablegram to New Orleans at once. But in the meantime try to extricate the boy in one way or another."

Bykov, raging, went below. More machine oil was thrown into the pipe; attempts were made to pull the boy out by yanking or by pulling steadily and carefully, but each move caused unbearable pain to Mitka and the stokehold resounded again and again with his wild screams. Mitka was sobbing and begged them to kill him right off—that would be better.

Things dragged on thus until evening. When evening came, Bykov, having exhausted his entire store of curses, went ashore. The stokers were quietly talking to one another as they listened to the muffled sobs.

"He won't hold out long," the Canadian remarked somberly. "That pipe's got to be cut with an acetylene torch, I tell you."

"Timmons won't allow it," another stoker commented.

"The low-down trash!" the Canadian got out hoarsely, hitting the pipe with his fist.

8

In the morning Captain Timmons received an answer to his special cablegram. He read it through in his cabin and his face grew stonier with every line. The shipowner had cabled that he would not tolerate any delay on account of some worthless Russian brat, and that he was placing the responsibility for the consequences of a late arrival upon Captain Timmons. "In America we can always find a captain who will be able to maintain the interests of the firm with greater loyalty," the cablegram concluded.

Captain Timmons shut his eyes—and saw his wife and the two youngsters as if they were actually before him. His face twitched. With an abrupt gesture he tore up the cablegram and went on deck. There Bykov was standing before O'Hiddy and, brandishing his arms, was heatedly explaining something to Zwiebel. Zwiebel caught sight of the captain and fixed him with his piteous intimidated gaze.

"Mr. Captain, do you already have an answer from America?"

"Yes," Timmons answered drily. "Interpret this to Mr Bikoff: I am not delaying for even one hour. This evening the fires must be started, and tomorrow morning we are off. If, through Mr. Bikoff's fault, this will not take place he will have to pay all the losses incurred by my firm and myself."

Bykov clenched his fists and launched into unsurpassable cursing.

"Ah, you thrice-accursed mongrel! If you'd only croak in that pipe, you sonvabitch!"

Leizer staggered back: "Whatever are you saying, Prov Kiriakovich—why, it's actually frightening even to hear it! Is the child to blame in any way that he should die in such a vile place?"

"Go to hell!" Bykov growled.

Captain Timmons was about to withdraw to his cabin, but he was stopped by the stoker with the scar who had come out on deck from the engine room hatchway.

"Pardon me, sir," the Canadian began. "The men are asking permission to cut the pipe. Can't wait any longer—the boy is barely breathing. We—"

Timmons' clean-shaven cheeks flushed slightly.

"I forbid it," he answered, without raising his voice.

"But that's murder, sir," the Canadian advanced threateningly. "We won't let it happen. We'll cut the pipe without your consent—"

"Try it!" said Timmons, still more quietly. "You know what mutiny on a ship means, and you know what the law has to say on that point. If you please . . . but I wouldn't give two cents for your hide if you go ahead. Is that understood?"

The scar on the Canadian's cheek became suffused with blood. His burning gaze seared Timmons, then he wheeled about and disappeared through the hatchway.

"Look after the men, O'Hiddy. You are responsible for the men in the engine room," Timmons informed the engineer with rancor and went off to his cabin.

Bykov and Zwiebel went down to the stokehold. Mitka no longer said anything in answer when they called to him but merely moaned, so faintly that you could hardly hear him. The dinner bell rang for the crew and the stokehold emptied. Bykov bent toward the pipe and for a long while listened closely. Then he straightened up and with a decisive gesture shoved his cap down over his eyebrows.

"Let's go to the captain," he commanded Zwiebel and started climbing up on deck.

Captain Timmons was enjoying a steak; he did not stop chewing as he fixed Bykov and Zwiebel with calm, dispassionate eyes.

"Did you get him out?" he asked, cutting off a piece that dripped blood.

"Nothings works, Mr. Captain. Oi, what a dreadful thing

to happen—" Leizer began, but Bykov cut him short; he
propped his hands on the table and his beet-colored face
suddenly paled.

"You tell him, Leizer," said he in a low voice, even
though nobody but Leizer could understand him, "that there's
no way of getting that little whoreson out, and as for paying
damages—why, I just can't do it. Where would I get such a
sum?" Bykov paused, noisily drew air into his lungs and then
got out dully together with the exhaled air: "Let him get the
fires going with the boy in there."

Leizer gasped.

"Oi, Prov Kiriakovich! How can one make jokes like that?
How will I tell such a thing to the American captain, that
he should kill the child with heat? Better do what you want
yourself, but I'm not going to. God will deny me and my
children for such a deed."

Bykov leant forward over the table.

"Listen, Leizer," he hissed, "I'm not joking with you. I'm
not going to be beggared because of a misbegotten brat. I
give you my word: if you won't tell this to the captain, I
swear on the Cross I'll inform the inspector of police how
last year you were marching on Deribassovskaya Street with
a red flag and yelling against the Czar."

Leizer felt ice-cold ants running down his back but he still
tried to resist.

"Well, and what of it?" he said with a pitiful and sickly
smile. "Mr. Police Inspector won't say anything. What Jew
didn't march at that time with a red flag and didn't shout all
sorts of foolishness?"

"Foolishness? Have you forgotten about the eagle? You
think I don't know?"

Leizer staggered back. This was a mortal blow. Bykov
knew about it, then. About what Leizer had been so painstakingly concealing all the while and had considered as completely grown over with the grass of oblivion. About how he,
Leizer Zwiebel, together with certain hot-headed students,
had torn down the sculptured double-headed Imperial Eagle
from over a pharmacy on Marazlievskaya Street and, in a
delirious frenzy, had trampled on its black wings. This was

far more frightful than any red flag. Leizer closed his eyes, but Bykov went on hissing: "And Schlickerman, now—do you remember him?"

Zwiebel let out a moan. He recalled the hideously mangled body of Schlickerman, who had been beaten to death by the police in the precinct house; heaving a bitter and profound sigh Leizer came to a decision. "It's a sin for you to do this, Prov Kiriakovich. Well, so be it—I'll tell the captain."

Leizer's hands were shaking and his lips quivered as he interpreted to Timmons what Bykov had said. Timmons heard him out in silence. Not the tiniest muscle twitched on his smooth face. He took the pipe out of his mouth and answered slowly: "Tell Mr. Bikoff that is his business. The boy is his and so is the enterprise. Let him arrange things as he thinks best—if he can manage to keep everything quiet from my crew and put it over on my men somehow. I haven't heard a thing and I don't know a thing. But the fires will be started this evening."

Bykov's lips tautened and he went on deck with Zwiebel. The beryl-tinted evening shadows were falling on the unruffled roadstead. The stillness of evening was over everything, broken only by the cries of the gulls squabbling over refuse close to the water. Bykov turned to Zwiebel and, his blood rushing to his face, whispered savagely and ominously: "One word of this to anybody, and I'll put you out of this world—remember that."

9

There was nobody in the stokehold except the young chimney sweeps. The Americans had not yet come back from mess. The little boys were talking in whispers, standing about the pipe in which the Rat was caught and into which Petka had thrust his head. Bykov grabbed him by his tarpaulin sack, which had buckled on his back, and yanked the boy toward him. Petka's eyes were popping out from fright, looking like white buttons against his black face.

"What are you shoving yourself in there for, you scum? Loafing again? I'll kill all of you, by the Devil and his dam!" Bykov growled, holding Petka up in the air.

"Why, we're all through, Prov Kiriakovich!" Petka squeaked. "We finished all the pipes at one clip, honest to God! If it wasn't for the Rat we would have been all done by one o'clock!"

Prov Kiriakovich looked up over his shoulder at the square opening of the hatch with the sky showing blue above it, drew Petka close to him and fell to muttering: "Crawl to the Rat in the pipe, this minute. Here, tie this rope around your foot and crawl in there. When the Britishers come back from supper I'm going to start pulling you out of there, and you'll scream loud as you can. Like you weren't Petka any more but the Rat."

"What's that for, Prov Kiriakovich?"

"Just keep on questioning me and see what you get! Well, when I pull you out, you start bawling like a cow—that's how overjoyed you are. There, get going—or I'll send you to the Devil's dam before you can count two! The rest of you, keep quiet when you get home or I'll flay ten hides off of each one of you!" he shouted at the other three boys.

Petka disappeared in the pipe, with the rope dangling out of it. The hatchway darkened and the treads of the trap ladder thundered under the feet of the descending Americans.

Zwiebel sighed noisily and ventured to touch Bykov's elbow.

"Prov Kiriakovich," he managed to say with great difficulty and much trembling, "do you yourself really want to do in an innocent child in that way?"

Bykov merely gave him a look: "What a very pitying nation you are!" he said with contemptuous incomprehension. "That must be why they're killing you off in every land!" And suddenly, his rancor coming to a boiling point, he yelled: "Is he yours, or what? What business is this of yours? I found him, and I'm the one that will have to answer for him. He's got nobody, anyway—he's homeless, nobody's going to ask about him. But if anyone's going to ask, I'll say he ran off, that he sailed with the limeys. Git, you!"

Leizer sprang back. The stokers, back by now, crowded about the pipe. Bykov grunted, seized the rope and, straining, tugged at it. Petka set up a howl within the pipe. The rope began to give.

"Pull! Pull!" Bykov yelled and the stokers, grasping his meaning, also took hold of the rope. Petka's feet appeared, then his back, and at last his whole body slipped out. The boy, his arms flung out, crashed with his face against the metal deck strewn with jagged clinkers. He hurt his forehead badly and burst into bawling that was no longer feigned. The stokers, breaking into excited talk, picked him up and dragged him up the trap ladder to the deck. The Canadian wiped the blood off Petka's injured forehead with his bandanna and was about to wipe the rest of his face which was covered with a greasy black coating of lubricating oil, but Bykov snatched the boy out of his hands and dragged him off toward the gangplank. On the way he ran into O'Hiddy, who had emerged to find out what the hubbub was all about.

"What's up?" asked the engineer.

The Canadian hurriedly told him that they had succeeded in getting the boy out.

O'Hiddy approached Bykov. The engineer wanted to say something encouraging and kindly to the rescued lad, and he put his hand on Petka's grease-covered hair. Petka turned his head and opened his mouth and the engineer caught sight of black carious teeth that did not in the least resemble Mitka's dazzling stockade of teeth. O'Hiddy took his hand away and his perplexed eyes followed Bykov, who had dashed down to the pier, dragging Petka after him. As soon as the two had disappeared around the corner of a bonded warehouse the engineer left the railing and went down into the stokehold.

The boys, having gathered their implements, were getting ready to leave in their turn. O'Hiddy, having bided his time till they had clambered up the trap ladder, picked up a firebar and thrust it far into the pipe. The firebar encountered a yielding obstacle and O'Hiddy caught a barely audible sound that resembled piteous mewling.

He threw down the firebar and went up the trap ladder, taking several treads at a time. On deck he moderated his steps and tapped at the door of the captain's cabin.

Timmons looked in wonder at the engineer, at his pale face with the cornflower-blue eyes distended, at the beads of sweat on his forehead.

"What's the matter with you, Dickie?" he asked.

"Fred—" the engineer gasped, "a crime has been committed. That swindler Bikoff has taken us in. It was another boy he pulled out of the pipe. The victim was left there. He's almost dead—he can't answer, even—"

Captain Timmons was fidgeting with his pipe. His face had become ponderous, utterly immobile.

"That's just what I thought," said he slowly.

"What! You know about this?" the engineer backed away.

"I don't know, but that's what I supposed." Timmons clenched the pipe in his teeth and, after striking a match on the sole of his shoe, got the tobacco to burn. But that doesn't make any difference. We have no way out. We must sail tomorrow morning, as soon as we take on the last bag of fertilizer. At ten tonight you'll get the fires going."

"You're out of your mind! And what about the child?"

Captain Timmons raised his head. His eyes had become greenish and cold, like chips of ice.

"Hear me out, my friend! If I don't carry out the owner's orders I'll be thrown out and black-listed. There isn't a line that will take me on. You're a single man. I have a wife and children. I am aware that a crime has been committed, if you want to look at things from the viewpoint of morals in general. But in the present instance my viewpoint is that of personal morals. I am a man, and I don't want my family to die in the gutter. My children are dear to me. You may not understand this, perhaps, but when I think of what will become of my children I take the responsibility for this upon myself. And you wouldn't want to make my children the same sort of waifs and beggars as this urchin—"

"But the crew—"

"The crew won't find out anything if you don't tell them. And tell them you won't, because you don't desire the death of my children. At any rate, there's no saving the boy by now. Two or three hours more and he'll suffocate. At ten we're coaling the fires. That's an order!"

O'Hiddy squeezed his temples. It seemed to him that his head was expanding like a rubber balloon and that it would burst at any moment.

"Very well! I won't say anything. And may the Lord forgive me and you, Fred!"

10

The *Lizzie Waldon* sailed out of Odessa harbor exactly at noon, after taking on a full cargo. The pier was deserted, and there was only one pitifully squirming figure in a long threadbare jacket lurking near the bonded warehouse. Leizer Zwiebel had come to see the ship off because he had nine hungry children and a heart which nobody had any use for but which felt pity for children. When the ship had turned the promontory of the breakwater he left the pier, carrying off on his bowed back a frightful burden which no one could see.

The *Lizzie Waldon* had no trouble passing through the Bosporus and the Strait of Gibraltar. The engines worked well; the coal taken on in Odessa was of an excellent grade; the men worked splendidly, and only O'Hiddy, the chief engineer, kept drinking himself into stupefaction from the break of day and lying in his cabin, all bloated and frightful to look at.

After the Strait of Gibraltar the ship entered the Atlantic, starting on a path laid down five centuries previously by a certain stubborn Genoese, and on the very first night out in the Atlantic Chief Engineer O'Hiddy, before the eyes of the sailors on watch, leapt overboard from the spar deck. The weather was freshening, the wind was raising heavy seas and it would have been risky to lower the boats. Captain Timmons marked this sad event by a brief entry in his logbook.

For eleven days the *Lizzie Waldon* cut the ocean waves and on the twelfth moored at her berth in her home port of New Orleans. Her owner, together with the head of the firm of Shelby, Shelly, Shelty & Co., a crisp gentleman in a white tophat (it was summertime), came up on deck to thank Captain Timmons for the successful trip and his exemplary service.

"We are giving you a special reward, in addition to the

bonus, and Mr. Shelby, for his part, has also found that a bonus is called for because of your efforts. Incidentally, how did you make out with that hitch in Odessa?"

"Thank you," Captain Timmons bowed. "A mere trifle. Not worth mentioning."

As always, he had on a blue cap with gold braid, and a captain's pipe with a gnawed mouthpiece was clenched between his teeth. Captain Timmons' face was unruffled and serene.

That night, when the crew had been given shore leave and had left the ship, except for one man on watch, Captain Timmons went down into the stokehold. After tightening every screw to close the hatch he took a long firebar, thrust it into the vent of the ill-fated pipe and poked about in its depths for a long while. Several thoroughly charred bones fell out on the metal grating of the deck; then, with a reverberating and hollow thump, a small round skull tumbled out. The firebar, introduced once more, dragged out something that rang as it fell on the deck. Timmons bent over and picked up a small metal box, of the sort used for packaging cheap candy drops. The box had a dark coating of carbon. The captain took out his pocketknife and, thrusting it under the lid, pried the box open. Lying on its bottom were a few copper coins and a silver dollar blackened by fire. He snapped the box shut and shoved it into his pocket. Then, getting down on his knees, he spread a handkerchief and gathered the bones and skull in it. When he emerged on deck he walked over to the railing and threw the handkerchief, knotted together, into the black, barely stirring water.

In his cabin he walked over to the table, picked up a bottle of whiskey and filled a tumbler to the brim—but did not drink it. Having stood thus for a minute or so he passed his hand over his face, as if he were brushing away the twitching of a muscle under his jaw, after which, going over to an open port, he splashed the whiskey through it.

When Captain Timmons went ashore the next morning he dropped in on a jeweler he knew and asked him to set the fire-darkened dollar into the lid of his silver cigar case.

"Where did you get this thing, Timmons?" asked the jeweler, turning the dollar in his puffy fingers.

"I don't feel like talking about it," Captain Timmons frowned. "An unpleasant affair. But I want to keep this coin as a memento."

He politely said good-bye to the jeweler and went out into the street. He was on his way home, rejoicing over the fact that he would very shortly see his wife and children and make his family happy by telling them of the bonuses he had received because of the fast freight. He was serene and feeling secure about tomorrow. And he trod firmly among the noise and rumble of the street, past buildings behind the plate-glass windows of which, screened halfway up with hangings of green pongee, there was beginning to seethe, amid the clatter of adding machines, the arid, measured work of human greed.

1927

Michael Michaelovich ZOSHCHENKO

[1895-1958]

Zoshchenko, a native of the Ukraine, was the son of an artist of noble descent. Dropping the law course at the University of St. Petersburg, he volunteered in 1914, served as an officer and was gassed and wounded. In 1918 he volunteered again, this time for the Red Army; after the Revolution came his wander years: he was a carpenter, trapper, cobbler, policeman, detective, gambler, clerk, actor. In 1921 he was one of the founders of the literary circle, the Serapion Brotherhood, which was to become so famous, and published his first story in 1922. According to his friends, Zoshchenko was a confirmed hypochondriac and much given to melancholy.

Like Leskov and Shchedrin-Saltykov, Zoshchenko has evolved a language of his own (an English approximation of it can be found in the stories of Ring Lardner and Damon Runyon). Just as there is Babel's recognized Odessa language, so is there a Zoshchenko language, critically acknowledged, which the reader finds a delightful concomitant to the story itself. "It is usually maintained," the humorist himself has written, "that I am mangling the beautiful Russian language, that purely for comic effects I employ words outside their rightful meanings, that I write in a twisted medium with the intention of provoking belly laughs. But all that is erroneous. I hardly twist anything: I write the same language that the man in the street thinks and talks in." * To laugh is human; to see ourselves as others see us is divine, and since the Russians are a most humorous people it was not unnatural for Zoshchenko to become, next to Chekhov, the Russians'

* As quoted in Marc Slonim's excellent *Modern Russian Literature*. Oxford University Press, New York, 1953.

most popular humorist (although he has hardly a smidgen
of the older humorist's compassion).

The crooked mirror has always been a dominant symbol
in Russian literature. As held up by Zoshchenko it showed
the eternal Russian Philistine with the Old Adam of bourzhu-
ism still strong within him, but with a few peacock feathers
of socialistic slogans and shibboleths stuck into the rather thin
coating of Sovietism: Pray to God, but don't go sassin' the
Devil, neither. What Soviet catoptrics demands of its artists,
however, is the Pepper's Ghost of the New Soviet Man, and,
inevitably, this "brainless, pornographic scribbler" got his
lumps when, in 1946, Zhdanov came down on him like a ton
of theologically ideological bricks for the story "The Adventures of an Ape." In 1947 the "vagabond of literature" attempted a recantation and, in 1950, a full comeback. Both
proved futile. It is axiomatic, by now, that no Soviet writer
can possibly die in his bed and of natural causes but, according to non-Soviet and therefore reputable press dispatches,
those were the incredible circumstances of Zoshchenko's
death.

The number of Russians who saw Lenin plain is not exceeded even by the number of places where Washington slept.
In fact, it is amazing that Lenin managed to accomplish
anything at all besides his personal appearances, since, at a
most conservative estimate, the quantity of stories, poems,
etc., on this theme seems at least three times greater than the
entire population of the USSR. "A Historical Story" is so
deft a parody on this *halturish* genre that it obviates the need
for actual representation. "A Medical Case" is typical of the
quandaries, for the most part bizarre, in which Zoshchenko's
Ivan Ivanovich Sovietskys find themselves.

A HISTORICAL STORY

It's no good lying about this sort of thing. Happen you did
see Vladimir Ilyich, say that you saw him in such-and-such

a place, under such-and-such circumstances. But if you didn't see him, keep your yap shut and don't go sounding off all for nothing. History will be better off that way.

And as for Ivan Semionych Zhukov bragging that he saw Vladimir Ilyich at a meeting, and that Vladimir Ilyich kept looking him right in the face all the time, why, that's just a lot of bosh and out-and-out nonsense. Ilyich couldn't have looked him in the face—a face like any face, with a coarse beard that sticks right out, the nose common and twelve-to-the-dozen. Ilyich just couldn't have looked at a face like that, all the more so since Ivan Semionych Zhukov opened a stand the other day; he's in business now and, like as not, his weights got no inspection seals on them.

I'm liable to spit in this same Zhukov's shameless eyes for lying like that, when I meet up with him.

As a general thing, such lying can't help but get history all balled up.

Me, now, I did see our dear leader Vladimir Ilyich Lenin —and I ain't lying.

Me, now, I may have gone to particular trouble to get me a pass into the Smolnyi from Martynov; I may have spent two or three hours walking up and down corridors like a damned soul, waiting. And I'm not making any fuss about it; you don't catch me bragging about it. And if I do say anything about it now I'm doing so only for the sake of history.

Well, I took my place in the corridor at exactly three in the afternoon. I took my place and I stood there, like a damned soul. And there was a man in a fur coat standing near me and jigging, on account of it was cold.

"What are you standing there for," I asked him, "and jigging your legs like that?"

"Why," he said, "I'm froze. I," he said, "am Lenin's chauffeur."

"No!" said I.

I looked at him—just an ordinary person, with an outsize mustache. And a nose.

"Allow me to introduce myself," said I.

We got to chewing the rag.

"How do you drive him?" I asked. "Ain't you afraid? That's no ordinary passenger you got there. And there's all kinds of pillars and posts all around you. You gotta watch out you don't run smack into something—"

"Why, no," said he. "I'm used to the work."

"Well, watch out," I told him. "Drive carefully."

By God, that's just what I told him. And you don't catch me bragging about it. And if I do say anything about it I'm doing so only for the sake of history. As for the chauffeur, he was the right sort; he looked at me and he said: "Why, to be sure—I'll try my best."

By God, that's just what the man said. "I'll try my best," that's what he said.

"Well," said I, "try your best, little brother."

At that he kinda waved at me, as much as to say "All right!"

"That's it, then," said I.

I wanted to write down our historical conversation but— bingo!—no pencil. I rummaged in one pocket: matches, cigarette papers, an unopened package of Number Eight tobacco, but no pencil. I rummaged in the other pocket: no pencil either. I ran up to the second floor, to an office—they give me a stub. I got back, fast as I could—no chauffeur. There he'd been, just a little while back, standing in his fur coat and jigging, but right then he just wasn't there. And neither was his fur coat.

I looked here, I looked there—he wasn't around.

I ran out into the street: the chauffeur was sitting in the car; the car was making noises and then it started off. And inside the car was our dear leader, Vladimir Ilyich, sitting, and his dear little coat collar was turned up.

I put my hand up to the brim of my cap and wanted to start hurrahing, but I got kinda leery of the sentry and stepped aside to the left.

I stepped aside—and you don't catch me bragging about it. I don't go around shouting about from the rooftops: There, now, I, too, seen Ilyich!

There, I seen him, and that's that. For my own part, I'm

happy, and if there's some folks as might be wanting to learn the particulars from me, let them get in touch with me directly.

1923-1933

A MEDICAL CASE

All my life, I may say, I've been cussing out village healers and all that sort of medical assistants' helpers. But right now I'll stick up for them for all I'm worth. On account of a real holy case happening that I seen with my own eyes.

Main thing was, all the medicos refused to treat this little wench. They'd just shrug her off—the Devil alone knew what was wrong with her. Medicine was at a loss here, you might say. But here just an ordinary fellow comes along, without even a middling education, and maybe a sonvabitch and a crook at heart, and he laid his peepers on the little wench, figgered awhile on the why and wherefore—and, if you please, you got a healthy personality instead of an ailment.

And what happened to the little wench was as per the following.

Such a small little wench, she was. Thirteen. Some little boys had frightened her. She'd gone out into the yard to attend to some personal business. And the little boys wanted to play a joke on her, to frighten her a little. And they pitched a dead cat at her. And because of that there the gift of speech left her. That is, she couldn't get a word out after a fright like that. She just kept yammering something, but wouldn't even try to get a whole word out. And she don't ask for something to eat, even.

As for her parents, they wasn't from amongst our leading citizens, of course. They wasn't in the vanguard of the Revolution. They wasn't rich parents—just handicraftsmen in a small way. They turned out bootlaces. And the little wench also turned something for them. A wheel of some sort. But when this thing come along, she could neither turn the wheel nor did she have the gift of speech.

So the parents kept on and on dragging her to all the physicians, and after they run out of those they up and took her to a special fellow. You couldn't say about him that he was a professor or doctor of Tibetan medicine. He was simply a natural-born healer.

So they brought their child to Shuvalovo, where this here specialist was living. They made known to him the why and wherefore of the business.

"Tell you what," said the healer. "Your little one's gift of speech was took away on account of a great fright. And," he said, "here's the way I figger it: I'm going to scare her right back into speaking, you see. Maybe, now, little draggletail that she is, I'll have her speechifying again. The human organism," said he, "is deserving of universal wonder. The doctors," he said, "and all them different professors, even," he said, "are up against it when it comes to finding out the why and the wherefore and the facts of what is going on in the human body. And," he said, "I'm in perfect agreement with them as to that and," said he, "I'd be up against it to tell you where somebody may have his liver located, or his spleen, now. One man," he said, "may have it here, whilst another might not have it here. One man," he said, "may be having a pain in his guts, whilst another may have had his gift of speech took away, even though his tongue is lolloping regular enough. The only thing required," said he, "is that you gotta find the proper cause for everything and then take a stick to it and drive it out. And that," he said, "is my strong point and my knowledge. I get at the cause," said he, "and I root it out."

Naturally, the parents got leery and didn't advise him to sock that little wench with no stick.

"Come now—come, now!" said the medico. "I ain't going to sock her with no stick," he said. "But," said he, "I'm going to take me a Turkish towel, for instance, or something of the sort; then I'm going to take your little whippersnapper," he said, "and place her on that there place, and let her squat there for three minutes or so. And after that," said he, "I'll pop out from behind the door, quiet like, and go *smack!* with the towel. And, maybe, she'll get straightened out. Maybe she'll get one hell of a scare and, the way I figger it, maybe she'll get so that you'll have her talking again."

Then he took a soft-woven towel from under a closet, seated the little wench as required, and went out.

A couple minutes later he tiptoed to her, quiet as quiet, and went *smack!* with the towel at the nape of her neck.

And that little wench, did she start squealing, did she go off into convulsions, on account of how bad she was frightened.

And, do you know, she started in talking.

She talked and she talked—there just was no stopping her. And she was asking to be took home. And holding on to her mom. Although her eyes had become more disturbed than ever and sort of—well, now, sort of crazy.

"Say," her parents spoke up, "ain't she likely to become a little idiot after all this here?"

"That's something I can't tell you," said the man of medicine. "My business was to impart the gift of speech to her. And that, as you can see, I've done. And," he said, "it ain't so much your three roubles that interest me; I find it more amusing to see such results as that."

The parents handed him his three roubles and took off.

As for the little wench, she got to talking, for a fact. True enough, she was drove a trifle crazy; she's become sort of foolish, like. But she's talking all right, sure as shooting.

1923-1933

Alexander FADEYEV (or BULYGA)

[1901—]

Fadeyev, although a native of Central Russia, was brought up and educated in Vladivostok, to which city his father, an M.D. of the Second Grade, had moved during Alexander's boyhood. While still in his teens the future writer went through the civil war as a Red Partisan, being wounded twice, and was also an active Party worker in Siberia and Ukraine. His best known work, *The Rout* (or *The Nineteen*), which tells the story of the last stand of a group of Siberian Partisans surrounded by Whites and Japanese interventionists, is based upon the author's own experience, and its publication in 1927 brought him into prominence as an exponent of Soviet Realism.

This novel marked, in effect, one of the turning points in the still young literature of the Soviets. During the decade since the October Revolution Leo Tolstoi's aberrant theories on art had come to bulk greater in the canon of Soviet aesthetics than even the dicta on art of Marx and Engels. The thematics of Proletarian Literature were all cut and dried, for what else was there to write about except the New Heroic Soviet Man? The rub was in the schematics. For although this Hero of His Time was invariably cut out of whole cloth, an arshin wide and duly stamped *Made in USSR* on the selvage, with every care taken to show him as a Man of Action, and neither a Bourgeois Individualist nor one of your Dostoevskian mooncalves tainted with introspection, there was just no breathing any life into the rag doll. Fadeyev's achievement lay in boldly adopting some of the Tolstoian artistic devices; his partisans in their Siberian Alamo, all psychologically portrayed, were alive and convincing. The cause of Psychological

Soviet Realism was further strengthened by Fadeyev's important critical essay, "The Road of Soviet Literature" (1928), a plea for drawing living characters and rendering Soviet reality truthfully. By 1932 Fadeyev, Gladkov and others, joined by many of the Fellow Travelers, were victorious over the anti-psychologists and came to exert a decided influence upon the development of Soviet literature in the 1930's and 1940's.

The Last of the Udegs, published in 1936, ranks next in importance to *The Rout* among Fadeyev's works and also deals with the civil war and the Japanese intervention, but at much greater length.

ON POVERTY AND RICHES

That fall we expelled Nicholai Kamkov, a woodsman, from the Party.

His father, Ivan Stepanovich Kamkov, a forester, had been well-to-do in his time; he had a big homestead and a house neighboring our settlement of Utessnoye, where the Red Partisan collective now is. We took away his homestead only in 1922, when the power of the Soviets became well established in our region. But we didn't do anything to the old man himself, because during the years the war was going on he used to hide the partisans at his place, and was famous in our region as a lumberman who knew his business.

We expelled Nicholai Kamkov because of a drunken debauch he staged at the collective. He came that fall to visit his father (his father is engaged in forestry hereabouts to this very day), and he happened to arrive on a holiday, when we were dividing the year's take. And that's when the thing happened to him.

When it came to investigating this mixup of his, they called us in as well—those of us who had left the settlement of Utessnoye, Party members who were scattered throughout the region. All of us had known Nicholka well in our youth and had faith in him, but after the civil war we had lost track of him. But now we saw that we shouldn't have had any faith in him even before, and we actually wondered how we could have been so mistaken about people at that time, and how a man like that could have stayed on in the Party to this very day.

In former times education was out of our reach, and we mouzhik kids were very much taken with the idea that Nicholka Kamkov, the son of a learned gentleman who was known to everybody in the region, was associating with us and making us his friends. As soon as he'd come visiting after school closed for the summer he would sling his gun over his shoulder and join us. And then he'd be with us for weeks and months at a time. He'd go with us to the fields, and fishing, and to our evening gatherings; he'd eat with us out of the same bowl, and the clothes he wore were no different from ours.

Sometimes, on holidays, we would have an all-out fight with some other lads nearby. Our village was on the poor side, while the one next to us was sort of well-to-do and, I remember, Nicholka Kamkov was always with us, on the poor side. Even in his youth he was a big fellow, heavy; his eyebrows were thick, his voice blared like a trumpet. He used to bowl everybody over, one after the other, until he'd come up against Alexashka Chikin, the miller's son. That fellow was nimble, quick both of hand and eye, and a beast for fair. If he managed to hit you he'd strike you in the most horrible places and show no mercy. They'd be fighting for an hour or thereabouts, and then Kamkov would be the first to hold out his hand.

"That's enough. I got respect for you," he'd say.

"That's the way, my gentleman!" Alexashka would laugh. "Well, if you honestly mean it, I've nothing against it."

We also had another mouzhik, not much of a one, though, by the name of Anton Guriev; a vagabonding fellow; even in the time of the czars he didn't acknowledge either God or priests. He had no livestock whatsoever, not even a hen; his hut had just a handful or two of straw for a roof, without any outbuildings or fences whatsoever, and it stood all by itself on the very edge of the village.

He didn't acknowledge anything like work, either: "That's the only point," he used to say, "that I agree on with Our Lord God Jesus Christ," and he would be away from the village for months at a stretch. The only one that worked was his wife; she worked without a drop of blood in her face, she worked both on the Chikin and the Kamkov lands; as for his little ones—and there was a host of them—they went around begging.

So this Anton Guriev would come back from his vaga-bonding, and go traipsing through the settlement practically mother-naked, his head with no neck to it setting spang on his shoulders, his trunk short, his legs long, his face with clumps of rusty-red hair all over it and solemn-looking, and jabbering all the time: "There's a great evening-up amongst people coming soon. Prepare yourselves!"

"What sort of evening-up, Antosha?"

"We're going to divide evenly the property of the lords of the earth."

"Come, will there be enough for everybody? Guess there's as many people on earth as there are stars in the sky."

"There will be enough for clothes, for food, and after that we'll all be living on the poor side," he would say, solemn-like.

And it was with this Antoshka Guriev that Nicholai Kamkov palled around most of all; quite often he'd even pass the night at his place, up in the unfinished attic. They'd get drunk, the both of them, and sit there with their legs dangling over the eaves of the hut. Antoshka would be spouting heaven knows what nonsense, while Kamkov would take him around and, all in tears, start singing:

> "Russia, my Russia, beggarly!
>   Your sad songs borne on the wind,
>   Your huts crushed down by poverty,
>   The tears of first love bring to mind. . . ."

And, for a fact, our settlement was a miserable one! About a hundred and thirty-five miles from the railroad; the wildest

forests all around, and swamps. We had to go for months
without kerosene, without salt. On a holiday, coming back in
the evening after hunting, you'd walk up to the ferry, and
you would hear a steady moaning rising from the village—
that's how many drunk people there were in it. Even the kids
of five—why, even they liked to play at being drunk.

And there was a lot of merciless poverty amongst us in
the settlement of Utessnoye—the Blinkovs, the Komlevs, the
Anchishkins; but then, how could you count all of us, people
who toiled greatly, people to whom life was bitter and cruel?
However, we, too, had a secret pride, seeing that with our
own hands we had built a road leading here, had made those
frightful forests part to either side, had stirred this bitter soil,
had killed off countless ferocious beasts, and had preserved
a conscience and a flame within the heart.

And when our first soldier Bolsheviks came home from
the German front we grasped that we were deserving of a
better lot on earth.

During the civil war the greater part of our settlement
joined up with the partisans. All of us joined—the Blinkovs,
the Komlevs, the Anchishkins: there was no numbering us.
Anton Guriev joined up too. And Nicholai Kamkov, too,
joined us. But it was now, while we were investigating this
Kamkov affair, that we old fighters recalled that these two,
both Guriev and Kamkov, had their quirks even at that
time.

Maybe we would capture an estate, or a mill, or a railway
station, and Guriev would start screeching: "Burn it all down
—to the Devil's dam with it!"

So he would be told: "Why burn it down? We built all
this; all this is ours. Make this clear to him, Nicholai, seeing
as how you're an educated man amongst the toiling peas-
antry."

But Kamkov would think it over awhile, and then say:
"But maybe he's right, at that? What do we need all this for?
I," he would say, "have experienced in my own person what
sort of thing riches are, and how much evil there is on earth
because of them."

The civil war set many of us on the right path. When you

get to thinking of the fine friends and comrades you fought side by side with, and where they are today—why, they're all great workers, well-known people, people with an education. The mouzhiks established the collective already without us, and battled for it every bit as hard as we did in the civil war. When we uprooted the Chikins their litter cluttered our lives for a long time. And what a lot of grief we went through until we learned to work honestly in the collective for every-body and for ourselves! For so much poison was still left in everyone's soul from the old days.

And who turned out to be among the haters of our Red Partisan collective? Why, Anton Guriev! Perhaps, by that time, he had feathered his nest and had something to lose? No; his hut stood the same way it had always stood, and just as before he wouldn't acknowledge any work, and he himself remained the way he had been. His older sons and daughters got away from him and joined the collective, while his wife, that martyr, died, and he took up with a widow that had been a *koulak;* she had four children, and no one knew where she came from. His beard, which stuck out in clumps like a hound's, had turned gray, and malevolence had come to birth in his eyes. For days on end he would go from hut to hut and talk in bywords: "You all right, my workers for the Soviets' might? They say toil is sweet—but will you ever eat?"

During the first difficult years there were folks who listened to him, but then things changed. From those very things which in the old days had always been our misfortune, new riches came to the collective—linden honey from our impass-able forests and rice, heavy and white as sugar, from our swamps. And that was when the folks perked up. And things also fell out so that just about that time they finished a road that connected our settlement of Utessnoye with the main rail-road and with the sea. And our damp black soil began work-ing wonders.

Anton Guriev happened to get lost for a month somehow, and when he came back we all gasped: we had already put up a school, but he, the vagabond, brought a priest back with him.

"Since I have come to believe in God," said Anton, "I have

the right to break the seal on the church—" Our church had been standing with its doors nailed up for eight years by now. "As for the man of God, I have brought him to you for conscience's sake, so's you would have a conscience. There, now, you'll hear from his lips what sort of brotherhood Our Lord Jesus Christ was teaching us!"

However, the priest ran off the next day. Guriev had taken him in: he had told him the call had come from the faithful, but the faithful answered that God saw and heard everything anyway, without any outside help.

In 1934 our collective won third place in the entire district. And suddenly the names of our people became shining lights throughout our region. And the remarkable thing was that it wasn't the old fighters who had gained new glory; what was remarkable was that the new people had emerged from utterly obscure depths, out of the most benighted families, who had not been known for anything in the village either in the old times, nor during the civil war, nor soon after it.

Grandpa Maxim Dmitrievich Gorchenko, about whom it had not been generally known even in the old days whether he was still among the living or whether he had already died —Grandpa, who had stagnated through a lifetime over his estate of ten primitive rotted hives, suddenly took incalculable quantities of honey from the collective hives and was appointed inspector of the entire apiary. Brigadier Agathea Semenovna Blohina (even I had never heard this name in the old days) had produced on her tract out in the swamps so many centals of good rice that, according to science, it just couldn't have happened. And yet you must know that previously she had left her husband, a loafer and a drunkard, with a baby at her breast. And there was so much milk in her mighty breast that in a year's time she nursed not only her own baby but the baby of an ailing woman neighbor.

And there were many such people, great and small, who sprang up in our settlement during that year. And after that came a crop of people who were just beautiful. Their chief beauty was that they showed off before one another with their labor, and had consideration for everybody, and respected one another in matters of labor or brains. And there was nothing in the world these people feared any longer.

And even outwardly life had become more beautiful. Our young women took to wearing slippers with high heels. They started bringing to our settlement suits of store clothes, neckties, phonographs, radio sets, books, toys for the youngsters —all those things which are not the most important ones in life but which do adorn it.

It was then that Anton Guriev struck up a different song: "Aha, my dear little collective farmers," said he, "so you've grown rich, have you? You've forgotten about equality and fraternity? People ought to be all equal," he says, "but what are you doing? There, you're sporting jackets, and we walking around in torn pants!"

So they told him: "Well, who can you blame for that? Come and work with us, and you shall be paid according to your labor."

But all he did was to gnash his teeth in malice. People began looking at him as if he were touched.

And so, in the fall of 1935, the year of our best crops, Nicholai Kamkov showed up in our settlement. We hadn't seen him in a rather long while; he'd been working all these years somewhere outside our region. Everybody knew he was a Party man, engaged in forestry, and they took offense because he hadn't put up at the house of anybody in the collective, and didn't want to stay at his father's, even, but for old times' sake clambered up to that small attic of Anton Guriev's.

Nobody knows what the tie between them was, but all the days before the holiday they went about under a full head of steam. Kamkov was all bloated, and he had a lost look about him, somehow.

Peter Theodorovich Blinkov, the chairman of our collective, a tall mouzhik, well built and good-looking, clever, and you just couldn't keep him back when it came to working (they called him Czar Peter in the collective), happened to meet the two friends in the street.

"What are you doing, Nicholai Ivanovich?" he asked. "Or have you lost something?"

The other gave him a look from under his brows, and said: "It's my youth I'm looking for—happen to see it, by any chance?"

"Brother, every man is as young as he feels," Czar Peter laughed. "I'm older than you, sort of, yet I'm getting younger all the time; but look at how old age has overcome you!"

"Yes, I can see that all of you here are grown plenty fat."

An answer like that riled Czar Peter: "How would you have me understand that?"

"Why, just so. I guess you, too, have got yourself a talking machine?"

"Well, what of it? Your dear late mother had a grand piano, even—the only thing was, us mouzhiks weren't let in to see it."

"You hear that?" Kamkov asked Guriev.

That's all that was needed to start the other off.

"They have staked all their souls on those pretty little things," he said, "and lost!"

"No," said Czar Peter, the chairman of our collective. "Our souls can't be lost gambling; they're beyond price. But as for you two, you've got alcohol fumes for souls; you ought to sleep them off."

Kamkov, altogether drunk by then, came to the collective banquet without Guriev.

At first, as usual, the prizes were distributed and there were speeches, and everybody was all excited. But after a while people had eaten and drunk their fill, dancing began, everybody felt gay. Well, it seems that Kamkov, too, had had a glass or two too much, and that's when he couldn't hold back any more. He got up at the table, all big and heavy, his eyes wild, his hair like a bear's, and he started to yell: "So you're dancing, are you, but you're keeping Antoshka Guriev in a hut without a chimney to it! It's your conscience as poor folk that you're keeping in that hut!"

First off, they didn't catch on to him, seeing only a drunken man yelling. But in a short while Grandpa Maxim Dmitriev Gorchenko, who was sitting next to him, took offense: "You ought to be ashamed of yourself, Nicholai Ivanovich," said he. "Whoever is holding him in that chimneyless hut? He's staying there of his own accord. And the soul within him is a *koulak's* soul—if not worse—from way, way back. What sort of a poor-folk soul could a drone have?"

"Aha—so you've gotten at bread! Got your bellies filled?" Kamkov kept roaring.

Czar Peter, being hot-tempered, couldn't hold back and he upped and yelled at him: "Whose voice are you chiming with? It's only the Trotskyist bandits that sing pretty little songs like that! Is it them you learned those songs from, eh? Guess you'd like to see us going hungry all our lives, wouldn't you? And to have darkness in our souls all our lives long, with you watching and admiring that?"

Kamkov went for him, spoiling for a fight. They tried to calm him down, but there was no getting near him.

"Come on!" he yelled. "I'll fight you one-handed! Call Alexashka Chikin here—we'll make an all-out fight of it. Call him here—he's lonely enough now and would like to see some folks!"

When he called out that name everybody quieted down. As far back as the time we were getting rid of *koulaks* Alexashka Chikin had killed the secretary of a Young Communists cell and had run off, and ever since there had been nor word nor sign of him.

While they were tying Kamkov, it occurred to Serghei Maximovich Gorchenko, the chairman of our village council, to send some people to Guriev's hut and there, up in the attic, they found Alexashka Chikin, dead drunk. He was filthy, with scabs all over him and a beard that was enough to frighten anybody; by that time there wasn't anything about him that looked human.

When we were expelling Nicholai Kamkov we kept saying all the time: there, it wasn't in us, as human beings, the man was interested, but in our poverty; he sang songs about it and shed tears over it. But when we became competent and fully privileged on this earth, all his interest collapsed, and he got to hating us, while he himself sank to the level of a beast.

1936

Andrei Michaelovich SOBOL

[1888-1926]

In dealing with war and revolution Sobol wrote from personal
and drastic experience. One-fifth of his life, eight of the best
years of a man's life, were spent in penal servitude and exile
(1906-14), a sentence meted out for his membership in the
Social Revolutionary Party. He was Commissar of the 12th
Army under Kerensky, but went over to the Soviets after the
October Revolution. A collection of his short stories (simply
titled *Stories*) was brought out in Moscow in 1926, the year
in which he killed himself.

Panopticum is the great grotesque of the Great Revolution.

The Malinin and Burenin, mentioned as having influenced
the reading of Solomon were: Alexander Fedorovich Malinin
(1835-1888), a pedagogue known as the author of school-
books on different branches of mathematics, written entirely
by himself or in collaboration with Victor Petrovich Burenin
(1841—[?]), poet, novelist and critic.

PANOPTICUM

I

1

White days and white nights: everything white as white.

Snowdrifts high as a man, behind gates in yards, behind
wattled fences in gardens; virgin mountains of snow in the
truck gardens; not a speck, not the least spot between sky and
earth, while below are little bobtail houses and runty beat-up

huts, scattered like raisins in a tasty fluffy loaf. It's the second year in the life of the town of Red-Selimsk—as the small town of Czarevo-Selimsk it had known hundreds of years. But—the Czar's reign got it in the neck from the Reds; they shot the chief of police on Goat Hill; there is a quadrangular whitish space on the wall of the precinct house instead of a portrait with crown and scepter—however, on the adjacent wall, covered with the same wallpaper, fusty and thickly speckled with fly mementos, hangs a new portrait, that of the garrison commander at Kuban, in whose house the Regional Committee meets; a shrine with the skin and bones of a saint was taken out of the cloister at Borissovo-Glebsk and sent off in a freight car marked *Fish;* a Petersburg Futurist in an open-neck sweater started a Studio of Poetics, and the snow kept falling, falling.

Before the snow, during the wet aguish autumn, Red-Selimsk was in darkness: there was no firewood at the electric powerhouse, the Red-Selimskians were tracking down kerosene the way rare game is tracked down on prairies; Eudokimov, the leading black-marketeer, reeked of naphtha, black mineral oil and something else, so that you could smell him five blocks away; one girl, after an evening seminar at the Studio of Poetics, had slapped the Petersburg Futurist's face and screamed in a strained voice: "You have deceived me, you scoundrel!" and the Futurist had, toward morning, decamped with his official papers and his mandate without letting any grass grow under his feet; an ancient crone in a bread queue shed bloody tears and threatened to tell God about all the nasty things people were up to, and the rain kept lashing, lashing.

Rain is over Red-Selimsk, clouds spread like felt over all the fields, gullies and country roads; Peter's Town is sopping wet, Kostroma is sopping wet; there's mire on Moscow's streets, even the main ones; turbid torrents are running through Kanavino, near Nizhni Novgorod; regiments, divisions, are wading knee-deep in the Urals, in Siberia, in the Ukraine; water-logged cannons, water-logged wagon trains, water-logged decrees on water-logged Russian fences—and Russia slogs along through puddles, Russia slogs along and is

unafraid, slogs along and, through the clouds, carries on a
conversation with the sun:

"Come on, now!"

. . . Rain, rain, go away. . . .

2

In November, immediately after the celebration of the
town's first anniversary as Red-Selimsk, an important visitor
from Moscow looked in on it. He had a private railroad car,
with a platform attached to it for his automobile. Twice did
the siren horn yap, stirring up the short streets, lanes and
dead ends, frightening horses and the young men of twenty-
five who had dodged registering for military service, but the
third yap was cut off short: the automobile got stuck, and
right on the main street at that; it had been sucked down into
the mire, it had gone astray in the dark—and that was precisely when Red-Selimsk firmly and resolutely declared war
against darkness.

Darkness disappeared, the way a vanquished devil dis-
appears through a trap door in the stage; electrical wonder-
workers raced one after the other, and after a long hiatus, to
the joy of little boys, messengers and Soviet young ladies, a
sign—rather cachectic, true enough, of three miserable little
bulbs all in all, yet dazzling just the same—burst into glow
on Spasso-Kudrinskaya Street:

PANOPTICUM

—on Spasso-Kudrinskaya Street, now known as the Triumph of the Revolution Street, practically the main one of the
town, the local Soviet was not too far off; there, too, was
the office of the Central Administration, as well as the
boarded-up, half-burned building of the Ochrana. The sign
blazed, beckoned, summoned, lured, attracted—and how it
blazed, and how it beckoned, and what wonders it promised!
Rain, mire, slush, rain, rain, dark-brown gurry underfoot,
overhead a sky as drab as a hospital blanket—but just the
same:

PANOPTICUM

But, as soon as the first blizzard started howling, why,
everything went to rack and ruin in the Panopticum.

And it was the Skeleton of a Merman which started off
the run of ill-starred days.

Unexpectedly, for some unknown reason, he let go of his
supports and fell all to bits and pieces, but in such a way
that his ribs reclined on his kneecaps, while one of the shin-
bones fell across his jaws. He who up to that time had stood
with hauteur (and even supercilious hauteur) on his dais just
as if he were a sovereign ruler exalted above the insignificant
mob with but one face, had now turned into a ludicrous heap
of yellow bones—no, not even bones, but hollow, rubbishy
bits of bone.

It must have been for some unknown reason: it may have
been due to the cold—there had been no heat all through
November; possibly even to the blues: the patrons, far and
few between, bestowed but scant attention upon him, while
the shooting out in the street came all too often and so palpa-
bly close that the skeleton's finger bones shuddered, like the
prismatic doodads that dangle from a crystal luster; and it
may also have been due to resentment and bitterness: only
the day before some sailor or other had stuck a spit-sodden
butt between the merman's teeth and had smacked the crown
of the merman's skull with his palm, adding: "You damned
clown, you idiotic sonvabitch, you!"

And he tumbled from his throne and fell low, this merman
—a poor bird blown here from unknown lands by chance
winds, and he ended his days to the shrilling of a Russian
winter wind, on Spasso-Kudrinskaya Street, now the Triumph
of the Revolution Street, Number 3, in the Pushchevsky Precinct.

And at almost that very time the Chief of Militia (or the
People's Police) was composing an awesome, rigorous docu-
ment about the immediate closing of the Special Exhibit for
Ladies Only because of its indecent character.

3

The lady clerk in the People's Police, with her hair in
bangs and wearing government-issue felt boots, tapped it out
on her Underwood: ". . . in twenty-four hours . . . as having not even a trace of any scientific interest . . . nothing

but pornography and attracting only the undesirable elements of the town—"

And so the Special Exhibit for Ladies Only, with its Friday showing of fetuses in jam jars and of plaster casts of sexual organs, intestines and syphilitic sores in a glass-topped showcase, and, behind a blue curtain, of pictorial representations of the phases of pregnancy, and of Celebrated Courtesans— the Special Exhibit for Ladies Only closed down.

Closed down irrevocably, its closing as final as the merman's passing into nonbeing, after first joining potato peelings, broken glass, sundry sweepings; emerging from the mysterious depths of the sea, making its way via London, Tula, Pekin, Libau, Calcutta, through decades, centuries, fogs, the tropics, snows, past cathedrals, circuses, policemen, opera hats, gendarmes, kepis, soldiers, teachers, Moscow leather jackets, Parisian gamins, prostitutes, transpiercing revolutions, wars, riots, on his way to the cesspool in the back lots of the house that had once belonged to Chashin the merchant.

4

It was Tsimbaleuk himself, gray, courteous and of respectable appearance, who lectured on the syphilitic sores and so forth, while it was Margarita who took charge of the photographs and pictorial representations; it was she, too, who every day except Friday was the Woman with Her Heart on the Right Side—on the right, without any faking: you could put your ear to it and hear the living heart beating there, beating for real, the way the heart beats in all the others who have their hearts on the left.

5

Margarita, hardening her right-sided heart, lugged the jam jars with the fetuses to a cubbyhole of a lumber room and shoved the prints and photographs of the courtesans (from the loves of Pharaoh Rameses to the Circassian favorite of Abdul Hamid) behind the painting of *Cleopatra on Her Couch*; Tsimbaleuk crated the showcase with the sores and, come Saturday, after counting the week's take, dejectedly shook his beard, cut *à la* Falieri, and that night beat up

Margarita—beating her left side, cautiously avoiding the right.

And, as if there weren't trouble enough, something went haywire inside the chest of the Wounded Boer and he stopped breathing: he gave a grunt, gagged and was still. Then suddenly the waxen Maid of Tyrol, with a slot in her side for the preliminary coins, took to winking in a lazy sort of way, just as if she had entered into a conspiracy with the Wounded Boer. She winked reluctantly, so abominably, kind of; one couldn't sense any of her former gumption, and she didn't sparkle with the same playfulness as before, when for a Czarist five kopeck copper she used to wink subtly, seductively, as if she were inviting one to join her in pleasant pastimes.

No one winking, no one breathing—everything dead as dead, even as out in the street where the snow dust swirled and swept past houses that were beyond waking. No one breathing, no one winking slyly; hardly anyone approached the case with the coins of sundry Ludovics, Carls and John Lacklands, even though Tsimbaleuk pompously proclaims that Louis Quinze, the Sixteenth, had held such and such a coin in his own hands, while rosy-cheeked Marie Antoinette in a powdered wig uselessly confirms this statement with a regal smile of her crimson lips—Marie Antoinette, the queen executed by the people for her excesses and her dissolute life; in vain is Brest-Litovsk going up in flames inside its box with two peepholes, and all the prancing and caracoling of a little potbellied Corsican on the Bridge of Arcole is an utter fiasco.

And were it not for Skin-and-Bones Zboiko, the Living Skeleton; Zharikova, the Quarter-of-a-Ton Beauty; Clara Anisimovna, the Girl with a Nine-Foot Braid; *and* Alphonse Maté the Lilliputian, the same being one Egor Sushkov, a burgher of Klinsk—were it not for all these Margarita would have made a beeline for the river and there, at a greenish hole in the ice, would have settled in full and simultaneously for all the bridges, for all the sores and all revolutions—both for the one during which there were executions for those leading dissolute lives as well as the one during which none could find firewood and Mitka the locksmith refused to repair the Wounded Boer without a written order.

During the December frost, a frost turned to substance, so that you could grasp it, almost, and that was punishing out in the deserted streets, during the December cold, which hung on tenaciously even inside houses, and during which the frosted designs on the windows were of a triple thickness, while beyond the windows there lay a triple stillness, an expanse of whiteness and a white death—during the frost and the cold the following were struck off the account books: the Boer, in an Austrian jacket and Red Army puttees, the Tyrolean Lorelei, the tiny fetuses in muddy jars that had once been filled to the top with stickily sugared and crystallized raspberries, and the little two-headed monster, wall-eyed, dead-white and wilted, like a defunct young frog.

And on the eve of a Christmas that was blizzardy, famishing, hamless, filled with nothing but annulled food cards, hoarse from its snowstorms, driving in a sleigh packed with frostbitten beets—on the eve of Christmas the living exhibits followed the lifeless ones of gypsum, of wax.

The first to do the vanishing act was the quarter-of-a-ton Zharikova, after snitching a kerchief of Margarita and the velvet slippers of that great tragedienne Rachel, a Jewess with a hooked nose on a wax face the color of saffron. After plunging out of sight the kerchief and slippers bobbed up at the New Market, where they were exchanged for horse meat and sauerkraut: deprived of kraut, the Quarter-of-a-Ton Beauty hiccuped with never a stop, experiencing a particular tension in her taut, swollen breasts with their hard, jutting nipples.

The next to go, with a brave flip of her nine-foot braid, very much like a fish flipping its tail to get as far as possible from a hook, was Clara Anisimovna, and ten days later with her hair bobbed short, all in little curls, she was a *nymphe de macadam* pestering Red Army men with quickly acquired patter, mooching for cigarettes for a "weak little chick who's a fellow-traveler Bolshevik."

Skin-and-Bones Zboiko was wasting away from day to day

and, although you couldn't notice it on him—except that his face was becoming ashy gray and his ears dangled still lower, like those of a setter—Margarita nevertheless hadn't a doubt that he, too, would run off: it wasn't for nothing that he kept going up to the windows, breathing on the panes and letting his hungry eyes rove over the neighboring chimneys; he could see the curly wisps of smoke, could hear the clatter of spoons.

And Margarita placed all her last hopes on the Lilliputian, on Alphonse Maté, on his flabby little cheeks, on his slender little feet and hands, on Egor Sushkov, on his opera hat and his trim little jacket, on Egorushka, faithful and never changing, on his great devoted soul in a diminutive bit of a body.

But the snowstorm, now—the snowstorm was spreading itself out, spreading itself out.

It drowned the five gaunt little fir trees on the Haymarket; it drowned out the peal of the Christmas bells; it sent the sleigh of the Chairman of the Soviet spinning into Little Fox Ravine just when the chairman was hurrying to a meeting with a new decree from the Center, and that decree was mighty important, and that ravine was small but deep and its brinks were coated with ice. It did in Clara Anisimovna, dazed and crazed by the blues, freezing her to death under the gateway of a speak-easy. It deprived the man who supplied the Commissariat with firewood of a suckling pig—the only one in town—for when they came in the night to arrest him for trying to fob off aspen wood for birchwood, the snowstorm blew the suckling pig all the way to the other end of town. It howled as a beast howls in the chimney of Minichkina, sibyl and chiromancer, and it frightened half to death the wife of Rear Admiral Koproshmatin who had come, neither for the first time nor the last, to learn from the diamonds and spades when the Bolsheviki would leave, and the present whereabouts of her son, a colorbearer in the cavalry and an Adonis with a flaxen-fair mustache.

6

And, having for a moment rent the snowstorm apart, Anton Razvozhaev, leader of the Anarchists-Egocentrists, emerged out of the snow, out of its white welter.

He tapped once or twice on the door of the Panopticum—on the portals of the temple of Tsimbaleuk—disrupting the quiet of the sole sanctuary of Margarita, the Woman with Her Heart on the Right.

And that heart, functioning in the same way as all other hearts, although they may be located on the left, began to pound in uncanny premonition, then swooned away, growing cold, when Razvozhaev, after colliding with Marie Antoinette, called out: "Where's the boss?"

As for Marie Antoinette, she had been unable to sustain the onslaught and the jolt; she began to sway, rocked, fell at full length, and with a short snap her head bounced off—bounced off and rilled along the floor, strewing gypsum dust: bluish-white blood dried to a powder.

II

1

On the square before the cathedral, behind the knoll of a mass grave, Yashka Maznikov cornered a little mouzhik who was turning to ice, with the business end of his horse pistol made the fellow turn his lumber sledge around, rewarded him with the promise of a pound of the vilest shag and some posters on thin paper that could be used for rolling cigarettes as crooked as a dog's hind leg and, toward noon, had moved over into the Panopticum all the property of the group from its former quarters in a mansion which the Anarchists-Egocentrists had had to evacuate in a hurry.

The lumber sledge scrunched along, carrying to the Panopticum fonts of type, sawhorses, Seraphima's baby carriage, a printing press, iron stoves, a samovar and literature.

The people on Little Swamp Street started telling one another in whispers: "The Bolsheviks are getting out."

The wife of Rear Admiral Koproshmatin, stupefied by a joy past all description, got down on her knees and crept along the floor in prayer; two bashlyks, or Caucasian cowls with earflaps so long they could be used as a neck muffler, started off at a trot for Durylinskaya Street, to the dean of the cathedral, and on the way one bashlyk was suggesting to the other that they ought to sound the biggest bell, the Vladimir-sky, right off; the lady clerks in the local Party headquarters were swarming and besieging the treasurer to pay them their salaries for three months in advance, right then and there.

As for Yashka, he took but one thing from the mansion for himself (hefting it when no one was looking, wrapping it up in a tulle curtain so's Razvozhaev mightn't notice): a mechanical elephant, with a howdah, with a mahout who kept tap-tapping the elephant's knobby head—an intricate and whimsical toy, one of the last remnants of the Grand Ducal wealth. The Grand Duke had been a distiller; the pot stills worked for him loyally and honestly, multiplying his riches; the Grand Duchess was on the Committee for Cadets, corresponded with the Countess Pannina, and acquired elephants for luck: there were elephants on her dressing table, elephants on whatnots, an itsy-bitsy elephant dangling from a bracelet. She kept acquiring and acquiring them and then went and lost them all: the first, the one on her dressing table, became damaged in April, 1917, the last, complicated one, from the Turin Exposition, fell into Yashka's hand, to bring him luck; the Grand Duke himself was in Paris now, trying to see what he could do for Russia and making up suitable laws both for Russia and for his own pot stills.

As for that small heavy trunk bound with strips of brass, Yashka moved it by itself, without taking his eyes off it, keeping his hand on it all the way, placing a mattress under it, and when he got it to its destination he and none other than Razvozhaev carried it over into the back room which, Razvozhaev declared, he was taking for himself.

And the people on Big Swamp Street began telling one another, mouth to ear: "The Bolsheviks are carting off the gold."

And two new bashlyks went off at a gallop, overcoming the snowdrifts in an instant, to Colonel Sedenko, retired, whose feet had been twisted into doughnuts by gout for the past ten years and who had an antediluvian berdanka rifle cached in a lumber room, and on the run one bashlyk was drilling the password into the other, as the two of them brandished mittens that had turned to boards from the frost.

During the day those in the group gathered, coming one by one from all the ends of the town.

Solomon, a Jew with a twisted hump to his nose and with eyes goggling from Basedow's disease, showed up on foot. It did not take him long to come upon the Wounded Boer, read the sign on his belly about the Boer being able to breathe, put his hands on the wax figure, put his ear against the figure's chest and right then and there, without taking off his over-coat, begin tinkering with a penknife. He tinkered and tink-ered until his tinkering paid off: the Boer began to breathe, while Solomon, after having stood there awhile, broke into a smile which may have been one of surprise or of gratifica-tion; but suddenly scowled, stepped away and lay down on the nearest divan, pulling his cap over his ears.

Lesnichy and Vassenka drove up in a carriage, Lesnichy carrying some sun-cured fish, Vassenka a huge round flat loaf of bread; Vassenka humming and carefree, Lesnichy more glum than a fiend out of a bog, chucking the fish viciously into the lap of Rachel the great tragedienne, who was sitting in a rocker.

Zina Kirkova, a round-shouldered girl in eyeglasses, in one of those caps of gray caracul which at one time used to be worn all year round by actors in Little Russian troupes and by buyers-up of horses, and wearing small boots of brightly colored morocco from the wardrobe of some municipal theatre, dashed up in a broad-beamed sleigh with a bearskin rug, driven by some individual in a long coat of deerskin.

2

As for grandfatherly Marius Petrovich, bald-headed, look-ing like an apostle, he came carrying a heap of newspapers and papers, passing by all objects, as always, without bother-ing to look at where fate may have tossed him again; in no time at all he contrived to unearth a bottle of ink, sat him down at a little table directly opposite a diminishing mirror—and the mirror's surface reflected a tiny Peter the fisher-man, a fisher of men, in an old, discolored sweater.

3

The pen began scratching, scratching away: Mankind
would achieve happiness—that was bound to come about;
man would be proud, and daring—man would become an
eagle, while earth, now dark and lying manacled and
shackled, would become a free forest, without limit or bound.

At dinnertime Yashka brought Grandpa some barley porridge and a piece of fish. Grandpa chewed away—and the
other grandpa, the one in the mirror, also moved his lips, and
also left a little porridge and two or three scales on his beard.
And the pen once more was running over the old blanks of
the Military Supplies Committee: Man would be a free god;
a second, a fifth, a seventh revolution would break out—
let it, let it! And blood held no terrors nor did the smoke of
conflagrations: blood is rain; behind the smoke is a purifica-
tory smoke—all that is vile will be swept away.

And at ten in the evening Yashka, in keeping with the communal usage, led Grandpa to bed, to take off his shoes and,
while he was at it, his trousers as well: the stretch he had
done in Sakhalin had left an inheritance to Grandpa—an
inability to bend over.

The following day Razvozhaev brought over Seraphima
and her child.

The snowstorm by now was raging like Satan himself; it
had squeezed all of Red-Selimsk into a snowball; it had
compelled all to keep silent—but it couldn't do that when it
had come to Seraphima.

"Let me go," she begged as they rode along. "Get me a
safe conduct and a train ticket. I can't stand this any more. I
beg you, by Christ and by God—let me go."

Razvozhaev said nothing; with white flake-stars strewn over
him, his face darkening, looking straight ahead of him
through the closely woven net of snow, he was stooping over
more and more, slumping lower and lower.

4

Toward evening, as in those days which Tsimbaleuk would
never forget, the days of Extra Gala Programs, all the elec-

tric bulbs in the Panopticum flared up: a pink one (romantic) over Cleopatra, and a violet (effective), lighting up an Arab in a burnous and with his teeth bared, looking like a refugee from a tobacco poster, and a green (dramatic) over Rachel, half-reclining in a rocking chair, and some hidden ones where the concave, distorting, diminishing and magnifying mirrors glimmered.

All the electric bulbs awoke, rousing Spasso-Kudrinskaya Street out of its white torpor; they enticed a stray or two toward them—one restless figure in a cap with long flapping earlaps and a short fur-lined coat of a Romanov cut actually shoved its hand into a pocket for money, while a hound, gaunt as a last year's sun-cured fish and as blotched from enforced leisure, ran up the front steps of the Panopticum and scratched at the door.

And in a small room off to one side, which used to be the office of the manager, with a ledger, portfolios, varicolored posters of Siamese twins, the Half-Woman Half-Fish and the Three-Headed Little Girl from Oberland, there sat, huddled close to one another, Zboiko the Skin-and-Bones Man, the Lilliputian, Margarita and Tsimbaleuk himself.

The beard *à la* Falieri had become disheveled, the noble eyebrows were drooping, while the Lilliputian had folded his toy hands and, holding his breath, was a clump at the feet of the weeping Margarita: Zboiko had just reported that the showcase with the ancient coins was being used for cutting bread and drinking tea, that Rachel had been thrown off her rocking chair, that they were sawing wood close to the mirrors and were likely to start chopping it right there—and when he was telling them about the bread his stubborn, insatiable gaze never shifted from the door.

And it was not for nothing that Tsimbaleuk had yelled at him in despair, calling him the lowest kind of a whore: the Skin-and-Bones Man hadn't gone off with the rightful owners of the Panopticum, had not sunk out of sight together with them in the snow, had not gone astray, shoulder to shoulder with the others, in the icy labyrinth of hoarfrosted by-streets; he had remained, had been taken on by One-Armed Yashka as a special messenger, had been enrolled by Lesnichy a little later as a member of their commune, had been initiated into Anarchism-Egocentrism by Grandpa. Grandpa hadn't paid much attention to his thinness—Grandpa himself was thin as thin could be; he had not surmised that he was face to face with a unicum, because Grandpa considered every man a unique, a freak, while at the same time he fenced himself off from all people, from all immediate pain, by putting up a wall, stronger than any wall of bricks and stone, consisting of black-lettered lines in books. And Grandpa, rustling his papers, his nose, livid from age, pecking at the inside of a book—Grandpa said that at the very last all would arrive at the great idea, that he was welcoming the new fellow member, the new fighter for the liberation of the individual from the chains of collectivism in the name of the future, and that that future was not over the hills and far away: it was approaching, it was nigh, and that nothing could stop it.

As for Yashka, he gave the living skeleton something to eat; after feeding him he counted his ribs over, studied his spine, examined his hand with the light behind it (lighting a candle especially for this purpose) and, stunned and transfixed by amazement, lost no time in offering his friendship to Zboiko. And life became gayer for Yashka; he now had two cronies, the living skeleton and the mechanical elephant, each more amusing than the other. Two things to solace him: for daytime, a living skeleton who could crawl through any crack without straining himself, could bend in two without a single bone crackling and shove his head between his legs, the way you shove a thumb between your index and middle fingers to show somebody a fig; for the evening, an elephant with a trunk that moved up, down, right, left—an exquisite, excellent thingumbob.

"Bourgeois rubbish!" Lesnichy muttered on seeing the toy.

Tap-tap went the tiny hammer, and a smile stirred in the midst of Lesnichy's shaggy beard, while Yashka wound the spring still tighter. There, the tiny hammer goes *tap-tap,* and the howdah rocks, and the elephant walks along, shifting one foot after the other, and moves his trunk about, and Machmutka his mahout—a tiny chocolate-colored mannikin—squirms in his seat.

Yashka is content of a wintry evening when almost everybody is out, while he is left on duty to guard the communal property and Seraphima's little boy. He lies down flat on his belly on a bunk, his face bent close to the floor, nudging Machmutka and smiling with delight at every *tap-tap*—this Yashka Maznikov, who had become the One-Armed, having lost an arm in the battle at Czaritzin; the One-Armed, who had impudently and bravely escaped after being captured by the Cossacks, outracing the very bullets of a firing squad while other prisoners were scraping in their last, premortal throes at the dank, blood-soaked earth that no longer seemed their own Russian earth but alien, inimical.

Tap-tap—from Gzhatsk, through Czaritzin, the Caspian region, Kuban and the Bashkir steppes, heading for the commune, for the quiet of somnolent Red-Selimsk's winter evenings, for the Egocent . . . Yashka couldn't even get the word out—Grandpa, however, knew how the word ought to be pronounced.

Tap-tap—from the district police, past Hindenburg, Kerensky, by way of Riga, Warsaw, past Trotsky, Wrangel, Grandpa Marius Petrovich, to Machmutka.

The spring unwinds, winds, and unwinds anew.

5

Rachel was lying on the floor, face up (Zina Kirkova had fallen in love with the rocking chair and had made it her own); Rachel's hooked nose had become sharpened to a point, every bit like that of a dead woman. And in the mute sorrow of the five or six minutes before the lights were turned on Tsimbaleuk, the ex-manager of the Panopticum, stood for a space over the old-new departed one, having stolen up to her, having in his grief crumpled up both fear and cowardice. And he would even have wept awhile, save that the sound of steps came from close by, and he would have gotten down on his knees also in final farewell, save that there would be no straightening up afterward for one crushed, beaten to his knees by the mortal wrong done him.

And Tsimbaleuk retreated, backing away, hugging the wall,

hugging the wall ever more closely, while Rachel's nose pointed higher and higher in reproach.

They had all lain down side by side—Rachel, and Marie Antoinette (decapitated a second time), and the Samoyed with his quiver; the coins had tarnished, the fetuses had grown haggard in their jam jars, the distorting mirrors had clouded over, while the living in the small office did not know what to do with themselves. The Lilliputian lay awhile in one corner, then crawled over into another; his tiny starched collar was all dusty, his little cravat of light blue, which had been so elegant a couple of days back, was now nothing but a string and its polka dots were wrinkled. Margarita kept clutching at her left side, by mistake—yet it was on the right that she had a nagging, burning pain. Tsimbaleuk had rolled some placards into a tube and with this tube he was tapping on the table softly, ever so softly. Ever so softly, when he wanted to pound with a hammer, with a sledge hammer and to yell, yell without tiring, without stopping for breath, that he was cursing the Revolution, that the little monster with three heads was the only thing that was near and dear to him in accursed Russia.

In the morning Zboiko shoved a sun-cured fish on a piece of string through the doorway. Tsimbaleuk *scat!*-ted at him. Zboiko yanked at the string—and the fish sprang away.

"Judas!" Tsimbaleuk yelled; the Lilliputian wrung his tiny hands and let out a sob.

About three o'clock they began chopping wood; the mirrors rattled and tinkled; Tsimbaleuk, trailing the tube of rolled-up placards as if it were a gun, made a dash for the main hall and ran into Lesnichy, glum and hairy. Tsimbaleuk whined and whimpered womanishly; then bowed low, pleading; then started shaking his tube of rolled-up placards—his last surviving symbol; then threatened Lesnichy with the wrath of God.

But hairy fellows have no fear of the wrath of God, or of anybody else, for that matter, because, to hear him talk, Lesnichy didn't give a hoot in hell for anybody, not even for the biggest one of all, the fellow on the portrait, should Tsimbaleuk ever make his way to Moscow and complain to

the Central Executive Committee, and he refused to acknowledge any law except the one which is called *I*, and is written
with a capital letter.

Lesnichy refused permission for the removal of the wax
figures, the mirrors and the coins; all he allowed them to do
was to take their wearables and some bedding—and not too
much, either. And so Tsimbaleuk loaded himself up to his
eyebrows, and Margarita was crushed under a bundle, and
Egorushka started dragging his little hamper of tiny neckties
and colored cuffs into the unknown, into space, dragging himself there as well.

But on their way out they ran into towering, indefatigable
Vassenka, and he, at full tilt, as always, as on all occasions
in his headlong and never-look-back life—he decided the
Lilliputian's fate.

6

"What's all this?" Vassenka drawled, poking a finger in
the Lilliputian's puny shoulders.

A minute later he was warbling in the corridor: "Solomon!
Solomon, come here! Solomon, I have a most remarkable
idea; Solomon, we're going to keep this little mannikin with
us." And, grabbing Egorushka by the scruff of his neck, he
lifted him off the floor like a bit of down. "Little mannikin,
we want to uplift all of humanity to the heights. And we'll
uplift you as well."

Egorushka's little yellow shoes jerked in his upward flight.
Margarita gasped and let her bundle drop.

"Lord God! Comrade!" squeaked the Lilliputian. "Mister
Comrade!"—and, closing his little eyes, grown lifeless now,
he let his little head, with its smooth, wide parting, droop.

"You fool!" Solomon told Vassenka quietly. "What will we
feed him with?" And he thrust out his thick Negroid lower
lip in disdain.

Tsimbaleuk and Margarita, plunging through the snowdrifts, were departing; Margarita was moaning and impul-
sively attempting to turn back to the Panopticum but Tsimbaleuk kept prodding her in the back with the bundle he was
carrying in front of him.

The snow was falling, falling—had a hole burst through the bottom of the heavens, or what?—and it kept on and on, throwing its pall over all things; it kept crushing against the earth the town that had been the Czar's but that now belonged to the Reds.

A town all in white: everything white as white.

III

1

Up to Christmas the inhabitants of Red-Selimsk managed to hold on, somehow or other; they even permitted themselves, ever so rarely, to dream a little about roast goose—not too seriously, with a bit of a mocking smile, as if in jest; but just the same, dream they did, amid the asphyxiating fumes of their self-built little stoves: they put flatirons on the stoves and poured water on the hot flatirons so as to create steam which would help to keep the room, the habitation, the corner, the kennel, from turning into a tundra, into Siberia.

But the city itself, taken as a whole, with its churches, its graveyards, its boarded-up shops, its unemployed monks, its Proletarian Culture Center, its kids covered with carbuncles from malnutrition, its monument to Lassalle, its black market —the city itself, bordered on the north, the west, the south and the east by dead, barren fields, had long since expanded into a tundra and, long since, its contours had congealed into a death's grin of hunger and cold. Had congealed hard, as if for all time, as if until doomsday, until the archangels blew their horns—nor did the New Year loosen the bony jaws; the teeth actually clenched still harder.

After Epiphany they took to killing dogs; they hunted hounds, bitches, puppies; there were lone hunters, each one relying on his own skill and doing his own tracking, and there were those who hunted in groups. The chairman of the house committee of a building on Gorshechnaya Street formed a group of Nimrods, with assessments for current expenses and office supplies. And on Meshcherskaya another co-operative society sprang up, consisting entirely of ex-reservists in the militia.

The first to die an inglorious death during the initial hunt of the ex-reservists was the decrepit fox terrier with dove-gray markings belonging to the widow of Rear Admiral Koproshmatin. The widow herself soon followed her dog in death. She had borne everything: ruin, and the execution of her husband by a firing squad, and the death of her son, the cornet, as divined through the ebony-hued spades and revealed for a pound and a half of dried mushrooms—but she had not borne the execution of her fox terrier: she kneeled over on her back and found eternal rest by her small stove, close to a pot of half-cooked peas.

Over at the Panopticum they finished their last round loaf. Yashka collected all the crusts and, having sprinkled them thickly with salt, toasted them over the stove. Lesnichy was scuttering all over town: he had charge of the commissary, he fed the brotherhood, while secretly he sustained himself by small doses of spirits—absolutely homeopathic, each practically no more than a thimbleful, but without which he could not have lived through a day. The only one who knew about this "vice" of his was Solomon, and he advised him not to sentimentalize, to remember his mouzhik origin, not to ham it up as a repentant nobleman, to pleasure his free peasant soul, to stop his dull-witted self-flagellation for every sip, and to drink, drink, as much as he wanted to and—

"As much as you're given, as much as you can get hold of."

"Let's you and me have a drink."

"I don't drink. I'm drunk as it is, without any likker."

"Stop playing the fool. In what way do you get drunk?"

"In a Jewish way," Solomon would answer, with a snicker. Everything about him was snickering at that moment: his lips, and the crooked little hump on his nose, and even his Basedowed pop eyes that looked like peeled hard-boiled eggs. They all snickered, knowing why; they were laughing slyly, knowing what they were laughing at.

As for hairy Lesnichy, he, having gotten drunk on his first glass, sitting in his corner under Cleopatra in her gilt frame, was punishing himself in bitter sorrow and inwardly pledging his word of honor not to disgrace in the future the good name of an Anarchist-Egocentrist.

2

The first hall, the one without the distorting mirrors, went unheated; it was off to one side and its door was guarded by a Samoyed with a quiver: cold was no novelty to him.

Behind the Samoyed was a small mattress of felt, and on the mattress was Egorushka, and on Egorushka was a small collar that had become the breadth of three fingers too wide for him—whenever Egorushka lifted his head his neck wobbled. The Samoyed's garments were warm—true, they were moth-eaten, but the fur was on the outside, and if you nestled close, really close to it, hanging on to the quiver, why, you not only got some warmth but caught a glimpse of Margarita as well: not too clearly, as if through a slight haze, but just the same you saw her before your eyes.

Zboiko brought him food; Egorushka squirreled in the Samoyed's quiver any leftovers for supper and against early morning, until Zboiko might happen to think of him.

It's the second day now that the quiver hasn't had as much as a crumb in it.

3

Lesnichy had tried everywhere; in all honesty he did not even think about spirits, directing his efforts toward getting bread, sugar and so forth; he made his way unannounced into places where you absolutely had to be announced; in one place he would put up an argument, in another would act insolently, in a third would be gentle and persuasive, yet would come back with mighty little to show.

"They're looking at us askance," he told Vassenka. "Won't give us a damned thing. They've nabbed the Anarchists in Moscow and they say they'll nab us too."

"Well, they'll be feeding us at least," Solomon remarked, and resumed his previous occupation: standing before a magnifying mirror he thrust out his gray-coated tongue, and watched it grow, expand, and fill the whole room.

As for Vassenka, he started yelling that it was a shame for an Egocentrist to be eying government grub when one should be proud, daring and overturning the world.

"We'll overturn it, all right," Solomon answered leisurely, with one eye squinting at the other Solomon, whose head was plunging into the ceiling, into infinite space. "We'll starve for quite a bit, fly into a rage and attack the Soviets. Peace on our humble cabin and down with the palaces of the commissars. We'll take the reins of power into our own hands, and as for you, Vassenka, we'll appoint you Governor General of Anarchy."

Vassenka spat, disdainfully called Solomon a "catastrophic fool" and hurried off to a soap refinery where he had a cell; the cell consisted of five workers and one office clerk. He didn't find the workers in: they had gone off on a hunt for flour; the office clerk, muffling himself in his wife's shawl, asked: "Well, when are we going to start?" and slipped Vassenka two cakes of soap as tokens of moral support.

Until evening Lesnichy's boots scraped along as he went from room to room, frenziedly yanking at his beard which by now was like a thicket: anarchy was anarchy, the stuff in Razvozhaev's small trunk was all very well in its way, but you couldn't do without porridge for Grandpa—without his evening porridge Grandpa went all to pieces: he became limp, he drooped. And there was also an ailing little boy, his dislocated leg in a splint, and without milk that little boy was as good as done for. In Moscow they were shooting up an Anarchists' hideout; the world, the universe would be shaken by confusion, destruction and reconstruction—but how was he to get the coveted blue order for food from the Red-Selimsk Committee of Supplies?

Grandpa says that the individual is everything, while the collective is a herd, and that the individual, the intellectual individual must—*must*—find a way out; each such individual bears on his shoulders a source of mighty power—his head; if you willed, it would throw light on everything or, if you willed, it would plunge everything into impenetrable darkness. Only yesterday Grandpa had read aloud from a leaflet: " 'Within me, the individual, lies that famous point of support which the world has been seeking in vain for thousands of years, which Archimedes knew not—yet we have come to

know it, and all the soldiery of the human herd cannot erase
the simple design which—' "

And so Lesnichy bent his steps toward Zina Kirkova, that
kindhearted friend of humanity who had all the instructions,
all the warehouses and all of the Red-Selimsk existence written down in a notebook which she kept in a pocket of her
leather jacket.

He headed for a feminine nook with a bed near which was
placed a pair of morocco bootees that had at one time liltingly
danced the mazurka at some Polish opera ball; Zina, however,
decided that the old times were back again, that the shaggy
head would once more lie upon her insatiable gaunt breast,
and she threw back her blanket, holding out her benumbed
hand to him in the darkness.

But after Lesnichy had said two or three words in that
feminine corner—where the Maid of Tyrol was leaning with
her face to the wall, where one could smell egg-shampoo soap,
and where, on a table, a broken comb with half its teeth
gone and the others clogged with combings of stringy, ashy
hair was lying side by side with a pair of old, no longer
elastic garters—a voice said, with a sigh: "Very well, comrade, I'll see to it tomorrow."

4

Grandpa was always saying that the collective is a blind
force, while the individual is a radiant, creative one—and
may the ego, the *I*, be at the center of all things.

And for a long while Zina Kirkova wept, with her feet
tucked in under her, her whole body gathered in a crumpled
ball—wept with her eyes open, yet of light, of light, now,
there wasn't a speck, neither around her nor within her soul.

And there was another feminine corner, and there, night
after night, and for many nights in unbroken succession,
another woman, a Cossack woman of the steppes with arched
eyebrows and an aggressive will as taut as a bowstring—
lo, an arrow would be loosed at any moment and go flying
through the air—kept on saying to Razvozhaev: "I hate you.
I want to be out in the steppe. I want to be out in the
feather grass. I want to be out in the open, away from these

false faces, these wax puppets. I am sick of your misbegotten monsters, I am sick of your own self. I hate you. There, just as much as I loved you before, when I would have cut myself into small pieces for your sake, that's how much I hate you now."

And Razvozhaev kept silent, but did not bend his knobby forehead with its transversal scar, and when Seraphima would fall asleep, having filled her soul with hatred to the very brim, racked by yearning and tindery wrath, her stubborn, unsated lips remaining tightly closed even in sleep, as though she were on guard even in her slumber, Razvozhaev would slowly go off to his place: to his bed, to his printing press, as yet standing idle, and to his trunk, throw back the lid of the trunk, take off the old newspapers, paw the rags aside, and eye the contents: there, lying peacefully close to one another, looking like fruit not grown on home soil but brought from far-off lands, were his bombs.

Toss one down from a belfry, and a third, a fifth after it— and Red-Selimsk would cease to be; the steeds of fire would rear, the dread tidings would rush off on wheels of fire to Peter's Town, to Moscow, to London, to Rio de Janeiro—and an answering hurricane would arise, encircling the whole terrestrial globe, making pole collide with pole, piling tropic upon tropic.

"You're stupid, Antoine," Razvozhaev let drop, and tapped the middle bomb with a bent finger; a taut, rancorous wrinkle formed a cross with the scar on his knobby forehead.

Beyond the wall, above Marie Antoinette minus her head, the fetuses, the Arab, Grandpa Marius Petrovich in his checkered drawers, the crazy mirrors, knowing nothing, foreseeing nothing, wearied from hunting dogs, from standing in queues and waiting their turns, lugging sleds, haunting commissions, crowding in waiting rooms, worn out by the squirrel-cage wheel of the daily run-around, the daily hurly-burly, the daily bickerings, exhausted by the nightly melancholy, the nightly wariness, the nightly stagnation, the Red-Selimskians dozed, slept and, amid dreams that reflected the same daily befuddlement and the same nightly spookiness, they tossed and turned on their beds and mattresses, these reservists of

the second category, nonworking individuals, passé collaborators, executives, chairmen of house committees, priests,
shopkeepers without shops, ex-bureaucrats, specialists, ac-
countants, nursing mothers, mothers who were not nursing,
housewives who went out to work, housewives whose house-
holds had broken up, army deserters and young ladies who
pounded Remingtons.

5

Yashka was the first to suggest that the dummies ought to
be stripped and their rags disposed of on the market: you
take a horse before an attack—it's not so easy to saddle it—
the beast is cutting up; but you just loosen the girth—and the
horse is again what a horse should be. The girth was pulled
tight, said Yashka; there was no use perishing when they
could forage so close to home. And Lesnichy went to Solomon for counsel.

Solomon was heating two flatirons on his small stove; in
one hand he was holding a small volume of French verse—
either Verlaine or Mallarmé—and, in the other, a teakettle
filled with water, using it just as if it were a watering pot.
And, spilling water at rare intervals upon the irons, as if he
were watering his beloved garden, Solomon was reading
aloud, speaking through his nose, as if he were blowing down
a chimney to clean it. The water hissed, tiny bubbles sprang
up, spinning madly; the place smelt like a Turkish bath.

"Make it a referendum," Solomon advised him.

"Are you for the plan?"

Solomon lifted one leg, then the other: "*Oui*, twice."

"And must I ask Anton, too?" Lesnichy shrank into himself, tugging at his beard.

"You coward!" Solomon began to yell. "You Russian slave
soul! An Egocentrist, and yet he shivers before someone in
authority," and with that he emptied the teapot. The small
stove, overwhelmed, emitted a tinny squeal; steam billowed
impetuously; Mallarmé sank out of sight in the steam while
the Basedowed eyes broke into sly snickering—eyes with a
jeering, mocking glint in them, the eyes of Solomon Briller,
quondam candidate for the rabbinate, for a pastorate over the

souls of Jewesses in ritual wigs, of Jews in long-skirted caftans, quondam Menshevik, quondam lecturer at the University of Lausanne, son of the celebrated *tsaddik,* or saintly sage, of Lida.

Those goggling eyes had bored into the Talmud, into God, the Only Begetter; had bored right through them, rejected them, covered them over with Malinin and Burenin and Russian grammar and, having broken through the structure of the universe like a battering ram, were brought up short before the jam jars with the fetuses. Those eyes were like hard-boiled eggs with the shells off; everything had been husked, all the bits of shell have been thrown away: the chair at the University of Lausanne and the flatirons on the small stove; Bergson and the Wounded Boer, who breathes though he is out of kilter; the universe cloven in two and the sun-cured fish gotten in exchange for the burnous of the Arab—pour, water, pour on the flatirons; snort, you homemade small stove of the year 1919: everything is steam, everything is steamy.

Vassenka, contrary to his wont, did not bristle up, did not start waving his arms, as long as whips, but answered quietly, really too submissively: "Sell the stuff."

Luckily for Lesnichy, Razvozhaev had gone away—no one knew why, where, or when he would return. Zina Kirkova, racked by the curse, merely nodded and crawled under the fur coat to resume writhing on the bed in uncontrollable pain. As for Grandpa, covered with ink spots, even on his bald head, he put his pen in his mouth (nib first) and, after giving the matter some thought, ordered half the proceeds to be set aside for the propaganda fund.

Zboiko and Yashka did the stripping.

They divested Marie Antoinette, had their hands full with Rachel (the stubborn Jewish girl held out to the last, fending them off with her nose all the time), took the Red Army puttees off the Wounded Boer and made the Arab lose face.

Egorushka leeched on to the Samoyed; Zboiko had run in that morning, had made his last offering—a moldy rye rusk —and had told the Lilliputian that the dummies would be dragged off to market.

Taking the Samoyed away meant finishing Egorushka off;

for a Lilliputian, as well as for all others, there are the same 365 days in the year, and in a Lilliputian's thirty-seventh year it is just as frightful for him to lose the last things remaining to him as it is for any six-footer you like. For where was he to find Margarita, how was he to find her, how was he to get to her, to ford, without drowning, the stretches of snow, how was he to track her down, without getting lost in the labyrinth of white, unfamiliar by-streets and dead ends? Taking the Samoyed meant grinding Egorushka into powder, rubbing him out. And so the little jacket was buttoned to its last button, although the neck—the neck, now—was wobbling in the roomy collar; his little mattress was rolled up, his tiny hands clenched in wrathful determination: come on, you ruddy-yellow snakes, you hairy devils!

But they forgot about the Samoyed—or, perhaps, the Skin-and-Bones Man had had a touch of human decency and had not reminded them about the figure.

And the Samoyed's parka (moth-ravaged) was left, and the quiver (empty) was also left.

They stripped all the others.

The Maid of Tyrol gasped: *"O mein Gott!"* and a Germanic blush mantled her cheeks; the Arab, the frenzied Arab who had stepped out of the cigarette-box cover: *Buy KATYK —with the Tube Filters,* turned his face away and drove his spear two inches into the floor; Rachel sniffed disdainfully in the direction of the brazen gallery gods, while Marie Antoinette was about to clutch her head but recalled just in time that she had been minus a head long, long since, and let her chiseled hands drop; the Wounded Boer heaved a sigh and, like a true soldier, hit the hay.

Brest-Litovsk kept right on burning, and the steed bearing the Corsican was still prancing on the Bridge of Arcole.

Seraphima's little boy Shurka, with his little leg in splints, was whining ever so softly and begging to be told fairy tales; Seraphima was on the alert, listening to every rustle—it might be Anton coming. Eh, how the free feather grass curls in the free steppe! The accursed winter evening of Red-Selimsk is howling in the chimney; two eyebrows—two hawks —have drawn together, have come to hover above darkened eyes: the hour will come, and they will swirl upward, will dart headlong and soar away—feather grass, feather grass, make way, welcome me, shelter me!

"*O-oh!* . . ."

6

They arrested Yashka at the market place for purloining and selling national property and certain articles of military supplies—the same being those Red Army puttees.

Tsimbaleuk was hanging around the market place. Margarita was close by with a small bast basket; the bast basket held a pie and a half and two small paper-wrapped cubes of sugar. Tsimbaleuk immediately recognized the bolero jacket of the Maid of Tyrol, and that bolero jacket started the whole thing off.

Yashka, with his one hand, mowed down one of the People's Police, then another—the third started shooting as he went after him. Yashka took to his heels, zigzagging as he had been taught in the army, but Margarita threw herself under his feet—under his feet, with the guttural screaming of an eagle; under his feet, to pay him out for the distorting mirrors, for the collection of coins, for Alphonse Maté, the Lilliputian. And a living mound of bodies, of police overcoats, went rolling over the snow, over rags, over skirts, over spread-eagled trousers.

A couple of hours later Lesnichy was standing before Marius Petrovich, getting him into his overcoat and hurrying him: "Get over to the town Soviet as fast as you can, Grandpa. You're an old-time Siberian convict—they'll treat you with respect. Fast as you can. . . . Things didn't work out right, Grandpa."

On Greater Swamp Street, on Gorshechnaya and on Lesser Swamp Streets they were nailing down the shutters—there was a riot going on on the market place, the Anarchists were taking over; the reservists of the second category were salting down dog meat, stocking up betimes.

Vassenka set out with Grandpa as his guide—and both got stuck in a snowbank. Lesnichy wandered flat-footedly through the rooms, shying away from the dummies—the dummies had tripped him up! He spat to ward off their spells—the accursed ones, the accursed ones! And, toward evening, he was standing by Solomon's small stove, just about as lively as a bump on a log.

Solomon was sitting on his bed, with his legs up, American fashion, and was drawling, syllable by syllable: "Pan-op-ti-cum. . . . Pan-op-ti-cum—" and his thick Negroid lips were grinning slyly.

They were interrogating Yashka, Tsimbaleuk and Margarita at the Cheka; Margarita kept tugging at the broad belt of Yashka's overcoat and sobbing: "What did you do with my boy? Why did you make Egorushka stay behind with you?"

"Leave off, you foot-clout washerwoman!" Yashka snarled back at her, with his head cast down.

Late in the evening Razvozhaev drove up—or he may have walked home; after all, there are many means of locomotion —on foot, on horseback, by rail. At midnight he brought back Grandpa and Vassenka, cooked some porridge for Grandpa with his own hands from what was left of the barley, and helped him undress; then, at two in the morning, shouted for Lesnichy and asked him to collect everybody for a meeting.

IV

1

They held the meeting in Grandpa's room so as not to get him up again, the mirror room with its concave, distorting, magnifying, diminishing mirrors. Solomon stretched out into a tapeworm a mile long, Lesnichy turned into the stubbiest of mushrooms, Kirkova's cheeks, ears, eyebrows started crawling and crisscrossing every which way, while Grandpa swelled up, spreading out in width over his green pillow which looked like a haystack.

They called in Zboiko too; the Skin-and-Bones Man took his stand near the doorway most unassumingly, and looked exactly like a suicide hanging limply from a trouser belt.

"New member?" asked Anton, letting his dry eyes glide indifferently over Zboiko, as if he had run a knife over glass. "I declare the meeting open."

"Sorry," Solomon raised his hand. "Order of the day. Not all of us are present. I move we call in the others."

"What others?" asked Anton, without turning to look at him.

Solomon, rising, licked his lips: "First of all, he that is least among you—the Lilliputian, first of all."

"What Lilliputian?"

"The most ordinary kind, twenty-one inches in height."

"Where did he come from?"

"Where all of us also came from: out of the depths of the earth. Next, call in all the wax effigies, as competent and capable members of society."

"That'll do!" Vassenka leapt up and leaned over the table. "This is the devil knows what—"

"Hold on, Vassia," Anton requested quietly. "I did not give you the floor—" and he looked deeply into Solomon's Basedowed eyes.

And those eyes did not avert their gaze; they merely twitched for an instant, just the least bit, only to become rounded again and to congeal, either in mockery or in pain.

Lesnichy sniggered.

"Your head is made of pine wood or of beech wood, you blockhead," Solomon turned on him. "There's nothing to laugh at—I was never more serious."

Anton stood up.

"I am putting the motion to a viva voce vote," he said calmly, looking in turn at each one of those present. "Who is in favor of Comrade Solomon's motion?"

"I protest!" Vassenka dashed forward. "We're on the brink of ruin, yet Solomon is clowning around—"

"Comrade Chairman," Solomon drawled, "I request your protection against insults which I do not deserve. In days of great upheavals everyone has the right to make any motion, however dizzy it might be, whereas I am making a motion that is elementary, most ordinary. After all, I'm not making a motion that Vassenka should take to wife the wax doll who has a coin slot in her side. I am merely—"

Vassenka sprang up from his place.

"I'm leaving!"

"I am putting the motion to a viva voce vote," Anton repeated imperturbably. "For the second time: Who is in favor of Comrade Solomon's motion? One vote. The motion is defeated. Let us proceed. Next on the agenda: Today is Thursday; we are ordered to vacate the premises by midnight, Sunday. No extensions whatsoever. They will not permit us to occupy any other premises. They are not releasing Yasha. If we refuse to leave they will surround the place and compel us to leave. What course are we to follow: are we leaving or are we putting up a defense? What are we to do: blow up the Cheka, setting Yasha free, or are we heading for Moscow, scattering every which way? I . . . I have brought back a little money, sufficient for everybody if we leave. Well, then, are we leaving or are we remaining? I am in favor of the latter: rescuing Yashka, holing in here until the very end. Grandpa, you have the floor. Pipe down, Vassya!"

2

Everyone was long asleep, and Grandpa had long since managed to draw up the protocol of the group's resolution, both as an edifying example and as material for his five-volume opus concerning Man as Center, while Anton was still carrying on a search for the Lilliputian.

He burned match after match, left effigy after effigy behind him, slowly, heavily taking step after step—and he found him; he stumbled on the small mattress behind the Samoyed's back and for an instant held his last match—an unreliable torch— over the diminutive body.

Darkness—and the Lilliputian's tiny fists were swallowed up in it, while two others, knotty, strong, large, closed abruptly, impetuously, as though they had seized long-coveted prey and would never again let it go.

Darkness—and a little face no bigger than a little saucer, a wrinkled autumn apple, disappeared in it, and another face, with high cheekbones, aggressive, with a fleeting evil smile slashed across it.

Darkness—and the dark is outside the windows and within one's soul.

3

At dawn the Skin-and-Bones Man vanished: he had slipped flatly out the back way—the bony one—had crept through a narrow crack, and yet he could have flung the front door wide open and flitted like a flat spot through the courtyard.

In vain did Lesnichy call out his name that morning—no skin, no bones, and the samovar cold; in Yashka's room (which was also Zboiko's) the bed was untouched—the be- numbed living skeleton had not as much as left a crease on it during the night; the mechanical elephant was freezing by the window, dark-skinned Machmutka no longer pounded the elephant's head with his hammer; the last of the Grand Duke's elephants, which was to bring luck to Yashka, to the One-Armed, was drowsing, and amid the frosty drowsiness its tropical soul was being crushed to death by the decreasing readings on the thermometer.

Lesnichy barged into Solomon's room.

"Our special messenger has run off. A fine how-d'you-do!"

Solomon thrust his curly, feather-sprinkled head out from under the blanket: "He did the right thing. Make tracks yourself. He did it out of cowardice; you go ahead and do it because you're a smart boy."

And a little later, when he was already dressed and, scald- ing himself, was drinking some sort of hot, greenish slops by way of tea close to the red-hot small stove, he was saying: "Get going, Lesnichy. I'm speaking to you seriously," and, as a generous treat, he proffered on the palm of his hand what was left of a piece of rock candy. "You have a mighty pair of shoulders on you, all of you is like a hundred-year-old oak. There are only shallow waters hereabouts. Hereabouts they do things only in a cultured sort of way; everything's boring—so they'll explode a bomb, and another bomb, maybe—so what? Make tracks!"

"Where to?"

"Idiot!" Solomon yelled at him. "Plenty of forests in Russia?"

"Plenty."

"And are you fond of having someone in authority over you?"

Lesnichy smirked and gave a grunt.

"Run, run, you wild critter. Into forests, into wildwoods. Russian forests for a Russian wild critter. And God save you from taking any female woman along with you! The forest Zinkas are raspberries; those hereabouts are squashed currants. Ah, if only I had your height, your nose like an onion! Your truly Russian nose, your magnificent, snub national ornament! Anybody would follow a nose like that without a second thought!"

And again the teapot was emptied over the hot flatirons and anew the stifling steam enveloped the Basedowed eyes—no longer snickering: they were sorrow-laden.

"Get going, get going!" and he kept nudging Lesnichy toward the door. Lesnichy, perplexed, was balky:

"Why, what are you saying . . . what are you saying—" he kept repeating in his embarrassment and confusion, yet he was already throwing his shoulders back; his chest stuck out like a wheel and he was distending, blowing out his nostrils, as if he were already following tangled trails and sniffing the smoke of a campfire and trying to get, through the forest odor, resinous, eternal, at the faint scent, human, lasting but a brief day.

At dinner Zina Kirkova demanded a second meeting, submitting a declaration to Anton: "I insist on a reconsideration of our resolution. Today's issue of the Red-Selimsk *News* informs us that the Anarchist movement is growing, *crescendo*, in Spain. It is senseless to die here when we are greatly needed there as active individuals."

"No meetings whatsoever!" vociferated Vassenka and, seven feet tall, pointy as a spire, he strode through the rooms as if he were on stilts, jarring the mirrors and throwing the denuded, cowering wax dolls into fear and trembling. "What's decided is decided. We're giving battle; we're not giving up our positions. It's shameful to back out."

"I adore Spanish women," said Solomon. "Let's have a meeting, let's have a meeting!"

In his room Lesnichy was repairing a duffle bag . . . the

green trails would run, would wind, dart forward, race into
the distance; the wildwood, nobody's mother and the mother
of all, would sough, sway, rumble . . . "Who goes there?"—
"Lesnichy."—"Give the password!"—"Cossack free troops."
—"Pass!" . . . walk your horse on and on through the
forest; then give him his head, shout, let him get a taste of
the quirt—and it's not a steed but a sure-enough swamp
demon, all in foam, snorting—over field, over steppe, straight
ahead, always straight ahead, as a bird, as free as freedom,
freedom inexhaustible.

Halfway through a stitch the sailmaker's needle fell out of
his hands; Lesnichy became bemused as he stared at it,
smiling, and that smile breaking through his beard was like
a ray of the morning sun in a thicket of evergreens.

4

Anton paid two visits to the Lilliputian that day.

The first time he stood for a while before him in silence,
merely looking him over intently, as though he were measur-
ing him; the Lilliputian straightened out his little jacket,
while his tiny legs shook in their diminutive trousers; the
second time Anton brought him something to eat.

Egorushka pushed the plate away with a sullen look.

"Eat," Anton urged him and took him by his shoulder.

The Lilliputian tore himself free and threw himself down
on his little mattress; the pale-pink nape of his neck under
the scanty hair, with a senile look about it, quivered, but
this quivering was gradually subsiding.

Anton bent over him.

"What's the matter with you? Don't be afraid," and the big
man knelt. "I'm not a bear. What's your name?"

A voice like that of a show-booth Punch squeaked on the
little mattress: "Egor."

"And how old are you?"

"Thirty-seven."

Anton sprang to his feet and broke into peals of laughter.

He laughed for a long while, a very long while, but his eyes
were not laughing, and the stubborn vertical furrow across
his scar did not leave his forehead, while Egorushka buried

himself deeper in his little mattress: if Margarita had been
there she would have picked him up in her arms, would have
pressed him to her right-sided heart, warming him and lovingly bearing him away from this laughter, frightful and un-
godly; as for the Samoyed, he stuck there like a scarecrow
and was no help at all to a heart that was Lilliputian, true
enough, yet a human heart just the same and one all upset.

And he kept clenching, clenching his little mattress in his
tiny fists, tiny fists turned blue from the cold.

Anton entered Seraphima's room without knocking. The
small kerosene stove was humming; Shurka was asleep, his
dislocated leg lying high on a pillow.

And Anton stood for a space over Shurka also, and also
looked him over from head to foot, intently, as he had done
just a little while ago with the Lilliputian.

"Turn off the burner," Anton requested. "It's making a lot
of noise. And there's something I want to tell you."

Seraphima went quickly to the kerosene stove and began
pumping it hard; the flame flared more intensely, the gadflies
of blue fire hummed still more furiously.

"For spite?" asked Anton.

The eyebrow-hawks—the black, angry birds so familiar—
oh, so painfully familiar to him—drew together and said,
without uttering a word: There is nothing to talk about.

"There is," said Anton and turned off the burner.

Quiet fell. Shurka's breathing became more audible—and
so did that of another in the room, panting under a gray
dress.

"I'm letting you go. The horses will be here at ten Sunday
evening. There's a train leaving at twelve. By eleven you will
already be at the station."

"With Shurka?"

"With Shurka," Anton answered—and smiled a little.

There was a thud against the floor: Seraphima was on her
knees—one could not tell whether she was weeping or
praying.

She had simply passed over Anton's sly smile without noticing it, and how could she have noticed it when her eyes—
blue lakes over a dead swell—had first stirred after many

days and long, upon seeing a light that did not die out, that was ineffable?

And—howl, howl indefatigably, thou thrice-accursed wintry wind of Red-Selimsk, for in spite of everything the silkily silver curly feather grass will twine; it will spread apart, being of her kindred; it will receive her, will give her shelter.

"Are you glad?" asked Anton, and his voice broke—for but an instant, yet break it did.

And the eyebrow-birds, twin raptors, fluttered up in frank and joyous answer.

5

The evening meeting did not come off and the original resolution sloughed away: evening was coming on when Lesnichy left the commune.

In the Hall of Mirrors he bowed in all four directions, just as a pilgrim might before the graves of those near and dear to him before starting on a long pilgrimage: he bussed Solomon, muttered a thank you, and that was the last you saw of the fellow with his shaggy head, shoulders as broad as the shafts of a cart are long, and legs like tree stumps; accept a new wayfarer, thou U-Ess-Ess-Ar-ian highroad, as untamable as in the days of old!

And, ten minutes later, close to the Maid of Tyrol, eyeglasses and brightly colored small boots flung themselves on a bed with a squeal; the high cap of gray caracul rolled off to one side; briny streams coursed behind the eyeglasses, the tips of the small morocco boots beat a tattoo. The Maid of Tyrol fluttered her eyelashes and wanted to wink, for the first time not alluringly but to show her sympathy—and could not: a cigarette butt—the only trace of Lesnichy— was stuck in the coin slot in her side.

Late that evening Zina Kirkova withdrew her motion about Spain, dressed and went into town.

Early next morning the sleigh with the bearskin laprobe glided up to the door; seated in the sleigh was the long overcoat of deerskin carrying a brief case, waiting while Zina Kirkova was collecting her belongings.

Solomon walked up to the window, rubbed a peephole

through the intricate design of hoarfrost on the pane, and said to Vassenka: "National Commissariat of Food Supplies. Zinka is going to get fat."

"What's to be done?" asked Vassenka.

"Well, according to Chernyshevsky, you might open a dressmaker's shop. However, Chernyshevsky is old stuff by now. The best thing, the way I see it, would be to get a length of rope and soap it. Your cell in the soap refinery, now—"

"You're always joking," Vassenka commented despondently and shuffled away from the window in none too cheerful a mood; he had suddenly become shorter, as though his stilts had broken off under him.

But the Basedowed eyes could be kindly also—Solomon caught up with Vassenka: "You're foolish, Vassiuk—my, but you're foolish. We'll go away together. I won't leave you behind, Vassenka, because I am fond of you—because you gape at everything like a young jackdaw. Never mind, Vassilii; the world is wide, we'll find ourselves another Panopticum. And we'll start going from one Panopticum to another Panopticum, you and I. And we're going to study—*studeamus raporticum humanum.* Were you ever in Turkestan? Never? Well, I never was there either. Let's travel there: we'll be the Eastern Sartsko-Bukharian Group of Anarchists-Egocentrists —light cometh from the East. Cheer up, Vassiuk!"

And the stilts took on new life: they were mended in an instant.

Those stilts will start striding—they cannot help but stride onward as long as the world is a whirligig about the sun and shows to the avid, insatiable gaze of man now a steel network of new rails, now the venturesome mountain trails, or the riotous, illimitable vistas of the sea.

As for Grandpa, he was sitting before a diminishing mirror and kept on writing, writing.

The same Grandpa was in the mirror, but there he was diminutive; and the sheets of paper were the same, but in the mirror they were teeny-weeny, like square scraps of paper for some children's game. But the pen scraped and scraped, on and on: man would be—he was bound to be—sole sovereign over the universe, he would be God.

V

1

On Saturday, toward evening, Anton led the Lilliputian into the room that had been Zina Kirkova's. On the other side of the wall was Seraphima's nook: right alongside Egorushka heard the boy crying and complaining that his leg hurt him. The Samoyed was left all by his lonesome in the cold; he wrapped his fur skins tighter about him, adjusted his quiver and in his grief launched into a long-drawn-out song— his Samoyed, cannibalistic song—about the tundra.

Anton got the stove going; Egorushka warmed up: the stove was far ahead of the Samoyed's moth-eaten fur; it was fine and warm to be sleeping on Zina's broad bed, but when the heart beats intermittently because of anxiety even a Lilliputian cannot sleep.

In the meanwhile the tall man, the new master, does not leave: he sits before the small stove, looking at the fire and smiling slyly all the time. Egorushka sees through the metal bars at the head of the bed that the other is smiling slyly: the blazing pieces of wood cast a shifting glow on his face; it is dark all around but the face is in the light, and lurking on that face is a crafty smile.

"Sleep," says the master. "Me, I'm going to sit here for a bit."

He spoke in a kindly way, almost the way Margarita used to speak, yet that smile did not disappear.

Thus an hour passed, and another: the face lit up, the sly smile, the corners dark, the windows covered with down, dove-gray, the wood in the stove crackling.

"Why aren't you sleeping?" asked the master. "You ought to sleep. We'll be on our way tomorrow."

Thus still another hour passed, the third: firelight on the face; the face immobile, crackling of firewood in stove; the little boy on the other side of the wall crying in his sleep— and ahead lies some road or other, an unknown road that had suddenly appeared from somewhere or other. . . . Lord God, whom would he be going with—this fellow with high cheek-

bones, perhaps, and where to, this time? . . . The tiny head
lolled, the parting, all rumpled, beat against the metal rods
at the head of the bed; Lilliputian grief wept.

And he was in tears that were as scalding as those of big
men, whose stature is human and not meant to be exhibited
for money. And, softened by a warmth he had not experienced for so long, in a timorous, tremulous drowsiness—
there, there, it would start up in fright and fly from his sub-
missive eyelashes—Egorushka nevertheless submitted his tor-
ment-exhausted body to it.

And when he awoke: murkiness, quietness, the master not
there, no fire, no sly smile—a Lilliputian's frightening nightmare.

2

And for Anton it was a frightening, endless night, the torture of an untamable soul, sheer waste—on this night all
things were jumbled together: waxworks, bombs, Lilliputians,
Shurka—the boy engendered one mad night on the bank of
the Kuban—black eyebrows and a black love: What is thy
beloved more than another beloved? Reaching to the level
of my heart—yet it turned out she didn't come up even to
my belt.

All things in one tangled ball: Yashka the One-Armed, porridge for Grandpa, Man-the-God, man-dryrot, distorting mirrors, distorted phizes, theatrical rags sold on the flea market,
the snow in Red-Selimsk, the Kremlin in Moscow (a nut no
one could crack, that), Grandpa's manuscript (the Newest
Testament, the Third, the Gospel according to Marius, an
apostle in checkered drawers), and again the Lilliputian, and
anew the hawk-eyebrows—how in the labyrinthine, the infernal darkness was one to find the slender clue, how un-
tangle the ball?

Long the night, long as sorrow; in the night steps rever-
berate, the ancient floorboards groan and complain resent-
fully: human feet, absurd and restless, give them no peace.

And the wax effigies gloated over the punishment being
meted out to the humans: the Wounded Boer breathed more
quickly and his innards rumbled; Rachel, forgetting her

nudity, was laughing tragically; the Arab was twirling his spear. And a shudder ran through the mirrors: Anton was awaking Grandpa. Both Grandpa and Anton were reflected dimly—you could barely, barely see their reflections.

"So you say, Grandpa, that one mustn't act like that? Why, everything is permitted to a free man. You yourself taught that."

Grandpa pulled his nightshirt up to his chin, just like a woman caught undressed, and said in a low, nocturnal voice, with a break in it: "That wasn't what I taught you—"

And then, in the darkness, he groped for Anton's hand, trying to capture it: "Anton!"—to capture that taut-sinewed hand on which he had placed all his hopes, a hand as firm as the joining of steel dagger and its hilt, a hand predestined to wreck the mechanism of the universe.

But the hand would not submit—a stubborn hand.

"No one who was over me succeeded in staying in power: nor God, nor Czar, nor the workingman. I admit no dominion over me: neither that of the workers, nor the peasants, nor the gentlefolk; only I have dominion over myself: only Razvozhaev dominates Razvozhaev. And yet Seraphima held me, held me fast. I want to even up the score."

"Anton!"—but the hand kept slipping away.

"I want revenge, Grandpa. It's the most pleasing sort of thing, revenge is. Just as I love—I do love, Grandpa, I do—without a second thought, so do I crave revenge, without a second thought. She'll unwrap the blanket in the warm car after the sleigh ride to take Shurka out—and find the midget. All wrinkled, bald-headed, spidery hands—" and Anton guffawed.

The mirrors rattled; faint was their gleam, faint their rattling.

"And then, Grandpa . . . then you and Shurka and I . . . then we'll go wherever you say—to pluck out the Dalai Lama's beard, to blow up London—"

Whereupon Grandpa bent in two, overcoming the injuries Sakhalin had scarred him with: "Let her have Shurka—let her have him!"

And Grandpa caught the hand and clung to it with his old, bitter lips.

"Let her have him!"—and, weakening, beginning to tremble, the hand gave in.

Dawn—

Dawn glided over the mirrors, removing the night's hangings from them, revealing two enormous heads close together on a green pillow that swells out like a haystack: one head bald, the other ruddy-fair.

3

Solomon and Vassenka were walking to the station through the town—a white town, everything white as white.

The snow was blinding the Basedowed, hopelessly tired. eyes. Long-legged Vassenka was breaking his way through the snow with zest; his hot red blood was laughing at the snowdrifts.

4

Grandpa did not leave Anton's side until the sleigh clattered up to the entrance.

And it was Grandpa as well who himself carried the muffled-up Shurka to the sleigh, hard as he found the task.

"Farewell, Anton," said Seraphima and, bending quickly, seized his hand and kissed it—and stumbled at the threshold, for the ruddy-fair head quickly drew back from her as he cried: "Two kisses in one day—it's too much!"

A little later another sleigh glided up.

Grandpa hurriedly gathered manuscripts, composition books, old newspapers from his table and mumbled toothlessly: "About that little trunk, now—what are we going to do about that little trunk?"

"Don't worry about it, Grandpa," Anton told him. "We'll take everything along. The midget, too."

"What midget?" asked Grandpa, and then, suddenly remembering, muttered: "Take him along, take him along: everything will come in handy."

Grandpa was bustling about; Anton was bringing Egorushka out of the room that had been Zina's and leading him to the sleigh; Egorushka, his knees buckling, was dragging a little hamper after him, containing his brightly colored ties, his cuffs.

"Hold on, Grandpa!" Anton called out. "I almost forgot—" and he dashed back through the front door.

Anton dragged wax figure after wax figure over to the windows, stuck their faces, one after the other, flat against the panes and, as he went to and fro, turned on all the switches. The lights ran over the snow, scattered, jostling the darkness of Red-Selimsk, stirring the somnolent winter stagnation.

The sleigh started off.

Anton was riding away, standing up in the sleigh, his stony face turned toward the Panopticum. The Lilliputian sobbed snufflingly from time to time; Grandpa was already dozing.

At midnight five long military uniforms stepped out of the gates of the local Cheka; a shaggy Caucasian felt cloak at their head kept grumbling, sibilantly: "Less noise!"

As in those days never to be forgotten by Tsimbaleuk, the days of Extra Gala Programs, all the electric bulbs in the Panopticum were radiant with color: lights romantically pink, dramatically green, violet for special effects.

Stiffly upright at the windows, their dead eyes staring out into the night, Rachel, the Maid of Tyrol, the Arab and headless Marie Antoinette were awaiting their guests.

Kraskovo—Moscow
1921-1922

Evgenii Ivanovich ZAMIATIN

[1884-1937]

Zamiatin was born in that very Lebedyan which was celebrated for its thimbleriggers, gypsies, horse fairs and the raciest Russian speech, and described with such fondness by Leo Tolstoi and Turgenev. In 1905, for his participation in the revolution of that year, Zamiatin served several months in solitary confinement in a St. Petersburg prison; early the next year he was banished to his native city, but from the summer of 1906 to 1911 he lived illegally in the northern capital and, in 1908, even graduated from the St. Petersburg Polytechnical Institute as a marine architect; later on he was to write a great deal in his specialty. In 1911 he was again banished to Lebedyan and did not return to St. Petersburg until he was amnestied in 1913. In 1908 his first short story appeared in a magazine; his first book, a novel, was published in 1911; his second, also a novel, *Out in the Sticks* (1914), led to the confiscation of the periodical in which it appeared and a court trial for its "subversive depiction of the Imperial Army"; the author was acquitted.

In 1916 he was sent to England to build icebreakers for the government. His regret at having missed the February, 1917, Revolution was "immense"; in the famous October of that year he hurried back to Russia. But his enthusiasm for this revolution was of the briefest. On the other hand he did not oppose the revolution to the extent of becoming a White Guard or abandoning his Russia. He remained and took a very active part in lecturing, writing, teaching others to write—"in 90-proof ink." The young writers who had about 1920 formed themselves into the Serapion Brotherhood proclaimed him their Nestor and their Mentor. In 1925 he dramatized Leskov's marvelous humoresque, "The Steel Flea"; produced by the Second Moscow Art Theatre as *The Flea* it proved extremely popular, since it had injected new blood into the Soviet theatre, which by that time was decidedly anaemic. However, his other play, *The Fires of St. Dominick,* published in Moscow and Berlin in 1923, met with official criticism; true, the drama was antireligious, but the characters contending against the Inquisition were doing so as glorified "solitary individualists." Even *Impious Tales* (1927) failed to satisfy the official critics.

The situation was growing more and more unbearable for Zamiatin. The crisis was brought on by *We.* According to nonofficial sources it had been written as early as 1920; a reading of it was given in 1924, at a meeting of the [Russian] Writers' League, and although it was never brought out in Russia its content was well known in the literary circles of both capitals. Its publishing history, while by no means unparalleled in the rigorous annals of Russian literature,* is not entirely without interest. It first appeared in New York (December, 1924), in an English version by the late Dr. Gregory Zilboorg. This was followed, in 1926 or 1927, by a Czech translation in a Brno newspaper. The first appearance of *We* in the original language was in 1927, in the *Will of Russia,* an exceptionally well-edited liberal émigré periodical published in Prague; the text was, however, very considerably abridged and purported to be a re-translation from the Czech—probably to make things easier for the author. In book form, complete and in Russian, *We* was first brought out only in 1952

* "The book from the publication of which it [Russian literature] dates as a modern literature, was first published neither in Russian nor in Russia." The reference is, of course, to the *Satires* of Prince Antioch Cantemir (1708-44), published in the author's own language and land in 1762, twelve years after its publication in a French version in London, and eighteen years after his death." Ya.Chort-Poluslepoi, *Korotkii Exquise Russkoi Literatury* (*Brief Sketch of Russian Literature*), Moscow, 1894; Vol. V, p. 678. The case of Pasternak's *Doctor Zhivago* is too recent to require more than mention here.

and again in New York, by The Chekhov Publishing House. And, in the three decades between 1929 and 1959, this utopia has been translated into seven more languages. The translation submitted herewith is new, complete and unexpurgated. It must also be pointed out that the style (most effective—at least in the original) which Zamiatin seems to have evolved especially for this masterpiece is quite elliptic and rather surrealistic. The translator has preferred to pumice it as little as possible in English.

The publication of *We* abroad intensified the attacks made on Zamiatin by the professional proletarians who had been long gunning for him because of his vitriolic insistence that the new Russian literature should be contemporaneous rather than quotidian, and in 1929, when what may be called the New Economic Policy in Soviet literature came to an end, his position became impossible and he resigned in protest from the All-Russian Union of Writers. However, it must be stated that it was also in 1929 that his collected works were brought out in four volumes, in Moscow. In 1931 he wrote a letter to Stalin, which was transmitted through his friend and admirer Gorki, asking to be permitted to leave Russia for a while; through Gorki's further intercession this request was granted, and Zamiatin went to Paris in 1932. Here he was very active as a critic, but kept away from the footling émigrés; he died five years later from an unassailably nonpolitical heart ailment.

Zamiatin is generally pigeonholed as a Neo-Realist; he shared with Prishvin and Remizov their great admiration for Leskov; in considering him as a satirist of stature, it must be remembered that he called Gogol a friend of his youth. At the same time it is utter banality to drag out the tears-through-laughter chestnut in his case: his satyricon, whether he attacks the bourgeoisie of the West, as in *The Islanders* (1922), or socialism in his own land, is never diluted.

Ordinarily one would be loath to add even a drop to the ocean of commentaries lapping at the continent of Utopia, but in the case of *We* it would be churlish to refrain. That wrathy Hebrew Isaiah sounded the basic theme of the Utopia-as-Ideal-Commonwealth no less than three times; Sir Francis

Bacon introduced a sour note into his rendering; Sir Thomas
More borrowed the Greek word for *nowhere* as a generic
label for this sort of composition; Bellamy's may well be
called the last straight-forward Utopia of any significance.

It was inevitable that the droller writers should discover,
fairly early (Lucian among the earliest) the satiric possibili-
ties of donning the motley of futurity and then belaboring
with the traditional blown-up pig bladders the rump of the
present. Rabelais discovered a very chain of Ever-Ever
Islands; the last and most amusing Unideal Commonwealth
lies, according to Butler, beyond a mountain range. And it
was equally inevitable that this still legitimate branch of the
grand old Utopia family should, about the middle of the
1870's, beget (but on the wrong side of the blanket) a line
of what may (and should) be described as Aipotus—to coin a
word for the pseudo-Utopia. Where is the vigorish, said the
more astute wags to themselves, in the by no means safe tilt-
ing against windmills? And so, faithfully following the paper-
patterns so plethorically furnished by Wells, each bear-and-
furbear aipotuist set to turning out a line of standardized men
of straw and then demolishing them with a valor that was
practically undistinguishable from extreme prudence.

The stigmata of these brain-hashing aipotuists are ever
present and never varying: a preternatural keenness of vision
in the perception of every mote, no matter how minute, in the
eye of the horripilant future, a total imperception of any
beam, even if of the size of a sequoia, in the eye of their own
present* and, above all, a most touching and obsessive concern for man's spiritual status, the fill-the-belly-and-kill-the-
soul complex, to use the psychological jargon of today—for,
as everybody knows, there is something peculiarly and infalli-

---

* With, naturally, the usual rule-proving exceptions. Prior
to his *We*-stenciled aipotus, Orwell had written a sociological
bit of orthodox objectivity about being hard up in Paris and
London. After describing how England handled her unemployed by perpetually churning them from town to town,
from government-sponsored doss-house to government-sponsored doss-house, he fearlessly contributes his solution to the
problem: Make the doss-houses a little more comfy. . . .

bly ennobling and salutary about a ventral vacuum. (Oddly enough, this particular variety of ventriloquism simply cannot be performed by the aipotuan ventriloquist except from a full belly.) The supreme formulation of this obsession is, of course, the "Grand Inquisitor" chapter in *The Brothers Karamazov*—a magnificent piece which is also remarkable in that the master managed to evade the present by sidling over into the past: no slight or common feat.

We, despite certain superficial resemblances, should not be confused with any aipotu; it differs in all the important respects. Official Soviet criticism errs in styling it a pasquinade against the socialistic *future:* Zamiatin may have fallen into the error against which the hardly radical Lord Macaulay warned, that of condemning a construction or a revolution while either is still incomplete and, as of now, Mayakovsky was an infinitely more percipient prophet than Zamiatin; nevertheless the latter did not play quintain with his own times; his Benefactor was no Big Brother scarecrow but none other than Lenin himself; he did not write either to fill his belly or on a full belly, and paid at an exorbitant rate for the courage of his convictions. Finally, since none of his exceedingly many copyists had his wit or his puissance in satire, *We* remains the best satire-fantasy, or sardonic Utopia, of our times. The only mark against it, and it is indeed a black one, is that it has proven to be the matrix for all the brave new Huxleys and Orwells.

It is very much to be doubted if any revolution would have won the full-hearted approval of this stormy petrel. Zamiatin could well have sat for Kamkov, in the Fadeyev story included in this anthology, and the reader will have little difficulty in perceiving that E-330, the chief heroine of *We,* is really the author's mouthpiece, his proponent of revolution-for-revolution's-sake. Above all, he was of kin to the famous White Sail of Lermontov:

> Lonely and far a white sail soars. . . .
> Beneath the azure current churns,
> Above the golden sunlight glows;
> Yet for a storm the sail still yearns—
> As though in storms one found repose. . . .

WE

FIRST ENTRY: *An Announcement. The Wisest of Lines. A Poem.*

I am simply transcribing, word for word, what appeared in today's *State Gazette:*

> In 120 days the construction of the *Integral* will be completed. The great, the historic hour is near when the first *Integral* shall soar into universal space. A thousand years ago your heroic ancestors subdued the entire terrestrial globe to the domination of The One State. Now a still more glorious deed lies before you: that of integrating, by means of the glazed, electrified, fire-breathing *Integral,* the endless equalization of all Creation. There lies before you the subjugation of unknown creatures to the beneficent yoke of reason—creatures inhabiting other planets, perhaps still in the savage state of freedom. Should they fail to understand that we are bringing them a mathematically infallible happiness, it will be our duty to compel them to be happy. But, before resorting to weapons, we shall try words.
>
> In the name of The Benefactor it is hereby proclaimed to all the numbers of The One State:
>
> Everyone who feels able to do so is obligated to compose treatises, poems, odes and/or other pieces on the beauty and grandeur of The One State.
>
> This will be the first cargo to be borne by the *Integral.*
>
> All hail to The One State; all hail to the numbers; all hail to The Benefactor!

I am writing this—and I feel my cheeks are flaming. Yes—we must carry through the integration of the grandiose, endless equalization of all Creation. Yes—we must unbend the wild curve, we must straighten it out at a tangent—at an asymptote—to a straight line! Inasmuch as the line of The One State is a straight line. The great, divine, exact, wise straight line—the wisest of lines!

I, D-503, the builder of the *Integral*—I am but one of the mathematicians of The One State. My pen, accustomed to figures, has not the power to create the music of assonances and rhymes. I shall merely attempt to record what I see, what I think—to be more exact, what *we* think (*we*, precisely, and let this *WE* serve as the title of the entries I am making). However, these things will be a derivative of our life, of the mathematically perfect life of The One State, and if that be so, will not all this be a poem *per se*, whether I will it or not? It will be a poem—I believe it and know it.

I am writing this—and I feel that my cheeks are flaming. Probably what I am going through is similar to what a woman experiences when for the first time she senses within herself the pulsation of a new homunculus, as yet tiny, blind. It is *I* and, at the same time, it is not *I*. And for months and months it will be necessary to nourish it with one's own juices, one's own blood, and then, enduring pain, to wrench it away from oneself and lay it at the feet of The One State.

Yet I am ready, even as every one of us (or almost every one) is. I am ready.

SECOND ENTRY: *Ballet. Harmony of the Square.* X. Spring. From beyond the Green Wall, from the wild plains that lie out of sight, the wind brings the honeyed yellow pollen of certain flowers. The lips become dry from this pollen; you run your tongue over them every minute or so and, in all probability, all the women you come across have sweet lips now (which must hold true of the men also, of course). This interferes with logical thinking, to some extent.

But then, what a sky! Blue, unmarred by a single cloud (how extremely primitive in matters of taste were the ancients, since their poets could find inspiration in those absurd, sloppily shaped, foolishly jostling masses of vapor). I love—I am sure I do not err if I say that we all love—only such a sky as the present one, sterile, irreproachable. On days such as this the whole universe is molded out of the same immovable, eternal glass as our Green Wall, as are all our other structures. On days such as this, one sees the blue depth of things, one sees certain of their equations, amazing and unknown until that moment—one sees them in something that may be ever so ordinary, ever so prosaic.

Why, consider even this, for example: this morning I was at the launching site where the *Integral* is under construction —and I suddenly caught sight of the work benches. Sightlessly, in self-oblivion, the globes of the regulators rotated; the cranks, glittering, bent to right and left; a balanced beam swayed its shoulders proudly; the blade of a gouging lathe was doing a squatting dance in time to unheard music. I suddenly perceived all the beauty of this grandiose mechanical ballet, flood-lighted by the ethereal, azure-surrounded sun.

Then, continuing my train of thought, I asked myself: Why is all this beautiful? Why is this dance beautiful? The answer was: Because this was *nonfree* motion, because all of the profound meaning of the dance lay precisely in absolute, æsthetic submissiveness, in ideal *nonfreedom*. And if it be true that our ancestors abandoned themselves to dancing at the most inspired moments of their lives (religious mysteries, military parades), it signifies only one thing: the instinct of nonfreedom is organically inherent in man from the times of old, and we in our life of today are only consciously————

I will have to finish this thought later: the intercommunication board clicked at this point. I looked up—O-90, of course. In half a minute she herself will be here; she is coming to fetch me for a walk.

Darling O-! It had always seemed to me that her looks matched her name; she is 10 centimeters or so shorter than the Maternal Norm, she is as rounded as if she had been turned on a lathe, while that rosy *O*, her mouth, is open to meet every word of mine halfway. And another thing: she has a tiny crease around her chubby wrist—the sort of crease you see in children.

When she entered, the flywheel of logic was still humming at full speed inside me, and through inertia I began telling her about the formula I had just arrived at which embraced not only all of us but the machines and their dance as well.

"Wonderful—isn't it?" I asked her.

"Yes, it is wonderful. It's spring," O-90 gave me a rosy smile.

There, now, if you please—spring! It was spring she was talking about. Women! . . . I fell silent.

We went down. The avenue was full of people—in such weather we usually spend the after-lunch Personal Hour in a supplementary walk. As always, the Musical Factory was chanting with all its pipes The March of The One State. The numbers—hundreds, thousands of numbers—all in light-blue unifs,* all with gold badges on their chests, each badge bearing the State number of the particular he or she—the numbers were pacing along in even ranks of four each, exaltedly pounding their feet in time to the music. And I—together with the other three in our unit of four—was one of the countless waves in this mighty torrent. O-90 was on my left (if one of my hirsute ancestors were writing this a thousand years ago he would probably apply the funny word *my* to her); on my right were some numbers or other whom I did not know, one female, one male.

The sky of beatific blue, the suns, tiny as children's toys, reflected in all the badges, faces unclouded by the insanity of thoughts—rays, these, you understand: all this was formed of some unique, radiant, riant matter. As for the brazen beats— *tra-ta-ta-tam, tra-ta-ta-tam*—these were steps of brass that sparkled in the sun, and with every step you rose higher and higher into the vertiginous azure. . . . And then, just as it had happened this morning at the launching site, I again saw all things as if I were seeing them for the very first time in my life—I saw the irrevocably straight streets, the ray-spurting

---

* Probably from the ancient word *uniform*.

glass of the roadways, the divine parallelepipedons of the transparent dwellings, the square harmony of our gray-blue ranks. And so it struck me that it had not been the generations upon generations before me but I—precisely I—who had conquered the old God and the old life; that it was precisely I who had created all this. And, as if I were a tower, I was afraid to move my elbow lest I send the walls, cupolas, machines tumbling in a cascade of fragments.

And the moment after there followed a leap through the ages, from + to —. There came to memory (evidently an association by contrast)—there suddenly came to memory a painting in a museum, depicting an avenue of *their* twentieth-century days, a deafeningly jangling, motley, confused crush of people, wheels, animals, posters, trees, colors, birds. And, to be sure, they say that this sort of thing really existed—it could have happened. This struck me as so improbable that I could not restrain myself and suddenly burst into peals of laughter. And I immediately heard an echo of laughter on my right. I turned my head: directly before my eyes were white (extraordinarily white and sharp) teeth, and an unfamiliar feminine face.

"Do forgive me," said she, "but you were surveying everything with such an inspired air—like some mythological god on the seventh day of creation. To me you seem so certain that you, and no one but you, created me along with all the rest. I feel so very flattered—"

All this without a smile—even with a certain deference, I would say (perhaps she was aware that I am the builder of the *Integral*). However, I don't know whether it was her eyes or her brows, but there was some sort of strange, irritating X about her, and no matter how I tried I could not capture it, could not give it a numerical formulation. For some reason I became embarrassed and, somewhat haltingly, began giving a logical motivation for my laughter. It was perfectly clear that this contrast, this uncrossable abyss between the things of today and those of that time—

"But why uncrossable? [What white teeth!] It's possible to throw a small bridge over an abyss. Just use your imagina-

tion: drums, battalions, ranks—why, all that sort of thing also
existed before, and consequently————"

"Well, yes—that's clear!" I exclaimed. This was an astounding intersection of thoughts: she had uttered—almost in my
very words—what I had been writing down before the walk.
"That is true even of thoughts, you understand. That is because nobody is *one,* but *one of.* We are so alike—"

"You are sure?" she put in. I caught sight of eyebrows
quirked at an acute angle toward the temples, like the sharp
horns of the upper half of an *X.* For some reason I was again
thrown off balance; I looked to the right, to the left, and . . .

She was to the right of me—E-330 (I can see her number
right now), slender, hard, willfully pliant as a whiplash; to
the left was O-90 (or simply O-), altogether different, made
up entirely of circumferences, with a small crease like a
child's around her wrist, while at the other end of our half-
squad was a male number whom I did not know, some
fellow formed in a double curve, on the nature of the letter
S. We were all unlike. . . .

E-330, the one on my right, apparently intercepted my dis-
tracted glance and said, with a sigh: "Yes, alas!"

In reality, this "alas!" was quite appropriate, but again
there was something odd about her face—or was it in her
voice?

"There's no alas about it!" said I, with a brusqueness which
was unusual for me. "Science is expanding, and it is clear
that if not now then in fifty years or a hundred years
hence—"

"Even the noses of all—"

"Yes, the noses!" I was almost shouting by now. "As long as
there is a basis for envy, no matter to what extent . . . if I
have a nose like a button, while somebody else has one
like—"

"Well, now, when it comes to your nose I'll grant it is
rather *classic,* as they used to say in the old days. But as for
your hands—no, no, do let me see your hands!"

I can't bear to have people looking at my hands; they're
all grown over with hair, shaggy—some sort of ridiculous

atavism. I held out my hands and said, making my voice as objective as I could: "They're simian."

She glanced at my hands, then at my face: "Yes, there is an exceedingly curious accordance." She was running her eyes over me, as if she were weighing me; I had another glimpse of the tiny horns at the tips of her eyebrows.

"He is registered in my name," O-90's mouth opened in rosy joy.

It would have been better if she had kept quiet; her remark was an utter *non sequitur*. This adorable O- is, in general— how should I put it? . . . In her case the velocity of the tongue is not calculated correctly: the velocity of the tongue per second should always be a trifle slower than the velocity per second of thought, and not by any means the reverse.

The big bell of the Accumulator Tower was booming 17:00. The Personal Hour was over. E-330 was about to leave with that *S*-shaped male number. His face was of the sort that inspired respect and, as I perceived by then, it actually seemed familiar. I must have met him somewhere but simply could not recall the occasion.

As she was leaving E-330 smiled at me slyly, in that same *X*-ish way: "Look in at Auditorium One Hundred and Twelve, day after tomorrow."

"If I get an assignment to the auditorium you have just mentioned—" said I, with a shrug.

"You will," she said with an odd assurance which I could not understand.

This woman had the same unpleasant effect upon me as an irrational component which strays into an equation and cannot be analyzed. And so I was glad to be left alone with dear O-, if only for a brief while. Arm in arm we passed four intersecting avenues. At the last corner she had to turn to the right and I to the left.

"I would like so much to come to you today and lower the blinds. Precisely today—right now—" O- timidly looked up at me with her rounded eyes of blue crystal.

How amusing she is. There, what could I say to her? She had been at my place only yesterday and she knows as well as I do that our next Sexual Day is day after tomorrow. This is simply that same tendency of hers of "getting ahead of thought"—a phenomenon analogous to the occasionally damaging one of the ignition spark getting ahead of the motor.

At parting I kissed her twice—no, let me be exact: I kissed her three times on her wonderful eyes of blue, unmarred by as much as a speck of a cloud.

THIRD ENTRY: *A Jacket. A Wall. A Table of Commandments.* I have looked over everything I wrote yesterday, and I see that I did not write clearly enough. That is, it is perfectly clear to any one of us; but how is one to know—it is possible that you, whom I do not know, and to whom the *Integral* will come bearing these notes of mine—it is possible that you have read in the great book of civilization only up to the very page our ancestors reached 900 years ago. Possibly you do not know even such *a-b-c*'s as The Tables of Hourly Commandments, Personal Hours, the Maternal Norm, the Green Wall, The Benefactor. I find it droll, and at the same time most difficult to talk of all this. It is exactly the same as if a writer of some twentieth century or other, let's say, were faced with the need of explaining the nature of *jacket, apartment, wife.* However, if his novel were translated for savages, is it conceivable that annotations concerning such a thing as *jacket* could be avoided?

I feel certain that the savage must have reflected as he viewed a *jacket:* "There, what's that for? It's nothing but a nuisance!" It seems to me that your views, too, will be every bit the same as that savage's when I tell you that not a one of us since the times of the Two Hundred Years' War has set foot beyond the Green Wall. But, dear friends, you will have to think—at least to some extent. It does help, quite a lot.

For this much is clear: all human history, insofar as we have any knowledge of it, is a history of the transition from nomadic forms to ever more sedentary ones. Does it not follow from this, then, that the most sedentary form of life (ours) is at the same time the most perfect one (ours, again)? If men did dash about from one end of the earth to the other, why, it was only in the prehistoric times, when there were such things as nations, wars, traffickings, discoveries of sundry Americas. But who needs all that nowadays, and what for?

I admit: the habit of this sedentariness came about not without toil and not all at once. When, during the Two Hundred Years' War, all the roads became ruined and overgrown with grass it must have seemed very inconvenient at first to be living in cities cut off from one another by green wildwoods. But what of that? After the falling away of his tail, man also did not learn all at once how to drive off the flies without its aid. Indubitably, he must have felt depressed at first without his caudal appendage. But now—can you picture yourself as having a tail? Or can you picture yourself naked out in the street, without a *jacket?* (It is possible that you are still strolling about without *jackets.*) Well, that is precisely the situation here: I cannot conceive of a city that is not girt about by a Green Wall, I cannot conceive of a life that is not enrobed in the figured chasubles of The Tables of Hourly Commandments.

The Tables of Hourly Commandments. . . . Why, at this very moment, from the wall in my room, it is looking into my eyes sternly yet kindly, with its figures of purple against a background of gold. One is involuntarily reminded of the object the ancients used to call an *icon,* and a desire springs up within me to compose verses or prayers (which are one and the same). Ah, why am I not a poet, so that I might fittingly chant your praises. O, Tables of Hourly Commandments, O, you who are the heart and the pulse of The One State!

We all (and perhaps all of you also) have read as school children that greatest of all the monuments of ancient literature which have come down to us: *Time Tables of All the Railroads.* But place even that classic side by side with The Tables of Hourly Commandments and you will see, side by side, graphite and diamond. Both contain the one and the same element—C, carbon: yet how eternal, how transparent the diamond, and how refulgent! Who can help but catch his breath as he thunders and races headlong through the pages of the *Time Tables?* The Tables of Hourly Commandments, however, really does transform each one of us into the six-wheeled steel hero of a great poem. Each morning, with six-wheeled precision, at the very same minute and the very same second we, in our millions, arise as one. At the very same hour we monomillionedly begin work—and, when we finish it, we do so monomillionedly. And, merging into but one body with multimillioned hands, at the very second designated by The Tables of Hourly Commandments we bring our spoons up to our mouths; at the very same second, likewise, we set out for a walk, or go to an auditorium, or the Hall of Taylor Exercises, or retire to sleep.

I will be quite frank: even we do not have an absolute, exact solution to the problem of happiness: twice a day (from 16:00 to 17:00 and from 21:00 to 22:00) our mighty unipersonal organism disintegrates into separate cells; these are the Personal Hours, as fixed by The Tables of Hourly Commandments. During these hours you can see the blinds chastely lowered in the rooms of some; others you can see traversing with measured tread the main avenue—and the brazen steps of The March of The One State, as it were; still others may be sitting at their desks, just as I am sitting at my desk right now. Yet I firmly believe (let them call me an idealist and phantaseur!)—I believe that sooner or later the day will come when we shall find a place in the general formula for these hours also, a day when all of its 86,400 seconds will be included in The Tables of Hourly Commandments.

I have had occasion to read and hear many incredible things concerning those times when people were still living in a free—i.e., an unorganized, savage—state. But the one thing that has always struck me as the most improbable was precisely this: How could the governing power (let us say even a rudimentary one) allow the people to live without anything resembling our Tables of Hourly Commandments, without obligatory walks, without exact regulation of meal-times—how could it allow them to get up and go to bed whenever they got the notion to do so? Certain historians even assert that, apparently, in those times the streets were lit all through the night—that, all through the night, people walked and drove through the streets!

Now *that* is something that my mind simply cannot grasp. Why, no matter how limited their intelligence may have been, they were nevertheless bound to understand that such a mode of life was nothing but downright wholesale murder—even though it was slow murder, protracted from day to day. The State (in its humaneness) forbade the outright murder of one person, yet did not forbid the half-murdering of millions. Killing one person—i.e., decreasing the sum total of human lives by 50 years—was criminal, but decreasing the sum total of human lives by 50 million years—*that* was not criminal. Come, now, isn't that laughable? Any ten-year-old number among us can solve this mathematically moral problem in half a minute, but all of their Kants taken together couldn't do it—inasmuch as not a one of their Kants struck on the notion of constructing a system of scientific ethics, i.e., a system of ethics founded on subtraction, addition, division, multiplication.

Or take this: isn't it an absurdity that the State (it dared to call itself a state!) could allow sexual life without any control whatsoever? Anybody, any time, and as much as one wanted to. . . . Completely unscientifically, like brutes. And, like brutes, they bred offspring gropingly. Isn't it laughable—to know horticulture, poultry culture, pisciculture (we have definite data that they had knowledge of all these), and yet be unable to reach the last rung of this logical ladder: child culture. To be unable to reach the logical conclusions: our Maternal and Paternal Norms.

This is so laughable, so incredible that, after having written the above, I am apprehensive: what if you, my unknown readers, should take me for a malicious wag? What if you should suddenly get the notion that I am simply intent upon making cruel sport of you and, with a serious air, am telling you utterly unmitigated bosh. But, first of all, I am incapable of jesting, inasmuch as the covert functioning of falsehood is a component of every jest, and secondly, Science in The One State affirms that the life of the ancients was precisely as I have described it—and Science in The One State is infallible. And besides, where was any logic of government to come from at that time, when people were living in a state of freedom—i.e., like brutes, like apes, like herded cattle? What could one demand of them, when even in our time one hears at rare intervals a wild simian echo issuing from the shaggy depths, from somewhere close to the very bottom? Fortunately, only at rare intervals. And, fortunately, we have only the unimportant failures of small parts—it is easy to repair them without stopping the grand, eternal progress of the whole Machine. And in order to throw out the warped bolt we have the skillful heavy hand of The Benefactor, we have the experienced eyes of the Guardians. . . .

Yes, by the way—I have just thought of something: that male number yesterday, the one in a double curve, shaped like the letter *S*—it seems to me that I chanced to see him coming out of the Bureau of Guardians. Now I understand why I felt that instinctive respect for him, and why I experienced a certain embarrassment when that peculiar E-330, right in his presence———— I must confess that that female number————

The bell has just rung; time for bed: 22½. Will resume tomorrow.

FOURTH ENTRY: *The Savage with a Barometer. Epilepsy. If Only—* To me, up to now, everything in life seemed clear (it is not merely by chance that I seem to be rather partial to this very word, *clear*). Today, however . . . I don't understand. First of all, I actually was assigned to Auditorium 112, just as she had told me I would be. Even though the probability of such an assignment was

$$\frac{1,500}{10,000,000} = \frac{3}{20,000}$$

(1,500 represents the auditoria, and there are 10,000,000 of us numbers). And secondly—however, it will be better to take things in their proper order.

The Auditorium: an enormous half-globe of glass massifs, shot through with sunlight. Circular rows of noble, globular, closely clipped heads. With my heart pleasantly missing a beat or two I looked about me. I think I must have been on the lookout: perhaps I would catch a glimpse, above the blue unif-waves, of a bright, rosy crescent—the dear lips of O-90. There—I caught sight of somebody's extraordinarily white and sharp teeth, so much like those of . . . no, they weren't. This evening, at 21:00, O- is coming to my place: my desire to see her here was perfectly natural.

There, the bell sounded. We stood up, sang The Hymn of The One State—and the phonolecturer was on the platform, gleaming with cleverness and a gold loudspeaker.

"Estimable numbers! Archaeologists recently unearthed a certain book of the twentieth century. The ironical author of this book tells a story about a savage and a barometer. The savage noticed that every time when the barometer indicated *rain,* rain actually fell. And since the savage had his heart set on getting rain he tinkered with the barometer until he had let out just enough quicksilver to bring it to the level of *rain.* (The screen showed a befeathered savage, tinkering with the quicksilver. Laughter.) You're laughing—but doesn't it strike you that the European of that epoch is far more deserving of being laughed at? The European wanted rain, just as the savage did—but the European wanted his rain with an upper-case *R,* an algebraic rain, but he stood before that barometer like a wet hen. The savage at least had more daring and energy and logic—even though it was wild logic. He was able to establish that there was a connection between effect and cause; having tinkered with the quicksilver he had been able to take the first step on that great path along which—"

At this point (I repeat, I am writing without keeping anything back)—at this point I became impermeable for a space, as it were, to the vivifying currents pouring out of the loudspeakers. It suddenly appeared to me that I had come here uselessly (why *uselessly,* and how could I do anything but come here, when the directive to do so had been issued?); everything seemed empty, no more than a husk. And I had difficulty in switching my attention on again, succeeding only when the phonolecturer had already passed on to its basic theme—that of our music, to the mathematical composition of music (the mathematician was the cause, music was the effect), to the description of the recently invented musicometer.

". . . By merely turning this handle any one of you can produce up to three sonatas an hour. Yet what toil and moil your ancestors had to go through to attain this sort of thing! They could create only by working themselves into seizures of *inspiration*—some unknown form of epilepsy. And now you will hear a most amusing demonstration of what they managed to achieve: the music of Scriabin, a *composer* of the twentieth century. This black box (a curtain toward the rear of the platform parted, revealing the oldest instrument of the ancients)—this box they called a Royal Grand, conveying thereby its *regal* nature, which is another superfluous proof to what extent their music—"

And again I don't remember what was said next, very possibly because I— Well, yes: I'll come right out with it: because she—E-330—had walked up to the Royal Grand. Probably I had simply been overcome by her unexpected appearance on the platform.

She was clad in a fantastic costume of some epoch of antiquity: a black, clingingly enveloping garment that strikingly emphasized the white of her bared shoulders and bosom and that warm, shadowy valley, wavering with her breath, between her———— And her teeth, too—dazzling, almost wicked. . . .

A smile: a bite, aimed down here. She took her seat; began playing. Something wild, spasmodic, motley, just as all their life was in those days—without a shadow of rational mechanicalness. And of course they—those around me—were right: all of them were laughing. Except for just a few . . . but why was I, too—I!—why was I one of them?

Yes, epilepsy is a psychic disease—a psychic pain. Slow, delectable pain, a bite—and oh, to have that bite penetrate still deeper, still more painfully! And then, slowly—the sun. Not our sun, not this bluishly crystalline and equable sun as seen through the glass bricks. No, but a wild, careering, scorching-searing sun—tear everything off yourself, shred everything into the smallest shreds. . . .

The number seated on my left looked at me out of the corner of his eye—and sniggered. One detail has, for some reason, remained with especial distinctness in my memory: I saw a microscopic bubble of saliva pop up on his lips—and burst. That bubble sobered me. I was I once more. Like all the others what I heard now was only the incongruous, fussy chatter of strings under percussion. I was laughing. Everything had become light and simple. The talented phonolecturer had given us too lively a depiction of that wild epoch—and that was all.

With what delight I listened next to our contemporary music! (It was played toward the conclusion of the talk, to demonstrate the contrast.) Crystalline chromatic scales converging and diverging in endless series—and the summarizing chords of the formulae of Taylor, of McLauren; the full-toned, squarely-massive passages of the Pythagorean theorem; the pensive melodies of an expiringly oscillatory movement; vivid cadences, alternating with the pauses of Frauenhofer's lines—the spectral analysis of planets. . . . What grandeur! What irrevocable regularity! And how self-willed the music of the ancients, restrained by nothing save wild fantasies. . . .

All the numbers came out of the auditorium in their usual even ranks of four each. A familiar double-curved figure flitted by—I bowed to him with deference.

Adorable O- was coming in an hour. I felt pleasantly and usefully excited. On getting home I hurried to the office, handed my pink ticket to the clerk in charge and received a certificate entitling me to the Right of Blinds. This right is ours only on Sexual Days. Ordinarily, however, we constantly live in full sight of all, constantly bathed in light and surrounded by our glass walls that seem to be woven of coruscating air. We have nothing to conceal from one another. Besides, this lack of concealment lightens the onerous and exalted work of the Guardians. Otherwise, who can tell what things may happen? Quite possibly it may have been the *outré,* opaque habitations of the ancients which engendered their pitiful cellular psychology. "My (*sic!*) house is my stronghold"—that surely required cerebration!

At 22:00 I lowered the blinds—and at that very moment O- entered, a little out of breath. She held out to me her tiny pink mouth—and her small pink ticket. I tore off the stub, but I could not tear myself away from the rosy mouth up to the very last moment—22:15.

Afterward I showed her my "entries" and spoke—very well, apparently—of the beauty of the square, the cube, the straight line. She listened in such a rosily enchanting way— and then suddenly a tear trickled out of her blue eyes, and another, and a third, plopping right on the open page (the 7th). The ink ran. Well, now I'll have to transcribe it.

"Darling D-, if only you would . . . if only—"

Well, *if only* what? What is this *if only?* Is she again at her old refrain, about having a baby? Or is this something new, concerning . . . concerning that other one? Although, if it comes to that, it would seem as if . . . no, that would be too absurd.

FIFTH ENTRY: *The Square.* *Sovereigns of the Universe. A Pleasantly Useful Function.* Again, I don't seem to be starting off right. Again I am talking to you, my unknown reader, as if . . . well, let's say as if you were R-13, an old friend of mine. He is a poet, with Negroid lips—why, everybody knows him. Yet when it comes to you—well, now, you may be on Luna, on Venus, on Mars, on Mercury; who knows what you are up to—where you are and who you are.

Tell you what: picture to yourself a square—a living, beautiful equilateral quadrangle. It has to inform you about itself, about its existence. The last thing that would enter this quadrangle's mind, you understand, would be to say that all its four angles are equal: it simply no longer perceives this, since it finds this fact such a customary, everyday matter. Well, I too find myself constantly in this quadrangular situation. There, take those pink tags, for example, and all that goes with them: I take the whole matter as much for granted as the square does the equality of its angles, whereas for you it may be a harder nut to crack than Newton's binomial theorem.

Well, now. Some ancient sage or other once said something clever (by pure chance, of course): "Love and Hunger rule the universe." *Ergo,* in order to win sovereignty over the universe man must win sovereignty over the sovereigns of the universe. By paying a high price our ancestors gained victory over Hunger—I am speaking of the Great Two Hundred Years' War between city and village. The Christian savages, probably because of religious prejudices, held on stubbornly to their *bread*.* But in the 35th year before the founding of The One State the food we eat today, a derivative of naphtha, was devised. True, only 0.2 of the population of the terrestrial globe survived; but then, cleansed of its millennial filth, how glowing the face of the earth became! Then, too, the surviving two-tenths certainly came to know bliss in the many mansions of The One State.

Is it not clear, then, that bliss and envy are but the numerator and denominator of a fraction called happiness? Now, what would be the significance of all the innumerable sacrifices of the Two Hundred Years' War if, in spite of everything, there still remained any reason for envy? And yet a reason remained, inasmuch as there still remained "button noses" and "classical" noses (to quote the conversation during our recent Supplementary Walk), and inasmuch as the love of some was striven for by many, while the love of others wasn't striven for by any.

Naturally, having subordinated Hunger (a victory which was the algebraic = sign of the sum of external blessings), The One State launched an offensive against the other sovereign of the universe—against Love, that is. In the end this elemental force was likewise conquered—i.e., it was organized, mathematized—and 300 years ago, or thereabouts, our historic *Lex Sexualis* was promulgated: "Every number has the right of availability, as a sexual product, to any other number." As for the rest of it—well, that is already mere technique. Your case is subjected to thorough research in the laboratories of the Sexual Bureau, the content of sexual hormones is determined with the utmost exactitude, and a corresponding Table of Sexual Days is worked out for you. After obtaining this you fill out an application, stating that on your Sexual Days you desire to avail yourself of such and

* This word has survived only in the form of a poetic metaphor—the chemical composition of this substance is unknown to us.

such a number (or such and such numbers) and receive the appropriate book of coupons (it is pink). And that's all there is to it.

Clearly, there are no longer any grounds whatsoever for envy; the denominator of the fraction of happiness is reduced to zero—the fraction is converted into magnificent infinity. And that which served the ancients as the source of countless and exceedingly silly tragedies we have converted to a harmonious, pleasantly useful organic function, much as we have done with sleep, physical labor, the intake of food, defecation and so forth. Hence you can perceive how the great force of logic cleanses everything it may come in contact with. O, if you, whom I do not know, would but come to know this divine force, would but follow it to the end!

. . . Odd: today, all the while that I was writing about the loftiest pinnacles mankind has achieved during its history, I was breathing the purest mountain air of thought—yet within me everything was still clouded over, covered with cobwebs, and crisscrossed with some four-pawed X or other. Or it may have been an image of my own paws, and all because they have been before my eyes for so long, those shaggy hands of mine. I don't like to speak of them and I have no great love for them—they are a vestige of a savage epoch. Is it possible that there really is within me————

I was about to cross all that out, since it is outside the scope of this entry. But then I decided that I would not cross it out. Let my entries, like the most delicate of seismographs, present the curve of even the most insignificant of cerebral waverings, for at times it is precisely such waverings that serve as a precursor of————

Well, now, *that* is an absurdity; it really should be crossed out: we have set all the elemental forces to flowing in their proper channels—catastrophes of any sort are utterly out of the question.

And now everything is perfectly clear to me: that odd feeling within me stems entirely from that same quadrangular situation of mine which I spoke of at the beginning. And the X is not within me (that is out of the question); I am simply afraid that an X of some sort may remain within you, my unknown readers. But I believe that you will not judge me too harshly. I believe you will realize that it is harder for me to write than it has been for any other author throughout the history of mankind: some authors wrote for their contemporaries, others for their descendants, but not one of them ever wrote for his ancestors—or for beings resembling his savage, remote ancestors.

SIXTH ENTRY: *An Accident. That Accursed "It's Clear." Twenty-four Hours.* I repeat: I consider it my duty to write without any secret reservations whatsoever. Therefore, no matter how deplorable it may be, I must remark at this point that the process of the induration, the crystallization of life is, apparently, still incomplete, even among us. There are still a few steps left to attain the ideal. The ideal (it is clear) exists where nothing any longer happens, whereas among us———— Wait, here is an example, if you like: I see in today's *Gazette of The One State* that in two days from now a Festival of Justice will be held on the Plaza of the Cube. Which means that again some number or other has disrupted the progress of the great Machine of State, that again something unforeseen, unforecalculated has happened.

And, besides that, something happened to me. True, it was during a Personal Hour—i.e., during a period specifically set aside for unforeseen circumstances—but, just the same————

About 16:00 (or 15:50, to be more precise) I was at home. Suddenly the telephone rang.

"D, Five Hundred and Three?" came a woman's voice.

"Yes."

"Are you free?"

"Yes."

"It's me—E, Three Hundred and Thirty. I'm flying over right now to pick you up and we'll go to the House of Antiquity. Is that all right with you?"

E-330. . . . This E- female number irritates me, repels me—almost frightens me. But precisely for these reasons I told her "Yes."

Five minutes later we were in an aero: the May sky was

blue majolica, and the buoyant sun was droning in our wake in a golden aero all its own, neither getting ahead of us nor falling behind. But there, ahead, glaring as whitely as a wall-eye, was a cloud—an incongruous cloud, as puffy as the cheeks of an antique cupidon—and that was disturbing, somehow. The windshield was down, the wind buffeted us, making one's lips dry—willy-nilly one kept running the tongue over them constantly—and constantly kept thinking of lips.

By now we could see turbidly green splotches in the distance—there, beyond the Wall. Next: the slight, involuntary swooning of the heart; down, down, down we went, as if swooping from a steep mountain—and we landed close to the House of Antiquity.

All of this quaint, fragile, sightless structure was enveloped with a glass shell—if not for that it would have collapsed long ago, of course. Standing at the glass door was a crone, her face all wrinkled—but especially so her mouth, which consisted solely of pleats and folds; the lips had become withdrawn by now, the mouth seemed grown over, somehow, and it seemed altogether unbelievable that she would break into speech—but, just the same, that was just what she did.

"Well, now, darlings—have you come for a look at my house?"—and her wrinkles beamed (i.e., they had probably arranged themselves in raylike formation, which had, precisely, created the impression of *beaming*).

"Yes, Grandma, I'm hankering for another look," E-330 told her.

The wrinkles still beamed: "Feel that sun, now—eh? Well, well—what are you up to this time? Ah, ah, you scamp—you scamp! I know, I know all about it! Well, so be it—you run along by yourselves; I'll be better off here, in the sun—"

Hmm. . . . Probably my companion was a frequent visitor here. There was something I wanted to shake off, but there was something else that prevented me from doing so: probably that same persistent optical image of that cloud against the blue majolica of the sky.

"I love her—I love that crone," E-330 said as we were going up a wide dark staircase.

"For what reason?"

"Oh, I don't know. For her mouth, perhaps. And, perhaps, for nothing at all. Just so."

I shrugged.

"I feel myself very much at fault," she continued, smiling ever so slightly—or, perhaps, not smiling at all. "It is clear that there should be no *just-so love*—that it should be *because-of love*. All the elemental forces should be—"

"It is clear—" I began, but immediately caught myself on that word *clear* and looked at E-330 furtively—had she noticed it or not? She was looking off somewhere in a downward direction; her eyes were lowered—like blinds. I recalled something: in the evening, about 22:00, as you walk along an avenue, you will see among the brightly illuminated, transparent cubicles some darkened ones, with their blinds lowered, and there, behind those blinds——— What was going on there, behind her blinds? Why had she rung me up today, and what was back of all this?

I opened a ponderous, creaking, opaque door—and we found ourselves in a somber, disordered interior (an *apartment,* they used to call it). With that same peculiar *royal* musical instrument, and the same motley splurge of colors and forms, as wild, unorganized, insane as the music of that remote time. A white plane above; walls of dark blue; ancient tomes, bound in red, green, orange; the yellow bronze of candelabra, of a statue of Buddha; furniture the lines of which were epileptically distorted, which could not be reconciled in any equations whatsoever.

I found it hard to endure this chaos, but my companion had, apparently, a stronger constitution.

"I find this one the most lovable"—and suddenly she seemed to bring herself up short—with a smile that was a bite, showing white sharp teeth. "That is, to be more exact, the most incongruous of all their *apartments.*"

"Or, to be still more exact, the most incongruous of all their *states,*" I corrected her. "Thousands of microscopic states, forever warring, as merciless as—"

"Well, yes—that is clear," said E-330, apparently with the utmost sincerity.

We passed through a room where there were children's

cribs (during that epoch children, too, were private property). Then came more rooms, the glimmering of mirrors, grim wardrobes, unbearably motley-hued divans, an enormous *fireplace,* a vast bed of mahogany. Our modern glass—splendid, transparent, eternal—was in evidence here only in the guise of pitiful, fragile, small squares set in the windows.

"And to think—here they loved *just so,* were consumed with fire, tormented themselves—" (Again, the lowered blinds of her eyes.) "What a senseless, extravagant expenditure of human energy—isn't that so?"

Her utterances came from within me, somehow; she was uttering my thoughts. But, throughout, that irritating X was lurking in her smile. There, behind those blinds something was going on within her—I don't know what it was, but it was exasperating me; I wanted to contradict her, to yell at her (yes, *yell,* precisely), yet I was compelled to agree with her: it was impossible not to agree.

At last we came to a stop before a mirror. At that moment all I saw were her eyes. I was struck by an idea: why, man is constructed just as primitively as these preposterous *apartments:* human heads are opaque, and the only windows into the interior—the eyes—are tiny. She surmised my thoughts, apparently—and turned around. "Well, here are my eyes. Well?" (This, of course, without uttering a word aloud.)

I was confronted by two eerily dark windows—and the life going on within them was so unknown, so alien. All I saw was a fire—some *fireplace* all her own, blazing—and some figures or other that resembled———

This was natural, of course: I had seen myself reflected in them. But what was unnatural and unlike me (evidently it was the depressing effect of the surroundings) was that I definitely felt fear, felt myself captured, imprisoned in this barbarian cage, felt myself caught up in the wild hurricane of the life of antiquity.

"Tell you what," said E-330. "Step out into the next room for a minute or so." Her voice was coming from there, from within, from behind the dark windows of her eyes, where the *fireplace* was blazing.

I went out, took a seat. From a small bracket on the wall

the snub-nosed, asymmetrical physiognomy of one of their ancient poets (Pushkin, I think it was) was smiling right in my face with a barely perceptible smile. Why did I sit there and submissively endure that smile, and what was all this for —why was I there, and whence the preposterous state I was in? That irritating, repellent woman, the strange game going on. . . .

From the other room came the click of a wardrobe door, the swish of silk; I restrained myself with difficulty from going there and———— I don't recall exactly: probably I wanted to deliver a whole string of exceedingly cutting remarks for her benefit. But at that point she had already emerged. She had on a black hat, a short, antiquated, glaringly yellow dress, black stockings. The dress was of light silk: I could clearly see that the stockings were very long, reaching considerably above her knees, while the neckline was low, revealing that shadow between her————

"Listen, it is clear you want to have a fling at being original, but can it be possible that you—"

"It is clear," E-330 cut me short, "that to be original means standing out from others. Consequently, to be original means violating uniformity. And what in the idiotic language of the ancients was called *being banal* means among us only the fulfillment of one's duty. Inasmuch as—"

"Yes, yes, yes—precisely!" I could not restrain myself. "And you oughtn't—you oughtn't—"

She approached the statuette of the snub-nosed poet and, lowering the blinds over the raging fire of her eyes—there, deep within her, behind those windows of hers—said something that was most reasonable, this time apparently in all sincerity (perhaps it was to mollify me): "Don't you find it astonishing that once upon a time people tolerated such fellows as that? And not merely tolerated them—they worshiped them. What a slavish spirit! Isn't that so?"

"It is clear . . . that is, I meant to say—" That accursed phrase of mine—*It is clear!*

"Well, yes, I understand. But then, in reality, these were sovereigns more powerful than the crowned ones of that time. Why weren't they isolated, exterminated? Among us—"

"Yes, among us—" I began—and then, suddenly, she broke into laughter. There, I simply *saw* that laughter, saw it with my eyes; I saw the pealing, steeply climbing curve of that laughter, a curve as stubbornly springy as the lash of a whip. I was all aquiver, I remember. There, if one could seize her and . . . I don't remember the rest of it by now. It was necessary to take some action—it did not matter what. I mechanically opened the lid of my golden badge and glanced at the watch inside: it was 16:50.

"Don't you think it's time to be leaving?" I suggested as politely as I could.

"But what if I should ask you to remain here with me?"

"Look, do you . . . do you realize what you're saying? I am obliged to be in the auditorium in ten minutes—"

"—And all numbers are obliged to take the prescribed courses in art and science—" E-330 said, and her voice sounded like mine. With that she yanked her blinds up, by raising her eyes to mine: through the dark windows I saw the fireplace blazing. "I know a certain physician in the Medical Bureau—he is registered in my name. And if I ask him he'll issue a certificate for you, stating that you were ill. Is that satisfactory?"

I understood. I understood, at last, what this whole game had been leading up to.

"So that's it, actually! But do you know that, like every conscientious number, I am really obliged to go immediately to the Bureau of Guardians and—"

"Come, not really"—again that sharp-pointed smile-bite. "I feel frightfully curious—will you go to the Guardians or not?"

"Are you staying here?"—and I put my hand on the doorknob. The knob was of metal—and my voice sounded to my ears as hard and metallic as that doorknob.

"Just a moment. May I?" She walked over to a telephone, called up some number (I was so agitated that I failed to make a note of it, but it was a male one) and spoke loudly: "I'll be waiting for you at the House of Antiquity. Yes, yes—alone!"

I felt how cold the brass doorknob was as I turned it: "Will you let me take the aero?"

"Oh, yes, of course! Please do."

There, at the gate, like a plant in the sunshine, the old woman was dozing. I again found it astonishing when her mouth, overgrown so impenetrably, opened and she began to speak: "And your lady—well, now, is she staying behind by herself?"

"She's by herself."

The crone's mouth became grown over anew. She shook her head. Evidently even her weakening brain had grasped all the preposterousness and riskiness of that woman's behavior.

On the dot of 17:00 I was at the lecture. And at that point I for some reason suddenly realized that I had told the crone something that was not exactly true: E-330 was not there all by herself now. Perhaps it was precisely this fact—my having involuntarily deceived the crone—which was tormenting me and distracting me from listening to the lecture. Yes, she was not there all by herself: that was the rub.

After 21:30 I had a free hour; I could have gone to the Bureau of Guardians that very day and made my report. However, I had become exceedingly tired after that stupid incident. And besides, the legal time limit for such a report was two days: there was still a margin of 24 hours.

SEVENTH ENTRY: *An Eyelash.* Night. Green, orange, blue;
Taylor. Henbane and Lilies-of- the red royal instrument;
the-Valley. a yellow—orange-yellow—
dress. Then—a brass Buddha; suddenly he raised his brass eyelids—and, out of Buddha, sap began to flow. And sap was flowing from the yellow dress also; and gouts of sap were trickling over the mirror as well, and the vast bed of mahogany was oozing sap, and the children's cribs were doing likewise, and right then I myself felt the flow—and there was a certain lethally delectable horror about it all————

I awoke: diffused bluish light, the glass of the walls glimmering, the sight of the glass chairs, the glass table. All this calmed me; my heart stopped pounding. The sap, Buddha—what absurdity! I am unwell—that is clear. I have never had dreams before. Having dreams, they say, was a most ordinary and normal thing among the ancients. Well, if it comes to that, all their life was just such another dreadful merry-go-round—green, orange, Buddha, sap. We, however, know that having dreams is a serious psychic disturbance. And I do know this: up to now my brain was a chronometrically tested, sparkling mechanism, without a single speck of dust, whereas now . . . Yes, now that is precisely the trouble: I feel some foreign body or other there, in my brain, just as you feel a very fine eyelash that has lodged in your eye. You feel entirely yourself, but as for that eye with the eyelash in it—that's something you can't forget, not even for a second.

From the head of my bed came the brisk, crystal-clear ringing of a small bell: 7:00, time to get up. To the right and left, through the walls of glass, I seem to be seeing myself, my room, my clothes, my movements—but repeated a thousand times over. This is invigorating: one sees oneself as one enormous, mighty whole. And such precise beauty: not one superfluous gesture, deviation, turn.

Yes, this Taylor was, beyond a doubt, the greatest genius the ancients had. True, he had not attained the final concept of extending his method until it took in the entire lifespan, every step, and both night and day—he had not been able to integrate his system from the first hour to the twenty-fourth. But just the same, how could the ancients have written whole libraries about some Kant or other, and yet have barely noticed Taylor, the prophet who had been able to look ten centuries ahead?

Breakfast is over. The Hymn of The One State has been sung with one accord. With one accord, four abreast, the numbers headed for the elevators. The motors hummed barely audibly—and down, down, down we went, swiftly, with that slight sinking of the heart. . . . And at this point, suddenly, for some reason or other, came a repetition of that preposterous dream—or some indeterminate function of that dream. Oh, yes—it was the same yesterday, on the aero—that going down. However, all that is over and done with. Full stop. And it is a very good thing that I had been so resolute and harsh with her.

The subway car was bearing me headlong to the dock

where the exquisite body of the *Integral*, as yet motionless, as yet unanimated by fire, was sparkling under the sun. With eyes closed I dreamed in formulae: I once more calculated the initial velocity that would be needed to pluck the *Integral* loose from the earth. With every atom of a second the mass of the *Integral* changed, since there was an expenditure of the explosive fuel. The resultant equation was extremely complex, with transcendental magnitudes.

Here, in my bedrock universe of figures, I felt, as in a dream, that someone had taken a seat beside me and, after a slight jolt, had uttered an apology. I opened my eyes a little and at first (by association with the *Integral*) saw some object in impetuous flight into space; it was a head, and it was in flight because it had pink wing-ears sticking out at its sides. And, next, the curve of the nape of the neck, like an overhang, the rounded back, the double curve, the letter *S*. . . . And through the glass walls of my algebraic universe that intrusive eyelash penetrated—there was something, something unpleasant, which I had to attend to this day————

"Not at all, please—not at all," I smiled to my neighbor, and bowed. S-4711: I saw the glitter of his number on his badge: it became understandable why, from the very first moment, I had associated him with the letter *S*: it had been a visual impression which had not registered on my consciousness. Just then his eyes sparked: two sharply pointed little gimlets, revolving rapidly, were boring in, deeper and deeper, and now, at any moment would bore their way to the very bottom, would see that which I dared not confess even to my own self————

Suddenly that eyelash became absolutely clear to me: he was one of *them*, one of the Guardians, and it would be simplest of all to tell him everything right now, without putting the matter off.

"You see, I was at the House of Antiquity yesterday"—my voice sounded strange, flatted, uninflected; I attempted to clear my throat by coughing.

"Why, that's fine. It should be productive of material for very instructive conclusions."

"Yes, but—you understand, I wasn't alone; I was accompanying E, Three Hundred and Thirty, and then—"

"E, Three Hundred and Thirty? I am glad for your sake. A most interesting, talented woman. She has many admirers."

Why, he too—during that promenade . . . and perhaps he may actually be registered in her name? No, mustn't say anything to him about that. It's not to be thought of—that is clear.

"Yes, yes! To be sure, to be sure! Quite"—my smile was becoming broader and broader, more and more inane; that smile stripped me, made me foolish. The little gimlets had reached to the very bottom within me; then, revolving rapidly, had bored in reverse, back into his eyes; S- smiled ambiguously, nodded to me, slipped off toward the exit.

I hid behind my newspaper (it seemed to me that everybody was looking at me)—and soon forgot about the eyelash, about the little gimlets, about everything—that's how agitated I was by what I had read: "According to reliable information, new traces have been revealed of a still elusive organization which has set for itself the goal of liberation from the beneficient yoke of The State."

Liberation? It's amazing how very tenacious of life criminal instincts are in humankind! I use the word *criminal* deliberately. Liberty and crime are just as indissolubly bound together as . . . well, as the motion of an aero and its speed: let the speed of an aero = O, and the aero does not move; let the liberty of man = O, and man does not commit crimes. That is clear. The only means of delivering man from crimes is to deliver him from liberty. And yet, hardly have we been delivered from this (on a cosmic scale *hardly* is applicable to centuries, of course), than suddenly certain pitiful half-wits——

No, I can't understand: why I did not go yesterday, without putting the matter off, to the Bureau of Guardians. I'm going there today after 16:00, without fail.

I was out by 16:10—and, looking toward the corner, immediately caught sight of O-, all in a rosy rapture over our encounter. "There, she has a simple, rounded mind. This meeting is opportune: she will understand me and lend me her support." On the other hand, no—I needed no support; I was firm in my resolve.

The pipes of the Musical Tower were harmoniously thundering The March—still the same diurnal March. What inexplicable enchantment there was in its diurnalness, its repetitiveness, its mirrorousness!

"Out for a stroll?" O- seized my hand. Her round blue eyes were wide open—blue windows giving access within— and I penetrated within without catching against anything, and found nothing therein—i.e., nothing extraneous, unnecessary.

"No, I'm not out for a stroll. I have to go to—" I told her my destination. And, to my amazement, I saw the rosy circle of her mouth fold itself into a rosy crescent with its horns pointing down—as if she had tasted something sour. This made me explode.

"You female numbers are incurably corroded by prejudices, it would seem. You are utterly incapable of abstract thought. Excuse my saying so, but that's simply obtuseness."

"You're on your way to the spies—ugh! But I had to go to the Botanical Museum and get a sprig of lilies-of-the-valley for you—"

"Why 'But I'? Why this 'But'? Spoken just like a woman!" I snatched the sprig away from her—angrily, I confess. "Well, here they are, your lilies-of-the-valley—right? Here, take a sniff—they have a lovely smell, haven't they? Do use some logic, then—no matter how little. Lilies-of-the-valley do have a lovely smell—granted. But then, you cannot say about a smell, about the very concept of *smell*, that it is either lovely or nasty. You simp-ly can-not—right? There is the smell of lilies-of-the-valley—and there is the abominable smell of henbane: each one is a smell. An ancient state had its spies— and so do we have spies—yes, spies. I have no fear of words. But then, it is clear—there the spies were henbane—here they are lilies-of-the-valley. Yes, lilies-of-the-valley—precisely!"

The rosy crescent was quivering. As I write this I realize that I was merely imagining it, but at the time I felt certain she would break into laughter. And so I began shouting still

more loudly: "Yes, lilies-of-the-valley! And there's nothing
funny about it—nothing funny at all!"

The rounded, smooth globes of heads were floating past—
and looking back. O- took my hand tenderly:

"You're somehow odd today—aren't you feeling well?"

My dream—the yellow hue—Buddha. . . . At once it became clear to me that I must go to the Medical Bureau.

"Why, yes, that's so—I don't feel well," I said with joy
(there is an utterly inexplicable contradiction here: there
wasn't a thing to rejoice about).

"Then you must get to a doctor at once. Surely you understand—you're under an obligation to be well; it's ridiculous
to have to prove that to you."

"Why, O- darling, why, you're right, of course. Absolutely
right!"

I did not go to the Bureau of Guardians; there was no help
for it—I had to visit the Medical Bureau; there I was detained until 17:00. And in the evening (however, that did
not matter: the other Bureau was closed by that time)—in
the evening O- came to see me. The blinds were not lowered.
We diverted ourselves by solving the problems in an ancient
textbook of mathematics: this sort of thing soothes and clari-
fies one's mind very much. O-90 was sitting over her exercise
book with her head inclined toward her left shoulder and was
trying so hard that she had thrust her left cheek out with
her tongue. This was so childlike, so charming. And everything within me was so fine, precise, simple. . . .

She left. I was alone. I took a couple of deep breaths (this
is very beneficial before going to sleep). And at that point I
caught an unexpected smell—and one that brought something
very unpleasant to mind. . . . It did not take me long to find
its source: the sprig of lilies-of-the-valley had been hidden in
my bed. At once everything rose up in a whirlwind—everything that had been at the bottom swirled up. No, it had been
simply tactless on her part to leave that sprig of lilies-of-the-
valley there like a foundling. Well, yes—I had not gone to
the Guardians, true enough. But then, I couldn't be blamed
because I wasn't feeling well, could I?

EIGHTH ENTRY: *An Irrational*   This happened so long ago,
Root. A Triangle.   during my years at school,
when this $\sqrt{-1}$ befell me. Everything is so clear, so deeply
engraved in my memory: a sphero-hall flooded with light,
hundreds of rounded little-boy heads—and Plyappa, our
mathematical instructor. We had nicknamed him Plyappa: he
was considerably second-hand by that time, with all his bolts
sprung, and when the monitor put the plug in his back the
first thing that always issued from the loudspeaker was *plya-
plya-plya-tshhh,* and the lesson would come only after that.
One day Plyappa told us about irrational numbers—and, I
remember, I cried, pounding my desk with my fists and
wailing: "I don't want this square root of minus one! Take
this square root of minus one out of me!" This irrational
root had become ingrown as something alien, outlandish,
frightful; it was devouring me; it could not be rationalized,
could not be rendered harmless, inasmuch as it was outside
any ratio.

And now there was this $\sqrt{-1}$ all over again. I have looked
over my entries, and it is clear to me that I was being foxy
with myself, that I was lying to myself—anything not to perceive that $\sqrt{-1}$. It was all bosh about my being sick and so
on: I could have gone to the Guardians; I know that only
last week I would have gone, without giving the matter a
second thought. Well, why not now? Why?

Take even today, for instance. Today, exactly at 16:10, I
was standing before a glittering glass wall. Overhead was the
golden, solar, pure glow of the letters on the sign of the
Bureau of Guardians. Deep within one could see through the
blocks of glass a long queue of bluish unifs. Their faces had
the warm glow of lampads in an ancient church: they had
come to perform a great deed—they had come to commit to
the altar of The One State those they loved, their friends,
themselves. As for me, I was drawn to them, to being with
them. And I could not stir: my feet were fused deeply into
the glass of the pavement; I stood there, dully staring, unable to move from the spot.

"Hey there, mathematician—lost in daydreams?"

I was startled. Dark eyes, lacquered with laughter, were

contemplating me; the lips were thick, Negroid. It was R-13, the poet, an old friend of mine, and the roseate O- was with him. I faced them angrily (I think that if they had not disturbed me I would in the very end have torn that $\sqrt{-1}$ out of me, flesh and all; I would have entered the Bureau).

"It wasn't daydreams I was lost in," I retorted quite brusquely, "but I was lost in admiration, if you like."

"Oh, certainly, certainly. You oughtn't to be a mathematician, dear fellow, but a poet. Yes, a poet! Really, now, come over to our side—join the Poets, eh? I'll arrange everything in no time at all, if you like—eh?"

R-13 splutters when he talks; the words simply spurt out of him, his lips become sprinklers; every *P* is a fountain—*poets* became one also.

"I have served knowledge and will continue to serve it," I frowned. I am not fond of jokes and do not understand them —yet R-13 has the bad habit of joking.

"Oh, come, now—knowledge! Your knowledge is nothing but cowardice. What's the use of arguing—that's a fact. You simply want to fence in, to wall in the infinite—but when it comes to taking a peek behind that wall you're scared. Yes! And if you should peek out you would have to close your eyes—yes, sir!"

"Walls are the basis of everything that's human—" I began. R- sprayed like a fountain; O- was laughing rosily and roundly. I gave up—let them laugh; it didn't matter. I had no time for that; I had to find something that would take the taste of that accursed $\sqrt{-1}$ out of my mouth, that would smother it.

"Tell you what," I suggested, "come over to my place; let's sit awhile and solve some pretty mathematical problems." I recalled the quiet hour I had spent with O- yesterday— perhaps today's would turn out as well.

O- looked at R-; then, clearly, roundly, she looked at me; her cheeks colored, ever so faintly, taking on the tender, agitating hue of our coupons.

"But today I . . . my coupon calls for him today," she nodded in R-'s direction, "but tonight he's busy. So then—"

"Well, now, even half an hour will suffice for the two of

us," the moist lacquered lips uttered good-naturedly and smackingly. "Am I right, O-? As for your pretty little problems, I have no overwhelming love for them. Let's simply go over to my place and sit awhile."

I had an uncanny feeling about being left all alone with my own self—or, more correctly, with this new self of mine, a strange self who only through an odd coincidence had the same number—D-503—as I. And I went along with R- to his place. True, he isn't accurate, nor rhythmical; he has some sort of inside-out, amusing logic, but just the same we are friends. It wasn't for nothing that three years before both of us had chosen this darling, rosy O-. This has formed stronger bonds between us than those of the years we had spent in school together.

We were shortly in R-'s room. Everything there was, apparently, the same as in mine: The Tables of Hourly Commandments, the glass of the chairs, the table, the wardrobe, the bed. But R- had hardly set foot in the room than he moved one chair, then another—the planes became displaced, everything departed from the accepted model, became non-Euclidean. R- is still the same—still the same. In the Taylor and mathematical courses he had always been at the tail end of his classes.

We reminisced about old Plyappa—how we urchins used to paste little notes of thanks all over his glass legs (we were very fond of Plyappa. We recalled, too, our Preceptor of Laws.* Our Preceptor of Laws was thunderous of voice—extraordinarily so; a veritable gale issued from his loudspeaker, while we children bawled the texts after him at the top of our voices. And we also recalled how that desperado, R-13, had one day rammed a lot of chewed paper down his amplifier: there wasn't a text without an explosion of spitballs. Of course, R- had been punished; what he had done had been nasty, of course, but just then we were laughing heartily—all three members of our triangle—for I must confess that I was laughing right along with R- and O-.

* Of course, I am not speaking here of a theologian and the Laws of God of the ancients, but about the Laws of The One State.

"But what if he had been one of those live instructors, such as the ancients used to have, eh? That would have been something—" the *B* sprayed like a fountain from the thick, smacking lips.

The sun came through the ceiling, through the walls; the sun was above, at the sides; it was reflected below us. O- was on R-13's lap, and the sun, in minute drops, was in her blue eyes. I had warmed up, somehow, had relaxed; $\sqrt{-1}$ had been smothered, was no longer stirring.

"Well, and how is your *Integral?* We'll be taking off soon, now, to enlighten the dwellers on the planets—eh? Well, you'd better speed things up—better speed them up, or else we poets will scribble so much stuff for you that even your *Integral* won't be able to get the load up into the air. We're at it from eight to eleven, every day—" R- tossed his head and scratched the nape of his neck—the nape of his neck looks like some kind of a small, square valise tied on behind (at this point I recalled an antique print, *In the Carriage*).

"Ah, so you too are writing for the *Integral?*" I became animated. "Well, suppose you tell me what you write about? There, take even today, for example?"

"Today I didn't write about anything. I had other things to keep me busy"—the *B* sprayed me right in the face.

"What other things?"

"Questions, questions!" R-13 made a wry face. "Well, if you must know, it was a death sentence. I was poetizing a death sentence. Passed on a certain idiot—one of us poets, no less. For two years he had sat alongside me; nothing wrong with him that you could see. And suddenly, out of a clear sky: 'I am a genius,' says he, 'and a genius is above the law.' My, and the things he popped out with! Well, what's the use of talking—" and he sighed with regret. The thick lips drooped; the lacquer had become eroded from his eyes. R-13 sprang up from his seat, turned around, began staring at some point through the wall. I was looking at the tightly locked little valise at the nape of his neck and pondering: What was he rummaging for now, in that little valise of his?

There was a minute of awkward, asymmetrical silence. It

was not clear to me just what was wrong, but something was.

"Fortunately, the antediluvian times of all those Shakespeares and Dostoevskys—or whatever they called them—are over," I said in a purposely loud voice.

R- turned around to face me. Words spattered, lashed out of him as before, but it appeared to me that there was no longer any lacquer of gaiety in his eyes.

"Yes, my most beloved mathematician—fortunately, fortunately, fortunately! We are the most fortunate arithmetical mean. How do you fellows put it—the integration from zero to infinity, from the cretin to Shakespeare. . . . So!"

I don't know why (apparently this was altogether inapropos) but there came to my mind that other one, the way she had spoken—some thread of the finest sort was extending itself between her and R-. (What sort of thread?) $\sqrt{-1}$ was again coiling itself. I opened the front of my badge: it was 16:25. They had 45 minutes left to avail themselves of that pink coupon.

"Well, time I was going." And with that I kissed O-, shook hands with R- and headed for the elevator.

After I had already crossed the main avenue I turned around: here and there in the enormous, sun-shot massif of glass which constituted the building there were gray-blue cells formed by the lowered blinds: cells of rhythmic, Taylorized happiness. On the seventh floor my eyes located the cell of R-13. He had already let down the blinds.

Darling O- . . . Dear R- . . . There is a certain something about him as well (I don't know why this *as well* has cropped up, but let the words come as they may)—there is a certain something about him as well which is not altogether clear to me. But just the same he, O- and I—we are a triangle; even if, admittedly, it is but an isosceles triangle, it is a triangle just the same. We, to speak in the language of our ancestors (perhaps, my planetary readers, that language is more comprehensible to you)—we form a family. And at times it is so pleasant to rest, if for but a little while, to isolate oneself, in a simple, sturdy triangle from everything which——————

A triumphant, bright day. On such a day one forgets one's failings, shortcomings, illnesses—and everything is imperturbably crystalline, eternal, like this new glass material of ours.

The Plaza of the Cube. Sixty-six gigantean concentric circles: the rostra, these. And sixty-six tiers of faces serene as lamps, of eyes reflecting the radiance of the heavens—or, it may be, the radiance of The One State. Flowers crimson as blood: the lips of women. Lovely garlands of children's faces —in the front tiers, closest to the scene of action. Intensified, austere, Gothic silence.

To judge by the descriptions which have come down to us, some emotion similar to this must have been experienced by the ancients during their *Divine Services.* They, however, held their services for their incongruous, unknown God, whereas our services are for a congruous God, known in the most exact manner; their God granted them naught but eternal, excruciating seekings, their God could think of nothing more clever than offering Himself as a sacrifice for goodness knows what reason, whereas the sacrifice we offer to our God, The One State, is a serene, thoroughly pondered, rational one. Yes, it was a solemn liturgy we chanted for The One State, a recollection of the crucial days and years of the Two Hundred Years' War, a majestic festival of the triumph of all over one, of the sum over the unit.

There: one unit was standing on the steps of the sun-swollen Cube. A white face (well, not actually white, but colorless by now), a glassy face, with glassy lips. And there were only his eyes—dark, sucking, gulping holes; these only, and that eldritch peace from which he was at only a few minutes' remove. The golden badge with this unit's number had already been taken from him. His hands were bound with a purple ribbon (a custom from antiquity: the explanation is, apparently, that in the ancient times, when such things were carried out not in the name of The One State, those condemned naturally felt they had the right to resist, and consequently had their hands fettered with chains as a rule).

And up there, on the Cube, near the Machine, was the figure, immobile, as if of metal, of Him whom we style The Benefactor. From below, where I sat, one could not make out His face: all one could see was that His face was confined within austere, majestic, rectangular lineaments. But then, His hands . . . As it occasionally happens in taking photographs, the hands, if they are too near the camera, in the very foreground, will come out enormous; they rivet your attention, they overshadow all else. Those heavy hands of His, as yet resting quietly on His knees—it was clear that they were of stone, and that the knees could barely sustain their weight.

And suddenly one of those enormous hands rose slowly— a slow, cast-iron gesture—and, coming down from the rostra, in obedience to the uplifted hand, a number approached the Cube. This was one of the State Poets to whom had fallen the great fortune of crowning the Festival with his verse. And iambics, divine and brazen, thundered forth over the rostra, telling of that madman with the glassy eyes, standing there on the steps and awaiting the logical consequence of his mad deeds.

. . . A conflagration. In iambics houses swayed, sent up showers of spattering liquid gold, came crashing down. Verdant trees writhed, bleeding sap, drop by drop, until they were reduced to nothing but blackened cruciform skeletons. But at this point Prometheus (by which we were meant, of course) came on the scene:

> And harnessed fire to steel machine,
> And forged on Chaos Chains of Law!

Everything was new, of steel: a steel sun, steel trees, steel men and women. Unexpectedly, some madman "chains loosed and fire freed"—and, once more, everything was perishing. . . . Unfortunately, I have a poor memory when it comes to verse, but I do remember one thing: more instructive and beautiful images could not have been chosen.

Again that slow, ponderous gesture, and another poet appeared on the steps of the Cube. I actually rose from my seat—could it be possible? But no, those thick Negroid lips were his; it was he! Why hadn't he said anything beforehand about his having been entrusted with something so lofty? His lips were quivering, livid. I could understand, this being before the face of The Benefactor, before the faces of the whole host of the Guardians; but still, to be so agitated. . . .

Chorees—abrupt, swift, falling like a keen ax. About an unheard-of crime, about sacrilegious verses in which The Benefactor was styled as——— No, I cannot bring myself to repeat the names.

R-13, all pale, without looking at anyone (I hardly expected such diffidence on his part), descended the steps, resumed his seat. For the very least differential of a second I caught a fleeting glimpse of someone's face—an acute black triangle—by his side, but immediately everything was erased: my eyes—thousands of eyes—were directed there, above, toward the Machine. There, for the third time, came that cast-iron gesture of a hand that was not mortal. And, swayed by an imperceptible wind, the criminal was walking, slowly; one step, another—and then came the stride that was the last he was to take in his life, and his face was toward the sky, his head thrown back: he was lying on his last couch.

Ponderous, stony, like fate, The Benefactor walked around the Machine, placed His enormous hand on a lever. Not a rustle, not a breath: all eyes were upon that hand. What a fiery, breathtaking whirlwind of emotion it must be to know that one is a weapon, that one is a force equivalent to hundreds of thousands of volts! How great a destiny!

An immeasurable second. The hand descended, switching on the current. The flash of the unbearably cutting blade of a ray; a barely audible crackling, like a tremor, within the tubes of the Machine. A spread-eagled body, all in an ethereal, glowing haze—and now, before one's eyes, it was melting, melting, dissolving with horrifying rapidity. And then— nothing: merely a puddle of chemically pure water that, only a moment before had been riotously and redly pulsing within a heart. . . .

All this was simple, all this was known to every one of us: yes, disassociation of matter; yes, the fission of the atoms in the human body. Yet, nonetheless, this was like a miracle each time; this was like a token of the more than mortal might of The Benefactor.

Up there, before His face, were the enkindled faces of half a score of female numbers, lips half open from excitement, flowers swaying in the wind.* In observance of an old custom half a score of women were adorning with flowers the unif of The Benefactor, which had not yet dried from the spattering it had received. With the majestic tread of a hierophant He slowly descended, slowly passed between the rostra—and His progress was marked by the upraised feminine arms that looked like tender white branches and the unimillioned tempest of our huzzahs. Then came much the same huzzahs, hailing the host of Guardians, who were invisibly present right there, in our ranks. Who knows: perhaps it was precisely these Guardians whom the fantasy of the ancient man foresaw when it created its gently awesome *archangels,* assigned to guard each mortal from the day of his birth.

Yes, there was about all of this celebration a certain something derived from the ancient religions, something purifying, like a thunderstorm or a tempest. You whom it may befall to read this—are such moments familiar to you? I feel pity for you if you know them not.

TENTH ENTRY: *A Letter. A Membrane. My Shaggy I.* Yesterday was for me precisely that sort of paper which chemists use to filter their solutions: all suspended particles, all extraneous elements remain on this paper. And so, this morning I went downstairs purified, distilled, pellucid.

Down in the vestibule the controller was seated at her small desk, consulting the clock as she recorded the comings and goings of the numbers. Her name is U- . . . however, I'd

* From the Botanical Museum, of course. I, personally, do not see anything beautiful about flowers—just as I do not see anything beautiful about everything which belongs to the wild world long since exiled beyond the Green Wall. Only that is beautiful which is rational and utilitarian: machines, boots, formulae, food, etc.

rather not give her number, for fear of writing something un-complimentary about her. Although, as a matter of fact, she is a most respectable woman of mature years. The only thing I don't like about her is that her cheeks sag somewhat—they look like the gills of a fish (no great matter, one might think).

Her pen scratched as she wrote; I saw myself—*D-503*—on the page and, right alongside, an ink blot. I was just about to call her attention to this when she suddenly raised her head and let an inky little bit of a smile sink into me: "Why, here's a letter. Yes. You'll get it, my dear—yes, yes, you'll get it."

I knew that the letter, which she had already read, had yet to go through the Bureau of Guardians (I consider it super-fluous to explain this normal procedure) and that it would be in my hands not later than 12:00. But I was confused by that same bit of a smile, the drop of ink had muddied the transparent-solution mood I had been in. And that to such an extent that later, at the building site of the *Integral*, I could not concentrate—and at one point actually made an error in my calculations, a thing which had never yet hap-pened to me.

At 12:00, again the pinkish-brown fish gills, again that bit of a smile, and I was holding the letter at last. I did not read it on the spot (I don't know why), but thrust it in my pocket and lost no time in getting to my room. I opened it, ran my eyes over it and—plumped down. It was an official notifica-tion that number E-330 had had me registered in her name, and that I would have to come to her at 21:00 that day. Her address was subjoined.

Never! Not after all that had happened, after I had so unequivocally shown what my attitude toward her was. In addition to that, she did not even know whether or not I had gone to the Bureau of Guardians, since there was no source from which she could have learned that I had been ailing—well, now, that I had been unable to make it, as a general thing. Yet, despite all this———

My head was in a whirl; there was a dynamo humming within it. Buddha . . . yellow; lilies-of-the-valley . . . a rosy crescent. Yes, and there was something else—there was also something else: O- had wanted to drop in on me today. Should I show her this notification concerning E-330? I don't know. . . . She wouldn't believe me (yes, really, how could she believe?) that I had had nothing to do with it, that I was perfectly——— And I do know: there will be a difficult, preposterous, absolutely illogical discussion. No, anything but that. Let the whole thing be solved mechanically; I will simply send her a copy of the notification.

I was hastily shoving the notification in my pocket—and I suddenly caught a glimpse of that horrible, simian hand of mine. I recalled how she—E-—had during that walk taken my hand and looked at it. Could it be possible that she was actually———

20:45, at last. A white night. Everything is greenish-glassy. But this is some sort of different, fragile glass; not our sort, not the real glass—this is a thin glass shell, and under that shell everything is swirling, rushing, humming. And I would not be surprised if right now the cupolas of the auditoria were to rise in rounded, slowly moving billows of smoke, and if the elderly moon were to smile inkily—like that female number at her small desk this morning—and if all the blinds in all the houses were to be lowered simultaneously, and if behind those curtains———

A strange sensation: I felt that my ribs were iron rods of some sort and that they interfered—absolutely interfered— with the heart; it was cramped, it hadn't space enough. I was standing at a glass door with *E-330* lettered in gold. E- was at a small table with her back to me, writing something. I stepped in.

"Here you are," I extended my pink ticket to her. "I received the notification today and have come."

"How prompt you are! Just a minute—may I? Sit down; I have only to finish this."

She let her eyes drop to the letter again—and what was going on there, within her, behind the blinds lowered over her eyes? What would she say—what was I to do in a second or so? How was one to find this out, how calculate it, when all of her came from there, from the wild, ancient land of dreams?

I was watching her in silence. My ribs were rods of iron;
I was cramped. . . . When she speaks her face is like a
rushing glittering wheel: there is no distinguishing the individual spokes. But right now the wheel was not in motion.
And I perceived a strange combination: dark eyebrows,
quirked high at the temples: an acute triangle of mockery;
and two deep, small wrinkles from the nose to the corners of
the mouth: another triangle, coming to an apex. And these
two triangles somehow contradicted each other, placing upon
the entire face that disagreeable, irritating cruciform *X:* it
was a crossed-out face.

The wheel began to turn; the spokes blended together:
"There, you didn't go to the Bureau of Guardians after all,
did you?"

"I was . . . I couldn't go—I was unwell."

"Yes. Well, that's just what I thought: something must
have kept you back—it doesn't matter just what [sharp teeth
—smile]. But then, you are in my hands now. You remember:
'Any number failing to make a report to the Bureau within
forty-eight hours is considered—' "

My heart pounded so hard that the rods of iron buckled.
Like a little boy—foolishly, like a little boy—I had fallen
into a trap; foolishly, I wasn't saying anything. I felt myself
all entangled—I couldn't stir hand or foot.

She stood up, stretching lazily. She pressed a button: with
a slight rattle the blinds fell on all sides. I was cut off from
the world—all alone with her.

E- was somewhere there, back of me, near a closet. Her
unif was rustling, falling; I was listening—I was all ears.
And something came to mind—no, something glimmered
there for one hundredth part of a second. . . .

I recently had occasion to calculate the curvature of a new
type of street membrane (these membranes, elegantly camou-
flaged, are now placed along all the avenues and record for
the Bureau of Guardians all conversations carried on out
of doors). And I remember that the concave, pink, quivering
tympanum was a strange creature consisting of but one organ:
an ear. Just then I was such a membrane.

There: a snap-button clicked at her collar—at her breast—

at a still lower point. The fiberglas silk swished over shoulders, over knees—along the floor. I heard—and that was still clearer than seeing it—one foot and then the other stepping out of the heap of grayish-blue silk.

The tensely stretched membrane quivered and recorded the stillness. No, not the stillness but the blows, abrupt, with endless pauses, of a sledge hammer against iron rods. And I heard—I *saw* how, standing behind me, she paused to think for a second. That was the sound of the closet doors; that other sound was the slamming of some chest lid—and, again, silk, silk. . . .

"Now, if you please—"

I turned about. She was in a saffron-yellow dress of an ancient cut. This was a thousandfold more wicked than if she had had absolutely nothing on. Two sharp points, glowing roseately through the thin tissue: two embers smoldering among ashes. Two tenderly rounded knees————

She was seated in a rather squat armchair; on a small square table before her stood a flagon of some poisonously green stuff and two diminutive stemmed glasses. In the corner of her mouth was the slenderest of paper tubes, sending up the smoke of that combustible substance the ancients used (I have now forgotten what they called it).

The membrane was still vibrating. The sledge hammer was pounding away there, within me, against the red-hot rods of iron. I distinctly heard every blow and . . . and what if she were hearing it too? However, she kept on sending up the smoke, glancing at me calmly from time to time, and negligently flicked the ashes from the tube onto my pink coupon.

"Look," I asked, with as much *sang-froid* as I could summon, "if that's the case, why did you have me registered in your name? And why did you compel me to come here?"

Apparently she had not even heard me. She poured some of the liquid in the flagon into one of the tiny glasses, sipped some off.

"An exquisite liqueur. Care for some?"

It was only then that I grasped what the green stuff was: alcohol. I saw in a flash of lightning the things that had taken place yesterday: the stony hand of The Benefactor; the un-

bearably bright blade of the electric ray; but above all, up
there on the Cube—that fellow with his head thrown back,
his spread-eagled body. I shuddered.

"Listen," I said, "you surely must know that The One
State is merciless to all who poison themselves with nicotine
and, especially, with alcohol—"

The dark eyebrows quirked high toward the temples: the
acute triangle of mockery: " 'The rapid destruction of a few
is more rational than giving to the many the opportunity of
working their own ruin'—then there's the matter of degenera-
tion, and so on. All that is true, to the point of indecency.
Yes—indecency! Why, if you were to let a little gang of such
baldheaded, mother-naked truths out into the street! No, just
imagine—well, now, take even that most immutable admirer
of mine—oh, yes, you know him. . . . Just imagine that he
has thrown off him all this deception of clothes and appeared
in public in his true shape. . . . Oh, my!"

She was laughing. But I could clearly see her sorrowful
lower triangle: the two deep creases from the corners of her
mouth to the nose. And somehow, because of these creases,
it became clear to me: that double-curved, stoop-shouldered,
wing-eared fellow had embraced her—the way she was now.
He!

However, right now I am trying to convey my (abnormal)
sensations of that time. Now, as I am writing this, I am perfectly aware that that is just how things should be and that
he, as every other honest number, has an equal right to the
joys of life, and it would be unjust to——— Well, yes, that
is clear.

E- kept laughing in a very strange way and for a very long
time. Then she looked at me—into me—intently: "But the
main thing is that I feel perfectly safe with you. You are such
a darling fellow—oh, I feel certain of that—that you won't
even think of going to the Bureau and reporting that I, now,
am drinking liqueur, that I am smoking. You will be unwell,
or you will be busy, or I don't know what else will be the
matter with you. More than that: I feel certain that right now
you will drink this enchanting poison with me—"

What a brazen, derisive tone! I definitely felt that right

then I was again hating her. However, why this *right then?*
I had hated her all the while.

She poured into her mouth the entire contents of the tiny
glass of green poison, stood up and, shimmering roseately
through the thin saffron tissue, took a few steps, halting
behind my chair. Suddenly her arm was about my neck, her
lips plunged into my lips—no, somewhere still deeper, still
more frighteningly. . . . I swear that this was utterly unexpected by me and, perhaps, merely because——— For I
could not possibly—right now I comprehend it with the
utmost clarity—I could not possibly have desired of my own
will what happened next.

Lips unbearably sweet (I suppose this was the taste of the
liqueur)—and then a swallow of searing poison was poured
into me—and another—and still another. . . . I took off
from the earth and, as an independent planet, rushed down,
down, following an uncharted orbit. . . .

What followed I can describe only approximately, only by
means of more or less close analogies.

The idea had never come into my head before—but then
the thing is precisely thus: we who live on this earth are
constantly walking over a burbling, blood-red sea of fire hidden there, deep within the maw of the earth. But we never
think of that. But now suppose that this thin shell under our
feet were suddenly to turn to glass, that we were suddenly to
see—

I had turned to glass. I saw into myself, deep within me.
There were two *I*'s. One *I* was my former self, D-503, the
number D-503, while the other . . . Up to now he had
merely shoved his shaggy hands just a little out of the shell,
but now all of him was crawling out; the shell was cracking,
any minute now it would fly into smithereens and . . . and
what then?

Grasping with all my strength at a straw (the arms of my
chair) I asked, so as to hear myself (that former self of
mine): "Where . . . where did you get this—this poison?"

"Oh, that! Easy: a certain medico, one of my—"

One of my—one of my WHAT? And that other *I* of mine
suddenly popped out and began yelling: "I won't have it! I

won't have anybody else but me . . . I'll kill anyone who
. . . Because I—I lo————"

This I saw: with shaggy paws he roughly seized her, tore
her delicate silk to ribbons, sank his teeth into her. My
recollection is precise on this point: *he used his teeth*.

I don't know just how, but E- slipped away—and there she
stood, with those damned blinds down over her eyes; she was
leaning back against a closet and listening to me. I remember
I was on the floor, clasping her legs, kissing her knees. And
I was imploring her: "Right now—yes, right now, this very
minute—"

Pointed teeth; the acute, mocking triangle of the pointed
eyebrows. She bent over, silently unfastened my badge.

"Yes! Yes, darling, darling!" I began to hurry about taking
off my unif. But E-, just as silently, brought up to my very
eyes the watch face within my badge. It was 22:25.

A chill ran through me. I knew what it meant to be seen
out in the street after 22:30. All my madness vanished as if
a wind had swept it away. I was *I*. One thing was clear to me:
I hated her—I hated, hated her!

Without saying good-bye, without looking back, I dashed
out of the room. Pinning my badge on as best I could on the
run, taking the steps a few at a time, I went down the back
stairs (I was afraid of encountering someone) and leapt out
into the deserted avenue.

Everything was where and as it should be—so simple,
usual, regular: the glass houses glowing with lights, the wan
glassy sky, the greenish quiescent night. But under that quiet
cool glass, those things that were riotous, blood-red, shaggy
were inaudibly rushing along. And, gasping, I raced on to get
home in time. Suddenly I felt that my badge, which I had
pinned on so hurriedly, was becoming loose; it loosened completely and clinked against the sidewalk. I stooped to pick it
up—and, in the momentary silence, caught the sound of
someone's steps behind me. I turned around: something small
and hunched was coming around the corner. At least it so
seemed to me. I resumed running with all my might and
main—all I could hear was the wind whistling in my ears. At
the entrance to my building I stopped: the clock showed I

had a margin of one minute. I listened: there was no one behind me. Plainly, it had all been due to my nonsensical imagination, to the effect of the green poison.

The night was excruciating. The bed rose under me, sank, rose again, then floated off at a sort of a curve. "All numbers"—I tried autosuggestion—"are duty bound to sleep at night. This is as much of a duty as working during the day. Sleep is necessary if one is to work in the daytime. Not to sleep at night is criminal—" But, just the same, sleep I could not. Simply could not.

I was done for. I was in no condition to fulfill my obligations to The One State. I————

ELEVENTH ENTRY:—*No, I* Evening. Fog, not too thick.
can't do it; let this go as it is, The sky is veiled over with
without any summary———— an aureately milky tissue:
one cannot tell what lies beyond, still further up. The ancients knew that their greatest skeptic, God, was being bored stiff up there. We know that all there is up there is a crystal-blue, naked, indecent nothing. I now don't know what's up there— I have come to know far too much. Knowledge which is absolutely sure of its own infallibility—that's faith. I used to have a firm faith in myself; I believed that I knew all that was in me. And then—

I am in front of a mirror. And for the first time in my life (yes, precisely so: for the first time in my life) I see myself clearly, distinctly, consciously; I see myself with amazement, as if it were somebody else's *I*. There he is, this *I*: black eyebrows, as straight as if they were drawn with a ruler and, between them, like a scar, a vertical wrinkle (I don't know if it was there before). Steely gray eyes, ringed with the shadow of a sleepless night, while behind that steel . . . well, it turns out that I had never known what was there. And out of there (this *there* is at the same time both here and infinitely far off)—from *there* I am contemplating myself (or *him*) and know that that fellow with his eyebrows as straight as if drawn with a ruler has nothing to do with me, a stranger whom I have met for the first time in my life. But I, the real *I*, am not he.

No—with a full stop. It's all bosh, and all those preposterous sensations are delirium, the result of yesterday's poisoning. Poisoning with what—with that swallow of green poison, or with her? It's all one. I am including this in my entry merely to show how strangely the human reason, which is so exact and keen, can become tangled and be thrown out of kilter. That reason which has been able to make eupeptic even that infinity, which the ancients found so frightening, by means of—

The indicator has just clicked: it announced R-13. Let him come, by all means; I am actually glad— Right now, to be all by myself would be————

20 minutes later:

Upon the plane of this paper, in a two-dimensional world, these lines run parallel, yet in another world. . . . I am losing my sensitiveness to figures: 20 minutes—that may be 200, or 200,000. And it is so wild to be calmly, deliberately bestowing thought on each word, to be recording that which took place between R- and myself. It would be tantamount to your sitting down cross-legged in an armchair by your bed and curiously watching yourself—your own self—writhing on that bed.

When R-13 entered I was perfectly collected and normal. With a feeling of sincere delight I began telling him how magnificently he had succeeded in trochee-izing the death sentence, and that it had been precisely those trochees more than anything else which had hewed that madman to pieces and annihilated him.

"And not only that, but if it were suggested to me to make a schematic sketch of the Machine of The Benefactor I would absolutely—absolutely!—introduce your trochees, in one way or another, into that sketch," I concluded.

Suddenly I saw all the luster leaving R-'s eyes and his lips taking on a leaden color.

"What's wrong with you?"

"What? What? Why . . . why, I'm simply fed up. Everybody around me keeps harping 'death sentence, death sentence.' I don't want to hear any more about it—and that's all there is to it. There, I don't want that!"

Glowering, he was rubbing the nape of his neck: that little valise of his, stuffed with extraneous impedimenta which was incomprehensible to me. Pause. There, he had found something in the little valise; he pulled the thing out, he was unrolling it, he had unrolled it at last: his eyes became lacquered with laughter—he sprang up.

"But there is something I'm making up for your *Integral* . . . yes, it's—it's really something, so it is!"

He was his former self; his lips smacking, spraying; words jetting forth like a fountain.

"It's an ancient legend, you understand, about Paradise [the *P* was a fountain]. For that legend applies to us, to our present time. Yes—you just think it over! Those two in Paradise were offered a choice: of happiness without freedom or freedom without happiness. They were not offered a third. They, the dunderheads, chose freedom—and what do you think happened? Naturally, for ages thereafter, they longed for shackles. For shackles, you understand—that's what *Weltschmerz* is all about. For ages! And it is only we who have again struck on a way of bringing happiness back. But just listen—listen, now! The God of the ancients and we sit side by side at the same table. Yes! We gave God a helping hand in overcoming the Devil for good and all. For it was the Devil who impelled mortals to transgress against the interdict, to taste of pernicious freedom—it was he, the subtil serpent! But we set a huge heel on this small ophidian head—and *crrunch!* And we're all set—Paradise once more. And, anew, we are simple of heart, innocent, like Adam and Eve. None of that crazy jumbled stuff about Good, about Evil; everything is as simple as can be, childishly, paradisiacally simple. The Benefactor, the Machine, the Cube, the Gas Bell Glass, the Guardians—all this is good, all this is majestic, splendidly beautiful, noble, exalted, crystal-pure. Inasmuch as all this safeguards our unfreedom—our happiness, that is. It's only the ancients who would at this point start to judge things, to dress them up, to rack their brains over ethics and nonethics. Well, let it go; in a word, what about a little paradisiacal poem like that—eh? And with all that the tone is ever so serious—you understand? Pretty little thing, eh?"

There, how could one fail to understand. I remember thinking: "How ludicrous and asymmetrical his appearance, and what a correctly reasoning mind!" And that is why he is so near to me—the real me (I still consider my former self the real one; everything that is happening to me at present is, of course, only an indisposition). R- apparently read all this on my face; he broke into laughter as he took me around the shoulders: "Oh, you . . . Adam! By the way, about Eve—" He rummaged for something in his pocket, drew out a notebook, turned its leaves: "The day after tomorrow—no, two days from now—O-90 has a pink coupon for you. How about you? Just as before? Would you like her to—"

"Well, yes—that's clear."

"I'll tell her so, then. For she herself feels embarrassed. . . . What an odd situation, I must say! Me she likes just so, in a pink coupon sort of way, but when it comes to you! . . . Yet there's not a peep out of you as to who has barged into our triangle and made it a quadrangle. Who is it? Confess, you sinner—come on!"

A curtain went up quickly within me, and I heard the swish of silk, saw the green flagon, her lips. . . . And for no good reason, altogether inapropos, I let the question escape me (if I had only restrained myself!): "But tell me, did you ever happen to. try nicotine or alcohol?"

R- pursed his lips, looking at me from under his brows. I could *hear* his thoughts, perfectly clearly: "When it comes to friends, you're a friend, sure enough. . . . But just the same—" And then he answered: "Well, how should I put it? Properly speaking, no. But I did know a certain woman—"

"E-!" I shouted.

"What—you . . . you were with her too?" He swelled up with laughter, gulped, and was on the verge of exploding.

My mirror was hung in such a way that in order to look into it one had to lean over the table; from where I sat all I could see were my forehead and eyebrows. And then I—the real *I*, caught sight in the mirror of my eyebrows as a distorted, twitching line, and my real *I* heard a savage, disgusting shout: "What's that *too* for? No—just what is that *too* for? No—I demand—"

Protruding Negroid lips. Eyes goggling. I (the real *I*) got a good grip on the collar of that other self of mine, wild, shaggy, breathing hard. I (the real *I*) said to him—to R-13: "Forgive me, for Benefactor's sake. I'm quite ill; can't sleep. Can't understand what's wrong with me—"

A smile flitted over the thick lips: "Yes, yes, yes! I understand, I understand! I'm familiar with all that sort of thing—theoretically, of course. Good-bye!"

In the doorway he turned, like a small black ball, came back to the table and tossed a book on it: "My latest. Brought it along on purpose—almost forgot—" The *B* spattered me; he waddled off.

I am alone. Or, more correctly, I am alone with that other *I* of mine. I am sitting in an armchair with my legs crossed and, out of some *there*, am curiously watching myself (my own self and no other) writhing on the bed.

Why—well, now, why did O- and I live for three years on such friendly terms—and now, suddenly, the mere mention of that other one, that E- . . . Is it possible that all that madness—love, jealousy—can exist outside the idiotic books of the ancients? But the main thing is that *I* should be involved! Equations, formulae, figures—and this! I can't understand a thing. Not a thing. No later than tomorrow I'll go to R- and tell him that————————

No, that's a lie. Neither tomorrow nor the day after—I'll never go to him again. I can't, I don't want to see him. This is the end. Our triangle has fallen apart.

I am alone. It's evening. There's a light fog. The sky is veiled over with a milkily golden tissue: if I could but know what's there, further up. And if I could but know who I am, and what I am like!

TWELFTH ENTRY: *The Limi-*   Just the same it seems to me
tation of Infinity. The Angel.   that I shall get well, that I
Meditations on Poetry.   can get well. I slept magnificently. None of those dreams or any other unwholesome phenomena. Darling O- will come tomorrow; everything will

be simple, regular and limited—like a circle. I'm not afraid of the word *limitation:* the work of the highest faculty man has, his reason, consists precisely of a ceaseless limitation of infinity, of fractioning infinity into suitable, easily digested portions—or differentials. That is precisely what the divine beauty of my element—mathematics—consists of. And yet an understanding of that same beauty is the very thing that that . . . female number doesn't have. However, that is just in passing—a chance association of ideas.

All of the above ideas occurred to the accompaniment of the measured, metrical clatter of wheels in a subway train. I was mentally scanning the clatter of the wheels and R-'s verse (in the book he had brought me yesterday) when I sensed that someone behind me was cautiously leaning over my shoulder and peeking at the open page. Without turning around, merely out of the corner of my eye, I saw pink, spread-out wing-ears, a double curve of a body . . . that fellow! I didn't want to interfere with him and I pretended that I hadn't noticed him. How he had bobbed up I don't know—when I was getting into the car he had apparently not been there.

This incident, insignificant in itself, exerted a particularly beneficial effect upon me; I might say it invigorated me. It is so gratifying to feel somebody's vigilant eye upon one, lovingly guarding one from the least mistake, from the least erring step. It may sound somewhat sentimental, but that same analogy again comes to my mind—that of the guardian angels, whom the ancients used to dream about. How many of the things which they merely dreamed about have materialized in our life!

At the moment when I had sensed this Guardian angel behind me I was enjoying a sonnet entitled "Happiness." I don't think I err in saying that this is a poem of rare beauty and profound thought. Here is the opening quatrain:

> Eternal lovers are these Two-Times-Two,
> Forever blent in a passionate Four;
> No others can so ardently adore
> As these inseparable Two-Times-Two!

And it goes on in much the same vein about the sage, eternal happiness to be found in the multiplication table.

Every authentic poet is, inevitably, a Columbus. America existed for eons before Columbus, but only Columbus succeeded in discovering it. The multiplication tables had existed for eons before R-13, but only R-13 had succeeded in uncovering a new Eldorado in a virginal forest of figures. And truly: is there anywhere a happiness more sage, more serene than in that wondrous universe of the multiplication table? Steel rusts; the God of the ancients created ancient man (i.e., man capable of error), and consequently He Himself had erred. The multiplication table is wiser, more absolute than the God of the ancients: it never (*never*—do you understand that?) errs. And there is no greater happiness than that of figures, existing in accordance with the harmonious, eternal laws of multiplication tables. No vacillations, no delusions. There is but one truth, and but one true path; and that truth is: two times two; and that true path is: four. And would it not be an absurdity if these happily, ideally multiplied two's were to get notions about some sort of freedom— i.e., about what is, clearly, an error? To me it is axiomatic that R-13 has succeeded in seizing upon the most basic, the most————

At this point I again felt (at first at the nape of my neck, then at my left ear) a warm, gentle whiff of my Guardian angel. Evidently he had noted that the book, now closed, was on my lap and that my thoughts were far away. But no matter: I was ready to lay open before him, right then and there, the pages of my brain—such a tranquil, comforting feeling, that, I remember I actually turned around to look at him, I gave him an insistent, beseeching look, but he failed to understand me or did not want to understand; he did not ask me about anything. There is only one thing left me: to tell everything to you, my unknown readers (right now you are as dear to me, and as near and unattainable, as he was at that moment).

Here is the course my thoughts took: from the particular to the general: the particular was R-13, the majestic general —our Institute of State Poets and Prosateurs. How could it have come about (I was thinking) that the ancients had not been struck by the whole preposterousness of their literature and poetry? The most enormous, magnificent force of the artistic words was expended by them utterly in vain. It is simply laughable: each one wrote about whatever happened to pop into his head—just as laughable and preposterous as the fact that the ancients permitted the sea to pound doltishly against the shore around the clock, while the millions of kilogrammeters imprisoned in the waves were utilized merely to warm up the emotions of enamored couples. Out of the enamored susurration of the waves we have obtained electricity; from a feral beast spattering foam we have made a domestic animal—and in precisely the same way we have gentled and saddled that once wild element of poesy. Nowadays poesy is no longer the unpardonable shrill clamor of a nightingale—poesy is service to the State, poesy is utility.

Take our famous *Mathematical Nones:* could we, at school, have come to love so sincerely and tenderly the four rules of arithmetic without their aid? And what about the classical imagery of *Thorns*—the thorns about the rose being the Guardians who protect the gentle Flower of State from the touch of coarse hands. Whose heart is stony enough to remain indifferent to the sight of the innocent lips of childhood babbling, as if they were reciting a prayer: " 'The pretty rose a bad boy seized,/But steel thorns stabbed his hand and squeezed;/The naughty child wept and wheezed,/And ran for home, none too pleased,' " and so on. And *Daily Odes to The Benefactor*—who, after reading them, can refrain from bowing piously before the self-denying toil of this Number of all the numbers? And the eldritch, crimson *Flowers of Legal Sentences?* And the immortal tragedy, *He Who Came Late to Work?* And that perennial favorite, *Stanzas on Sexual Hygiene?*

All of life in all its complexity and beauty is minted for all time in the gold of words.

Our poets no longer soar in the empyrean; they have come down to earth, they are striding side by side with us, keeping in step with the austere, mechanical March issuing from the Musical Factory; their lyre is the matutinal swishing of elec-

trical tooth-brushes, and the awesome crackling of sparks in
the Machine of The Benefactor, and the majestic echo of The
Hymn of The One State, and the intimate tinkling of a night
pot shaped like a vase and made of sparkling crystal, and the
exhilarating clatter of falling window blinds, and the joyous
voices of the latest cook book, and the barely audible susurration of the listening membranes under the streets.

Our gods are here, below, in our midst: in the Bureaus, in
the kitchen, in the workshop, in the lavatory—the gods have
become even as we; *ergo,* we have become even as the gods.
And we shall come to you, my unknown planetary readers—
we shall come to you to make your life even as divinely
rational and regular as ours.

THIRTEENTH ENTRY: *Fog. Thou.*   I awoke at dawn: a roseate,
An Utterly Preposterous Ad-   unmarred firmament met my
venture.   eyes. Everything was fine,
rounded out. O- was coming this evening. I was all well by
now, beyond a doubt. I smiled, went back to sleep.

The morning bell. I got up—and found everything entirely
different: fog—through the glass of the ceiling, of the walls,
everywhere, all over, through and through. Insane clouds,
growing constantly more ponderous, then becoming lighter
and drawing nearer, until at last there were no longer any
boundaries between earth and heaven; everything was flying,
melting, falling: there was nothing to seize hold of. There
were no longer any buildings: the glass walls had deliquesced
in the fog, like small salt crystals in water. If one looked up
from the pavement, the dark figures of those inside the buildings appeared like particles suspended in some phantasmagoric milky solution; some were dangling low, but one saw
them on higher and higher floors, up to the tenth. And everything was swathed in smoke: it might have been an inaudibly
raging conflagration of some sort.

Exactly at 11:45—that was the time I purposely looked at
the clock, so as to seize hold of the figures, so that the
figures, at least, might save me. At 11:45, then, just before
leaving to do some physical work, as designated in The

Tables of Hourly Commandments, I dropped into my room for a little while. Suddenly, the telephone rang; the voice was a long needle, protractedly plunging into the heart: "Ah, you are in? I'm very glad. Wait for me on the corner. You and I are setting out for . . . well, you'll see later on where."

"You know very well I am going to work right now."

"You know very well you will do as I tell you. Good-bye. In two minutes."

In two minutes I was standing on the corner. It was necessary to show her that it was The One State that was managing me and not she. "You will do as I tell you—" and mind you, she felt so assured about it: you could hear it in her voice. Well, I would have a showdown with her very soon.

Gray unifs, woven out of the raw fog, would materialize close to me for a second and unexpectedly dissolve back into the fog. I did not take my eyes off my watch—I was its pointing, quivering second hand. Ten minutes, eight . . . three minutes, two minutes to twelve—

It was all over. Too late to go to work. How I hated her! However, it was necessary for me to show her that————

On the corner, through the white fog—blood, a gash made with a keen knife: her lips.

"I must have kept you waiting, I think. But that makes no difference—it's too late for you to go now."

How I hated her! However, she was right: it was too late.

I was silently watching her lips. All women are lips—nothing but lips. The lips of one are rosy, resiliently round, a circle, a gentle enclosure against the whole world. And then these: but a second before they had not been here and then, in a moment—the knife, slashing, and the sweet blood still dripping.

She drew nearer, let her shoulder nestle against mine—and we were one. Something of her pouring into me—and I knew that that was as it should be. Knew it with every nerve, every hair, with every stroke of my heart, so delectable that it hurt. And it was such a joy to submit to this *as it should be*. Probably it is just as joyous for a bit of iron to submit to an inevitable, infallible law and to cleave to a magnet. Or for a stone, tossed upward, to hesitate a second and then plunge impetuously to earth. And to a man, after his agony, to breathe his final breath at last—and die.

I remember smiling in a muddled sort of way and saying, for no particular reason: "Fog . . . lots of it—"

"Dost thou love the fog?"

This ancient, long-forgotten *thou,* the *thou* of a master to a slave, plunged into me sharply, slowly: yes, I was a slave and that, too, was as it should be; that, too, was fine.

"Yes, it's fine," I said aloud to myself. And then, to her: "I hate the fog. I'm afraid of the fog."

"That means thou lovest it. Thou art afraid because it is stronger than thou; thou hatest it because thou art afraid of it; thou lovest it because thou canst not make it submit to thee. For one can love only the insubmissible."

Yes, that was so. And that was precisely why—precisely why I———

The two of us were walking—as one. Somewhere far off the sun was singing, its song coming ever so faintly through the fog; all things were swelling with yielding pigments: nacreous, aureate, roseate, red. All the universe was one unembraceable woman and we were in her very womb; we were as yet unborn—we were joyously ripening. And it was clear to me, incontrovertibly clear, that all things were intended for me: the sun, the fog, the roseate, the aureate— all were intended for me.

I did not ask where we were going. It did not matter: all that mattered was to walk—to walk, ripen, become ever more yieldingly swollen———

"Well, here we are," E- stopped before an entrance. "There's a certain doctor who happens to be on duty this very day. . . . I told you about him that time at the House of Antiquity."

Somewhat aloof, using only the sense of sight so as to conserve carefully what was ripening within me, I scanned the sign: Medical Bureau. I understood everything.

A room all of glass, filled with gold-tinted fog. Glass shelves holding bottles, jars of colored glass. Electric wires. Bluish sparks sparking away in glass tubes.

And a homunculus—the thinnest ever. As if he were a

paper cutout, and no matter which way he might turn it
wouldn't matter one bit: he would still have only a profile,
ground fine, his nose a glistening blade, his lips a pair of
scissors.

I didn't catch what E- was saying to him; I watched her
speaking and I felt that I was smiling irrepressibly, beatifically.
The blades of the lip-scissors gleamed, and the physician
said: "Right, right. I understand. The most dangerous disease.
I know of nothing more dangerous—" At that he laughed,
wrote something with his tissue-paper hand, turned the slip
over to E-; wrote again, handed the other slip over to me.

The slips certified that we were ill, that we could not report
for work. I was stealing my work time from The One State;
I was a thief, I was under the Machine of The Benefactor.
Yet all this was as remote and immaterial to me as if it were
something in a book. I took the slip without a second's hesita-
tion; I—my eyes, lips, hands—I knew that this was as it
should be.

We got an aero at a half-empty hangar at the corner. E-
again took the pilot's seat, as she had done that other time,
pressed the starter, and we took off and soared. And everything took off in our wake: the roseately aureate fog; the
sun; the thinnest-of-blades-profile of the physician, who had
suddenly become so beloved and near. Hitherto everything
had revolved about the sun; now I knew that everything was
revolving about me—slowly, beatifically, with puckered
eyes. . . .

The crone at the gates of the House of Antiquity. Her dear
mouth with the lips grown together and ray wrinkles all
around it. Probably the lips had remained grown together
from that other day to this one, and only now did they open,
smile: "Ah-ah, you naughty girl! There, instead of working
like everybody . . . oh, well, let it go! In case of anything—
why, I'll come on the run and tell you—"

The heavy, creaking, opaque door closed and at once,
painfully, the heart opened wide—wider still—to its widest.
Her lips were mine; I drank and drank, tore myself away
from time to time, gazed wordlessly in the eyes opened wide
for me, and again————————

The half-dusk in the suite; blue; saffron-yellow; dark-green morocco; the golden smile of Buddha; mahogany; the gleam of mirrors. And—that old dream of mine, now so comprehensible: everything was saturated with aureately roseate sap that would brim over at any moment, spurting———

The ripening was completed. And inevitably, as with iron and magnet, with delectable submission to an infallible, immutable law, I infused myself in her. There was no pink coupon, there was no accounting, there was no One State, there was no me. There were only the tenderly sharp, clenched teeth, there were eyes of gold opened wide for me— and through them I was slowly entering within, further and further. And there was silence. Save that in some corner— thousands of miles away—drops were dripping in a washbasin; and I was the whole universe, and between drop and drop there were eras, epochs. . . .

Throwing on my unif I bent over E- and absorbed her with my eyes for a last time.

"I knew it. . . . I knew thee—" said E-, ever so softly. She quickly got up, put on her unif and her usual sharp smilebite: "Well, now, my fallen angel. . . . For you're ruined and done for now. What, you're not afraid? Well, good-bye! You will go back by yourself. Well?"

She opened the mirrored door of a closet and waited, looking at me over her shoulder. I obediently went out. But hardly had I crossed the threshold when I felt the urge to have her shoulder nestling against mine—if for but a second, no more than that. I dashed back into that room where she was (probably) still fastening her unif before a mirror. I ran in— and stopped in my tracks. Yes, I clearly saw the old-fashioned ring on the key in the closet door still swinging, but E- was not there. She could not have gone anywhere—there was but one exit to the room—but just the same she was not there. I rummaged everywhere; I even opened the closet and ran my hands over the motley, ancient dresses in it: there was no one there.

I feel somehow embarrassed, my planetary readers, in telling about this utterly implausible happening. But what else is one to do, since all this happened in just that way? There,

hadn't that whole day, from the very morning, been full of
implausibilities—doesn't all this bear a resemblance to that
ancient disorder of seeing dreams? And if that be so, what's
the difference if there's one incongruity more or less? Besides
that, I feel certain that, sooner or later, I will manage to
include each and every incongruity into some syllogism or
other. This thought reassures me; I hope it will reassure you
as well.

 . . . How overwhelmed I am! If you but knew how overwhelmed!

FOURTEENTH ENTRY: *"Mine."* This is a continued record of
Mustn't. A Cold Floor. yesterday's events. The Personal Hour before going to bed was taken up with something
else and I could not finish the entry yesterday. But I have
retained everything as if it were graven within me, and therefore that unbearable cold floor sticks in my memory particularly—and probably forever. . . .

O- was to come to me in the evening—it was her day. I
went down to the clerk on duty to get a permit for lowering
my window blinds.

"What's wrong with you?" the clerk asked me. "You seem
somehow strange today—"

"I—I am unwell."

Strictly speaking, it was the truth; I was unwell, of course.
And immediately I remembered—why, yes, I had a certificate. I groped for it in my pocket; there, I heard it rustling.
Which meant that it had all happened—it had actually happened. . . . I held the paper out to the controller. I felt my
cheeks burning; without looking directly I saw that the controller was eying me and wondering.

And then it was 21:30. The blinds in the room to the left
were lowered; in the room to the right I saw my neighbor
poring over a book. His bald head, knobby and all hillocky,
and his forehead formed an enormous yellow parabola. In an
excruciating mood I kept pacing and pacing the room: after
all, how was I to behave with her, with O-? To my right I
clearly felt my neighbor's eyes fixed upon me, I distinctly
saw the wrinkles on his forehead—a succession of yellow,

illegible lines—and for some reason it seemed that those lines had to do with me.

At 11:45 a joyous rosy whirlwind burst into my room; a sturdy ring of rosy arms encircled my neck. And then I felt the ring slackening more and more—slackening, then parting; her arms dropped.

"You're not the same, you aren't what you were—you're no longer mine!"

" 'Mine'—what savage terminology. I never—" and at that point I faltered: it suddenly occurred to me that before, true enough, I had not been anybody's, but that now . . . why, now I was living not in our rational world but in the ancient, delirious world consisting of $\sqrt{-1}$'s.

The window blinds fall. There, behind the wall to my right, my neighbor let his book drop from the table to the floor and, through the narrow crack between floor and blind during the second before the latter's final fall, I saw his yellow hand clutching the book—and I felt within me an urge to clutch this hand with all my might.

"I thought . . . I wanted to meet you today during the walking period. There are so many . . . I have so many things I must discuss with you—"

Poor, darling O-! The rosy mouth a rosy crescent with its horns downward. However, I couldn't very well tell her everything that had happened—if only because that would make her an accomplice in my crimes, since I knew that she lacked the resolution to go to the Bureau of Guardians and, consequently————

O- was lying down. I was kissing her slowly. I kissed that naïve, chubby little fold at her wrist; her blue eyes were closed; the rosy crescent was slowly blossoming, unfolding—and I kissed her all over. Suddenly I clearly felt to what extent everything had been devastated, how everything had been given over to others. I couldn't, I mustn't. I had to—and I mustn't.

My lips instantly grew chill. The rosy crescent began to quiver; it dimmed, shriveled. O- threw a coverlet over herself, wrapped herself up in it—and buried her face in the pillow.

I was sitting on the floor near the bed (what a desperately chill floor that was!); I was sitting there in silence. The excruciating cold from below crept higher and higher. Probably the same taciturn cold reigns out there, in the blue, mute interplanetary spaces.

"Do understand—I didn't want this . . ." I mumbled. "I tried my utmost—"

That was the truth: I, the real *I*, hadn't wanted this to happen. But just the same, in what words could I convey this to her? How explain to her that the iron had not wanted to be attracted, but that the law is inevitable, infallible————

O- lifted her face from the pillow and said, without opening her eyes: "Go away," but because of her tears this sounded like " 'o 'way," and for some reason this nonsensical trifle also impinged on my memory.

Chilled to the bone, stiff with the cold, I stepped out into the corridor. Light, barely perceptible fog was swirling out there, outside the glass wall. But toward night that fog would again descend, blanketing everything with all its weight. What would happen during the night?

O- slipped past me without a word, heading for the elevator; the door thudded.

"Just a moment!" I called after her; fear overcame me.

But the elevator was already humming, going down, down, down.

She had taken R- away from me.

She had taken O- away from me.

And yet—and yet————

FIFTEENTH ENTRY: *The Bell Glass. The Mirrorous Sea. I am Condemned to Eternal Flames.*

I had barely set foot on the building site of the *Integral* when the Second Builder came toward me. His face had its usual look: it was a round plate of white faïence, and when he spoke he was offering you something unbearably tasty on that plate.

"You deigned to be ill, now, and during your absence, while we were without anyone in authority here, we had an incident, so to speak, yesterday—"

"An incident?"

"Well, yes! The quitting bell rang; we began letting all the workers out of the building site—and just imagine: the guard checking out the workers nabbed a man without a number. How he ever managed to get in is something I simply cannot understand. They took him away to Operational. There they'll get the why and wherefore out of the dear fellow"—this with a smile, a tasty smile.

Our best and most experienced physicians work at the Operational Division under the direct supervision of The Benefactor Himself. There you will find all sorts of instruments and, most important of all, the famous Gas Bell Glass. Essentially it is the same as the appliance used in the hoary experiment in elementary physics: a mouse is placed under a bell glass; the air within the glass is increasingly rarefied by means of an air pump. And so on, and so forth. But, of course, the Gas Bell Glass is a considerably improved apparatus, utilizing various gases; and, furthermore, there is no more of this business of abusing a small defenseless animal— the lofty purpose is to assure the security of The One State: in other words, the happiness of millions. Five centuries ago, or thereabouts, when the work of the Operational Division was still merely in its formative stage, there were simpletons to be found who compared the Operational with the ancient Inquisition. But really, that is as preposterous as placing on the same plane a surgeon performing a tracheotomy and a highwayman slitting a throat. Both wield a knife—much the same sort of a knife, perhaps; both do one and the same thing—cutting the throat of a living person. But, just the same, one is a benefactor, the other a criminal; one has the + sign, the other the − sign.

All this is exceedingly clear, all this takes but a second, but a single turn of the logical machine—and then its cogs engage a minus, whereupon something different becomes uppermost: the ring on the key in the closet door is still swinging a little; that door has evidently been just slammed closed, yet she, E-, is not there—she has vanished. This is something the machinery of logic could not turn up. A dream? Yet I feel, even now, the incomprehensible, delectable pain in my right shoulder, I feel E- nestling against my right shoulder, side by side with me in the fog. "Dost thou love the fog?" Yes, I love even the fog . . . I love everything, and everything is flexible, new, wondrous—everything is fine. . . .

"Everything is fine," I said aloud.

"Fine?" the faïence eyes were goggling. "Really, what's so fine about this? If that fellow without a number contrived to get in, it means that they are everywhere, all around us, all the time; they are here, they are near the *Integral*, they—"

"Come, who are *they?*"

"Well, how should I know who they are? But I can *feel* them—you understand? Feel them all the time—"

"But have you heard—seems they have worked out a certain operation for the surgical removal of fantasy?"

I really had heard something of that sort recently.

"Yes, I know. But what's that got to do with this?"

"Why, this—if I were in your place I'd go and ask them to perform this operation on myself."

Something lemonishly sour emerged distinctly on the plate. The dear man—even a remote hint that he might have fantasy struck him as offensive. But then, if it came to that, a week ago I, too, would probably have taken offense at the idea. But now . . . no, not now, since I know what's the matter with me, know that I'm ailing. And I also know that I don't want to be cured of this ailment. I don't want to, and that's all there is to it.

We went up the glass steps to the top stage. Everything below us was as clear as if spread out on the palm of the hand. You who read these notes, no matter who you are, you still have the sun shining over you. And if you, too, were ever afflicted as I am right now, you know what the sun is like— you know what the sun can be like—in the morning; you know its rosy, lucid, warm gold. The very air is so faintly rose-tinted, and everything is saturated with the gentle blood of the sun; everything is alive—the stones are alive and soft, iron is alive and warm, people are alive and every last one of them is smiling. It can so happen that within an hour everything will vanish; within an hour the roseate blood will be drained off, drop by drop—but in the meantime everything

is imbued with life. And I saw: something was playing irides-
cently and pulsing through the vitreous juices of the *Integral;*
I saw: the *Integral* was meditating on its great and awesome future, on its crushing cargo of inevitable happiness
which it would bear aloft to you, my unknown ones, to you,
forever seeking and never finding. You shall find, you shall
be happy—you are bound to be happy and now you will not
have to wait long.

The body of the *Integral* is almost ready: an exquisite,
elongated ellipsoid fashioned of our glass—eternal as gold,
flexible as steel. I saw: within they were attaching to the glass
body its transverse ribs and longitudinal stringers; they were
laying a foundation for the gigantic rocket engine at the stern.
Every 3 seconds—an explosion; every 3 seconds the mighty
tail of the *Integral* would eject flames and gases into universal
space—and it would speed on and on, a fiery Tamerlane of
happiness———

I saw: the workers below, in conformance with Taylor,
regularly and rapidly, all keeping time, were bending, straightening up, turning like the levers of a single enormous machine. They were holding gleaming tubes: with jets of fire
they were cutting apart and with jets of fire they were welding
together glass walls, set squares, ribs, angle bars. I saw:
monster cranes of transparent glass slowly rolled over glass
rails and, just as the workers were doing, they obediently
turned, bent, thrust their loads within, into the belly of the
Integral. And all this was but one unit: humanized machines,
machine-perfect humans. This was the loftiest, most staggering beauty, harmony, music. . . . I had to hasten down to
them as quickly as I could, to be with them!

And then I was shoulder to shoulder with them, welded
with them, caught up in a steel rhythm. Their motions were
measured; their cheeks were round as a rubber ball, their foreheads mirror-smooth, unclouded by the insanity of thoughts.
I was afloat on a mirrorous sea. I was in repose.

And suddenly one of them turned to me insouciantly:
"Well, now, is it over—better today?"

"Better? What do you mean?"

"Why, you weren't here yesterday. We thought you were

down with something serious"—his forehead was glowing, his smile was childlike, innocent.

My blood rushed to my face. I could not lie to those eyes—I simply could not. I was silent, I was drowning—

A face of faïence, glowing in its round whiteness, thrust itself through the hatchway above: "I say, D, Five Hundred and Three! Do come here, please! We've got the consoles jammed in the frame, you understand, and the tension readings aren't right—"

Without waiting to hear more I dashed up the ladder toward him: I was ignominiously saving myself by flight. I hadn't the heart to raise my eyes; there were spots before them because of the glittering glass steps underfoot, and with every step I was becoming more and more despondent: there was no place here for me, a criminal, a man filled with toxins. Nevermore would it be mine to blend with the faultless, mechanical rhythm, to float upon a mirror-smooth sea. My lot would be to burn forever, forever to dart about, to seek some cranny where I might hide my eyes—forever, until at last I would find the strength to pass through and————

And at this point an icy spark shot through me: as for me, let come what may, I did not matter; but I would have to think of her also, they would involve her too. . . .

I clambered out of the hatchway to the deck and stopped: I did not know where to go next, did not know why I had come there. I glanced aloft. There the sun, exhausted by its nooning, was dully climbing. Below was the *Integral*, grayish-glassy, lifeless. Its roseate blood had drained off. It was clear to me that all this was merely my imagination, that everything remained as it had been, and at the same time it was clear————

"Why, Five Hundred and Three—have you lost your hearing? Here I've been calling and calling you . . . what's the matter with you?" It was the Second Builder, shouting in my very ear; he must have been shouting like that for a long while.

What was the matter with me? I had lost my rudder. The motor was droning its loudest, the aero was shaking and rushing at full speed, but it had no rudder—and I did not know where I was rushing to: downward—and I would crash to the ground; or upward—and I would run into the sun, into the flaming mass————

SIXTEENTH ENTRY: *Yellow. A*   I have made no entries for
Two-Dimensional Shadow. An   several days. I don't know
Incurable Soul.   how many days: all days are
as one. All days are of one color—yellow, like sand calcined and made incandescent by the sun—and there isn't a patch of shade, not a drop of water, and I am walking over this yellow sand with no end in sight. I cannot be without her, whereas she, ever since the time when she disappeared so inexplicably in the House of Antiquity————

Since that time I have seen her only once, during a walk. Two, three, four days ago—I can't tell: all days are one. She flitted by, filling for a second the yellow, empty world. Arm in arm with her was that double-curved *S*, who reached only to her shoulder; there was also the tissue-paper doctor, and some fourth number—all I can remember of him was his fingers: they were fluttering out of the sleeves of his unif like clusters of rays—fingers unusually slender, white, long. E- raised her hand and waved to me, then leaned over the head of her short companion toward the number with the finger rays. I thought I caught the name *Integral:* all four looked over their shoulders at me, and then they were lost against the gray-blue sky, and again there was the yellow, calcined path.

She had a pink coupon for me that evening. I stood before the indicator and with tenderness, with hatred, was imploring it to click, to have it show *E-330* in its blank space as soon as possible. The door of the elevator opened noisily time and again; pale women, tall women, rosy women, swarthy women emerged; the blinds were clattering down everywhere. But she wasn't there. She did not come. And perhaps at that very minute, on the stroke of 22:00, as I am writing this, she, with her eyes closed, is nestling with her shoulder against somebody (as at that time) and (as at that time) is saying to that somebody: "Dost love?" Whom is she asking? Who is he?

That fellow with finger-rays, or thick-lipped, spluttering R-?
Or S-?

S-! Why, all these days, do I hear behind me his flat-footed
steps, that sound as if he were splashing through puddles?
Why, all these days, is he after me like a shadow? A gray-
blue, two-dimensional shadow—ahead of me, on either side
of me, behind me; people walk through it, people step on it,
but it is just as inalterably present, close by, bound to me
by an invisible umbilical cord. Is she, E-, this umbilical cord,
perhaps? I don't know. Or, perhaps, is it already known to
them—to the Guardians—that I——————

Suppose you were to be told that your shadow sees you—
sees you all the time. Do you understand? And then, suddenly, you have a queer sensation: your arms aren't your
own but some stranger's—they're in your way. And I catch
myself swinging my arms in a ridiculous fashion, completely out of rhythm with my walk. Or, suddenly, I *must*
look over my shoulder, yet it is utterly out of the question to
do so: my neck is in an iron clamp. And I run, run even
faster, and I sense with my back that the shadow is also
running faster after me, and there is no place—no place!—
where one may escape it. . . .

I am in my room at last. Alone. But here I am confronted
by something else: the telephone. Again I pick up the receiver: "Yes, E-330, please." And, anew, I hear through the
receiver a light stir, someone's light steps out in the hallway
going past the door of her room, and then silence. . . . I
drop the receiver. I can't stand this—I can't stand it any
longer. I must go there—I must go to her.

This was yesterday. I ran there and for a whole hour (from
16:00 to 17:00) I roamed near the building where she lives.
Numbers, rank after rank, paced past. Thousands of feet
pattered in time; millionpedal Leviathan,* swaying, was floating past. But I—I was all alone, cast up by a lash of the
storm on an uninhabited island, and my eyes were searching,
searching the gray-blue waves.

* Behemoth [?]—*Researcher 565316, Venusian Bureau of
Multilinguistics*.

Why, at any moment now, there would bob up the acute mocking angle of eyebrows quirked up toward the temples, and the dark windows of her eyes and there, within them, would be a fireplace flaming, and certain shadows flitting. And I would make my way in there, deep within, and I would call her *thou* (*thou*, without fail): "Surely, thou knowest I cannot do without thee. Why, then, dost thou treat me so?" But she would not say a word.

Suddenly I heard the silence; suddenly I heard what the Musical Factory was playing, and I grasped that it was past 17:00, that all the numbers had long since left; I was all alone —I was late. All around me spread a desert of glass flooded with the sun's yellow. I saw, as if reflected in water, the topsy-turvy sparkling walls suspended in the smooth expanse of glass, and myself, too, suspended therein topsy-turvily, mockingly.

I had to go, as quickly as I could, that very second, to the Medical Bureau to get a certificate that I was ailing, otherwise they would take me and———— But, perhaps, that would be best of all: to remain here and wait calmly until they saw me and handed me over to the Operational Department; it would be best to end everything at one stroke, at one stroke to redeem everything.

A slight rustle—and a double-curved shadow was before me. I felt, without looking, how quickly the two augers of gray steel bored into me. I summoned all my strength to smile and said (I had to say something): "I . . . I have to go to the Medical Bureau—"

"What's keeping you back, then? Why are you standing here?"

Blazing with shame, feeling that I was absurdly, topsy-turvily hanging with my feet up in the air, I made no answer.

"Follow me," said S- grimly.

I started walking, swinging my unnecessary arms, which apparently belonged to someone else. I couldn't raise my eyes; all this while I was traversing a wild, topsy-turvy world: over there were some machines or other, with their bases up, and people with their feet stuck antipodally to the ceiling and, still lower, was the sky, shackled by the thick glass of the pavement. The most humiliating thing of all, I remember, was the fact that, as the last sight of my life, all this should be thus, inverted, not as it really was. But raise my eyes I could not.

We came to a halt. There were steps before me. Just a step —and I would see figures in white surgical gowns, the enormous mute Glass Bell. . . .

Forcing myself, as if I were using some sort of inner worm-gear, I at last tore my gaze away from the glass underfoot: suddenly the golden letters of *Medical Bureau* spattered my face. Why he had brought me there and not to the Operational Department, why he had spared me—these were questions which at that moment did not even occur to me. I took all the steps at one leap, slammed the door tight after me— and heaved a sigh. Just as if, ever since morning, my lungs had not drawn a breath, my heart had not given one beat, and I had drawn my first breath only at that point, and only at that point had a sluice opened within my breast.

There were two medical numbers confronting me: one extremely squat, with legs as stubby and round as the iron posts one finds along curbs and eyes that seemed to be tossing the patients the way a bull might toss a victim on his horns; the other was as thin as thin could be, his lips a pair of glittering scissors, his nose a knife blade: the same fellow I had met before. I darted toward him as if he were a near kinsman, heading straight for the points of the three blades, babbling something about insomnia, dreams, a shadow, a universe all yellow. The scissors-lips glittered in a smile.

"You *are* in a bad way! Apparently a soul has formed within you."

A soul? That quaint, ancient, long-forgotten word. . . . We would occasionally say *soulmost, soulless, soul-destroying,* but who ever used that naked word *soul* itself?

"Is that . . . very serious?" I babbled.

"Incurable!" snipped the scissors.

"But, really . . . just what is it? Somehow, I—I can't conceive what it is—"

"You see . . . how am I to put it to you? You're a mathematician, aren't you?"

"Yes."

"Well, then, take a plane, a surface—there, this mirror will do. And you and I are on this surface—there, you see: we're squinting our eyes because of the reflected sunlight, and there's the blue electric spark in that tube, and just now the shadow of an aero has flitted by. Only on the surface—only for a second. But just imagine that through the application of some form of fire this impenetrable surface has suddenly softened, and nothing any longer glides over it—everything penetrates it, into that mirror-world which we eyed with such curiosity when we were children—children aren't at all as foolish as people think they are, I assure you. The plane has become a mass, a body, a world, and that which is within the mirror is within you: the sun, and the whirlwind from the propeller of the aero, and your quivering lips—and the lips of someone else. And, you understand, a cold mirror reflects, rejects, whereas my supposititious mirror absorbs, and re-tains a trace through all time of all things that have affected it. You may have once seen a barely perceptible wrinkle on someone's face—and that wrinkle is within you forever; you may have once caught the sound of a drop of water falling amid silence—and you are hearing that sound right now—"

"Yes, yes—that's it!" I seized his hand. I was hearing it right now: the sound amid silence of drops dripping slowly from the faucet of a washbasin. And I knew that sound would endure forever. But, just the same, why a *soul*, all of a sudden? I had lived on and on without it—and then, sud-denly . . . How was it no one had it, but I had to go and get it———————

I clutched that thinnest of hands still harder: I felt creepy about losing my life belt.

"How does it happen? But how is it that you have no feathers, no wings, but only shoulder blades—only bases for wings? Well, because there is no need for wings by now; the aero has been invented—wings would only be in the way. Wings are intended for flying, but we no longer have any place to fly to: we have finished our flight, we have found what we were after. Isn't that so?"

I nodded absent-mindedly. He gave me a look, broke into sharp, lancet-ish laughter. That other medical number heard him, stomped over on his stubby iron-pillar legs, tossed my thin-as-thin doctor on the horns of his eyes, then tossed me.

"What's going on here? What—a soul? A soul, you say? What the Devil! First thing you know we'll be getting back to cholera. I told you"—the ever-so-thin doctor was on the eye horns again—"I told you we must have fantasiectomy— wholesale fantasiectomy. Fantasy must be extirpated. Only surgery can avail here—only surgery and nothing else—"

He put on enormous Roentgen spectacles and for a long while walked around me and peered intently through my skull, right into my brain, jotting some notes into a book.

"Exceedingly curious—exceedingly! Look: won't you perhaps consent to . . . to being preserved in a jar of alcohol? For The One State it would be exceedingly . . . it would help us to prevent an epidemic. Unless you have special objections to it, of course—"

"You see," the ever-so-thin doctor interposed, "number D, Five Hundred and Three is the builder of the *Integral,* and I feel sure such a thing would result in disruption—"

"Ah!" the other muttered and stomped back to his office on his stubby iron-post legs.

We remained alone. The paper-thin hand rested lightly, kindly on mine; the face, practically all profile, bent close to me.

"I'll let you in on a secret," he whispered, "your case is not the only one. My colleague isn't merely spouting when he talks of an epidemic. Just think back, now: haven't you yourself noticed something similar—very similar, very near to it in the case of a certain person"—at this point he gave me an intent look. At what—at whom—was he hinting? Could it be———

"Look here!" I sprang out of my chair—but he had already begun speaking loudly of something else: "But as for insomnia, as for these dreams of yours, I can give you but one piece of advice: you ought to walk as much as you can. There, start tomorrow morning, go for a stroll . . . why not walk as far as the House of Antiquity, say?"

Again his eyes transpierced me, smiling the narrowest of smiles. And it seemed to me that I saw, perfectly clearly, a

word, a letter, a name—the unique name—wrapped up in
the fine tissue of this smile. Or was that only my fantasy
again?

I could barely wait until he wrote out for me a certificate
of ill health covering that day and the next, squeezed his hand
hard once more without a word, and ran out of the place.

My heart was as light, as swift as an aero and it was bearing me higher and higher. I knew that the morrow held some
joy for me. What joy would it be?

SEVENTEENTH ENTRY: *Through*   I am utterly bewildered. Yes-
Glass. I Died. Corridors.   terday, at the very moment
                                                    when I thought that every-
thing had been untangled, that all the X's had been found,
new unknown quantities bobbed up in my equation.

All the co-ordinates of this whole story have their starting
point at the House of Antiquity, of course. From this point
radiate the axes of the X's, the Y's and the Z's, upon which
of late my entire universe is built. I was walking along the
axis of the X's (59th Avenue) toward the starting point of
the co-ordinates. All the things of yesterday were a motley
whirlwind within me: the inverted houses and people, the
hands that were excruciatingly not my own, the glittering
scissors-lips, the grating *drip-drip* of the washbasin: things had
been like that, they had been like that once! And all this,
lacerating the flesh, was impetuously whirling there, under the
molten surface, where the *soul* was.

In order to carry out the doctor's instructions I deliberately chose a route that followed the two legs of a triangle
and not its hypotenuse. And before long I had reached the
second leg: the road running around the base of the Green
Wall. Out of the unencompassable ocean of greenery on the
other side of the Wall a raging billow of roots, flowers,
boughs, leaves came surging toward me; it reared up on end,
was on the verge of sweeping over me—and from a man, the
finest and most precise of mechanisms, I would be trans-
formed into————

But, fortunately, between me and the raging ocean of
greenery there was the glass of the Wall. Oh, the great,

divinely limiting wisdom of walls, of barriers! The wall is, probably, the greatest of all inventions. Man ceased to be a wild animal only when he had built his first wall. Man ceased to be a wild man only when we had built the Green Wall, when we had isolated our perfect machine world from the irrational, hideous world of trees, birds, animals—

Turbidly, dully, the blunt muzzle of some beast showed through the glass; its yellow eyes persistently kept repeating the same unvarying thought which was incomprehensible to me. For a long while we looked into each other's eyes, those shafts from the superficial world into that other world under the surface. And a thought began stirring within me: "But what if that yellow-eyed creature, living its uncalculated life among its ridiculous, dirty heaps of leaves, is happier than we are?" I swung up my arm: the yellow eyes blinked, backed away, disappeared in the leafage. The pitiful creature! What an absurdity—its being happier than we! Yes, happier than I, perhaps—but then I am only an exception: I am ill. And, even I———

I already saw the dark-red walls of the House of Antiquity —and the old woman's endearing mouth, the lips of which seemed grown together. I ran to the crone as fast as I could.

"Is she here?"

The grown-together lips opened slowly: "And just who may *she* be?"

"Ah, now—who indeed? Why, E-, of course. There, she and I came here the other day in an aero—"

"A-ah—so, so! So, so, so!" Ray-wrinkles about the lips, crafty rays from yellow eyes cautiously probing their way into me, deeper and deeper. And, at last: "Very well, then. She went by here not so long ago."

She was here. I noticed, at the crone's feet, a clump of silvery wormwood (the courtyard of the House of Antiquity was as much of a museum as the House itself, and was painstakingly kept in its prehistoric state). The clump had extended one of its stems until it was lying on the crone's hand and she was stroking the silky leaves; the sun had laid a streak of yellow across her lap. And for one instant I, the sun, the crone, the wormwood, the yellow eyes were one whole; we were fast bound by certain veinlets—and the same shared, tempestuous, magnificent blood was coursing through those veinlets. (I feel ashamed to write about it, but I promised to be frank, to the very end, in these notes. Well, then: I bent over and kissed that grown-together, soft, mossy mouth. The crone wiped her mouth and broke into laughter.)

I started off at a run through the familiar, murky, reverberating rooms, for some reason heading straight for the bedroom. It was only when I was at its very door and clutching the doorknob that it suddenly occurred to me: "But what if she's not alone there?" I stopped, listening intently. But all I heard was the *tick-tocking* of my heart—not within me, however, but somewhere in my vicinity. The great bed—untouched. A mirror. Another mirror, in the closet door and, in the keyhole of that door, a key with an old-fashioned ring. And no one in sight.

"E-! Are you here?" I called softly, and then, still more softly, with eyes closed, holding my breath and as if I were already on my knees before her: "E-! Darling!"

All was quiet. Except for water dripping hurriedly from the faucet into the white washbasin. Right now I can't explain the reason for it, but I did find this dripping unpleasant—I turned the faucet hard and left the room. She wasn't there—that was clear. And that meant she was in some other *apartment*.

I ran down a wide, gloomy staircase, tugged at one door, at another, at a third: all were locked. Everything was locked save that one *apartment*—"our" apartment—and no one was there.

Yet, just the same, I again went there, I myself don't know for what reason. I walked slowly, with difficulty: my shoe-soles had suddenly turned to cast iron. I distinctly remember thinking: "The idea that the force of gravity is constant is erroneous. Consequently, all my formulae———"

At this point—an explosion: a door slammed on the ground floor; someone tramped quickly over the flagstones. I— buoyant, most buoyant again—darted toward the railings, intending to bend over them and to put all I felt into a single shouted word, in a single cry of *"Thou!"*

And I turned to ice: below, sketched in the shadowy square cast by the window frame, flapping its pink wing-ears, the head of S- was sweeping along.

The bald conclusion came to me in a lightning flash—the conclusion only, without any premises (even now I don't know what the premises were): "He mustn't see me, under any circumstances." And on tiptoe, hugging the wall, I slipped upstairs, to that unlocked *apartment*.

I paused for a second at the door. The fellow was slogging up the stairs, to where I was. If only that door would not betray me! I implored that door, but it was of wood: it started creaking, squeaking. Something red, something green, the yellow Buddha—they all swept past like a whirlwind; I was now before the mirror in the closet door—I saw my ashen face; my very eyes, my lips were listening intently. . . . I heard, through the pounding of my blood, the door creaking again. It was he—he.

I seized the key in the closet door—and the ring on the key started swinging. This reminded me of something. Again there was an instantaneous bald conclusion without any premises—or, more correctly, a splinter of a conclusion: "That time, when E- ———" I quickly opened the closet door; once inside, in the darkness, I shut the door tight. One step—the floor rocked under me. Slowly, gently, I floated off somewhere in a downward direction; everything turned dark before my eyes; I died.

Later, when I had to write down all these odd happenings, I rummaged in my memory and in books, and now, of course, I understand: it was a state of temporary death, a state known to the ancients but, insofar as I am aware, utterly unknown among us.

I have no idea how long I was dead (5-10 seconds, most probably), but after a while I came back to life and opened my eyes. It was dark and I felt that I was going down, down. . . . I put out my hand, clutching: the rough-surfaced wall, quickly going past, scraped me; there was blood on one of my fingers—it was clear that all this was not merely the play of my sick fantasy. But what was it, then—what was it?

I could hear that my breathing was broken, wavering (I feel ashamed to make this confession; everything was so unexpected and incomprehensible). A minute passed, then a second, a third: I was still descending. At last there was a mild jolt: whatever it was that had been falling underfoot was now motionless. My groping hand came upon some kind of knob in the darkness: I pushed—a door opened—light showed dimly. Then I noticed, behind me, a small square platform—it was quickly going up. I made a dash for it but it was too late: I was cut off there—where this *there* was I didn't know.

A corridor. Silence, crushing as a thousand tons. Up on the vaulted ceiling—small electric bulbs in an unending, twinkling, tremulous dotted line. There was a slight resemblance to the tubes of our underground railways, except that this corridor was considerably narrower and was constructed not of our glass but of some other old-time material. There came a flitting suggestion of the catacombs in which, allegedly, people tried to save themselves at the time of the Two Hundred Years' War. Not that that made any difference: one had to go on.

I must have walked for twenty minutes, I think. I turned to the right: the corridor widened; the small electric bulbs brightened. I heard vague rumbling of some sort. It might have been that of a machine, it might have been that of voices—I did not know. All I knew was that I found myself standing before a ponderous opaque door: the rumbling came from behind it. I knocked; then I knocked again, more loudly. Things quieted down behind that door. Something clanked; the door opened slowly, ponderously.

I don't know which one of us was more petrified: standing before me was that ever-so-thin blade-nosed doctor.

"You? Here?"—and his scissors-lips simply clicked shut. And I—it seemed as if I had never even known as much as a single human word; I stood there, saying nothing, and understood absolutely nothing of what he was saying to me. Probably that I would have to leave the place, because the next thing he did was to shove me quickly with his paper-flat abdomen to the end of this better-lighted stretch of the corridor—after which he nudged me in the back.

"Allow me . . . I wanted— I thought that she . . . that E, Three Hundred and Thirty . . . however, there's someone following me—"

"Stay here," the doctor cut me short—and vanished.

At last! At last she was by my side, right there—and did it at all matter where this *there* was? The familiar saffron-yellow silk, the smile-bite, the eyes with the blinds down. . . . My lips, my hands, my knees were quivering, while the silliest of thoughts went through my head: "Vibrations are sound. Quivering must produce sound. Why, then, can't it be heard?"

Her eyes opened wide for me. I entered into them.

"I couldn't stand it any more! Where were you? Why—" Without taking my eyes off her I talked on as if in delirium, quickly, incoherently—possibly I may even have been merely thinking, without actually speaking. "There's a shadow— following me. . . . I died . . . coming out of the clothes closet. Because that doctor of yours . . . said with his scissors that I have a soul . . . it's incurable—"

"An incurable soul! My poor little boy!" E- began to laugh —and asperged me with her laughter; all the delirium passed, and the flakes of laughter were sparkling, tinkling everywhere and how fine—how fine!—everything was. . . .

The doctor came back from around the corner—the wonderful, splendid, ever-so-thin doctor.

"Well, now," he came to a stop close to her.

"It's nothing, nothing! I'll tell you about it later. He got here by chance. Tell them I'll be back in . . . fifteen minutes or so—"

The doctor flitted around the corner. She waited. The door closed with a thud. Thereupon E- slowly, slowly, plunging the sharp, delectable needle ever deeper into my heart, nestled against me with her shoulder, her arm, all of herself, and we walked off together—together, the two of us as one.

I don't remember at what point we turned off into the darkness—and then, in the darkness, silently, started mounting

endless steps. I did not see it but I knew that she was walking
the same way that I was: with eyes closed, like one blind, her
head thrown back, biting her lips and listening to the music—
the music of my barely perceptible tremor.

I came back to my senses in one of the countless nooks in
the courtyard of the House of Antiquity; there was some sort
of a fence, the exposed stony ribs and yellow fangs of half-
ruined walls were jutting out of the ground. She opened her
eyes. Said: "Day after tomorrow, at sixteen." And left.

Did all this actually take place? I don't know. I will know
—day after tomorrow. There is only one real trace: the skin
is scraped off the finger tips of my right hand. But today, on
the *Integral,* the Second Builder assured me that he himself
had seen me accidentally touch a polishing disc with those
very fingers—and that was that. Well, perhaps that was it.
Very likely. I don't know. I don't know a thing.

EIGHTEENTH ENTRY: *The Jun-*   Yesterday I lay down—and
gles of Logic. Wounds and a   at once foundered to the bot-
Plaster. Never Again.   tom of the sea of sleep, like
an overloaded ship when it keels over. Crushing masses of
swaying green water. And I slowly floated up from the bottom
and about halfway I opened my eyes: I was in my room; the
morning was still green, congealed. A splinter of the sun on
the mirror of the closet door was aimed at my eyes. This
interfered with my fulfilling the exact quota of sleep hours
prescribed by The Tables of Hourly Commandments. The
best thing of all would have been to open the closet door, but
I felt as if I were all cocooned in cobwebs, and the cobwebs
were in my eyes as well; getting up was beyond my strength.

But get up I did, just the same, opened the closet—and
suddenly, behind its mirror-door, extricating herself from her
dress, all rosy, was E-. By that time I had become so used to
the most improbable things that, as far as I can recall, I was
not even in the least surprised, did not ask a single question—
I lost no time getting into the closet, slammed the door to
and, gasping, hurriedly, blindly, greedily blended into one
with E-. I can see it all right now: a sharp sunbeam penetrated through the crack of the door and, in the darkness, it

zigzagged like lightning on the floor of the closet, on one of its walls, going higher—and then this cruel, glittering blade fell upon E-'s bared upturned neck: and this had about it something so terrifying to me that I could not endure it; I cried out—and opened my eyes again.

I was in my room. The morning was still green, congealed. A splinter of the sun rested on the mirror of the closet door. I was in my bed. So—a dream. But my heart was still beating riotously, fluttering, jetting; there was a nagging tingling at my finger and toe tips, at my knees. There was no doubt about these things. And right then I did not know which was dream and which reality; irrational quantities were sending up shoots through all that was solid, habitual, tridimensional, and instead of firm, polished planes there was something gnarled, shaggy around me. . . .

There was still plenty of time before the bell for rising; I lay there thinking—and an exceedingly curious logical chain unwound itself before me. For every equation, every formula in the superficial world there is a corresponding curve or solid. For irrational formulae, for my $\sqrt{-1}$, we know of no corresponding solids; we have never seen them. But that is precisely where the horror lies: these solids, though unseen, do exist, inevitably, ineluctably, because in mathematics, as if on a screen, their whimsical, prickly shadows—irrational formulae—pass before us: and mathematics and death are never in error. And if we do not see these solids in our universe, on the surface, there does exist—there must unescapably exist—an entire immense universe of their own there, below the surface.

I jumped up without waiting for the rising bell and took to dashing up and down the room. My mathematics, up to then the sole firm and unshakable island in my dislocated life, had in its turn broken away, had floated off, going round and round. Well, then, did that mean that this ludicrous *soul* was just as real as my unif, as my boots, even though I did not see them just then (they were behind the mirror-door of the closet)? And if the boots were not a disease, how did it happen that the *soul* was one?

I sought for a way out of the logical wildwood and could

not find it. This wildwood was much the same as the unknown and scary impenetrable forests beyond the Green Wall—and, at the same time, these forests were extraordinary, incomprehensible creatures who spoke without words. It appeared to me that I was seeing, through some sort of thick glass, an infinitely enormous and, at the same time, an infinitely small $\sqrt{-1}$, scorpioid, with a hidden yet constantly sensed minus sign for a sting. But then, perhaps this was nothing but my *soul,* which, like the legendary scorpion of the ancients, was of its own will stinging itself with all that which———

The bell. Day. All the above, without dying, without vanishing, was merely covered with daylight—just as visible objects are, without dying, covered over at nightfall with the darkness of night. My head was filled with a light, wavering haze. Out of the haze emerged long tables of glass; spheroid heads chewing slowly, silently, in perfect time. From some distant point the ticking of a metronome reached me through the haze, and to this customary and gentle accompaniment I, together with all the others, mechanically counted up to fifty: the fifty legalized mastications for each morsel. And, mechanically marking time, I went downstairs and checked off my name in the register of those leaving (just as all the others checked off their names). Yet I felt that I was leading a separate existence, alone, surrounded by a soft, sound-absorbing wall, and that my universe lay within this wall.

However, here is a point: If this world is only mine, how does it happen to be in these records? Why are those preposterous *dreams,* closets, endless corridors to be found herein? I perceive with much regret that instead of a well-constructed and strictly mathematical poem glorifying The One State I am turning out some sort of a romance of fantastic adventure. Ah, if it were really no more than a fantastic romance instead of my present life, full of X's, $\sqrt{-1}$'s and downfalls. . . .

Still, perhaps this is all for the best. Most probably you, my unknown readers, are children by comparison with us (after all, we have been reared by The One State—consequently we have attained the highest summits that man can possibly attain). And, like children, you will swallow all the bitter things I shall give you only when they are thoroughly coated with the thick syrup of adventure. . . .

Evening:

Are you familiar with the feeling of being in an aero, climbing at top speed up a blue spiral—the window is open, a strong wind, whistling, buffets your face, there is no earth, you forget about the earth, the earth is just as far removed from you as Saturn, Jupiter, Venus? That is how I am living now; a strong wind is buffeting my face, and I have forgotten about the earth, I have forgotten about dear, rosy O-. But, just the same, the earth exists; sooner or later one must plane down to it, and I am merely closing my eyes to avoid seeing the date marked with her name—with the name O-90—on my Sexual Schedule.

This evening the remote earth gave me a reminder of itself.

In order to carry out the doctor's recommendation (I sincerely, most sincerely, want to get well) I spent all of two hours rambling the glassy, rectilinear deserts of the main avenues. All the numbers, in conformance with The Tables of Hourly Commandments, were in the auditoria, and only I. . . . Properly speaking, I presented an unnatural sight. Imagine a finger lopped off a man, off his hand—a human finger, all hunched up and bent over, hopping and dashing over the glass sidewalk all by its lonesome. I was that finger. And the strangest, most unnatural thing of all was that this finger had no desire whatsoever to be on the hand, to be with the other digits; the finger wanted to be either the way it was, all by itself, or . . . Well, now, I no longer have anything to conceal: or to be with her, with that woman, transfusing as before one's whole being into hers through her shoulder, through interlaced fingers. . . .

I came back to my building only when the sun was setting. The roseate ashes of evening lay upon the glass of walls, upon the spire of the Accumulator Tower, upon the voices and smiles of the numbers one came across. Rather strange, isn't it: the rays of the sun as they are about to be extinguished fall at the same angle as those that are being enkindled in the morning, yet everything is altogether different, the roseate hue is of a different nature: at sunset it is most gentle, just the least bit on the bitter side, whereas when morning comes it will again be pealing, effervescent.

And then, in the vestibule, U- the controller rummaged at the bottom of a heap of envelopes covered with the roseate sun-ashes and, pulling out a letter, handed it to me. She is (I repeat) a most respectable woman, and I'm certain that she could not be better disposed toward me. But, just the same, every time I see those pendulous cheeks which look like fish gills I have an unpleasant feeling, somehow.

As she extended the letter to me with her knotty hand, U-sighed. That sigh, however, merely fluttered, so very slightly, the curtain which separated me from the world: all my being was projected at the envelope shaking in my hand and which (I had no doubt) contained a letter from E-.

At this point there came a second sigh, doubly underlined and so clear that I tore myself away from the envelope and beheld, between the fish gills and peeping through the jalousies of bashfulness over her lowered eyes, a tender, cocooning, blinding smile. And then: "You poor, poor dear"—this time the sigh was triply underlined and she gave a barely perceptible nod toward the letter—the contents of which she naturally knew, since it was her duty to read all letters.

"But really, I . . . what makes you say that?"

"No, no, my dear—I know you better than you know yourself. I have been keeping an eye on you for a long time now, and I perceive that what is needed here is for someone who has been a student of life for many years to walk hand in hand with you along life's path—"

I felt myself all gummed over by her smile: it was intended as a plaster to be applied to all the wounds which would shortly be inflicted upon me by the letter shaking in my hand. And finally there came through the jalousies of bashfulness, ever so softly: "I will think about it, my dear—I will think about it. And you may rest assured that if I should feel sufficiently strong . . . but no, no—I must think about it some more at first—"

Great Benefactor! Could it be that I was fated to . . . could it be that she was trying to say that———

There were spots before my eyes—thousands of sinusoids; the letter was simply leaping. I drew nearer the light, nearer the wall. There the sun was smoldering out, and, from there, more and more densely, the old-rose, tristful ashes were falling upon the floor, upon me, my hands, the letter.

The envelope was torn open; no time lost in getting to the signature—and the wound was dealt. The letter was not from E-, not from E- at all; the writer was O-. And another wound: a blot had spread over the lower right-hand corner of the small sheet: something had splashed there. I can't bear blots, it doesn't matter whether made by ink or by . . . no matter what. And I know that formerly I would simply have found it unpleasant; my eyes would have found it unpleasant—an unpleasant blotch like that. Why, then, did that grayish small blotch seem, at that point, a very cloud, and why did it make everything more and more leaden-hued, more and more somber? Or, was that the *soul* cutting up again?

Here is her letter:

> You know—or, perhaps, you don't—that I can't write well. However, that doesn't matter: right now you know that without you I won't have a single day, a single morning, a single spring. Because to me R- is only . . . however, that is of no importance to you. At any rate, I am very grateful to him, for if I were all alone these days, without him, I don't know what I would do. During these days and nights I have lived through ten—or perhaps twenty—years. And it seems as if my room were not square but round, and I walk round and round, without end, and it's always the same thing, over and over, and there are no doors of any kind anywhere.
>
> I can't do without you—because I love you. Because I see, I understand: you need no one now, no one in the world, except her, that other one—and, you understand, if I do love you, that is precisely why I must————
>
> I need only two or three days more to patch up out of the scraps of myself something that will have at least some resemblance to the former O-90—and then

I'll go and notify them that I am taking your name off my register, and things are bound to be better for you; you are bound to feel fine. Forgive me; I'll never bother you again.

O-.

Never again. It's better so—she is right. But why, then— why————

NINETEENTH ENTRY: *An Infinitesimal of the Third Order. A Glowering Glance. Over the Parapet.* There, in that queer corridor with its dotted line of tremulous, dim, small electric bulbs . . . or—no, no, it wasn't there; later on, when she and I were already in one of the lost nooks in the courtyard of the House of Antiquity, she had said: "Day after tomorrow." The day after tomorrow is today, and all things have wings and are in flight; the day is flying, and our *Integral* is winged by now: we finished the installation of the rocket motor and tried it out today with blank charges. What magnificent, mighty salvos, and in my ears each one of them was a salute in honor of her, the one woman—and in honor of this day.

At the first try (= blast) something like half a score of the numbers working on our site hadn't been fast enough in getting out from under the exhaust—and absolutely nothing was left of them except a few tiny nondescript fragments and a little soot. With pride I record here that the rhythm of our work was not broken even for a second by this, not a man was startled, and we and our lathes went on with our rectilinear or circular motions with the same precision as if nothing had happened. Ten numbers represent hardly 1/100,000,000th of our One State; for the purposes of practical calculation this is an infinitesimal of the third order. Pity based upon arithmetical illiteracy was something that was known only to the ancients: we find it mirth-provoking.

And I also find it mirth-provoking that yesterday I was capable of cogitating about some pitiful grayish blob, about some blot or other—and even of recording such cogitations on these pages. That was still that same "softening of the surface," whereas the surface must be as hard as a diamond, as hard as our walls (there is an ancient saying about "throwing peas against a wall").

Sixteen o'clock. I did not go for the supplementary walk: who knows, she might have gotten the notion of coming at precisely this hour, when all things are pealing because of the sun. . . . I am practically the only one in the building. Through the sun-shot walls I can see far to the right and left and downward—I can see the empty rooms, suspended in the air and catoptrically repeating one another. And only on the bluish staircase, darkened just a trifle by the shading of the sun, is there a shadow, gaunt, gray, slowly crawling upward. There, I can hear footsteps, and I can see—can feel—through the door that a plaster-smile has been slapped on my face; then she passes by and goes down another staircase.

The indicator clicked. Not just my eyes—all of me strained toward the instrument's white blank and . . . and some unfamiliar male number appeared thereon (consonants denote males—and the indicator showed a consonant). The elevator droned; its door popped open. I was confronted by a forehead that looked like a rakishly slanted and lowered cap brim, while the eyes . . . the eyes created a very odd impression: as though the fellow were speaking from under his eyebrows, as if speech were coming out of his eyes.

"Here's a letter for you from her"—this came from under his eyebrows, as if from under an overhang. "She asked that everything should be done without fail, as the letter says."

He glowered all around him from under his eyebrows, from under their overhang.

"Why, there's nobody here—nobody at all. There, let's have it!"

He glowered about him once more, thrust the letter at me, went away. I was left alone. No—not alone: the envelope yielded a pink coupon and a barely perceptible perfume—her perfume. It was she who had sent the letter; she would come, she would come to me. Let me see the letter without delay, so that I may read it with my own eyes, so that I may wholly believe this—

What! This just couldn't be so! I read the letter once more, skipping some lines: "The coupon . . . and do not fail to lower the blinds, as if I were really with you. . . . It is absolutely necessary for me to have them think that I . . . I feel very, very sorry—"

The letter is torn into scraps. I caught a second's glimpse of my distorted, broken eyebrows in the mirror. I picked up the coupon, to have it share the fate of her note———

"She asked that everything should be done without fail, as the letter says."

My hands weakened, grew lax. The coupon fell from them on to the table. She was stronger than I and apparently I would do what she wished. However . . . however, I don't know: we'll see; there is still a lot of time before evening. . . . The coupon remained lying on the table.

The mirror reflected my distorted, broken eyebrows. Why didn't I have a doctor's certificate for today as well, so that I might start out and walk, walk endlessly, all around the Green Wall, and then fall into bed, sink to the bottom of the ocean of dreams. . . . But no: one had to go to Auditorium No. 13, had to wind all of oneself tight, so as to sit for two hours without stirring . . . whereas one really felt like screaming, like stamping one's feet.

The lecture. It was very strange that the voice issuing from the sparkling apparatus was not the usual metallic one but a soft, shaggy, mossy voice. A woman's voice: I have a flitting image of what she must have been like in life: a tiny crone, all bent and bowed, something on the style of the one attached to the House of Antiquity.

The House of Antiquity . . . and at the thought everything at once spouted upward like a fountain, and I exerted all my strength to wind myself tight, so as not to drown out every sound in the auditorium with my screaming. The soft, shaggy words went right through me, and all that remained of everything that was said was something about children, about child culture. I was like a photographic plate: I was making a print within myself of everything with some sort of alien, aloof, senseless exactitude: reflected light formed a golden sickle on the loudspeaker; lying under this reflection, by way of a living illustration, was a child; it was stretching itself toward the reflected sickle; the hem of its microscopic unif was thrust into its mouth; one tiny fist was clenched, with the thumb on the inside; there was light, fluffy shading over the plump crease on its wrist. Like a photographic plate I was making a print: now there was a naked little leg hanging over the edge of the table; the toes, spread in a pink fan, were about to step on air—in a moment, in just a moment, the child would smash against the floor————

And—a woman's scream; with a sweep of the diaphanous wings of her unif she flew up on the platform, caught up the baby, put her lips to the crease at its chubby wrist, moved the baby to the center of the table, came down from the platform. The print within me: the mouth a rosy crescent, with the horns downward; the eyes blue, like small saucers filled to the brim. It was O-. And I, as if I were perusing some harmonious formula, suddenly felt the inevitability, the predetermination of that trifling occurrence.

She sat down behind me, just a little to my left. I looked at her over my shoulder; she submissively took her eyes away from the table with the baby on it, fixed them on me, within me, and, once more, she, I and the table on the platform constituted three points, and drawn through these points were three lines, the projections of certain events, inevitable but as yet unperceived.

Home, by way of a green, dusky street, by that time many-eyed with lights. I heard myself ticking all over, like a watch. And the watch hands within me were just about to overstep a designated figure; I would do something that would cut off all retreat. She found it necessary to have someone, somewhere, think that she was with me. Whereas she was necessary to me, and why should I concern myself with any "necessity" of hers? I didn't want to serve as a blind for anybody else; I didn't want to, and that was all there was to it.

Behind me, a familiar flat-footed walk, as if the walker were slogging through puddles. (By now I no longer turn around to look; I know it's S-.) He would tail me to the very door and then, probably, remain standing below, on the sidewalk, and keep boring upward with those small drills in his eyes, into my room—until the window blinds there fell, concealing somebody's crime.

He, this Guardian angel, had already put a period after everything. I had decided not to let him have his way. I had decided.

When I had gone up to my room and turned on the light switch I could not believe my eyes: O- was standing by my table. Or, more correctly, she was dangling there, the way a crumpled dress dangles after the wearer has taken it off. As if there were no longer even one spring under her dress; her arms, her legs had no springs; her voice was pendent, springless.

"I have come about my letter. Have you received it? Yes? I must know your answer; I must—this very day."

I shrugged. As I contemplated her blue, brimming eyes, I enjoyed taking my time about answering her, just as if she were to blame for everything. And, with enjoyment, plunging each word into her, I said: "The answer? Well, now. . . . You're right. Absolutely. About everything."

"That means"—a smile concealed the almost imperceptible tremor of her lips, but I perceived it. "Very well, then! I'm going right . . . right now."

And she continued dangling over the table. Her eyes, her arms, her legs—all were slack. The other woman's crumpled pink coupon was still lying on the table. I quickly spread this *We* manuscript of mine, covering the coupon with its pages (perhaps this covering up was more for my sake than O-'s).

"There, I'm writing all the time. One hundred and seventy pages by now. The result is something quite unexpected—"

"But do you remember"—her voice was the shadow of a voice—"the time . . . the time I let a tear fall on—on page seven of what you were writing, and you—"

The tiny blue saucers brimmed over; inaudible tears hurriedly trickled down her cheeks; words hurriedly pattering over the brim: "I can't bear this—I'm leaving right now. . . . I'll never again . . . and I don't care. But the only thing I want—the only thing I must have—is a child by you. Let me have a child and I'll go away—I'll go away!"

I saw: she was all aquiver under her unif, and I felt that I, too, would at any moment———— I put my hands behind me; I smiled:

"What? Are you hankering for the Machine of The Benefactor?"

And, as before, the words spurted at me, like streams overflowing dams: "I don't care! But then I shall feel . . . I shall feel the child within me. And if but for a few days . . . to see—to see, if only once, the fold in its flesh, right here. . . . Like that baby there, on the table in the auditorium. For just one day!"

Three points: she, I, and there, on that table, the chubby clenched little hand with the crease on its chubby wrist.

I remember the time when I, as a child, was taken with some others to the Accumulator Tower. At the very top flight I leaned over the glass parapet. Below, the people were tiny dots, and my heart gave a delectable thump: "But what if I were to jump? . . ." At that time I grasped the railing still harder; this time I leapt over.

"So you want to go ahead with this? Realizing perfectly that—"

Her eyes were shut, as if she were staring directly at the sun. Her smile was moist, refulgent.

"Yes, yes! I do want to!"

I snatched the other's pink coupon from under the manuscript and started for the stairs, to run down to the controller on duty. O- seized my hand and called out something —but I didn't understand just what it was until I came back.

She was sitting on the edge of the bed, her hands pressed hard between her knees.

"Was that . . . was that her coupon?"

"Does it make any difference? Well, yes—it was hers."

Something crackled. Most probably it was nothing more than O-, slightly shifting. She sat there, hands between her knees, without uttering a word.

"Well? Let's hurry—" I roughly squeezed her hand and red spots (tomorrow they would be black-and-blue marks) appeared on her plump wrist, where she has that babyish crease.

That was the last thing I remember. Then: the switching off of the light, the extinguishing of thoughts, and darkness, and sparks in the darkness—and I was falling headlong over the parapet.

TWENTIETH ENTRY: *The Discharge. Material for Ideas. Zero Cliff.* A discharge: that is the most appropriate definition. Now I perceive that this was precisely like an electric discharge. The pulse of my last few days is becoming more and more crisp, more and more frequent, more and more tensed. The opposite poles are drawing ever nearer; there is a crisp crackle; one more millimeter—then an explosion, followed by silence.

Everything within me is now very quiet and empty, as in a building when everybody has left and you are lying alone, feeling ill, and you hear so clearly the distinct, metallic clicking of your thoughts.

Quite possibly it was this *discharge* that cured me at last of my excruciating soul, and I again became like all of us. At least by now I can mentally visualize, without any pain, O-standing on the steps of the Cube, I can visualize her under the Gas Bell Glass. And, if she should name me there, in the Operational Department, I shall not care: I will devoutly and gratefully kiss at the last moment the punitive hand of The Benefactor. In my relationship to The One State I have the right to receive punishment, and this right I shall never relinquish. No number among us should renounce, or should dare to renounce this sole—and hence the most precious—right of his.

. . . Ever so quietly, with metallic distinctness, my thoughts keep clicking away; an immaterial aero bears me off into the azure heights of my beloved abstractions. And I see how there, in the purest, rarefied air, my argument about the "actual right" bursts with a pop like a pneumatic tire. And I see clearly that this is no more than an eructation of the preposterous prejudice the ancients had: their ideas of having any *right*.

There are ideas of clay—and there are ideas carved for all time out of gold, or out of our precious glass. And, in order to determine the substance of an idea, all that is needed is to apply a drop of strong acid to it. One of these acids was known even to the ancients: *reductio ad finem*. That, I believe, is what they called it; but they were afraid of this poison; they preferred to see some sort of heaven at least— even though of clay, even though toylike—rather than an azure nothingness. We, however—glory be to The Benefactor! —are adults, and we have no need of toys.

Well, then—suppose we apply a drop of acid on the idea of *a right*. Even among the ancients, the more mature ones knew that the source of right was force, that right was a function of force. Well, here is a pair of scales. On one is a gram, on the other a ton; *I* on one, *We,* The One State, on the other. Is it not clear, then, that the assumption that the *I* can have some *rights* or other in relationship to the State, and the assumption that a gram can counterbalance a ton—why, these two assumptions absolutely amount to one and the same thing. Hence the allocation: the rights to the ton, the duties to the gram, while the natural course from nullity to grandeur is to forget that you are a gram and to feel that you are a millionth part of a ton.

You florid-bodied, rosy-cheeked Venusians, you Uranians, sooty as blacksmiths—I, in my azure silence, can hear you murmuring in protest. But do understand this: everything that is great is simple; do understand, that the only things unshakable and eternal are the four rules of arithmetic. And only that morality which is built upon these four rules will prove great, unshakable, eternal. This is the ultimate wisdom; this is the pinnacle of that pyramid up which men, red from sweating, kicking out and hoarsely panting, have been clambering through the ages. And from that pinnacle one can see where, at the very base, something that has survived within us from the savagery of our ancestors is still stirring like a cluster of insignificant worms; from this summit O-, the illegal mother, and the murderer, and that madman who dared to toss a rhymed squib at The One State, are all alike. And alike is the judgment meted out to them—premature death. This is that same divine justice which the Stone-House People dreamt of as they were bathed by the roseate, naïve rays of the dawn of history: their *God* dealt out the same punishment for blasphemy against the Holy Church that He dealt out for murder.

You Uranians, grim and dark as the Spaniards of antiquity, who were ingeniously skilled in their *autos-da-fé*, you are silent; apparently you agree with me. But, my rosy Venusians, I hear you murmuring something about tortures, executions, a return to barbaric times. My dear ones, I feel sorry for you—you are incapable of thinking philosophically-mathematically.

Human history ascends in circles—like an aero. The circles vary in color, some golden, some bloody, but all alike are divided into 360°. Counting from zero we have 10°, 20°, 200°, 360°—and we are again at zero. Yes, we have returned to zero—yes! But to my mathematically reasoning mind it is clear that this zero is a new, altogether different one. We went from the zero to the right—we came back to the zero from the left—hence, instead of plus zero we have minus zero. You understand?

This zero I envisage as a somehow taciturn, enormous cliff, narrow and sharp as the cutting edge of a knife. Amid the feral, shaggy darkness we have, with bated breath, cut our moorings and set out from the black nocturnal side of Zero Cliff. For ages we Columbuses sailed and sailed; we circumnavigated the whole world and at last—hurrah! Salvos, and then up the masts we went, all of us: lying before us was the other, hitherto unknown side of Zero Cliff, lit up by the aurora borealis of The One State, a blue mass, the coruscations of rainbows, of the sun—of hundreds of suns, of billions of rainbows. . . .

What matters it if only the thickness of a knife blade separates us from the other, the black side of Zero Cliff? A knife is the most substantial, the most immortal object, the greatest work of genius among all the things created by man. The knife served as a guillotine; the knife is a universal device for cutting all knotty problems, and the path of paradoxes lies along the sharp edge of a knife—the only path befitting a fearless mind.

TWENTY-FIRST ENTRY: *An Author's Duty. The Ice Thickens. The Most Difficult Love.*

Yesterday was her day, and again she did not come, and again there was an incoherent note from her which explained nothing. But I am tranquil, perfectly tranquil. And if I still go through with whatever the note dictates, if I still carry her pink coupon to the controller on duty and then, having lowered the blinds, sit all alone in my room, I do so, naturally, not at all because I haven't the strength to go against her wishes. The very idea is mirth-provoking! Of course that's not it at all. The thing is very simple: in the first place, isolated by the blinds from all plastery, therapeutic smiles, I am able to write these very lines in peace. And, secondly, I am afraid of losing in her, in E-, the only key to the solution of all the unknown quantities (the incident of the clothes closet, my temporary death, and so on). And I consider it my duty to discover them, if only as the author of these records, to say nothing of the fact that the unknown is, in general, inimical to man, and *homo sapiens* is man in the fullest sense of that phrase only when his grammar has absolutely no question marks but exclamation points, commas and full stops exclusively.

And so, guided by what seems to me nothing but my duty as an author, I took an aero at 16:00 today and once more set out for the House of Antiquity, in the teeth of a strong wind. The aero had difficulty making headway through the aerial thicket with its translucent branches soughing and lashing. The city below seemed to be made entirely of blocks of blue ice. Suddenly a cloud cast a fleeting oblique shadow; the ice below turned to a leaden hue; it swelled up. That's the way it happens in spring, when you are standing on the river bank, expecting everything to start cracking, surging, swirling, rushing at any moment; minute after minute passes, however, yet the ice remains stationary, and you yourself feel that you are swelling, your heart pounds still more restlessly, still more frequently—however, why am I writing about this since, after all, there is no icebreaker that could possibly break the most translucent, the most solid crystal of our life————

There was no one at the entrance to the House of Antiquity. I walked around it and found the old woman who acted as gatekeeper standing near the Green Wall, shielding her eyes with her hand as she stared upward. There, beyond the wall, were the acute black triangles of some birds or other; cawing, they threw themselves into the attack, breasting the impenetrable fence of electric waves—then, repelled, soared again above the wall.

I caught fleeting oblique shadows sweeping over the dark wrinkle-covered face, a fleeting glance in my direction.

"There's nobody here—nobody, nobody! Yes, and there's no use your coming around here. Yes!"

There, just what did she mean by that *no use?* And what odd behavior, to consider me no more than somebody's shadow! But perhaps all of you are my shadows: was it not I who peopled with you these pages which only recently were quadrangular deserts of white? Come, if it were not for me, would you ever be seen by those whom I shall lead over the narrow paths of the lines I have written?

Naturally, I did not say all this to her; through my own experience I know that the most excruciating thing is to implant in an individual a doubt as to his or her being a reality—a three-dimensional reality rather than some other sort. I merely remarked to her drily that her business was only to tend the entrance, and she let me into the courtyard.

Emptiness. Quiet. The wind—there, beyond the walls— was far off, as on that day that we, shoulder to shoulder, two as one, emerged from below, from those corridors—provided that that ever really happened. I walked under stone arches of some kind and the sound of my footsteps, after rebounding from the damp vaults, fell behind me, as though someone were constantly striding at my heels. The yellow walls, with eruptions of red brick, were watching me through the square spectacles of their windows, watching me as I opened the singing doors of sheds, as I peered into corners, dead ends and crannies. A wicket door in a fence and a wasteland: a memorial of the Two Hundred Years' War—protruding from the ground, the bared ribs of stone, the grinning yellow jaws of walls, an ancient oven with the vertical of a chimney: a ship petrified forever amid lashing waves of yellow stone and red brick.

It seemed to me that I had already seen those identical yellow teeth once before—indistinctly, as if I had been at the bottom and looking up through masses of water—and I began my search. I fell into pits, stumbled against stones; rusty paws kept clutching at my unif, acrid-salty drops of sweat crept down my forehead and into my eyes.

It was nowhere! I could not find anywhere the exit through which we had emerged from the corridors below at that time; it did not exist. However, perhaps it was actually better so: there was a greater probability that this whole thing was one of my preposterous *dreams*.

Tired out, covered all over with dust and cobwebs, I opened the wicket door to re-enter the main courtyard. Suddenly, a rustle behind me, squelching footsteps—and the rosy wing-ears, the double-curved smile of S-, sprang up before me.

"Out for a stroll?" he asked, puckering his eyes and boring into me with their tiny drills. I made no answer. My hands were hindering me. "Well, what about it—are you feeling better now?"

"Yes, thank you. Apparently I am getting back to normal."

He dismissed me, lifted his eyes high. His head was thrown back—and that was the first time I noticed his Adam's apple.

From above, not too high (about 50 meters), came the droning of aeros. I recognized them by their slow flight, their low altitude and the observation tubes hanging down like black proboscises; I recognized them as belonging to the Guardians. There weren't just two or three of them, as usual, but from ten to twelve (I regret having to confine myself to an approximate number).

"Why are there so many of them today?" I made bold enough to ask.

"Why? Hm. . . . A real physician takes to treating a patient who is still well but who will be taken ill only to-morrow, or the day after—or a week later. Prophylaxis, to be sure!" He nodded, and started off with flapping steps over the flagstones of the yard. Then he turned and threw at me over his shoulder: "Be careful!"

I was alone. Quiet. Emptiness. Far above the Green Wall the birds and the wind were darting about. Just what did he want to convey by that phrase?

My aero glided swiftly with the air stream. Light shadows and heavy, cast by clouds; below, the blue cupolas, the cubes of glass ice were turning a leaden hue, were swelling up.

Evening:

I have opened my manuscript in order to include in its pages a number of thoughts which, I believe, will be useful (to you, my readers), concerning the great Day of Unanimity, which Day is almost here. However, I realized that I could not write just then. All the time I was listening intently; all the time I was looking behind me, expecting something. Expecting what? I don't know. And when the familiar brownishly pink fish gills appeared in my room I was very glad—I say this in all sincerity. She sat down, chastely straightened out a fold of her unif that had fallen between her knees, quickly pasted me all over with her smiles—a small patch of a smile to each one of my cracks—and I felt myself pleasantly, firmly bound.

"You understand, when I entered the classroom today"—she works in the Educational Plant for children—"what did I see on the wall but a caricature! Yes, yes, I assure you that's a fact. They made me look like some sort of fish. Perhaps I really do look like that—"

"No, no, whatever are you saying!" I hastened to protest (really, close at hand it is clear that there is nothing about her resembling fish gills, and whatever I may have written here about fish gills is utterly irrelevant).

"Well, after all is said and done, that is of no real importance. But, you understand, there is the act as such. Naturally, I called in the Guardians at once. I am very fond of children, and I consider that cruelty constitutes the most arduous, the highest sort of love. You understand?"

How else! What she said was on all fours with my ideas. I could not resist and read out to her a bit from my Twentieth Entry, beginning with: ". . . you hear so clearly the distinct, metallic clicking of your thoughts."

Without looking at her directly I saw how the brownishly pink cheeks were quaking and that they were drawing ever closer to me—and then dry, hard, even somewhat prickly fingers were placed in my hands.

"Let me have that, let me have that! I will have a recording made of it and make the children learn it by heart. It isn't so much the Venusians who need it as we—we, right now, tomorrow, the day after—" She looked about her and then said, her voice quite low: "Have you heard? They're saying that on the Day of Unanimity—"

"What . . . what are they saying?" I sprang up from my seat. "What about the Day of Unanimity?"

The snug walls were no longer there. I instantly felt myself cast out, out in the open, where the enormous wind was dashing about over the roofs and the oblique clouds of dusk were lowering more and more ponderously and ominously. U-took me around the shoulders with resolute firmness (although, in rationalizing my agitation, I noticed that her small bony fingers were trembling).

"Sit down, my dear; don't upset yourself. What won't people say? And besides, if you should but need me, I will be near you on that day. I will leave my schoolchildren in somebody else's care and shall be with you—because you, my dear, are also a child and you have need of—"

"No, no!" I gestured in protest. "Not for anything! You will really think then that I am some sort of child, that I can't be on my own. . . . Not for anything!" (I confess I had other plans for that day.)

She smiled; if spelled out, the text of that smile would have evidently approximated: "Oh, what a stubborn little boy!" Then she sat down. Eyes lowered. Hands modestly adjusting a fold of her unif which had again fallen between her knees. And she broached something else: "I think that I must decide . . . for your sake. . . . No, I implore you not to hurry me—I must give it further thought—"

I did not hurry her. Even though I understood that it behooved me to be happy and that there was no greater honor than serving as the crowning glory in the evening of someone's life.

. . . The whole night was beset by wings of some sort, and I kept on the go all the time, with my hands and arms protecting my head from these wings. And then—a chair. Not one of our modern chairs but of an ancient style, and wooden. With a horselike gait (right foreleg and left hindleg, left foreleg and right hindleg) this chair trotted up to my bed and climbed up on it; it was uncomfortable, painful—and I loved that wooden chair.

It is amazing: is it really impossible to contrive any remedy against this dreaming disease that would cure it or make it rational—perhaps even put it to some use?

TWENTY-SECOND ENTRY: *Comatose Waves. All Things Attaining Perfection. I Am a Microbe.* Picture yourself standing on the shore of the sea. The waves rise rhythmically— and, at their highest, suddenly remain thus, congealed, comatose. It was just as ghastly and unnatural a phenomenon when our walk, ordained by The Tables of Hourly Commandments, was suddenly thrown into confusion and, disrupted, came to a halt. The last time anything like that had happened was 119 years ago when, as our chronicles proclaim, a meteorite plunged into the very midst of the walkers with great noise and much smoke.

We were walking the way we usually do—i.e., as the marching warriors are depicted on Assyrian monuments: a thousand heads, two composite integrated legs, two integrated swinging arms. From the end of the great avenue—where the Accumulator Tower was awesomely droning—a marching quadrangle was coming toward us: guards in front, at the sides and in the rear, and in the center a group of three whose unifs no longer bore the golden numbered badges. And everything became horripilantly clear.

The enormous face of the clock on the tip of the Tower was a face: leaning out of the clouds and spitting down its seconds, it was apathetically waiting. And then, precisely at 13:06, a commotion sprang up within the quadrangle. It all happened quite close to me; I could see the most minute details, and I have an extremely clear recollection of a thin long neck and, at one of the temples, a tangled interweaving of small blue veins that looked like rivers on a geographical map of some tiny unknown world—and this unknown world was, apparently, a youth. Probably he had noticed someone in our ranks: he got up on tiptoes, craned his neck and stopped. One of the guards snapped the bluish spark of his electric whip at him; the offender sent up a high-pitched yelp, like a puppy's. And then—a distinct snap, approximately every two seconds, followed by a squeal: snap—squeal.

We were walking as before, rhythmically, Assyrianly— and, as I contemplated the exquisite zigzags of the sparks, I was reflecting: "Everything in human society is attaining infinite perfection—and it is in duty bound to attain it. What a hideous weapon the ancient whip was, and how much beauty there is here—"

But at this point, like a nut flying off a wheel going at full speed, a slender, resiliently flexible female figure detached itself from our ranks and shouting: "Enough! Don't you dare!" threw herself directly at the quadrangle. This paralleled the fall of the meteor 119 years ago: we froze in our tracks and our ranks turned to gray crests of waves welded into ice by sudden frost.

For an instant I regarded her extraneously, just as all the others did: she was no longer a number; she was merely a human creature, she existed merely as the metaphysical substance of the insult which had been inflicted on The One State. But a certain movement of hers (as she turned she twisted her hips to the left)—and it became clear to me that I knew (I *knew*) that body, as pliant as a whiplash; my eyes, my lips, my hands knew it—at that moment I was utterly certain of it.

Two of the guards ran to cut her off. In an instant, at a point of the pavement still clear, mirrorous, their trajectories would cross—in an instant they would seize her. My heart gulped, stopped—and, without reasoning whether the action was permissible or interdicted, whether it was preposterous or wise, I made a dash for that point. I felt upon me thousands of eyes goggling in horror, but this merely bestowed still more of a certain desperately lilting power upon that wild being with hairy hands who had burst out of me and

who was running faster and faster. There was just a stride or
two more, when she turned around————

Before me was a quivering, freckle-strewn face with rusty-
red eyebrows. . . . It wasn't—it wasn't E-!

Frenzied joy lashed at me. I wanted to shout something
like "Serve her right!" or "Grab her!" but all I could hear was
my lips whispering something. But by now there was a heavy
hand on my shoulder; I was being detained, led away, as I
attempted to explain things to them: "But listen, you really
must understand that I thought this was—"

Yet how could I explain myself entirely, how explain this
entire illness of mine as I have recorded it on these pages?
And I was extinguished, I went along submissively. A leaf
torn from a tree by an unexpected onslaught of wind drifts
down submissively, yet on its way it swirls, catches at every
familiar branch, bifurcation, knotty twig; in the same way I
caught at each of the speechless spheroid heads, at the transparent ice of the walls, at the blue needle of the Accumulator
Tower plunged into a cloud.

At this moment, when an asbestos curtain was about to
fall between me and all of this resplendent world, I saw at
not too great a distance a familiar enormous head with flapping rosy wing-ears floating over the mirror of the pavement.
And then came the familiar flatted voice: "I consider it my
duty to testify that number D, Five Hundred and Three is
unwell and in no condition to control his emotions. And I
feel certain that he was carried away by a natural indigna-
tion—"

"Yes, yes!" I clutched at the straw. "I even shouted for
them to hold her!"

"You weren't shouting a thing," came from behind me.

"Yes, but I wanted to—I swear by The Benefactor I did!"

For a second the gray, chill, tiny drills of S-'s eyes bored
right through me. I don't know whether he saw within me
that this was (almost) the truth, or whether he had some
secret purpose in sparing me again for a time, but he wrote a
brief memo, handed it to one of the guards holding me and I
was once more free—i.e., I was once more confined in the
orderly, endless, Assyrian ranks.

The quadrangle, together with the freckled face and the temple with a geographical map of small blue veins within the quadrangle, disappeared around a corner—for good. We walked along, a single million-headed body, and within each of us was that meek joyfulness which, probably, constitutes the life of molecules, atoms and phagocytes. In the world of antiquity this was understood by the Christians, our only (even though very far from perfect) predecessors: meekness is a virtue, while pride is a vice; they also understood that *WE* is from God, while *I* is from the Devil.

There I was, at that point, walking in step with all of them, and yet, despite everything, apart from them all. I was still shaking from the perturbations I had gone through, like a trestle over which a railway train of the ancients had just rumbled. I was conscious of myself. But then, consciousness of self, awareness of individuality, pertains only to an eye with a speck of something in it, to an infected finger, to an aching tooth; when an eye, a finger, a tooth is sound each seems nonexistent, as it were. Is it not clear that consciousness of self is only a disease?

It may be that I am no longer a phagocyte calmly and in a businesslike way devouring microbes (with blue-veined temples and freckle-strewn faces): it may be that I am a microbe and, again, it may be that there is in our midst a thousand such microbes by now, still pretending to be phagocytes, as I am pretending to be one.

What if today's happening, which, properly speaking, is of small importance—what if all this is only the beginning, only the first meteorite out of a whole series of rumbling, blazing stones which Infinity has showered upon our paradise of glass?

TWENTY-THIRD ENTRY: *Flowers. Dissolution of a Crystal. "If only—"* There are (so they say) certain flowers which blossom only once in a hundred years. Why, then, shouldn't there also be flowers which blossom only once in a thousand years—or once in ten thousand years? It is possible we may not have known about this only because this once-in-a-thousand years arrived precisely today.

And so, in a blissful and tipsy mood, I went down the

stairs to the clerk on duty, and all around me, before my
eyes, the millennial buds were quickly and silently bursting,
and armchairs, shoes, gold badges, small electric bulbs, somebody's dark shaggy eyes, the faceted balusters of the railing,
a handkerchief dropped on the stairs, the clerk's small desk
and, above the desk, U-'s cheeks of polka-dotted pastel brown
—all these were blossoming forth. Everything was extraordinary, new, tender, roseate, humid.

U- took my pink stub—and through the glass of the wall
one could see, hanging over her head from an unprecedented
branch, a light-blue, aromatic moon. I solemnly pointed my
finger at it and said: "The moon—you understand?"

U- glanced at me, then at the number on the stub—and I
saw that familiar, charmingly chaste movement of hers: she
was adjusting the folds of her unif between her angular knees.

"You look abnormal and ill, dear—because abnormality
and illness are one and the same. You are ruining yourself,
and there's nobody—nobody!—to tell you so!"

This "nobody" was, of course, equated with the number
on the coupon: E-330. Darling, wonderful U-! You are right,
of course: I'm not prudent, I'm ailing, I'm afflicted with a
soul, I'm a microbe. But then, isn't all florescence an ailment?
Isn't it painful for a bud to burst? And don't you think that
the spermatozoid is the most frightful of microbes?

I was upstairs, in my room. E- was sitting within the wide-
open calyx of the armchair near the bed. I was on the floor,
embracing her legs; my head was on her knees. We were
silent. Stillness; the pulse racing. And so: I was a crystal, and
I was dissolving in her, in E-. I felt with perfect clarity how
the polished facets defining me in space were dissolving, constantly dissolving; I was vanishing, dissolving in her knees, in
her; I was becoming smaller and smaller—and at the same
time expanding, increasing more and more, becoming more
and more unencompassable. Inasmuch as she was not she but
the whole universe. But then, for a second, I and that ecstati-
cally transfixed armchair were one. And the magnificently
smiling crone at the doors of the House of Antiquity, and the
wild, impenetrable forests on the other side of the Green
Wall, and certain ruins, silver against black and half-asleep

like the crone, and a door that had slammed just then somewhere unbelievably far off—all these were within me and,
together with me, were listening to the beats of the pulse and
careering through a beatified second. . . .

In absurd, confused, submerged words I strove to tell her
that I was a crystal, and hence there was a door within me,
and hence I felt how happy the armchair was. But the result
was such a nonsensical farrago that, for very shame, I
stopped. Then, suddenly: "Dear E-, do forgive me. I simply
can't understand— I'm spouting such foolish stuff—"

"But what makes you think that folly isn't a good thing?
If we had groomed and cultivated folly through the ages as
we groomed and cultivated intelligence, it is possible that
something exceedingly precious might have resulted from it."

"Yes—" It seemed to me that she was right; how could she
have been anything but right at that moment?

"And merely for your folly—for what you did yesterday
during the walk—I love you all the more . . . all the more."

"But why did you torture me, then; why didn't you come;
why did you send your coupons; why did you compel me
to—"

"Well, perhaps I found it necessary to put you to the test?
Perhaps I found it necessary to know that you would do
everything I wanted—that you were completely mine by
now?"

"Yes—I am completely yours!"

She took my face—all of me—between her palms, raising
my head:

"Well, now what about your 'obligations of every honest
number'? Eh?"

Sweet, sharp, white teeth; a smile. In the open calyx of the
armchair she was like a bee: there was a sting in her—and
honey.

Yes, obligations. . . . In my mind I turned over the pages
of my last entries: really, there was not the least idea in
them to the effect that, properly speaking, I was obligated
to———

I kept silent. I was rapturously (and, probably, inanely)
smiling, gazing into her pupils, shifting from one to the other

and seeing myself in each one; I, tiny, a millimeter high, was imprisoned in those tiny, iridescent dungeons. And after that, again the bee lips, the delectable pain of florescence.

There is in each one of us numbers a certain invisible, quietly ticking metronome and we, without looking at a watch, know the exact time, within five minutes. But just then the metronome within me had run down; I did not know how much time had passed and, in a fright, I snatched out from under the pillow my badge with the watch inside. Glory to The Benefactor—there were still twenty minutes left! But those minutes were so very short that one felt like laughing; they were bobtailed, they ran along, and yet there was so much that I had to tell her: I had to tell her everything, had to put all of myself in my story: I had to let her know about O-'s letter and that horrible evening when I got her with child; and for some reason I had to tell about my childhood years: about Plyappa the mathematician about $\sqrt{-1}$, and how, the first time I had attended the Festival of Unanimity, I had cried bitterly because, on such a day, my unif turned out to have an inkspot on it.

E- raised her head and propped herself on her elbow. The two long sharp lines at the corners of her lips and the dark angles of her raised eyebrows formed a cross.

"Perhaps, on that day—" she stopped, and her eyebrows turned still darker. She took my hand, squeezing it hard. "Tell me: you won't forget me? You will always remember me?"

"Why do you say such things? What are you hinting at, E- darling?"

She did not say anything and by now her eyes were looking past me, through me; they were remote. Abruptly, I heard the wind beating its enormous wings against the glass (naturally, this noise had been going on all the while but I had heard it only at that point), and for some reason I recalled the piercing cries of the birds above the towering Green Wall.

E- tossed her head, as if she were casting off something. Once more, for a moment, her whole body came in contact with mine—the way an aero comes in momentary resilient contact with the ground just before landing.

"There, let me have my stockings! Quick!"

The stockings had been thrown on my desk, on top of these records of mine (open at p. 193). In my hurry I jostled the manuscript; the pages scattered and I simply could not make an orderly stack of them but, above all, even if I did stack them there would have been no real order, anyway—there would still remain certain riffles, yawning gaps, *X*'s. . . .

"I can't bear to have things this way," said I. "There, you are by my side, and yet it seems as if you were after all, behind one of those opaque walls of the ancients; I hear rustling and voices on the other side of that wall—and I can't make out the words, I don't know what is going on there. I can't bear to have things this way. You're forever leaving things half-said, somehow; not once have you told me where I had found myself that time in the House of Antiquity, and what those corridors were for, and how the doctor came to be there—or is it possible that nothing of all that ever happened?"

E- placed her hands on my shoulder; slowly she entered deep into my eyes: "You want to learn everything?"

"Yes, I do. I must."

"And you would not be afraid to follow me wherever I might go, to the very end—no matter where I might lead you?"

"Yes—anywhere!"

"Very well. I promise you this: when the Festival of Unanimity is over, if only . . . Oh, yes—what about your *Integral*? I always forget to ask you—will it be ready soon?"

"No. Go on: 'if only' what? Are you putting me off again? 'If only' what?"

She said (already near the door): "You'll see for yourself."

I was alone. All that had remained behind her was a barely perceptible fragrance, something like the sweet, dry yellow pollen of certain flowers growing on the other side of the Green Wall. That, and certain questions fixed firmly within me, like those barbed little hooks which the ancients used for the capture of fish (specimens are on display at the Prehistoric Museum).

. . . Why this sudden question of hers about the *Integral*?

TWENTY-FOURTH ENTRY: *Limi-* I am like a machine set to go
tations of a Function. Easter. at an excessive number of
Delete All. revolutions: the bearings
have become red-hot; one minute more and the molten metal
will start dripping and everything will turn into nothing.
Quick—let's have the cold water of logic. I pour it in bucketfuls, but the logic sizzles on the hot bearing and spreads
through the air in an elusive white vapor.

Well, yes: it is clear that to establish the true significance
of a function it is necessary to take its limitations into consideration. And it is clear that yesterday's preposterous "dissolution in the universe," if taken as the very limit, is death.
Inasmuch as death is precisely the fullest dissolution of oneself in the universe. *Ergo,* if we designate Love by L, and
Death by D, it follows that $L = f(D)$, i.e., love and
death———

Yes, precisely—precisely! And that's just why I fear E-,
why I struggle against her, why I don't want to die. Yet why
are "I don't want to" and "I feel a want" side by side within
me? That's precisely wherein the horror lies, that I feel I want
that blissful death of yesterday; that's precisely wherein the
horror lies, that even now, when the logical function has been
thoroughly integrated, when it is evident that death is a covert
component in it, I nonetheless want her; my lips, my arms
want her, my breast, every millimeter of me wants her. . . .

Tomorrow is the Day of Unanimity. She, too, will be there,
of course; I shall see her, but only from afar. From afar: that
will be painful, because I have to be by her side, because I
am irresistibly drawn to her, so that her hands, her shoulder,
her hair . . . But I want even this pain of distance—let it
come.

Great Benefactor! What absurdity—to want pain! Who
does not grasp that painful sensations are negative quantities
which, added together, reduce the sum which we call happiness? And, consequently—

There, now, let's have no *consequentlies* of any sort. All
clean. All bare.

Evening:

A windy, feverishly flushed, disquieting sunset, seen

through the glass walls of the building. I turned my armchair so as not to face this hectically rosy eyesore, started leafing the pages of these records—and perceived that I had again forgotten that I am writing not for myself but for you, my unknown readers, whom I love and pity, who are still plodding along somewhere in the remote—and submerged—ages.

There, let's talk about the great Day, the Day of Unanimity. I have always loved it, since my childhood years. It seems to me that it is, for us, something in the nature of what their *Easter* was for the ancients. I remember that on the eve of this Day I would make me a sort of small hour-calendar; exaltedly one crossed out each elapsed hour—one hour nearer, one hour less to wait! Upon my word, if I felt certain that no one would see me, I would carry a little calendar like that with me even now and keep track with it of the time still remaining till tomorrow, when I shall see, even though from afar———

(An interruption. They have brought me a new unif, fresh from the factory. According to custom, new unifs for tomorrow are issued to all of us. There are footsteps out in the hall, and exclamations of pleasure, and hubbub.)

I continue. Tomorrow I shall see the spectacle which is repeated year after year, yet which stirs one in a new way each time: the mighty chalice of accord, arms uplifted in reverence. Tomorrow is the day of the annual election of The Benefactor. Tomorrow we entrust The Benefactor anew with the keys to the impregnable citadel of our happiness.

Naturally, this bears no resemblance to the disorderly, unorganized elections of the ancients when (it sounds so funny to say it!) even the result of the elections was actually unknown in advance. To build a state upon utterly uncalculated chance happenings, blindly—what could be more senseless? And yet, as it turned out, centuries were required for this to be understood.

Is it necessary to say that in this instance, even as in all things, we have no room for any chance happenings whatsoever—nothing unexpected can eventuate. And the elections themselves have a significance that is more symbolic than anything else: to remind us that we are one mighty, million-

celled organism, that we are (to use the words of the Gospel
of the ancients) the One Church. Inasmuch as the history of
The One State does not know of a single instance of even one
voice having dared to violate our majestic unison on this
solemn Day.

They say that the ancients conducted their elections in
some secret manner, concealing themselves like thieves; some
of our historians even affirm that these ancients attended the
election celebrations painstakingly masked (I can imagine the
fantastically somber sight: night; a plaza; figures in dark
capes stealing along the walls; the torches with their dark-red
flames dancing in the wind). What the need was for all this
mysteriousness has not been definitely clarified to this day;
most probably the elections were tied up with certain mysti-
cal, superstitious—perhaps actually criminal—rites. But as for
us, we have nothing to conceal or to be ashamed of: we cele-
brate our elections openly, honestly, in the light of day. I can
see how all give their votes for The Benefactor—all can see
how I give my vote for The Benefactor—and how can things
be otherwise, since *all* and *I* are the one *We?* How much more
ennobling, sincere, lofty this is than the craven, thievish *mys-
tery* of the ancients! Then, too, how much more expedient
our way is: for, even if we suppose the impossible (i.e., some
dissonance amid our customary monophony), why, the unseen Guardians are right there, in our ranks—they are able to
determine immediately which numbers have fallen into error
and to save them from further false steps, as well as save The
One State from them. And, finally, there is one more
thing———

Through the wall to the left I could see a female number
hurriedly unbuttoning her unif. A second's blurred glimpse of
eyes, lips, two pointed rosebuds. Then the blinds fell; all the
things of yesterday instantaneously sprang to life within me,
and I did not know what "finally, there is one more thing"
referred to, and I didn't want to write about it—I didn't want
to! There is but one thing I want: E-. I want her always, at
any and every minute, to be with me—and with me only. And
that which I have written just now about Unanimity—all of
it is unnecessary, it isn't the right thing; I feel like deleting

everything, tearing it into scraps, chucking it out. Inasmuch as I know (let it be blasphemy, yet it is true) that the holiday will be a holiday only with her, if she will be by my side, shoulder to shoulder with me. But without her tomorrow's sun will be a small disk cut out of tin, and the sky a sheet of tin daubed over with blue, while I myself—

I snatched the telephone receiver: "Is this you, E-?"

"Yes, it is I. Why are you ringing so late?"

"Perhaps it's not too late yet. I want to ask you . . . I want you to be with me tomorrow. Darling—"

I uttered *darling*—softly. And for some reason there flitted through my mind something that had taken place this morning at the building site of the *Integral:* just for fun someone had placed a watch under a hundred-ton hammer—a full swing, wind in one's face, and then the quiet contact of one hundred tons of gentleness with the fragile watch.

A pause. I imagined that I could hear someone whispering there, in E-'s room. Then I heard her voice: "No, I can't do it. Surely, you understand that I myself would . . . no, I can't do it. Why? You'll see tomorrow."

It is night.

TWENTY-FIFTH ENTRY: *Descent from Heaven. Greatest Catastrophe in History. The Known Has Come to an End.*

When, as a preliminary to the opening of the celebration, all stood up and The Hymn, compounded of hundreds of tubes in the Musical Factory playing and of millions of human voices chanting, spread over our heads like a slowly wavering, imposing canopy—I for a second forgot everything: I forgot something disturbing that E- had said concerning today's holiday; I even forgot, I do believe, E- herself. At that moment I was the very same little boy who on a time had cried because on this Day there had been a spot on his unif, a spot so tiny that it was not noticeable to anyone but himself. Even if nobody around me saw what black, ineradicable spots were all over me, I myself nonetheless knew that there was no place for me, a criminal, among these open—wide open—faces. Ah, if I could but have stood up right then and, with a lump in my throat, have made a clean breast of it by shouting everything about myself! Let the end come then—let it!—and yet, if for but a moment, to have felt myself as pure, as unclouded by thought as that sky of childlike blue!

All eyes were lifted up to where, in the pure, immaculate azure of morning, with the tears of night still not dried upon it, there was a barely perceptible speck, now dark, now clad in the rays of the sun. It was He, the new Jehovah in an aero, just as wise and cruelly loving as the Jehovah of the ancients, descending to us from the heavens. With every moment He drew nearer, and millions of hearts strained higher to meet Him—and then we were in His sight. And in thought I was surveying everything with Him from above: the concentric circles (marked with a fine blue dotted line) of the rostra, looking like the circles of a spider web strewn with microscopic suns (i.e., the glitter of our badges). And in the center of this web a white, wise Spider was about to land: The Benefactor in His white vestments Who had wisely cocooned us hand and foot in the beneficial nets of happiness.

But His magnificent descent from the heavens came to an end; the clangor of The Hymn fell silent, all seated themselves—and I at once understood: everything was truly the finest of spider webs; it was taut and quivering and, at any moment, would sunder and something incredible would happen———

Raising myself a little I looked about me, and my gaze met lovingly alarmed eyes that were shifting from face to face. There, one number had raised his hand and, wagging his fingers barely perceptibly, was signaling to another, whereupon a finger wagged back in answer. And a third joined in. . . . I grasped the situation: they were the Guardians. I also grasped that they were alarmed by something: the spider web was taut, it was vibrating. And within me, as if in a radio receiver tuned to the same wave length, there was a responsive vibration.

A poet was reciting a pre-election ode from a platform, but I did not hear a single word, only the measured swing of a hexametric pendulum, and with every sweep thereof a certain destined hour was drawing closer and closer. And I was still feverishly riffling face after face in the ranks, as if each face

were a page, and still did not see the only one, the one I was
seeking, and yet it was imperative to find it as quickly as
possible, because the pendulum was going to click at any
moment, and then————

It was he—it *would* have to be he! Below, past the platform, gliding over the glittering glass, flitted the rosy ear-
wings; the speeding body was reflected as a dark, double-
curved loop of the letter *S*: he was straining to reach some
spot in the labyrinthine passages between the rostra.

S-, E- —there is some sort of thread between them; I am
constantly aware of this thread—I still don't know its nature,
but some time or other I shall unravel it. My eyes fastened on
him: he was a rolling ball, and that thread was trailing him.
There, now, he had come to a stop; there————

I was transpierced, twisted into a knot by a lightning discharge of high voltage. In our row, only 40° from me, S-
came to a stop, bent over. I saw E- and, alongside her, R-13
with his repellently Negroid lips, smirking.

My first thought was to rush over there and to shout to
her "Why are you with him today? Why didn't you want me
to be with you?" But an invisible, beneficent spider web had
cocooned me hand and foot, immovably; gritting my teeth I
sat there as if I were of iron, without taking my eyes off the
group. As if I were experiencing it right now I remember that
poignant, physical pain in my heart. I remember the thought
that came to me: "If there can be physical pain from non-
physical causes, then it is clear that—"

Regrettably, I did not finish the construction of the conclusion: my only recollections are of some thought about the
soul flashing through my head, of the nonsensical ancient
saying about the *soul sinking into one's boots* flitting through
my mind. And I held my breath: the hexameters no longer
sounded. Something was about to begin. . . . What was it?

There was a five minute pre-election intermission—as established by custom. The pre-election period of silence—as
established by custom. But just then it was not the same truly
prayerful, reverential silence as always; just then it was as it
had been among the ancients, in the days when our Accumulator Towers were yet unknown, when the sky, still untamed,
would go on a rampage of *thunderstorms* from time to time.

Just then it was like that *lull before the storm* which the ancients knew.

The air consisted of transparent cast iron. One wanted to open one's mouth wide with every breath. One's hearing, strained until it hurt, was registering, somewhere in the rear, a disquieting susurration, like the gnawing of a mouse. Without raising my eyes I could constantly see those two—E- and R- —side by side, shoulder to shoulder, and a pair of shaggy hands, hands which were somebody else's, which I abominated, were trembling on my knees. . . .

All the numbers were holding their badge-watches. One. Two. Three . . . five minutes elapsed. A cast-iron, protracted voice issued from the platform: "All those *for*— please raise your hands."

If I could but have looked into His eyes, straightforwardly and devotedly as formerly: "Here I am, all of me. All of me! Accept me!" But I dared not, then. It was with an effort, as if all my joints had rusted, that I raised my hand.

The rustling of millions of hands. Somebody's muffled "Ah!" And I felt that something had already begun, that it was hurtling headlong, yet I could not grasp what it was, and I had not the strength, I had not the courage to look. . . .

"Those *against?*"

This had always been the most majestic moment of the celebration: all would remain seated, never stirring, joyously bowing their heads under the beneficent yoke of The Number of Numbers. But at that point I caught, with horror, a new rustling—the lightest of rustlings, light as a sigh, it was more audible than the brazen trumpets of The Hymn. A man will sigh like that, barely audibly, for the last time in his life— even as the faces of all those surrounding him are turning pale, their foreheads beading with cold sweat.

I raised my eyes—and———

It was but a hundredth part of a second, but a hair's breadth. I saw: thousands of hands beat, winglike, upward, *against*—then lowered. I saw: the pale face of E- with a cross marking it, her raised hand. Everything turned dark before my eyes.

Another hair's breadth; a pause; everything stilled; the

pulse pounding. Then—as if at the signal of some insane conductor, simultaneously on all the rostra: crackling, screams, a whirlwind of unifs billowing in flight, figures of Guardians distractedly darting about, the heels of somebody's shoes in the air before my very eyes—close to those heels somebody's mouth stretched wide and straining in an inaudible scream. For some reason that has become engraved in my memory most sharply of all: thousands of inaudibly bellowing mouths, as if in a silent film thrown upon a monstrous screen.

And, as if upon a screen, somewhere far below, for a second before my eyes, a flash of O-'s bloodlessly white lips. She was standing pressed against the wall in a passage, guarding her belly with her crossed arms. And then she was no longer there, washed away—or I may have forgotten about her, because————

This was no longer on a screen—this was within my own self, within my vise-gripped heart, within my temples, which had begun to pound. R-13 suddenly leapt forth on a bench over my head, toward the left—all red, frenzied, his lips spattering. In his arms was E-, pale, her unif torn from shoulder to breast, blood staining the white cloth. She was holding fast to his neck and he, making enormous leaps from bench to bench, repulsive and agile as a gorilla, was carrying her off, higher and higher.

Just as if at a conflagration among the ancients, everything turned red—dark-red—before me, and I had but one thought —to leap after them, to reach them. Right now I cannot explain to myself whence I found such strength, but I breached the crowd like a battering ram, stepping on somebody's shoulders, on benches—and then I was right near them, had seized R- by the back of his collar: "Don't you dare! Don't you dare, I tell you! Right now"—fortunately, my voice could not be heard: all were absorbed in their own screaming, all were running.

"Who's that? What's going on? What—" R- turned around; his lips, spluttering, were quivering—he probably thought that he had been seized by one of the Guardians.

"What? I'll tell you what—I won't have any of this—I

won't allow it! Put her down this minute!"

But he merely made an angry, plopping noise with his lips, tossed his head and ran on. And at that point I—I am unbelievably ashamed to write this down, yet it seems to me that I am nevertheless bound, absolutely bound to write it so that you, my unknown readers, might study the case history of my disease to the very end—at that point I swung back and struck him over the head. You understand? I struck him! I remember that distinctly. And I also remember the sensation of a certain liberation, of buoyancy in my whole body as a result of this blow.

E- quickly slipped out of his arms.

"Go away!" she shouted to R-. "There, you can see for yourself that he . . . Go away, R- —go away!"

R-, baring teeth as dazzlingly white as a Negro's, spattered some word or other in my face, made a dive, disappeared somewhere below. As for me, I picked E- up in my arms, clasped her hard to my breast and bore her off.

My heart was pounding—an enormous heart, and at every stroke there lashed out of it such a riotous, hot—such a joyous—wave. And what if something down there had burst into smithereens—let it, nothing mattered! The only thing that mattered was to carry her thus, to carry her on and on———

Same evening (22:00):

I am holding the pen with difficulty—so immeasurable is my fatigue after all the vertiginous events of this morning. Can it be that the salutary, centuries-old walls of The One State have crumbled? Can it be that we are again without shelter, in the savage condition of freedom, even as our remote ancestors had been? Can it be that The Benefactor no longer exists? *Against! Against,* on the Day of Unanimity? I feel ashamed, pained, afraid for their sakes. But then, who are *they*? And who am I, myself—am I with the *they*'s or the *we*'s? Really, do I know?

Well, now: she was sitting on the bench, its glass hot from the sun, on the topmost rostrum, where I had carried her. Her right shoulder and the beginning of that wondrous, incalculable curve just below it were bared, with the slenderest of small snakes, a red snake of blood, creeping over the flesh. Apparently she did not notice the blood, that her breast was bared . . . no, more than that: she saw all this, but it was precisely what she was in need of just then, and if her unif had been fastened she would have torn it, would have———

"But tomorrow"—she was breathing avidly through clenched, gleaming sharp teeth—"why, nobody knows what will happen tomorrow. Do you understand—I don't know, nobody knows—the thing is unknown! Do you understand that the known has come to an end? Henceforth the new, the improbable, the prodigious!"

There, below, people were churning, rushing, screaming. But all that was far off, and receding ever further, because she was gazing at me, she was slowly drawing me into herself through the narrow golden windows of her pupils. Thus for a long while, in silence. And for some reason the recollection came to me of how once I had been gazing through the Green Wall into certain incomprehensible yellow pupils, while birds were soaring above that Wall (or I may have seen those birds on another occasion).

"Listen: if nothing out of the ordinary happens tomorrow I'll bring you *there*—do you understand?"

No, I did not understand. Yet I nodded in silent assent. I had dissolved, I was an infinitesimal, I was a geometrical point. . . . In the final analysis, this punctual condition has a logic all its own (today's logic): a point has more unknowns in it than anything else has—it has but to move, to stir, and it can turn into hundreds of solid bodies, into thousands of various curves.

The idea of stirring frightens me: what will I turn into? And it seems to me that everybody is just as afraid of the least motion as I am. There, right now, even as I am writing this, all the numbers are sitting in their glass cages, cowering, and are awaiting something. One can't hear the humming of the elevator out in the corridor, so usual at this hour; one can't hear laughter, footsteps. Occasionally I glimpse numbers tiptoeing in twos through the corridor, looking over their shoulders, whispering. . . .

What will happen tomorrow? What will I turn into tomorrow?

TWENTY-SIXTH ENTRY: *The Universe Exists. Rash. 41° Centigrade.*

Morning. Through the ceiling the sky is as firm, as rounded, as rosy-apple-cheeked as always. I would have been less astonished, I think, if I had beheld some sort of unusual, four-square sun overhead, or people in varicolored garments of animal hair, or opaque walls of stone. Well, now, did that mean that the universe— *our* universe—still existed? Or was it merely inertia: the generator switched off, but the pinions still rumbling and revolving—two turns, three turns; on the fourth turn they would die down. . . .

Are you familiar with the strange state of waking in the night, opening your eyes to blackness, and suddenly feeling that you are lost? And quickly, as quickly as possible, you begin groping around you, seeking something familiar and solid—a wall, a small lamp, a chair. . . . That was precisely my sensation as I groped and searched through the *Gazette of The One State* quickly, as quickly as possible—and there it was:

> The Day of Unanimity, so long, impatiently and universally awaited, was held yesterday. The same Benefactor Who had so repeatedly proven His incontrovertible wisdom, was unanimously elected for the 48th time. The celebration was marred by a certain disturbance brought about by the enemies of happiness who through that very action have naturally deprived themselves of the right to become the building blocks of the foundation, renovated yesterday, of The One State. It is clear to every number that to have taken the votes of these delinquents into consideration would have been just as preposterous as it would be to consider as part of a magnificent, heroic symphony the coughing of sick persons who chanced to be present in the concert hall.

Oh, Wise One! Can it be that, despite everything, we have nevertheless been saved? But really, now, is it possible to contradict this most crystalline of syllogisms?

And, further on, there were a few more lines:

> A joint session of the Administrative and Medical Bureaus and of the Bureau of Guardians is to be held at 12:00 today. The promulgation of an important Act of The One State is scheduled for the very near future.

Nay, the Walls are still standing; there they are—I can run my fingers over them. And now there is no more of that strange sensation of being lost, of being no one knows where, of having lost one's way, and there's nothing at all astonishing about my beholding a blue sky, a round sun, or about the phenomenon that everybody is—as usual—setting out for work.

My step as I walked along the Prospect was particularly firm and resounding—and it seemed to me that all were walking along in much the same way as I was. But then I came to the crossing where I had to turn the corner, and I saw that everybody was going around the corner of the building somehow oddly, sidling away from it, as if a pipe had burst in its wall and were spurting cold water, making the sidewalk impassable.

Five steps more, then ten—and I in my turn was doused with cold water that made me sway, knocking me off the curb. Upon the wall, at a height of 2 meters or thereabouts, there was a square piece of paper, and staring from it were incomprehensible letters of a venomous green:

MEPHI

—while below it I saw a back bent in the form of an *S* and wing-ears transparently swaying from wrath or agitation. With his right arm raised and his left helplessly stretched back as if it were an aching, maimed wing, S- kept leaping upward to tear down the bit of paper—and couldn't manage it, missing it by the tiniest margin.

Probably each one of the passers-by had the same thing in

mind: "If, out of all these numbers, I should be the only one to approach him, isn't he likely to think that I am guilty of something and that it is for that very reason that I want to help him—"

I confess that I, too, had the very same thing in mind. But I recalled how many times he had been my veritable Guardian angel, how many times he had come to my rescue—and, boldly approaching, I stretched out my hand and tore down the small sheet.

S- turned around, quickly; ever so quickly he sank the tiny drills in his eyes into me, to the very bottom, got something out of there. Then he cocked his left eyebrow, sort of winked with that brow in the direction of the wall where the *mephi* thing had been hanging. And the tail end of his smile flitted before me—to my astonishment it seemed to be actually a gay smile. But then, what is there to be astonished at? The physician will always prefer a rash and a fever of 40° centigrade to the exhausting, slowly rising temperature of an incubational period: the high temperature at least makes clear the nature of the disease. This *mephi* which has broken out on the walls is a rash. I understood his smile.*

The stairs leading down into the subway—and underfoot, on the immaculate glass of the steps, again a small white sheet: *MEPHI*. And on the wall of the platform—on a bench—on a mirror in the car (evidently these stickers had been slapped on in haste, carelessly, crookedly): the same white, gruesome rash was everywhere.

In the stillness the distinct humming of the wheels was like the pounding of enfevered blood. One of the numbers felt a touch on his shoulder—startled, he dropped a bundle of papers. And another number, to the left of me, was reading the selfsame line, the selfsame line, the selfsame line in his newspaper—and the newspaper was barely perceptibly trembling. And I felt the pulse of all things—of the wheels, hands, newspapers, eyelashes—quickening more and more, and it is possible that today, when I will find myself with E- in *that*

* I must confess that I found the exact solution for that smile only after many days that were chock-full of the strangest and most unexpected events.

place, the temperature will reach 39°, 40°, 41°, marked off on the thermometer with black lines. . . .

The same silence, humming like a distant, unseen propeller, prevailed on the building site of the *Integral*. The lathes were standing silent, as if they were sulking. And only the cranes, barely audibly, as if on tiptoe, were gliding, leaning over, seizing with their chelae blue blocks of frozen air and stowing them in the tanks along the sides of the *Integral:* we were already readying it for a test flight.

"Well, now, will we be through loading in a week?"

I was questioning the Second Builder. His face is of faïence, decorated with little flowers of sweet blue and tender pink (his eyes, his lips), but that day they were faded, washed out, somehow. We were tallying aloud the cubes of frozen air when I broke off suddenly, in the middle of a word, and stood there with mouth gaping: there was a barely noticeable small white square of paper pasted on a blue block of frozen air which a crane had lifted high, under the very cupola. And my whole body was shaken—by laughter, perhaps. Yes, it was laughter—I could hear myself laughing. (Are you familiar with the sensation of hearing your own laughter?)

"No, do listen," I said. "Just imagine that you're in an ancient airplane; the altimeter reads five thousand meters; one of the wings has broken off, you're falling like a tumbling pigeon—and yet on the way down you're figuring: 'Tomorrow, from twelve noon to two I'll do so and so . . . from two to six, there'll be this and that . . . at six there'll be dinner—' Come now, wouldn't that be ridiculous? And yet, right now, that's precisely how we're acting!"

The little blue flowers stirred; they were popping out. Suppose I were made of glass, and he had seen that three or four hours later, let us say, I———

TWENTY-SEVENTH ENTRY: *No*   I was alone in the endless
Summary—Impossible!   corridors—those same corri-
dors. The sky mute, of poured concrete. Water dripping on stone somewhere. The familiar heavy, opaque door—and muffled rumbling on the other side of it.

She said she would come out to see me at 16:00 on the

dot. But it was already five minutes past the hour, then ten, fifteen minutes—and no one had come. For a second I was my former *I*, who felt frightened lest this door should open. Another five minutes, no more, and if she did not come out—

Water dripping on stone somewhere. No one had come. With rather rueful joy I felt I was saved. I slowly walked back along the corridor. The tremulous dotted line of small electric bulbs on the ceiling was becoming dimmer, ever dimmer.

Suddenly, from behind me, came the hurried banging of a door, the patter, reverberating against the ceiling, the walls, of hastening feet—and there she was, a winged creature, yet slightly winded, panting from her haste.

"I knew it," she said, "I knew you would be here, that you would come! I knew it—thou, thou. . . ."

The spears of her eyelashes moved aside, letting me enter, and . . . How can I convey what this ancient, preposterous, wonderful rite does to me, when her lips touch mine? Through what formula can I express this whirlwind which sweeps everything out of my soul except her? Yes, yes, out of my *soul*—laugh at me, if you like.

Slowly, with an effort, she raised her eyelids—and her words came with difficulty, slowly: "No, that's enough . . . later . . . let's go now."

A door opened. Steps—trodden down, old. And unbearably cacophonic din; whistling; glaring light. . . .

Almost four and twenty hours have passed since then, and by now everything within me has settled down to some extent, yet nonetheless it is exceedingly difficult for me to give a description that would be even approximately accurate. My head feels as if a bomb had been exploded within it, while gaping mouths, wings, screams, leaves, words, stones are alongside me, heaped up, trailing one another. The first thing that occurred to me, I remember, was: "Go back, quick—at breakneck speed!" Because it was clear to me that, while I had been waiting there, in the corridors, they had blown up or demolished the Green Wall, and everything that had been beyond it had rushed in like a tidal wave and inundated our city which had been immunized against the inferior world. I must have said something of the sort to E-.

"Why, not at all!" she broke into laughter. "We have simply gone beyond the Green Wall—"

It was then I opened my eyes—and was face to face, in reality, with that very sort of thing which up to then none of those living had seen other than diminished a thousand times, weakened, smudged over by the turbid glass of the Wall.

The sun—it was no longer that sun of ours, proportionately distributed over the mirror-like surface of the pavements; this sun consisted of some sort of living splinters of incessantly bobbing spots which blinded one's eyes, made one's head go 'round. And the trees—like candles thrusting into the very sky, like spiders squatting flat against the earth on their gnarled paws, like mute fountains jetting green. . . . And all these things were going on all fours, stirring, rustling; some sort of rough-skinned little ball darted out from underfoot. As for me, I stood there rooted to the ground; I could not make a step, because the surface underfoot was not a flat plane—not a flat plane, you understand, but something repulsively soft, yielding, alive, green, springy.

I was stunned by all this, I gulped (that is, perhaps, the most appropriate word). I stood there, clutching a swaying branch with both hands.

"That's nothing—nothing at all! You feel that way only at first—this feeling will pass. A little more courage!"

Somebody's profile, the thinnest of profiles, scissored out of paper, was side by side with E-, against the background of a green, crazily bobbing net. No, not *somebody's* profile, for I knew whose it was. I remembered: it was the doctor. Yes, yes—I understood everything very clearly. And I also understood when the two of them grabbed me under the arms and laughingly dragged me onward. My feet were weaving, slipping. There, ahead, were cawing, moss, tussocks, gurgling, boughs, tree trunks, wings, leaves, whistling. . . .

And—the trees scattered. A bright meadow. On the meadow—people . . . or—really I don't know how to put it —perhaps it would be more correct to call them creatures. Here comes the most difficult part. Because this went beyond

any bounds of probability. And it is clear to me now why E-
always maintained such a stubborn silence about all this
before: I wouldn't have believed anyway—not even her. It is
possible that tomorrow I won't believe even my own self—
even this very entry of mine.

On the meadow a crowd of three or four hundred . . .
people (let *people* stand: I find it difficult to use another
word) were making a lot of noise around a bare rock that
looked like a skull. Just as out of the sum total of faces of
those filling the rostra you would at first flush perceive only
those familiar to you, so in this instance I at first saw only
our gray-blue unifs. But another second passed—and among
the unifs I distinguished, perfectly clearly and starkly, dark-
colored, rufous, gold-tinted, dark-bay, roan, white people—
people, apparently. They were all unclothed and all were grown
over with short, glossy pelage, somewhat like that of the
stuffed *horse* which anyone may see at the Prehistoric Museum. The faces of the females were, however, exactly the
same—yes, yes, *exactly* the same—as those of our women,
delicately rosy and not overgrown with hair; their breasts—
large, firm, of splendidly beautiful geometrical forms—were
likewise free of hair. Among the males only a part of the face
was not hirsute, much the same as with our ancestors.

All this was improbable to such a degree, to such a degree
unexpected, that I stood there calmly (calmly—I absolutely
assert that) and looked on. You take a pair of scales, now:
overload one of the pans, and then you can put as much as
you like on it—the arrow won't budge any way.

Suddenly I was alone; E- was no longer with me—I did not
know how or where she had vanished. All around me were
only these . . . beings, with the sun giving a satiny sheen
to their pelage. I clutched somebody's hot, stalwart, dark-
colored shoulder: "Listen, for Benefactor's sake—did you
happen to see which way she went? Just now, just this minute—"

He turned his shaggy eyebrows sternly upon me: "Shhh!
Not so loud," and the eyebrows shaggily nodded in the direction of the central point, where the skull-yellow boulder was.

There, at a height, above their heads, above all of them, I

saw her. The sun, on the other side of her, was shining straight into my eyes, and because of that all of her, against the blue canvas of the sky, was sharply drawn, coal-black: a coal-black silhouette against blue. Just a trifle above her the clouds were sailing along, and this made it seem that it was not the clouds which were in motion, but that the boulder, and she herself, and the crowd and the meadow following her example, were all gliding inaudibly, like a ship, while the earth, the buoyant earth, was floating away from underfoot. . . .

"Brothers [she was speaking]—brothers! There, in the city within the Wall, they are building the *Integral*. And you know that the day has come for us to raze this Wall—all walls—so that the green wind may blow over all the earth, from one end of it to the other. But the *Integral* is going to carry those walls upward, into thousands of other earths whose lights will this night come murmuring to you through the black nocturnal leaves—"

Waves, spume, wind beat against the boulder: "Down with the *Integral*! Down with it!"

"No, brothers—not 'down with it!' The *Integral* must be ours instead. On the day when it first casts off its moorings and sails into the sky *we* will be aboard. Because the Builder of the *Integral* is with us. He has abandoned walls; he has come here with me to be in your midst. All hail to the Builder!"

An instant—and I was somewhere up there; below me were heads, heads, heads, mouths distended in clamor, hands plashing upward and subsiding. All this was extraordinarily strange, inebriating; I felt myself superior to all, I was I, a world by itself, I had ceased to be an item, as I had always been, and had become an integer. And then, with my body rumpled, suffused with happiness, crumpled as if after the embraces of love, I was down to earth, near the very boulder. The sun, voices above, the smile of E-. A woman with golden hair (and all of her was satiny-golden, redolent of grasses) was holding a chalice, apparently of wood; her red lips drank off a little and she held out the vessel to me—and avidly, closing my eyes, I drank to drown the fire within me; I drank

the sweet, prickly, cold sparkles. And then, my blood and
all the universe raced a thousand times faster; the light earth
flew like down. And all things were, to me, light, simple,
clear.

There, I caught sight of those familiar, enormous letters
MEPHI on the boulder itself—and for some reason this
seemed so necessary; it was a simple stout thread that bound
all things together. I caught sight (perhaps it had been on
that same boulder) of a crude depiction: that of a winged
youth with a transparent body, and in the place usually occupied by the heart there was a dazzling ember, smoldering
with a dark-red glow. And I comprehended that ember—or,
rather, that's not quite it: I sensed it, just as, without actually
hearing it, I sensed every word uttered by E- (she was speaking up there, on the boulder), even as I sensed that all those
there were breathing as one and that they were about to take
wing to somewhere, all of them as one, just as those birds had
done above the Wall at that time. . . .

From behind, out of the deeply breathing thicket of bodies,
rose a stentorian voice: "Why, this is madness!"

And apparently it was I—yes, I think it was none other
than I—who leapt up on the boulder, and from there the view
was one of sun, heads, the serrature of a green saw against
blue, and I was shouting: "Yes, yes—precisely! And we must
all go mad, it is imperative for all of us to go mad—as speedily as possible! It is imperative—I know it is!"

E- was by my side; her smile was drawn in two shaded
strokes—up, at angles, from the corners of her mouth. And
the ember was within me—and its penetration had been
instantaneous, easy, just the least bit painful, splendidly beautiful. Of what came afterward only oddments remain lodged
in my memory like slivers, like shards:

A bird, in low, slow flight. I perceived it was alive, even
as I was; it turned its head to the right, to the left, even as
man does, and its black beady eyes held me fast as if with
screws.

Also: a back, covered with glossy pelage the hue of old
ivory. An insect of a dark color with tiny transparent wings

was crawling down this back; the back twitched to get rid of the insect, then it twitched again.

Also: leaf-shadow, interwoven, reticulate. People lying in this shadow-shape and chewing something similar to the food of the ancients; one of the women thrust some of it—an elongated yellow fruit and a hunk of something dark—into my hand, and I found the thing amusing, since I did not know whether I could eat it.

And, anew: the throng, heads, legs, arms, mouths. Faces bobbing up for a second only to disappear, to burst like bubbles. And, for a second (or perhaps I merely may have imagined them)—translucent, flying wing-ears—

I squeezed E-'s hand with all my might. She looked at me over her shoulder; "What is it?"

"He's here. It seemed to me—"

"Who's *he?*"

"S-. There, just now, in the crowd—"

Coal-black, slender eyebrows quirked up toward the temples: the acute triangle of her smile. It was not clear to me why she was smiling—how could she smile?

"You don't understand, E-; you don't understand what it means if he, or any one of that lot, is here."

"Funny fellow! Come, would it ever enter the head of any-one there, inside the Wall, that we are out here? Think back; take yourself for example—did you ever imagine that this was possible? They're hunting us there—let them hunt! You're raving."

She smiled, lightly, gaily, and I smiled as well; the earth, inebriated, gay, light, was floating along. . . .

TWENTY-EIGHTH ENTRY: *The Two of Them. Entropy and Energy. An Opaque Part of the Body.*

Look: if your world is similar to the world of our remote ancestors, suppose you picture yourself as having happened to stumble upon a sixth (or even a seventh) continent one day, an Atlantis or something of that sort, and finding there labyrinthine cities, people soaring through the air without the aid of wings (or even aeros), stones levitated through the power of a glance—in short, such things as could never occur to you, even if you were afflicted with the dream-sickness. Well, that was precisely the case with me yesterday. Because (you *must* grasp this) not a one of us, ever, had been beyond the Green Wall since the days of the Two Hundred Years' War—which I have already spoken to you about.

I know that I owe you the duty, my unknown friends, of telling you in greater detail about this strange and surprising world which revealed itself to me yesterday. But I am in no condition as yet to revert to that topic. More and more new things are happening, there is something very like a cloud-burst of events, and there isn't enough of me to catch all of it—I hold up the flaps of my unif, I hold out my cupped hands, but just the same bucketfuls splash past me and only droplets fall on these pages.

The first thing I heard beyond the wall of my room was raised voices, and I recognized *her* voice, the voice of E-, resonant, metallic, and another voice, almost inflexible, like a wooden ruler, the voice of U-. Then the door flew open with a crash and shot both of them into my room. Precisely that: it shot them into the room.

E- placed her hand on the back of my chair and smiled over her right shoulder at the other—with her teeth only. I wouldn't want to stand up against that smile.

"Listen," E- spoke to me; "this woman seems to have made it her aim in life to guard you against me as if you were a little child. Is this with your permission?"

Upon which the other spoke up, her gills quivering: "Yes, and he is a child. Yes! That's just why he doesn't even see that you're doing all this to him only in order to . . . he doesn't see that all this is a comedy. Yes! And my duty is—"

An instant's glimpse in the mirror of the broken, jumpy line of my eyebrows; then I sprang up and, with difficulty restraining that other fellow within me, whose hairy fists were shaking, with like difficulty getting each word out through clenched teeth and quite sibilantly, I shouted right at her, at her very gills: "Out—this very second! This very second—"

The gills puffed up, red-brickishly, then subsided, turned gray. She opened her mouth to say something and then, with-

leaving until you tell me about those people, because you love . . . them, while I don't even know who they are, where they have come from—"

"Who are they? They are the half which we have lost. You have H two and O, but in order to get H two O—streams, seas, waterfalls, waves, storms—it is necessary for these halves to unite."

I remember, distinctly, every movement of hers. I remember how she had picked up my glass triangle from the table and, all the while that I had been talking, had held its sharp edge against her cheek, until a white weal had appeared there; then, as she took the triangle away, I saw the weal filling with rosiness, disappearing. And, amazingly, I cannot recall her words—especially when she began—but only certain images, colors.

I do know that at first she told about the Two Hundred Years' War. And there it was: red against the green of grasses, against dark clays, against the bluish tint of snows— puddles of red that would not dry. Then yellow grasses burnt by the sun; yellow men, naked, with matted hair, lurking side by side with dogs whose hair was also matted, much too near bloated carrion, canine carrion or, perhaps, human. . . . All this, of course, beyond the Walls, since the city had already proven victorious; the city already had our present-day food, a derivative of naphtha.

And, drooping almost from the sky to the earth itself, were black heavy folds, folds swaying over forests, over villages— slowly rearing pillars of smoke, these. Muffled howling: black, endless files of people being driven into the city so that they might be forcefully saved and trained to happiness.

"You knew almost all this?"

"Yes—almost."

"You didn't know, however, and there weren't many who did, that a small part of these people survived in spite of everything and stayed on to live there, beyond the Walls. Naked, they took to the forests. There they learned from the trees, beasts, birds, colors, sun. They became hirsute, but to make up for that they had preserved warm, red blood under their hirsuteness. It was much worse with all of you: you became overgrown with ciphers; ciphers are crawling all over you like lice. You ought to be stripped of everything and driven naked into the forests. Go ahead and learn how to tremble with fear, with joy, with frenzied wrath, with cold; go ahead and pray to fire. And we, the Mephis, we want—"

"The Mephis? Hold on a minute—what's this Mephi thing?"

"Mephi? It is an ancient name.* Mephi is he who . . . you remember, the youth depicted on that boulder. . . . But no—I'd better talk your language; you'll grasp it more quickly then. Look: there are two forces in this world— entropy and energy. The first leads to beatific quietism, to a happy equilibrium; the other, to the destruction of equilibrium, to excruciatingly perpetual motion. It was entropy which our—or rather your—ancestors, the Christians, worshiped as a god. But we are anti-Christians, we—"

At that moment there was a tap at the door, a whisper of a tap, and that same flattened fellow with his forehead shoved down over his eyes, who had more than once brought me notes from E-, sprang into the room. He came toward us at a run, halted, wheezing like an air pump—and could not utter a word; he must have been running for all he was worth.

"Well, now, speak up! What's happened?" E- seized his hand.

"They're . . . coming here," the air pump puffed out at last. "The patrol . . . and that fellow with them—well, now, what's his number . . . short, sort of hunchbacked—"

"S-?"

"Why, yes! They're in the next building. They'll be here right away . . . hurry, hurry!"

"Bosh! There's plenty of time—" E- was laughing, while sparks, tiny tongues of flame leapt gaily in her eyes.

This was either preposterous, unreasoning pluck—or else something was involved in this which was still incomprehensible to me: "E-, for Benefactor's sake! Do understand— why, this is—"

* Mephi [stopheles] (?)—*Researcher* 565316, *Venusian Bureau of Multilinguistics.*

"For Benefactor's sake?"—with that acute triangle of a smile.

"Well . . . well, for my sake, then. I implore you!"

"Ah, there was still another thing I had to talk over with you—but no matter; tomorrow will do." She nodded to me gaily (yes, *gaily*); the other nodded to me also, peeping out for a second from under his overhang of a forehead. And I was alone.

I sat down at my table—and lost no time in doing so. I spread out the manuscript of these entries and picked up a pen, so that they might find me at this labor for the benefit of The One State. And suddenly every hair on my head became alive, isolated, horripilant: "But what if they should take it into their heads and read just one page of this—one of the most recent ones?" I sat at that table without stirring, and I saw how the walls were quivering, how the pen in my hand quivered, how the letters rocked, blurring together—

Hide them? But where—there was nothing but glass around me. Burn them? But then those in the corridor and in the adjoining room would see. And, after all, I was unable, I hadn't the power, to do away with this excruciating (and perhaps the dearest to me) bit of myself.

By then there were distant voices, footsteps out in the corridor. All I had time for was to grab a batch of pages and thrust them under me, and there I was, riveted to the armchair, every atom of which was in convulsions, while the floor was a deck, heaving, dropping away. . . .

Shrunk into a tiny lump, cowering under the overhang of my own forehead, I saw (somehow stealthily, from under my eyebrows) how they were going from room to room, starting at the right end of the corridor and coming ever nearer. Some of the occupants were sitting as cataleptically as I; others (the lucky ones!) would spring up to meet the inspectors and fling the doors open for them. If I could but have done the same!

"The Benefactor is a disinfection, brought to the utmost pinnacle of perfection and indispensable to humanity, and consequently there is no peristalsis whatsoever in the organism of The One State—" I was squeezing out this utter balderdash with a jumpy pen and bending lower and lower over the table, while a crazy smithy was furiously pounding in my head, and I heard (with my back) the clatter of the doorknob; a gust of wind enveloped me, the armchair launched into a tarantella under me—

It was only then that I managed, with difficulty, to tear myself away from the page and turn to those who had entered (how difficult it is to be playing a comedy . . . ah, who was it spoke to me today about comedy?). S- was in the lead, his eyes somberly, silently, quickly drilling wells in me, in my armchair, in the sheets twitching under my hand. Then, for a second, I caught sight of certain familiar, everyday faces in the doorway, and shortly one of these separated itself from the others: the palpitating rosily brown gills emerged. I recalled everything that had taken place in this room half an hour before, and it became clear to me that at any moment she would——— All my being was pounding and pulsating in that (fortunately) opaque portion of my anatomy with which I had shielded my manuscript.

U- approached him, this S-, from behind, cautiously plucked at his sleeve, and spoke to him in a low voice: "This is D, Five Hundred and Three, the builder of the *Integral*. You have heard of him, surely? He's forever sitting at his desk like that—he absolutely never spares himself!"

There, what hadn't I been thinking about her! What a wonderful, amazing woman. . . . S- glided off in my direction, bent over my shoulder toward the table. I placed my elbow in such a way as to screen what I had written, but he said sternly in a loud voice: "I must ask you to show me at once what you have there!"

Blazing with shame I handed him the sheet. He read it through and I saw a smile slither out of his eyes, dart down his face and then squat, with its tiny tail barely twitching, somewhere in the vicinity of the right corner of his mouth: "Somewhat ambiguous but, just the same—well, now, do go on; we're not going to bother you any further."

He flapped off, as if he were whacking water with paddles, toward the door, and at his every step I felt my feet, hands, fingers gradually reverting to me; my soul was once more distributing itself proportionately throughout my body; I was drawing breath again—

The last bit: U- managed to detain herself in my room, walked up to me, bent to my very ear and uttered in a whisper: "It's a lucky thing for you that I—"

I cannot understand: what had she wanted to convey by that?

Later on, in the evening, I found out that they had taken along three numbers. However, nobody speaks of this out loud, just as they don't talk aloud about all the things new taking place (here you have the educational influence of the Guardians, who are invisibly present in our midst). Conversations deal for the most part with the rapidly falling barometer and the change in the weather.

TWENTY-NINTH ENTRY: *Filaments on the Face. Seedlings. An Unnatural Compression.*

A strange thing: the barometer is falling, yet there is no wind: a calm prevails. There, above, the storm which is as yet inaudible to us has already begun. The clouds are scudding along at full speed. So far there are not many of them—just separate jagged fragments. And so it seems as if some city has already been razed up there and segments of walls and towers are hurtling downward, growing bigger and bigger before one's eyes with terrifying rapidity, yet fated to hurtle on for days through the blue infinitude until they crash to the bottom, where we are, far below.

Here, below, calm prevails. Filaments—inexplicable, so fine as to be almost invisible—float in the air. They are wafted here every autumn from beyond the Wall. They float along slowly—and suddenly you feel an invisible foreign substance on your face; you want to brush it off, but no, you can't, there's no getting rid of it. These filaments are especially prevalent when one is walking near the Glass Wall, as I had been doing this morning. E- had told me to meet her at the House of Antiquity, in that *apartment* of ours.

When I was only a short distance away from the enormous,

solid, rust-red pile of the House of Antiquity I caught the
sounds of hard breathing, the patter of somebody's hurried
footsteps behind me. I turned around and saw it was O-,
trying to catch up with me. All of her was somehow peculiarly, resiliently rounded in a painstakingly finished fashion.
Her arms, and the inverted chalices of her breasts, and all
her body which I knew so well, were in the round, and making
her unif taut: there, at any moment, the thin material would
be rent and everything would be out in the open, under the
sun, in the light. A picture sprang up before me: out there,
in those green wildwoods, the seedlings just as stubbornly
struggle to break through the ground in the spring so that they
may put forth twigs, leaves as speedily as possible and, as
speedily as possible, burst into flower. For a few seconds her
eyes shed their blue light upon my face; then: "I saw you
that time—on the Day of Unanimity."

"I saw you too—" and immediately the recollection came
to me of how she had stood there hugging the wall in the
narrow passage below and protecting her belly with her arms.
I involuntarily glanced at the round belly bulging out her
unif.

She must have noticed my glance, became spherically rosy
—even her smile was rosy: "I am so happy—so happy! I am
filled—filled to the very brim, you understand. And so I walk
about and hear nothing of what's going on around me, but
am all the time listening to what's going on inside me, within
my own self—"

I kept silent. Some foreign substance was clinging to my
face, bothering me, and I simply could not get rid of it. And
suddenly, unexpectedly, the blue light beaming a still more
intense blue, she seized my hand—and I felt her lips upon it.
This was my first such experience in all my life. It was some
sort of an ancient caress which I had known nothing of up
to then, and it shamed and pained me so much that I snatched
my hand away—likely as not I may even have been rough
about it.

"Listen, you're out of your mind! And it isn't so much
this—you are, in general——— What are you rejoicing
about? Really, can you possibly forget what is awaiting you?

It makes no difference—if not now, then in a month, in two months—"

She was extinguished; all her circumferences sagged, warped. As for me, I felt an unpleasant (even a sickly) contraction, linked with a feeling of pity, within my heart (the heart is nothing but an ideal pump: to speak of compression, contraction in connection with a pump's suction of a liquid is a technical absurdity; hence it is clear to what an extent all these *loves, pities,* etc., etc., which bring about such a contraction, are essentially absurd, unnatural, sickly).

The calm prevailed. To the left, the turbidly green glass of the Wall. Ahead, the dark-red pile of the House of Antiquity. And these two colors coming together gave me as a resultant an idea that struck me as brilliant.

"Hold on! I know how to save you. I will extricate you from this situation of beholding your child for one moment—and dying the next. You will be able to rear it—you understand?—you will watch it growing, rounding out, ripening like a fruit even as you dandle it in your arms—" She simply shook, simply clutched at me, clung close. "You remember that woman—well, it was long ago, that time we were all taking our collective walk. She happens to be here right now, in the House of Antiquity. Let's go to her, and I guarantee that I'll arrange everything without delay."

In my mind's eye I already saw E- and myself leading O- through those corridors; why, she was already there, outside the Wall, among all those flowers, grasses, leaves. But she backed away from me; the tiny horns of her rosy mouth-crescent were quivering and twisting downward. "It's that same woman," said she.

"Well—" I became embarrassed for some reason. "Well, yes—it's the same one."

"And you want to have me go to her, have me beg her, have me . . . Don't you ever dare speak to me of this again!" All slumped over, she quickly walked away from me; then, as if reminding herself of something else, she turned around and shouted: "And I will die—yes, so be it! And it's none of your business—isn't it all the same to you?"

The calm prevailed. Segments of blue towers and walls

were hurtling downward from above, growing bigger and bigger before one's eyes with terrifying rapidity, but they were fated to hurtle on through infinitude for hours yet— perhaps for days; invisible filaments were floating slowly through the air, settling on one's face—and there was no shaking them off, no getting rid of them.

I was walking slowly toward the House of Antiquity. In my heart I felt an absurd, excruciating contraction.

THIRTIETH ENTRY: *The Last Number. The Error of Galileo. Whether 'Tis Better—* Here is the conversation I had yesterday with E- there, in the House of Antiquity, amid the motley clamor of red, green, bronze-yellow, white, orange, colors so loud that they drowned out any logical course of thoughts. And, throughout the conversation, we were under the smile, frozen in marble, of that snub-nosed ancient poet.

I shall reproduce this conversation literally because, as it seems to me, it will be of enormous, decisive importance for the fate of The One State—and, what is more, for the universe. Then, too, you may find therein, my unknown readers, some justification for me.

E- let me have it right off, straight from the shoulder and without any preparation: "I know that you're having a first, trial flight of the *Integral* day after tomorrow. On that day we're going to take it into our own hands."

"What! Day after tomorrow?"

"Yes. Sit down; don't get excited. We mustn't lose even a minute. There were a dozen Mephis among the hundreds whom the Guardians happened to haul in yesterday. And if we let two or three days slip by those twelve are done for."

I did not say anything.

"They are bound to send you electro-technicians, mechanics, physicians, meteorologists to observe the progress of the test flight. And exactly at noon—remember this—when they ring the bell for lunch and all pass into the dining salon, we'll stay behind in the corridor, lock all the others in there—and the *Integral* is ours. This, you understand, is necessary, come what may. The *Integral* in our hands—why, it will be a weapon which will help to end everything at once, quickly, painlessly. Their aeros—bah!—they'll be no more than a swarm of midges against a hawk. Then, too—if this should prove unavoidable—we can direct the motor exhausts downward and by that means alone—"

I sprang up. "This is unthinkable! This is preposterous! Is it possible you can't see clearly that what you're stirring up is revolution?"

"Yes, revolution! But why is that preposterous?"

"It's preposterous because there can't be any revolution. Because our revolution—it is I who say it and not you—was the last. And there can't be any other revolutions. Everybody knows that—"

"Dear man, you're a mathematician"—her eyebrows were a mocking acute triangle. "Even more—you're a philosopher, because of your mathematics. Well, then: name the ultimate number for me."

"What do you mean? I . . . I don't understand—what ultimate number?"

"Why, the ultimate, the supreme, the greatest number of all."

"Come, E—, that's preposterous. Since the number of numbers is infinite, what number would you want to be the ultimate one?"

"Well, and what revolution would you want to be the ultimate one? There is no ultimate revolution—revolutions are infinite in number. The ultimate revolution—that's for children. Infinity scares children, yet it is necessary for children to sleep soundly of nights—"

"But what sense—just what sense is there in all this, for Benefactor's sake! What's the sense, since everybody is already happy?"

"Let's suppose . . . very well, let's say that is so. But what comes next?"

"That is funny! An utterly childish question. You tell a story to children, all of it, to the very end, but just the same they will inevitably ask: 'But what comes next? But why?' "

"Children are the only venturesome philosophers. And venturesome philosophers are, inevitably, children. And that's what we must always ask, precisely like children: 'But what comes next?' "

"Nothing comes next! Full stop. Throughout the universe there is everywhere an equable flow of—"

"Aha—*equable, everywhere!* There it is, that very same entropy—psychological entropy. To you, a mathematician— isn't it clear to you that it is only in differences—differences! —in temperature, only in thermal contrasts, that life lies? But if everywhere, throughout the universe, there are only equally warm—or equally cool—bodies, they must be thrust out of the way—so that there may be fire, an explosion, Gehenna. And thrust them away we shall!"

"But, E-, do understand—you must!—that our ancestors did precisely that during the Two Hundred Years' War—"

"Oh, and they were right—right a thousandfold. They committed but one error: later on they came to believe that they were the ultimate figure—such as doesn't—simply doesn't!— exist in nature. Their error is the error of Galileo: he was right in maintaining that the earth moves around the sun, but he did not know that the entire solar system also moves about a certain center; he did not know that the real orbit of the earth—not the relative but the real orbit—is not at all a naïve circle—"

"But what about all of you?"

"Well, we know, for the time being, that there is no ultimate number. It may be that we will forget that. No, not maybe but surely, we will forget that when we will have grown old, as all things must, ineluctably. And then we too will drift downward, as autumnal leaves drift down from a tree, as on the day after tomorrow you—no, no, dearest—not you! For you are with us—you are with us!" All ablaze, cyclonic, coruscant—never yet had I seen her like that—she embraced me with herself, with all of her. I vanished———— At the last, looking steadfastly, firmly into my eyes: "Remember, then: at noon."

And I said: "Yes, I remember."

She went away. I was alone amid the riotous, discordant clamor of blues, reds, greens, bronze-yellows, orange-reds. . . . Yes, at noon . . . and suddenly that preposterous sensation of some foreign substance that had settled on my face, something there was no brushing off. And, as suddenly, the events of yesterday, in the morning, U- and the things she was shouting into E-'s face at the time. . . . Why this recollection? How absurd—

I hastened to get outside—oh, to get home, home, as fast as I could! Somewhere behind me I heard the piercing cries of birds above the Wall, while ahead of me, seen against the setting sun as if they were fashioned of raspberry-hued crystallized fire, were the globes of cupolas, enormous flaming cube-buildings, the spire of the Accumulator Tower like a bolt of lightning frozen in the sky. And all these things, all this impeccable, geometric beauty, I would have to destroy myself, with my own hands! Could it be that there was no escape, no other way?

My course lay past some auditorium (I don't recall its number). Within the benches were stacked high; in the middle were tables covered over with sheets of snowy fiberglas; against the whiteness of one of these was a blotch of rose-tinted sun-blood. And lurking in all this was an unknown—and therefore eerie—tomorrow. It is unnatural for a thinking, seeing being to live amid irregularities, unknown quantities, X's. There, suppose they were to blindfold you and compel you to go about thus, groping, stumbling, and you knew that lying somewhere close by—entirely too close to you—was the very brink: one step more, just one, and all that would be left of you would be a squashed, mangled piece of flesh. . . . Wouldn't that be the very same situation as mine just then?

. . . But what if, without waiting, one were to dive head first off the deep end on one's own initiative? Wouldn't that be the only and the proper thing, which would immediately disentangle all things?

THIRTY-FIRST ENTRY: *The Great Operation. I Have Forgiven Everything. Trains in Collision.*

Saved! At the very last moment, when it seemed that there was not a straw to clutch at, when it seemed that everything was over and done with . . . as if you had already mounted the steps to the awesome Machine of The Benefactor, and its glass bell had already clangorously covered you, and for the last time in your life your eyes were quickly, quickly gulping the blue sky . . . and suddenly all this turned out to be only a *dream*. The sun was rose-tinted, riant; and the wall of my room—what a joy it was to run one's hand over the coolness of that wall; and the pillow—why, one could drink in forever the beauty of the depression one's head made in that white pillow!

There you have an approximation of what I experienced when I read the *Gazette of The One State* through this morning. The nightmare had been frightful—and it was over. Yet I, pusillanimous fellow, I, of so little faith—I had already been meditating willfully taking my own life. I now feel ashamed to read the last lines I wrote yesterday. However, it doesn't matter; let them remain—let them!—as a reminder of that incredible event which might have been—and which now will never be—yes, never!

The front page of the *Gazette of The One State* was lambent with:

REJOICE!

For henceforth you are perfect! Up to this day your own offspring, your various mechanisms, were of greater perfection than yourselves.

IN WHAT WAY?

Every spark of a dynamo is a spark of purest reason; every thrust of a piston is an immaculate syllogism. But then, does not the same inerrable reason dwell within you as well?

The philosophy of cranes, presses and pumps is as finished and clear as a circle drawn with a pair of compasses. But then, is your philosophy any less circular?

The beauty of a mechanism lies in that which is undeviating and exact, as in a pendulum, as in rhythm. But then you, who have been nurtured on the Taylor System from your very childhood—have you not become as exact as pendulums?

There is, however, one point of difference:

MECHANISMS HAVE NO FANTASY!

Did you ever see a wool-gathering, senselessly dreamy smile spread over the physiognomy of a pump cylinder while it was working? Did you ever hear any cranes tossing restlessly in bed and sighing of nights, during the hours appointed for rest?

YOU NEVER DID!

And yet the Guardians have more and more often (well may you blush!) seen these smiles and heard these sighs among you. And (you may well hide your eyes!) the historians of The One State are tendering their resignations so that they may be spared having to chronicle sundry ignominious occurrences.

However, you are not to blame for these things—you are sick. And the name of your sickness is

FANTASY!

Fantasy is a worm whose boring leaves black furrows on your brows. Fantasy is a fever which drives you on to further and further flight, even though this *further* point may begin where happiness ends. Fantasy is the last barricade on the road to happiness.

And yet,

REJOICE!

That barricade has been dynamited. The road lies clear ahead.

The location of the Center of Fantasy is the latest discovery of science in The One State. This Center is a miserable little cerebral node in the region of the Bridge of Varoli. A triple cauterization of this node with x-rays, and you are cured of Fantasy—

> PERMANENTLY!
> You are perfect; you are on a par
> with machines; the road to 100 per-
> cent happiness lies clear ahead. Hasten,
> then, all of you, young and old—
> hasten to submit yourselves to the
> Grand Operation! Hasten to the audi-
> toria, where the Grand Operation is
> now being carried on!
> All hail to the Grand Operation!
> All hail to The Benefactor!

You, if you had read all this not in these notes of mine,
which are so much like some whimsical novel of antiquity,
but if instead had this newspaper sheet, still redolent of
printer's ink, quivering in your hands as it is quivering in
mine, if you knew, as I know, that all this is the most actual
reality (if not today's then tomorrow's)—would not your
sensations be the very same as mine? Would not your head be
spinning, even as mine is spinning right now? Would not
these same eerie, delectable needlets of ice be darting over
your back and arms? Would you not feel that you were a
Titan, an Atlas, and that if you were to stand up straight your
head would inevitably bump against the glass of the ceiling?

I grabbed the telephone: "E-, Three, Three, Naught. Yes—
Three, Three, Naught." And then I was spluttering loudly into
the instrument: "You're speaking from home, aren't you?
Have you read—oh, you're reading it now? Why, it's . . .
it's—it's amazing!"

"Yes"—followed by a long, obscure silence. The receiver
was humming almost inaudibly; she was pondering something. Then: "I have to see you today, without fail. Yes, at
my place, after sixteen. Without fail."

The darling! Such a dear, dear darling. "Without fail!" I
felt I was smiling, and I simply couldn't stop, and I would
go forth like that, bearing this smile through the streets like
a lantern, high above my head!

Out of doors the wind swooped down on me. It whirled,
whistled, lashed, yet this made my mood all the blither. Howl,
yowl—it makes no difference: you won't throw the Walls
down! And the clouds, rolling as if they were of cast iron,

were tumbling down overhead: Go right ahead and tumble; you will never darken the sun—we have fastened it with chains to the zenith for all time—we, who are Joshuas, the sons of Nun!

A tight knot of us Joshuas, the sons of Nun, were standing near a corner building, their foreheads glued to the glass of a wall. Inside, some number was already stretched out on a dazzlingly white table. One could glimpse his bare soles diverging at a yellow angle from under the whiteness; medicos in white were bending over the upper end of the table; a white hand extended to another white hand a syringe filled with a liquid.

"Well, what about you—why don't you go in?" I asked, addressing nobody in particular—or, more correctly, all of them.

"Well, what about *you?*"—somebody's globular head turned in my direction.

"I'll do it later on. There are still some things I must attend to first—" I backed out, somewhat abashed. I really did have to see my E- first. But why *first?* That was something I couldn't explain to myself.

The construction site. The *Integral,* bluishly icy, was glistening, sparkling. In the engine room the dynamo was humming, caressingly, endlessly repeating some word, just one, a word that sounded familiar, as if it were a word of my very own. I bent over, stroked the long, chill tube of a motor. A darling—what a . . . what a darling of a tube! On the morrow you will come to life; on the morrow, for the first time in your life, a shudder will run through you because of the fiery, searing jets within your belly————

With what eyes would I have regarded this mighty monster of glass if everything had remained as it had been yesterday? If I were to know that on the morrow, at noon, I would betray—yes, betray—it?

A cautious tap on my elbow, from behind. I turned, confronting the Second Builder's dish face.

"You already know," said he.

"What—about the Operation? How all these . . . these things are coming about so . . . suddenly—isn't that true?"

"Why, no—that's not what I meant. The test flight has been put off till the day after tomorrow. All on account of this Operation. All this rush, all our efforts, and all for nothing—"

"All on account of this Operation—" What a peculiar, limited fellow. Can't see anything beyond that dish face of his. If he but knew that if it weren't for the postponement because of the Operation he would be sitting in the glass cage of the *Integral's* dining salon at noon tomorrow, dashing about on the inside and trying to scramble up its walls.

I was in my room at 15:30. I entered—and saw U-. She was sitting at my table—bony, erect, unyielding, her right cheek planted on her right hand. She must have been waiting a long time, because when she sprang up to greet me the impressions of the four fingers and thumb remained for quite a while on her face. For a second that other unfortunate morning was resurgent within me: yes, she had been at that spot close to the table, standing in a rage by E-'s side. But for a second only, for at once everything was washed away by today's sun—the way it happens when, on a bright day, you absent-mindedly turn the light switch as you enter a room: the electric bulb begins to glow, yet it seems not to be there at all, so ludicrous it is, the poor little thing, so unnecessary.

I unhesitatingly held out my hand to her, forgiving her everything; she clutched both my hands hard, squeezing them with prickly fingers, while her cheeks, which dangled like antique ornaments, quivered from time to time, and she said: "I was waiting for you—I've dropped in for just a minute. Merely wanted to tell you how happy I am, how I rejoice on your account! Tomorrow or the day after, you understand, you will be absolutely well, you will be reborn—"

I caught sight of a sheet of paper on the table—the last two pages of my entry for yesterday; they were lying there just as I had left them the evening before. If she had but seen what I had written on them! However, it didn't matter; now it was all history; now it was so ludicrously remote, as if viewed through reversed binoculars.

"Yes," said I. "You know, I was walking down the Prospect just now, and there was a man ahead of me, and he was casting a shadow on the pavement. And, you understand, his shadow was luminous! And it seems to me—no, I feel certain of it—that on the morrow there will be no shadows whatsoever—neither of a single human being nor of a single thing; everything will be shot through with sunlight!"

"You're a phantaseur!"—this was uttered tenderly and sternly. "I would never permit the children in my school to talk like that—" and she went on with something or other about the children, and how she had taken them, the whole pack of them, straight off to the Operation, and how it had become necessary to tie them up there, and that "it is necessary to love mercilessly—yes, mercilessly," and that, apparently, she would at last decide to——

She adjusted the gray-blue cloth between her knees; plastered me silently, quickly with a smile; went out.

Fortunately, the sun had not stopped that day; it was still running, and at last it was 16:00. I was pounding at a door, my heart was pounding against my ribs—

"Come in!"

I sank on the floor near her chair, embracing her legs, throwing my head back so as to look into her eyes, now into one, now into the other, and saw myself in each, held in wondrous captivity—— But there, beyond the wall of the room, the storm was ripening, the clouds were turning into heavier and heavier cast iron—well, let them! My head was thronged; my words rioted, brimmed over, and I, as if I had been uttered aloud, I was in flight together with the sun for some unknown destination . . . or no, for by that time we knew where we were heading; and the planets were trailing me: planets spattering flames and populated by fiery, singing flowers, and planets that were mute, blue, where rational stones were united into organized societies—planets that had, like our earth, attained the pinnacle of absolute, 100 percent happiness——

And suddenly, from above: "But don't you think that the pinnacle consists precisely of these stones united in an organized society?" And, with the triangle becoming ever more acute, ever darker: "As for happiness . . . well, now, desires are excruciating things, after all—isn't that so? And it is clear that happiness comes into existence only when there are no longer any desires—not even a single one. What an error, what a preposterous prejudice it was for us to be putting a plus sign before happiness up to now; a minus—the divine minus!—should, of course, be placed before absolute happiness."

"Absolute minus is two hundred and seventy-three degrees," I remember murmuring absent-mindedly.

"Minus, two hundred and seventy-three degrees—precisely. Rather cool, but doesn't that very thing prove that we are at the pinnacle?"

As at that time, long ago, she was somehow speaking for me, through me, unfolding my thoughts to the end. But there was about this something so ghastly that I could not bear it, and with an effort I dragged a *no* out of me. "No," said I. "You're . . . you're jesting—"

She broke into loud—much too loud—laughter. Quickly, within a second, she laughed until she reached some brink, took a step—and went over. . . . A pause. She stood up. Placed her hands on my shoulder. Looked at me—long, deliberately. Then drew me to her—and there was nothing save her keen, searing lips.

"Farewell!"

This came from afar, from above, and was slow in reaching me—it may have taken a minute, or two minutes.

" 'Farewell'? What do you mean?"

"Why, you are ill; you have committed crimes because of me—come, didn't you find that excruciating? And now there is the Operation—and you will be cured of me. And so this is farewell."

"No!" I cried out.

The triangle was mercilessly acute, black against white: "What? You don't want happiness?"

My head was splitting, its fragments bounding apart: two logical trains of thought had collided, were piling up on each other, wrecking everything, ear-splittingly turning to matchwood—

"Well, now, I'm waiting. Choose: the Operation and one hundred percent happiness, or—"

"I cannot be without you, there's no use living without

you," I said, or I may have merely thought it: I don't know
which it was, but E- caught it.

"Yes, I know," she answered me. And then, still keeping
her hands on my shoulders and with her eyes holding mine
fast: "Until tomorrow, then. Tomorrow, at noon. You remember?"

"No, not tomorrow—the trial flight has been put off for a
day. It's the day after tomorrow—"

"So much the better for us. At noon, then—day after tomorrow—"

I was walking alone through the twilit street. The wind
spun me, bore me up, drove me along like a scrap of paper;
broken segments of the cast-iron sky were hurtling on and on;
they were fated to hurtle on through infinitude for a day, for
two days yet. . . . The unifs of those I met flicked me, yet
I walked alone. It was clear to me that all were saved, but
that there was now no salvation for me: *I did not want to be
saved—*

THIRTY-SECOND ENTRY: *I Have* Do you believe that *you will*
No Belief. Tractors. A Small *die?* Yes: man is mortal; I
Human Sliver. am a man: *ergo* . . . No,
that's not it—I know that you know all that. But what I am
asking is this: have you ever had occasion to *believe* in this,
to believe it definitely, believe it not with your mind but your
body, to feel that the fingers holding this very page will one
day be yellow, icy———

There, of course you don't believe—and that is why, up to
now, you haven't jumped out of a tenth floor window to the
pavement, that is why, up to now, you keep on eating, turning pages, shaving, smiling, writing—

That is the very state—yes, the very same—I am in today.
I know that this small black hand on the watch will, toward
midnight, crawl down to here, then it will climb up, slowly,
will take a step across a certain ultimate line—and the improbable tomorrow will be here. This I know but, just the
same, I somehow *have no belief in it* or, perhaps, it seems to
me that the four and twenty hours are four and twenty years.
And that is why I can still do something, hurry somewhere

or other, answer questions, clamber up the trap ladder to get aboard the *Integral*. I am still able to feel its rocking on the water and I comprehend that I must grab at the handrail— and can sense the chill of the glass under my hand. I can see how the translucent living cranes, bending their necks which are like those of the birds they are named after and extending their beaks, are cautiously and tenderly feeding the *Integral* with the terrible explosive food it needs for its motors. And below, on the river, I see clearly the blue veins, the nodes puffed up on the water by the wind. But all of this is very much apart from me, extraneous, flat—like a plan drafted on a sheet of paper.

And it was strange that the flat, schematic face of the Second Builder should suddenly speak up: "Well, now, how much motor fuel are we taking on? If we reckon on three hours—or on three hours and a half, let us say—"

Before me—in projection, as if on a draft—is my hand holding a computus, a logarithmic dial, the figure 15. "Fifteen tons. No, you'd better take on . . . yes, take on a hundred tons"—this because I knew, after all, that on the mor- row——— And, from the side, I saw my hand with the logarithmic dial beginning to tremble, barely perceptibly.

"A hundred tons? But why such a world of fuel? Why, that's enough for a week. A week, did I say? Longer than that!"

"Never can tell what'll turn up—who knows—"

I did know.

The wind whistled; all the air was crammed, to the limit, with something one could not see. I found difficulty in breath- ing, difficulty in walking—and with difficulty, slowly, never stopping, the hand was creeping on the clock of the Accumu- lator Tower, there, at the end of the Prospect. The Tower's spire, up among the clouds, was dull, blue and howling in a muffled way as it sucked in the electricity. Howling, too, were the tubes of the Musical Factory.

As always, the numbers were walking in ranks, four to each. But the ranks were, somehow, unstable and (perhaps because of the wind) wavering, sagging. More and more, right along. There, these groups had collided with something at the corner, had rolled back, and then frozen into a solid, tight, quickly breathing wad; all of them, instantaneously, acquired the elongated necks of geese.

"Look! No, look over there—quick!"

"There they are! They, and no others!"

". . . Well, I wouldn't do it for anything! Not for anything! I'd rather shove my head under The Benefactor's Machine—"

"Not so loud! Are you crazy—"

The door of the auditorium on the corner was gaping and out of it issued a slowly, ponderously trampling column of fifty men. However, *men* is not at all the word: they did not have legs but some sort of heavy, forged wheels turned by an invisible drive; not men, these, but some sort of humanoid tractors. Over their heads, flapping in the wind, was a white banner with a sun embroidered in gold—and, amid the rays of this sun, the inscription: WE ARE THE FIRST! WE ARE ALREADY OPERATIONED! FOLLOW US—ONE AND ALL!

Slowly, irresistibly they plowed through the crowd—and it was clear that if, instead of us, there had been a wall, a tree, a building they would, nevertheless, have plowed unhesitatingly through wall, tree, building. They had already reached the center of the Prospect. Screwed together by their arms they stretched out in a chain, their faces toward us. While we, a tensed wad with all its heads bristling, waited. Necks goosishly extended. Clouds. Wind whistling. Abruptly the wing tips of the chain, to the right and to the left, curved inward and, at an ever increasing tempo, like a heavy machine going downhill, the chain headed for us, ringed us in tightly —and drove us toward the gaping door, through the door, within the auditorium———

Somebody's piercing scream: "It's a dragnet! Run!"

Everything in a tidal surge. Near the wall of the building there was still a small, narrow living gateway—all stampeded toward it, their heads momentarily sharpening into wedges, their elbows, ribs, shoulders, hips becoming acute. Trampling feet, fluttering hands, unifs—all these sprayed out like a fan and came showering down all around me, like water under high pressure escaping through a firehose. For a second a doubly-curved, *S*-shaped body, a pair of translucent wing-ears, impinged on my eyes—then their owner was no longer there, had vanished through the ground, and I was alone in the midst of instantaneous arms, legs; I was on the run————

A brief respite to catch my breath, at some entrance, with my back pressed hard against the door—and immediately a tiny human sliver was flattened against me, as if driven by the wind.

"I've been . . . I've been running after you all the time. I won't have any of this—you understand? I won't have it! I am ready to—"

Rounded, diminutive hands on my sleeve, the eyes round, blue—it was she, O-. And then, somehow totally, she slid down the wall, slumped to the ground. She contracted into a small ball down there, on the cold steps, and I stood over her, stroking her head, her face . . . and found my hands were wet. It was as if I were very big, while she was utterly little—a little part of my own self. This was an altogether different emotion from that which I felt for E-, and at that moment I had a notion that there might have been something of that sort among the ancients in their attitude toward their private children.

Coming from below, made barely audible by the fingers covering her face, I heard: "Every night I . . . I won't be able to bear it if they should give me this cure. Every night, alone in the darkness, I keep thinking of the baby, of what he will be like, of how I will be holding him. . . . If I am given this cure life will hold nothing I can live on—do you understand? And you are obligated—you are obligated to—"

A preposterous feeling, yet I truly felt certain that, yes, I was obligated. Preposterous, because this obligation of mine was but an additional crime. Preposterous, because white cannot at the same time be black, because obligation and crime cannot coincide. Or, there is neither black nor white in life, and color depends solely upon a basic logical premise. And if the premise here was that I had unlawfully given her a child————

"Very well, then; only you mustn't . . . mustn't object," I

said. "You understand, I'll have to bring you to E-, as I suggested that other time, so that she may—"

"Yes"—this she said in a subdued voice, without taking her hands away from her face.

I helped her to her feet. We walked in silence through the darkening street, amid the mute leaden buildings, in and out and between the resisting, lashing branches of the wind, she absorbed in her own thoughts, I in mine—or it may have been that both of us were thinking of one and the same thing.

At a certain perceptive, tense point I caught, through the whistling of the wind, familiar footfalls behind me, sounding as if the walker were sloshing through puddles. As I was about to turn a corner I looked back: among the clouds scurrying across the dull glass of the pavement in inverted reflections I espied S-. Immediately my arms became extraneous, their swinging was off-beat, and I began telling O- loudly that tomorrow—yes, tomorrow—the first flight of the *Integral* would take place, that it would be something utterly unprecedented, wonderful, awesome. . . . O-, in amazement, was looking with rounded blue eyes at me, at my noisily swinging arms; I, however, gave her no chance to utter a word but kept on talking, talking. Yet an isolated thought was feverishly buzzing and tapping away within me (only I could hear it): "You can't . . . you can't be the means of leading him to E-! You must somehow throw him off your track—"

Instead of turning left I turned right. A bridge offered its submissively, slavishly arched back to the three of us—to O-, to me and to that S- fellow behind us. Bright lights from the buildings on the other side were cascading into the water and shattering into thousands of feverishly leaping sparks that were aspersed by raging white foam. The wind was droning somewhere not too high, like a taut hawser. Strung on a giant's bass viol. And, through the bass notes, constantly flap-flapping behind——

My building, at last. At the entrance O- paused, began babbling something like: "No! Why, you promised me—" but I would not let her finish, hurriedly pushed her through the doorway and we were inside, in the vestibule. Hovering over the controller's desk were the familiar pendulous cheeks, shuddering every so often in agitation; numbers surrounded her in a compact crowd—there was some sort of a dispute going on; heads were hanging over the railings of the second floor; numbers kept running down the staircase, but each by himself or herself. But more about this later, later. I lost no time in drawing O- to a corner away from the desk, sat down with my back to the wall (I could see a dark, big-headed shadow gliding back and forth over the sidewalk there, beyond the wall), and drew out my memo pad.

O- was slowly sagging in her armchair—as though her body were evaporating, thawing under her unif, and there seemed to be nothing in that seat but this empty garment and those empty eyes, engulfing one in their blue emptiness. Then, wearily: "Why have you brought me here? Did you deceive me?"

"No—not so loud! Look over there—do you see what's beyond the wall?"

"Yes. A shadow."

"He is tailing me all the time. I can't go with you. You understand, I mustn't. I'll write a few words; you take the note and go on by yourself. I know he'll remain here."

Under her unif the sap-swollen body stirred anew, the belly grew just the least trifle rounder, a barely glimmering dawn, a morning glow, appeared on her face. I thrust the note into her chilled fingers, clasped her hand hard, my eyes drank for the last time from the blue of her eyes.

"Farewell! Perhaps, some day again—" She took her hand away. All bent, she walked off slowly, took two steps, quickly turned around—and was again by my side. Her lips moved—with her eyes, her lips, with all of her she was saying some word to me, one word, the one and the same word, over and over, and how unbearable her smile was, how poignant her pain——— And then the bent, tiny human sliver was in the doorway, turned into a diminutive shadow beyond the wall, moving without a backward look, quickly, ever more quickly—

I approached U-'s small desk. Puffing out her gills agitatedly, indignantly, she addressed me: "You understand, they all seem to have gone out of their minds! That number over there, for instance, assures me that he apparently saw with his own eyes some sort of a man near the House of Antiquity, all naked and grown over with coarse animal hair—"

A voice rose from the vacuous pack, with every head in it bristling: "Yes! And I repeat once more—I did see him! Yes, I did!"

"Well, how do you like that—eh? What delirium!"

And this *delirium!* of hers was so full of conviction, so inflexible, that I asked myself: "Really, now, isn't all that which has of late been going on within me and all around me truly delirium?" But I happened to glance at my hairy hands, and I recalled what E- had said: "Most probably there's a drop of forest blood in you. . . . Perhaps that's just the reason why I—"

No: fortunately, all this was not delirium. No: unfortunately, all this was not delirium.

THIRTY-THIRD ENTRY: *No summary for this; jottings, in utmost haste; this is the last—*

This day has come. No time lost in getting at the *Gazette.* I read it with my eyes (the phrase is precise: my eyes just then were like a pen, like a computus, objects which one holds, feels in one's hands; my eyes were extraneous, they were instruments).

The proclamation was in such large type that it took up all of the front page:

THE ENEMIES OF HAPPINESS ARE NOT NAPPING. HOLD ON TO HAPPINESS WITH BOTH HANDS! TOMORROW ALL WORK WILL BE SUSPENDED — ALL NUMBERS WILL REPORT FOR OPERATION   "OPERATION."

ABSENTEES ARE CANDIDATES FOR THE MACHINE OF THE BENEFACTOR.

Tomorrow! Could there possibly be, would there be, a tomorrow?

Through the inertia of daily habit I stretched out my hand (an instrument) toward the bookshelf to put today's *Gazette* together with the other issues in a binder ornamented with gilt. And, even as I was doing this, it occurred to me: "What's this for? Does it make any difference? For I will never again enter this room—never—" and the newspaper fell out of my hands to the floor. Yet I stood there and looked around the room, all over the room, at every inch of that room; I was hastily taking along with me, feverishly stuffing them in an invisible portmanteau, all the things I regretted leaving here. Table. Books. Armchair. E- had sat in that armchair, at that time, while I was sitting on the floor at her feet. . . . Bed—

Then, for a minute or two, I ludicrously awaited some miracle: perhaps the telephone would ring, perhaps she would tell me that I was to————

No. No miracle.

I am going away, into the unknown. These are my last lines. Farewell to you, my readers, whom I never knew, whom I loved, with whom I have lived through so many pages, to whom I, who have contracted a soul, have revealed all of myself, down to my last smallest stripped screw, to the last broken spring.

I am going away.

THIRTY-FOURTH ENTRY: *The Manumitted Ones. A Sunlit Night. A Radio Valkyrie.* Oh, if I could but have smashed myself and all the others to smithereens, if I could but find myself, together with her, somewhere beyond the Wall, among the wild beasts baring their yellow fangs, if I had but never returned here! Things would be a thousand—a million—times easier. But now—what next? Go and choke the life out of that ████████████████████ But would that help in any way?

No, no, no! Get a grip on yourself, D-503! Plant yourself on a firm logical axis; if for but a little while pit all your weight and might against the lever and, like a slave of antiquity, turn the mill wheels of syllogisms until you have recorded, until you have thought over, everything that happened.

When I came aboard the *Integral* all were already mustered, all were at their posts, all the cells of the glass beehive were filled. Through the glass of the decks one could see the people below, tiny, like ants, standing by the telegraph instruments, dynamos, transformers, altimeters, ventilators, dial indicators, pumps, tubes. In the wardroom some numbers (probably assigned by the Scientific Bureau) were bent over tabulations and instruments, with the Second Builder and his two assistants standing by. These three had their heads drawn in between their shoulders like turtles; their faces were gray, autumnal, anything but beaming.

"Well, how do you feel?" I asked.

"So-so. Kind of scary," one of the trio smiled, grayishly, without beaming. "We may have to land no one knows where. And, in general, everything is unknown—"

I found it unbearable to look at these three—these, whom an hour later I would, with these same hands of mine, cast out forever from the snug figures of The Tables of Hourly Commandments, whom I would forever tear away from the maternal breast of The One State. They reminded me of the tragic figures of *The Three Manumitted Ones,* whose story is familiar to all our schoolboys. The story has to do with three numbers who were manumitted from labor for a month, as a sort of experiment: each was told he could do what he liked, could go where he liked.* The unfortunates kept loitering around their customary place of work and peeping within with hungry eyes; they would stop at the public squares and for hours on end go through the motions which, at set times during the day, became an actual physical need: they sawed

---

* This took place a long time ago, in the third century after the giving of The Tables of Hourly Commandments.

and planed the air, or clanged and pounded with invisible sledges upon invisible ingots. And at last, on the tenth day of their manumission, they could no longer bear the strain: linking hands, they went into the water and, to the sounds of The March, immersed themselves deeper and deeper, until the water put an end to their torments.

I repeat, I found it oppressive to look at these three; I was in a hurry to get away. "I'll just check in the engine room," I said, "and then we're off."

They were asking me things: what voltage to use for the blast-off; how much water was needed as ballast in the tank at the stern. There was some sort of a talking machine inside me: it replied to all the questions quickly and precisely; yet incessantly, subliminally, I was thinking thoughts of my own. And suddenly, while I was in a narrow little passageway, something found its way there, into that subliminal self of mine—and it was from that moment, strictly speaking, that everything began.

Gray faces, gray unifs flitted through that passage, and for a second one face stood out against the others: the hair was a cap pulled low over the forehead, the forehead an overhang above the eyes: it was that messenger of E-'s. I surmised that those of whom he was one were here, and that there was no place I could escape to from all this, and that only minutes— a few decads of minutes—remained. An infinitesimal, molecular tremor ran all through my body (nor did it cease to the very last)—just as if an enormous motor had been placed within me, but the construction of my body was too light, and consequently its walls, partitions, cables, rafters, lights, all were trembling.

I still did not know if she was on board. But just then there was no time to find out: I had been sent for in haste to go up to the commander's roundhouse: it was time to be off . . . to where?

Faces gray, not beaming. Blue, tensed veins on the water below. A laminated sky of crushing cast iron. And it was as hard for me to pick up the speaking tube as if both hand and tube were of cast iron. "Up—at forty-five degrees!"

A muffled blast; a jolt; a frenzied white-green mountain of

water at the stern; the deck (yielding, rubbery) recedes from underfoot, and all things below, and one's whole life, recede also—forever. A second's view, as all things fell deeper and deeper into some sort of funnel and all their surroundings contracted—the city's blue-ice layout, the round bubbles of its cupolas, the lonely leaden upthrust finger of the Accumulator Tower. Then, for an instant, a cotton-wool curtain of clouds. We went through it and into the sun, into the blue sky. Seconds, minutes, miles: the azure hardened, became bloated with darkness, the stars emerged as beads of cold, silvery sweat.

And then it was night—eerie, unbearably bright, black, starry, sun-shot. Just as if one had suddenly become deaf: the tubes were still roaring, but you merely saw that—the tubes were mute, silence prevailed. The sun was like that—mute.

That was natural; that was precisely what one should have expected. We had left the earth's atmosphere. But everything had come about so rapidly, somehow, so overwhelmingly, that all those around me were stunned, subdued into silence. As for me, things actually seemed easier under this fantastic mute sky, as though, having gone through my last spasm, I had already set foot across the inevitable threshold and my body were somewhere there, below, while I was careering through a new world where everything was naturally bound to be dissimilar, topsy-turvy.

"Keep her on course!" I called down the speaking tube—or rather it was not I who did so but the machine within me, and it was also this machine which with a mechanical, hinged hand thrust the mouthpiece of the tube upon the Second Builder, while I, clad from head to toe in a most exquisite molecular tremor which I alone was aware of, ran down in search of——

The door of the wardroom was still open—only an hour later was it to clang, locking itself. Near the door was some number whom I did not know, a squat little fellow with one of those faces that are turned out by the hundred, by the thousand, and are lost in a crowd, but with arms inordinately long, the hands coming down to his knees, as though through a hasty error they had been taken from another set of human fittings. One of the long arms stretched out, barring my way: "Where do you wish to go?"

It was clear to me that he did not know that I knew everything. So be it—perhaps things had to be thus. And so, towering above him, I said in an intentionally brusque tone: "I am the builder of the *Integral*. And I am in charge of the trial flight. Understand?"

The arm was no longer there.

The wardroom. Heads were bent over the instruments, the charts—heads circuited all over with gray bristles and heads that were yellow, bald, ripe. One quick look scraped them up and wadded them; then I was on my way back again, traversing the narrow passageway and going down the trap ladder into the engine room. There the tubes, incandescent from the blasts, were emitting heat and rumbling; the sparkling cranks were doing a drunken, desperate, squatting dance; the dial indicators were trembling with a barely perceptible tremor that did not cease for a second. And then I caught sight of him at last, standing near the tachometer with his forehead shoved down over a notebook.

"Listen"—I had to shout in his very ear on account of the rumbling—"is she here? Where is she?"

"She?"—this with a smile, from under the shadow of his overhanging forehead. "Over there. In the radio communication room—"

And I headed there. Three of them were in that room, all wearing winglike headsets, while she seemed to be a head taller than usual, winged, coruscating, in flight—like one of the Valkyries of the ancients—and it seemed, too, that the enormous blue sparks, from the radio aerial above were really emanating from her, even as that heady, after-lightning ozone was also an emanation of hers.

"One of you—well, you'll do," I said to her, panting (from having run, of course). "I have to transmit something to the earth, to the building site. Come, I'll dictate it to you—"

There was a cabin about the size of a matchbox next to the radio room. We sat down at a table, side by side. I found her hand and squeezed it hard: "Well, what's what? What's going to happen?"

"I don't know. Do you understand how wonderful this is— to be flying without knowing the destination—and without caring what it is? There, it will be twelve soon—and no one knows what's coming! And when it's night . . . where will you and I be at night? On the grass, perhaps, on dry leaves—" Blue sparks emanated from her, and an odor of ozone, as after lightning, while the tremor within me was constantly increasing in frequency.

"Write it down," I told her loudly and still panting (from having run). "Time, eleven thirty. Speed, six thousand, eight hundred—"

She, from under her winged, helmet-like headset, softly, without taking her eyes off the paper: "She came to me last evening, with a note from you. I know—I know everything; don't say a word. However, the child is yours, isn't it? And I got her away; by now she is there, beyond the wall. She will live."

I was back again in the roundhouse. Again that delirious night with its black starry sky and blinding sun, again the hand on the clock, limping slowly from one minute to the next; and everything clad, as if in a fog, in the most delicate tremor, barely perceptible (and that only to me).

For some reason it struck me that it would be better if all this were to take place not here but somewhere down there, closer to the earth.

"Stop!" I shouted into the speaking tube.

The *Integral* was still making headway, through inertia, but slowly, more and more slowly. But then it caught, as if hanging on by a hair, and was motionless for an instant; next, the hair snapped and the *Integral* plummeted like a stone, faster and faster. Thus for minutes, for decades of minutes; I could hear my pulse; the minute hand before my eyes was drawing nearer and nearer to 12:00. And it was clear to me: I was the stone; E- was the earth. I was the stone thrown by someone, and there was an excruciating need for the stone to fall, to crash against the earth, so as to shatter itself into smithereens.

But what if . . . the firm blue smoke of the clouds was already below—what if————

The talking machine within me picked up the speaking tube with a hinged, unerring motion, issued a command for reduced speed: the stone ceased plummeting. And then there was the tired snorting of only four tubes, two fore and two aft, furnishing just enough energy to neutralize the *Integral*, which, with only an occasional slight shudder, was at a standstill in the air, as if it were anchored, a kilometer or so above the earth.

All poured out on deck (the 12:00 bell for lunch was just about to ring) and, bending over the glass gunwale, were swallowing, hastily and at one gulp, the unknown, beyond-the-Wall world lying there, below. Amber, green, blue: autumnal forest, meadows, lake. At the rim of a small blue saucer were some yellow, bony ruins and a yellow, mummified finger menacingly raised—the latter most probably the belfry of an ancient church which had remained standing through some miracle.

"Look, look! Over there, a little more to the right!"

In the distance some blotch or other was flying fast, like a brown shadow over the green desert. I had a pair of binoculars in my hands and mechanically brought it up to my eyes: a drove of brown horses with waving tails was galloping through chest-high grass, while perched on their backs were those dark-bay, white, raven-black . . . beings.

"But I'm telling you—I saw a face!"—this from behind me.

"Go on! Tell that to someone else!"

"Well, then, take the binoculars—there, take them!"

Horses and riders vanished. An endless green desert lay below. And then, in the midst of this desert, filling all of it, and all of me, and all of those there—came the shrill quavering of a bell—the bell for lunch; it was one minute to 12:00.

A microcosm scattered into momentary, disjointed fragments. Somebody's golden badge tinkled as it fell on the steps —and it did not matter to me at all to hear it crunch under my heel. A voice: "And I'm telling you it was a face!" A dark rectangle: the open door of the wardroom. Clenched white teeth, sharply smiling. And then, as the clock began to strike with infinite slowness, holding its breath between strokes, and the front ranks had already begun to move, the rectangle of the door was suddenly crossed out by two familiar, unnaturally long arms.

"Stop!"

Fingernails sank into the palm of my hand: it was E-, standing alongside me: "Who is he? Do you know him?"

"But—but isn't he one of you—"

He had already clambered up on someone's shoulders; his hundred-lot, thousand-lot face, yet unique among all faces, now reared above the hundred faces there: "In the name of the Guardians! You whom I am addressing—bear in mind that the Guardians can hear me, each one of them hears me. And I'll tell you this much—we know. We don't know your numbers, so far, but just the same we know everything. The *Integral* will never be yours! The trial flight will be carried out to the end, and you yourselves—you will not dare to stir now; you yourselves, with your own hands, will carry it out. And afterwards—however, I have finished."

Silence. The squares of glass underfoot were soft, cottonwoolly, and my legs, too, were cotton-woolly, soft. She, alongside, was smiling, the smile utterly white; frenzied blue sparks issued from her. She whispered in my ear, through clenched teeth: "Ah, so it was you? You *fulfilled your duty?* Oh, well—" She snatched her hand out of my hands; the Valkyrian, wrathfully winged helmet-headset was already somewhere far ahead of me. Solitary, silent, turned to ice, I went on toward the wardroom along with all the others.

"But then, it wasn't I—it wasn't I! Why, I didn't discuss it with anybody, I confided it only to those white, mute pages"—inwardly I was shouting this to her—inaudibly, desperately, deafeningly. She was seated across the table from me—and not even once did her eyes alight on me. Next to her was somebody's ripe-yellow bald head. I overheard E- saying: " 'Nobility of character'? But, my dearest professor, even a simple philological analysis of this phrase indicates that it is a prejudice, a survival of ancient feudal epochs. Whereas we—"

I felt myself paling and that at any moment all would

notice this. But the machine within me went through the pre-scribed 50 chews for every mouthful; I locked myself within me, as in an opaque house of ancient days; I blocked up the door outside with stones; I put hangings over the windows.

Then: the speaking tube in my hands again, and the flight, in the grip of an icy, ultimate melancholy, through clouds, into the starry–sun-shot icy night. Minutes, hours. And, evi-dently, a logical motor which I myself could not hear had been working all the time within me, feverishly, at top speed. Because, suddenly, at a certain point of the blue expanse, there was my desk, with the gill-like cheeks of U- bent over it and, lying on it, a couple of sheets of these entries—sheets I had forgotten to put away. And it was clear to me that no one but she could have lodged the information. It was all clear to me.

Ah, if I could but make my way to the radio room—if I but could! Winged helmets, the ozone odor of blue lightnings. . . . I remember I was telling her something, loudly; I re-member, too, her saying, looking through me as if I were of glass and with her voice coming from somewhere far off: "I am busy—I am receiving a message from down there. You can dictate to her"—indicating another female number.

In the tiny matchbox of the cabin adjoining I dictated firmly, after thinking the message over for a minute: "Time: fourteen forty. Descending. Cut off motors. Everything over."

The roundhouse. The machine heart of the *Integral* had been stopped; we were falling, and my heart could not keep pace with the fall: it lagged, it rose up, up into my throat. Clouds, and then a green blotch in the distance, becoming a more intense green, more distinct, rushing toward us in a whirlwind. The end at any moment——

The faïence-white distorted face of the Second Builder. Probably it was he who pushed me away with all his strength; I hit my head against something and, as everything was turn-ing dark before me and I was falling, 1 heard dimly: "Tail tube—full speed!"

A sharp leap upward. I remember nothing more.

THIRTY-FIFTH ENTRY: *A Hoop.* I did not sleep all night. I
A Carrot. A Murder. kept thinking of but one
thing.

After what happened yesterday my head is tightly band-
aged. And I feel that these are not bandages but a hoop;
an implacable hoop of glassy steel has been forged about my
head, and within that forged hoop I am thinking of but one,
never varying, thing: killing U-. Killing U-, and then going to
her, to E-, and telling her: "Now do you believe me?" Most
repulsive of all is that killing is somehow filthy, atavistic. The
idea of braining this creature brings a sensation of something
disgustingly sweet to my mouth and I can't swallow my
saliva; I keep spitting into my handkerchief all the time; my
mouth is parched.

I had in my closet a piston rod which had cracked after
casting; I had to examine the nature of the break under a
microscope. I rolled all my entries into a tube (let her read
all of me, to the last letter), thrust the piston rod into this
tube, and went down. The staircase was endless, the steps
were somehow repulsively slippery, fluid; I had to keep wiping my mouth with a handkerchief all the time.

I reached the ground floor. My heart plunged. I paused,
drew out the piston rod, headed for the controller's
desk———

But U- wasn't there. Just the bare, icy desk top. I recalled
that all work had been suspended for today; all numbers had
to report for the Operation and, understandably, there was no
reason for her to be here; there was nobody here for her to
register.

Out in the street. Wind. A sky of careering sheets of cast
iron. And, just as it happened at a certain moment yesterday:
the universe was shattered into isolated, sharp, individual
small bits, and each one of these in its headlong descent
paused for a second, hung before me in the air, and evapo-
rated without leaving a trace.

Suppose the black, specific letters on this page were suddenly to shift, each one going off lickety-split this way or that,
in its fright, and there wouldn't be a single recognizable

word, just a lot of meaningless pi: *igh* for *fright*, *ty-spl* from *lickety-split*. Well, that's just the way the crowd in the street was: out of alignment, barging straight ahead, backing off, crisscrossing, acting contrary. And then—nobody. Also, frozen for a second in headlong flight, there, up on a second floor, in a glass cage suspended in mid-air: a male number and a female number, in a kiss, standing; her whole body was bent backward, as if broken. This for the last time, for all time.

At one corner—a moving prickly bush of heads. Over these heads—apart from them, up in the air—a banner with the words: *Down with the Machine of The Benefactor! Down with the Operation!* And—apart from me—my *I*, thinking every second: "Can it be that each one of us bears such an inner pain that it can be plucked out only together with the heart, and that each one of us must do something before he can————" And for a second there was nothing in all the universe save a bestial hand (mine) holding a cast-iron-heavy parcel.

Next, an urchin; he was straining forward, all of him; there was a shadow under his nether lip. This nether lip was everted, like the cuff of a turned-up sleeve—for that matter, his whole face was everted; he was bawling and trying to get away from somebody as fast as his legs would carry him— I could hear the pounding of pursuing feet.

"Yes," I got out of him, "U- must be in school now; I must hurry."

I ran to the nearest subway entrance. As I was about to step in somebody informed me as he hurried past: "No trains! No trains running today! Something going on down there—"

I descended. Utter delirium prevailed. The gleaming of faceted crystal suns. A platform paved with solidly tamped-down heads. An empty train frozen on the rails. And, amid the silence, a voice. I could not see her but I knew that voice, resilient, flexible as a whiplash, lashing—I knew it; and somewhere over there was that acute triangle of eyebrows quirked up at the temples. "Do let me through!" I shouted. "Let me through there! I have to—" But somebody's nippers were holding, nailing down my arms, my shoulders.

And, amid the silence, a voice: "No; make haste up there! There you will be cured, there you will be fed with pastry-dough happiness until you can't swallow another mouthful, and you, with your bellies full, will doze in peace, in an organized way, all snoring metronomically—can't you just hear that great Snoring Symphony? You're funny—they want to give you a vermifuge against those question marks which squirm like worms, which gnaw excruciatingly like worms, yet you are standing here and listening to me. Make haste to get up there, to the Great Operation! What is it to you if I am left all alone here? What is it to you if I do not wish to have others do my wishing for me, if I wish to do my own wishing—if I wish for the impossible—"

Another voice—slow, ponderous: "Aha! The impossible? That means chasing after your damn-fool fantasies, while they twitch their tails in front of your nose? No; we grab them by their tails, crush them under us, and then—"

"And then you'll gobble them up, start snoring—and you'll need new tails in front of your noses. They say that the ancients had a certain animal—the ass. In order to make him go forward, go forward all the time, they would tie a carrot on a pole in such a way that the animal could not get at it. And if he did get at it, he would gobble it up—"

Suddenly the nippers let go of me; I dashed nearer the central point, where she was speaking—and at that moment everything turned into a crush, a spate; there was a cry from behind: "They're coming! They're coming this way!" The lights flared up, went out: someone had cut the cable—and then an avalanche of cries, gasps, heads, fingers————

I don't know how long we kept milling through the subway tube. At last there were stairs, dimness as of dusk but becoming ever lighter, and we were out in the street again, fanning out in different directions.

And then I was alone. Wind; twilight—gray, low, almost directly overhead. In the wet glass of the sidewalk, very deep within it—inverted lights, walls, figures moving about with their legs up in the air. And an unbelievably heavy parcel in my hands, dragging me into the depths, to the bottom.

U- was still not at her desk downstairs, and her room was empty, dark.

I went up to my room, put on the light. My temples, tightly bound by their hoop, were pounding; I paced the room, still encircled by that ring forged around me: the table, the white parcel on the table; the bed; the door; the table, the white parcel. The blinds of the room to the left were lowered. In the room to the right, a knobby bald head, and a forehead like an enormous yellow parabola, bent over a book. The furrows on the forehead were a series of yellow illegible lines of print. Now and then our eyes met—and I would then feel that those yellow lines had to do with me.

. . . The thing happened at 21:00, exactly. U- came herself. Only one thing has remained distinct in my memory: I was breathing so loudly that I could hear myself breathing, and all the time I was trying to breathe more quietly, somehow—and couldn't.

She sat down, straightened out the unif at her knees. Her rosily pink gills were flapping: "Ah, my dear—so it's true that you are wounded? Just as soon as I heard about it I immediately—"

The piston rod was in front of me on the table. I sprang up, breathing still more loudly. She heard me, broke off in the middle of a word, and also got on her feet for some reason. I already saw the right spot on her head for the blow; there was a disgustingly sweet taste in my mouth. I reached for my handkerchief but it wasn't there—I spat on the floor. That fellow on the other side of the wall, to the right, with the yellow, staring lines that had to do with me—it was necessary that he should not see; the thing would be even more repulsive if he were to look on. I pressed the button (very well; I had no right whatsoever to do it, but did that at all matter at that juncture?); the blinds fell. She evidently understood, instinctively, made a dash toward the door. But I headed her off and, breathing loudly, without taking my eyes for a second from that spot on her head———

"You've—you've gone out of your mind! Don't you dare—" She was backing away, sat down (or rather fell) on the bed, tremblingly thrust her hands, pressed palm to palm, between her knees. All wound up like a spring, holding her as firmly as ever on the leash with my eyes, I slowly stretched my hand toward the table (only my hand moved), seized the piston rod.

"I implore you! A day—just one day! Tomorrow—no later than tomorrow—I'll go and attend to everything—"

What was she babbling about? I swung my arm back————

And I consider that I did kill her. Yes, my unknown readers, you have the right to call me a murderer. I know that I would have brought the piston rod down on her head, if she had not cried out: "For . . . for the sake of . . . I agree—just a moment—"

With trembling hands she snatched off her unif; the expanse of yellow, flabby body threw itself back on the bed. And only at that point did I grasp the situation: she was thinking that I had lowered the blinds in order to . . . that I wanted to————

This was so unexpected, so silly, that I burst into peals of laughter. And immediately the tightly wound spring within me snapped; my hand weakened, the piston rod clattered to the floor. That was when I perceived, through personal experience, that laughter is the most dreadful of weapons: with laughter it is possible to kill everything—even killing.

I was sitting at the table and laughing—with desperate, ultimate laughter—and saw no way out of this preposterous situation. I don't know how all this would have ended if things had followed their natural course, but at this point a new, external factor suddenly emerged: the telephone rang.

I rushed over, grasped the receiver: perhaps it was she? And then, through the receiver, came an unfamiliar voice: "Just a minute—" Exhausting, endless buzzing. First at a distance, ponderous footfalls; then, approaching, ever more reverberatingly, more clangorous, like cast iron, and: "D, Five Hundred and Three? Aha! This is The Benefactor speaking. Come to me, without delay!" A click—the receiver hung up. Just a click.

U- was still lying on the bed, her eyes closed, gills widely distended in a smile. I scraped her garment up from the floor, tossed it at her, told her through clenched teeth: "There! Make it quick—make it quick!"

She raised herself on her elbow; her breasts splashed over to one side; her eyes were round; all of her had turned to wax: "What?"

"Just that. There, do get dressed!"

She (all tied in a knot, clutching the garment, her voice squashed in): "Turn around—"

I turned around, pressed my forehead against the mirror. It was black, wet; lights, figures, sparks were quivering within it. No: all this was I, all this was within me. Why had He called me up? Was it possible He already knew about her, about me, about everything?

U-, fully dressed, was at the door. Reaching her in two strides, I squeezed her hands very hard, as though I was trying to squeeze from those hands, drop by drop, what I had to know: "Listen: her number—you know whom I'm talking about—did you turn in her number? No? But tell me the truth, I have to know. It makes no difference about me—but tell me the truth—"

"No, I didn't."

"No? But why not, since you had already gone there and made a report—"

Suddenly her nether lip turned inside out, like that urchin's, and tears spurted from and rolled down her cheeks: "Because I . . . I was afraid . . . that if I named her, you . . . you would stop loving—oh, I can't do a thing like that—I couldn't have done it!"

I understood: this was the truth. Preposterous, funny, human truth! I threw the door open.

THIRTY-SIXTH ENTRY: *Blank Pages. The God of the Christians. About My Mother.*

It is odd: there seems to be a blank white page in my head. I don't remember how I made my way there, how I had to wait (I know I did wait); I don't remember a thing, not a single sound, not a single face, not a single gesture. As if all the wires connecting me with the universe had been cut.

When I came to, I was already standing before Him; I dreaded raising my eyes: all I saw was His enormous cast-iron hands lying on His knees. These hands were crushing His Own Self, they made His knees buckle. His fingers stirred slowly. His face was somewhere above, in the mists, and it seemed that it was only because His voice reached me from such a height that it did not roll like thunder, did not deafen me, but still bore a resemblance to an ordinary human voice: "And so—*et tu?* You—the builder of the *Integral?* You, to whom had been granted the opportunity of becoming the greatest of all conquistadors? You, whose name was to inaugurate a new, illustrious chapter in the history of The One State— you?"

The blood plashed up to my head, my cheeks, then— another blank page: there remains only the memory of the pulsing at my temples and the voice reverberating up there, above, but not a single word. Only when He fell silent did I come to; I beheld His hand stirring as if it weighed three thousand pounds; it crept forward, ever so slowly; a finger pointed rigidly at me: "Well? Why are you keeping silent? 'He is an executioner'—have I read your thought aright—yes or no?"

"Yes," I answered submissively. And from then on I heard every word of His clearly.

"Well, now, do you think I am afraid of that word? Come, did you ever try to get the shell off it and see what is inside? I will show you that right now. Recall: a mount in the blue dusk, a cross, a rabble. Some men, spattered with blood, on top of the cross, nailing a body to it; others, spattered with tears, at the foot of the cross, looking on. Does it not seem to you that the role of those on top of the cross is the most difficult, the most important? Why, if they were not in the cast, would all this magnificent tragedy have been staged? They were whistled off by the dark rabble—but then, to make up for that, the author of this tragedy—God—is obligated to remunerate them all the more generously. And what about the Most Merciful God of the Christians, Who is charking all the contumacious over the slow fires of Hell—is He not an executioner? Or take autos-da-fé and living torches—really, is the number of those who were burned by the Christians any smaller than the number of Christians who were burned? And yet, just the same—do understand this!—this God was, just the same, glorified for ages as the God of Love. An absurdity? No: on the contrary, it is a patent, written in blood, attesting the ineradicable common sense of man. Even when he was a shaggy savage he grasped that true, algebraic love for humanity is infallibly inhuman, and that an infallible sign of truth is its cruelty. Just as an infallible sign of fire is that it consumes by fire. Will you show me a fire that does not sear? Well, produce your arguments, do! Dispute with me!"

How could I dispute with Him? How could I dispute with Him, when these had been (up to now) my very thoughts—save that I had never been able to panoply them in such well-forged, glittering armor. I kept silent.

"If your silence signifies that you agree with me, why, let us talk as grownups do when the children have gone off to bed. Let's talk everything over to the end. I ask you: what have men, from their swaddling-clothes days, been praying for, dreaming about, tormenting themselves for? Why, to have someone tell them, once and for all, just what happiness is—and then weld them to this happiness with chains. Well, what else are we doing now if not that? The ancient dream of Heaven. . . . Remember, in Heaven they no longer know anything of desires, of pity, of love; there you will find only the beatified ones, with fantasiectomy already performed on them (that is the only reason they *are* beatified)—the angels, the servants of God. And now, at the very moment when we have already caught up with this dream, when we have already seized it like this [His hand clenched: had there been a stone in it, the stone would have squirted juice], when all that remained was to gut the prey and cut it up in pieces for general distribution—at that very moment you . . . you—"

The cast-iron rumbling unexpectedly broke off. I was all red, like pig iron on an anvil under a clanging sledge hammer. The sledge hammer was silently poised, and waiting for it to fall was still more . . . more frightening————

Suddenly: "How old are you?"

"Thirty-two."

"You are twice the age of a sixteen-year-old—but every bit as naïve! Listen to me: is it really possible that it did not occur to you even once, that they—we still do not know their numbers, but I feel certain we will learn them from you— that, after all, they needed you only as the builder of the *Integral,* only that they might, through you—"

"Don't! Don't!" I cried out. It was like putting your hands up as a shield and crying out to a bullet: you can still hear that funny "Don't!" of yours, but the bullet has already seared its way through you, you are already writhing on the floor. Yes, yes, I was the builder of the *Integral.* Yes, yes . . . and, immediately: a flash of U-'s infuriated face with its quivering, brick-red gills, on the morning when she and E- had come to my room together.

I remember most clearly: I broke into laughter, raised my eyes. Sitting before me was a baldheaded, a Socratically-bald-headed man. And with beads of sweat all over that bald head.

How simple, all this. All this, how magnificently banal, and so very simple that it was laughable. Laughter was suffocating me; it escaped me in billows. I put a hand over my mouth and dashed out of there pell-mell.

Stair steps. Wind. Wet, bounding fragments of lights, of faces. And, even as I ran, I kept thinking: "No, I must see her! I must see her, if only one time more!"

At this point there is another blank white page. All I remember is feet. Not people but, precisely, feet. Hundreds of feet, discordantly trampling, falling on the pavement from somewhere above: a downpour of feet. And some sort of rollicking, provoking song, and a shout (probably meant for me): "Hey! Hey! Come over here—join us!"

Then, a deserted plaza, crammed to the full with a taut wind. In the center of the plaza, a dully glinting, ponderous, sinister massif: the Machine of The Benefactor. And because of that Machine a certain remembered, reflected image, apparently unexpected, sprang up within me: a dazzlingly white pillow and on it a woman's head, thrown back, with the eyes half shut, the teeth a sharp, sweet streak. . . . And all this was somehow so incongruously, so horribly bound up with the Machine. I knew the nature of this bond, but I still did not want to see it, to name it aloud—I did not want to, I could not.

I closed my eyes, sat down on the steps leading upward to the Machine. It must have been raining: my face was wet. There were shouts, muffled, somewhere far off. But no one— no one!—heard me crying "Save me! Save me from all this!"

If I only had a mother—as the ancients did: a mother of my own—yes, precisely, *my own*. . . . And if only I were, as far as she was concerned, not the builder of the *Integral*, and not a number, D-503, and not a molecule of The One State, but a bit of common humanity, a bit of her own self— a trampled-upon, crushed, cast-off bit. . . . And whether I was crucifying or being crucified (perhaps both are one and the same), if she would only hear what no one hears, if only her lips, a crone's lips, grown over with wrinkles————

THIRTY-SEVENTH ENTRY: *In-* This morning, in the dining
fusoria. The Day of Judgment. hall, my neighbor to the left
Her Room. whispered to me in a scared
voice: "There, do eat! People are looking at you!"

I smiled, exerting myself to the utmost. And I felt that smile as if it were a crack of some sort on my face: I was smiling, the edges of the crack were crawling further apart, and this was causing me more and more pain.

This is what happened next: hardly had I speared a small cube of the naphtha food when the fork jiggled in my hand and clinked against the plate—whereupon the tables, the walls, the plates, the air all shuddered and rang, while out of doors an iron, rotund rumbling arose, enormous, reaching to the sky, passed over heads, over buildings, and died away in the distance in barely audible circles, like those from a stone thrown into water, but diminishing instead of spreading.

For a second I saw washed-out, faded faces, stuffed mouths braked to a dead stop at the height of their mastication, forks frozen in mid-air. Then everything became jumbled, jumped the rails that had lasted for ages, all sprang up from their places (without even singing The Hymn), finishing their chewing any old way, without keeping time, choking on their food, grabbing one another: "What's up? What happened?

What is it?" And these chaotic fragments of The One State, the mechanism of which had once been so well proportioned, so great, all poured out, heading downward, in elevators, down the stairs, their tramping on the steps and the fragments of their words making one think of the scraps of a torn letter swept up by a whirlwind.

They were pouring in the same way out of all the neighboring buildings, and a minute later the whole avenue was like a drop of water under the microscope: confined within the glassily transparent drop, the infusoria were distractedly darting to this side and that, upward, downward.

"Aha!"—in somebody's triumphant voice. I saw before me the nape of somebody's neck, and his finger aimed at the sky: I remember most distinctly the yellow-pink nail, and its white, like a crescent crawling out from under the horizon. And that finger was like a compass: hundreds of eyes, following it, were directed at the sky.

There, fleeing from an unseen pursuit, clouds were careering along, crushing one another, leap-frogging; there, too, tinted by the clouds, were the dark aeros of the Guardians with the black hanging proboscises of the spying tubes, while still further, over there, to the west, was something that resembled———

At first nobody understood what this was—not even I, to whom (unfortunately) more had been revealed. It resembled an enormous swarm of black aeros: barely noticeable speeding dots, at some unbelievable height. Drawing closer— hoarse, throaty sounds, like drops from above; finally, over our heads—birds. They filled the sky as black, piercing, falling acute triangles; the windstorm beat them down; they perched on cupolas, on roofs, on pillars, on balconies.

"Aha-a!"—the triumphant neck turned around. I saw the fellow whose forehead was an overhang. But all that remained in him now of his former characteristics existed in name only, so to speak; he had somehow clambered out clear from under his overhang of a forehead, and rays were sprouting like tufts of hair on his face about the eyes, the lips; he was smiling. "You understand?" he shouted to me amid the whistling of the wind, the flapping of wings, the cawing. "It's

the Wall—you understand? They've blown up the Wall! You-
un-der-stand?"

Cursorily I saw, somewhere in the background, flitting
figures, their heads bent forward as they hastened to get indoors, into the buildings. An avalanche was rushing down the
middle of the pavement, yet because of its ponderousness its
progress seemed slow—an avalanche of those who had been
subjected to fantasiectomy; they were slogging westward.

. . . Rays like tufts of hair about his lips, his eyes. . . . I
seized his hand: "Listen, where is she—where is E-? Is she
there, beyond the Wall, or . . . I have to see her—you hear?
At once—I can't stand this—"

"She's here," he shouted to me in a tipsy, gay voice (his
teeth were strong, yellow). "Right here, in the city, and
active. Oho—we sure are active!"

Who were *we?* Who was I?

Around him were half a hundred of just such men as he,
who had crawled out from under the murky overhangs of
their foreheads, who were noisy, gay, strong of teeth. Gulping the windstorm with their gaping mouths, casually swinging electrocutors (wherever had they gotten hold of them?)
that were so unassuming and innocuous to look at, they too
moved off westward, after those who had undergone the
Operation, but performing a flanking movement by taking the
parallel 48th Avenue.

I stumbled against the taut hawsers woven out of wind and
kept on running to her. What for? I did not know. I stumbled
on. Deserted streets; the city alien, barbarous; ceaseless,
triumphant din of birds; Judgment Day. Through the glass of
their walls I saw, in several buildings (this was deeply engraved on my memory), female and male numbers shamelessly copulating—without as much as lowering the blinds,
without any pink coupons, in broad daylight.

A building—her building—its utterly bewildered entrance
door wide open. Nobody at the controller's desk on the
ground floor. The elevator stuck halfway down the shaft.
Already winded, I started running up the endless staircase. A
corridor. Room numbers on doors flashing by, fast as the
spokes of a revolving wheel: 320, 326, 330 . . . yes, E-330's!

And, through the glass door, it was obvious that everything in the room was scattered, jumbled, crumpled. Chair overturned in the rush, all its four legs sticking up in the air, looking like a dead domestic animal. Bed moved away from the wall, somehow ridiculously, at an angle. On the floor, the pink coupons, like rose petals fallen and trampled upon.

I bent down, picked up one, a second, a third: all bore the number D-503; I was on all of them; each bore a drop of myself, molten, brimming over. And this was all that remained. For some reason it seemed impermissible for them to be lying thus on the floor, and to have everybody tramping over them. I scooped up another handful, placed them on the table, smoothed them out painstakingly, looked at them—and broke into laughter. I hadn't known it before; now I know it, and you know it too: laughter comes in different colors. It is only a remote echo of an explosion within you; it may consist of festal rockets, red, blue, golden; it may consist of gobs of human flesh blown skyward.

I caught a glimpse among the coupons of a number utterly unfamiliar to me; the figures made no impression on my memory—only the consonant, indicating a male, did: it was F-. I swept all the coupons off the table onto the floor, stamped on them, on myself, with my heel—there, take that! and that!—and left the room.

I sat for a while in the corridor, on a window sill facing her door, all the time awaiting something, dully, protractedly. Flapping steps, coming from the left. A codger, face like a bladder with the air let out of it and collapsed into pleats—and something transparent was still oozing out of the pinhole and trickling downward, very slowly. Slowly, dimly, I comprehended: the something was tears. And only when the codger was at a considerable distance did I come to and call after him: "Listen—listen! Do you happen to know where number E, Three Hundred and Thirty is?"

The old man turned around, dismissed me with a gesture of angry despair and hobbled on.

At dusk I came back home, to my room. In the west the sky was contorting at every second in a pale-blue convulsion, and a dull, muffled rumbling was coming from that direction.

The roofs were strewn with blackened, extinguished brands:
birds, these.

I lay down on the bed—and instantly brute sleep fell upon
me, suffocating me.

THIRTY-EIGHTH ENTRY: (*I*
don't know how to summa-
rize this. Perhaps the whole
summary can be reduced to
one item: A Dead Cigarette).

I awoke: the light was glaring, painful to look at. I
puckered my eyes; there was
an acrid blue haze in my
head; everything before me
was in a fog. And, through the fog, I was wondering: "Come,
I didn't turn on the light—how does it happen, then—"

I sprang up. Sitting at the table, with her chin propped up
on her hand, was E-, regarding me with a mocking smile.

I am writing at that same table now. Those ten or fifteen
minutes (a spring cruelly wound up to the very limit) are
already behind me, and yet it seems to me that the door has
shut behind her only just now, and that it is still possible to
catch up with her, seize her hands, and perhaps she will start
laughing and say————

E- was seated at the table. I rushed over to her: "Thou—
thou . . . I was over there—I saw your room . . . I thought
that thou————" But halfway through what I wanted to say
I was brought up short by the pointed, fixed spears of her
eyelashes: she had given me exactly the same look that last
time, aboard the *Integral*. And so, right then and there, I
had to tell her everything in the space of a second, I had to
have the skill to tell her everything in such a way that she
should believe—for otherwise there might never be another
opportunity———— "Listen, E-, I must . . . I must tell you
everything—no, no, just a moment; as soon as I take a drink
of water—"

The inside of my mouth was as dry as if it were all lined
with blotting paper. I kept trying to pour water into a tumbler
but simply could not manage it; I put the tumbler on the
table and got a firm grip on the carafe with both hands. It
was then I noticed that the wispy blue haze was coming from
a cigarette. She brought it up to her lips, inhaled, avidly
swallowed the smoke—just as avidly as I had swallowed the

water—and said: "No need to say anything. Keep still. It makes no difference: I have come anyway, as you can see. They are lying in wait for me there, downstairs. And do you want these few minutes, our last ones together, to be—"

She tossed her cigarette on the floor, leaned all the way back over the arm of her chair (the release button was in the wall, and was difficult to get at) and I remember how the chair rocked and two of its legs came up from the floor. Then the blinds fell.

She drew near, clasped me hard. Her knees, even through her unif, were a gentle, warming, all-absorbing, slow-acting venom.

And suddenly . . . There are times when you have already plunged into sweet and warm sleep—and suddenly something sharp goes right through you, you come to with a start and your eyes are wide open again. That's the way it happened then: I saw the trampled pink coupons on the floor of her room and, on one of them, the letter F- and some figures or other. They clotted into a lump within me, these figures, and plunged their hooks into me, and even now I can't tell what this emotion was, but I held her to me so hard that she cried out from pain.

Still another minute (out of those ten or fifteen minutes): her head thrown back on the dazzlingly white pillow, the eyes half closed, the teeth a slashing sweet streak. And all the while this reminded me importunately, preposterously, excruciatingly of something or other which one must not think about, which it was not necessary to think about just then. And, ever more tenderly, ever more cruelly, I clasped her to me; the black-and-blue marks of my fingers stood out more and more distinctly. She said (without opening her eyes, I noticed): "They say you were at The Benefactor's yesterday. Is that true?"

"Yes, it is."

And thereupon her eyes flew wide open—and I watched with gratification how quickly her face paled, became obliterated, vanished: only the eyes were there.

I told her everything. And there was one thing only which I passed over in silence (why, I do not know—no, that isn't

true: I do know): what he had been saying toward the very
end, that they had needed me only because————

Little by little, as on a photographic plate in a developing
solution, her face emerged: cheeks, white streak of teeth,
lips. She got up, walked over to the mirror on the closet door.
My mouth was again dry. I poured water for myself, but it
was revolting to drink it; I put the glass on the table and
asked: "Was that just why you came here—because you had
to find out?"

A mocking acute triangle of eyebrows quirked up toward
the temples looked at me out of the mirror. She turned
around to tell me something but in the end did not say a
word.

There was no need. I knew.

Should I say farewell to her? I shuffled my feet (not
really mine: they were some stranger's), ran into the chair—
it overturned, dead, like that other one there in her room.
Her lips were cold—one time, 'way back, the floor had been
just as cold right here, in my room, near the bed.

But when she left I sat down on the floor, bent over the
cigarette she had tossed away————

I can't write any more—I don't want to write any more!

THIRTY-NINTH ENTRY: *Finis.*   All this was like the last grain
of salt thrown into a saturated solution: bristling with needles,
the crystals have begun to crawl, to solidify, to congeal. And
it was clear to me: everything was decided, and tomorrow
morning *I would go through with it.* It was every bit the same
as killing myself but, perhaps, it would be only then that I
would truly rise again. For, after all, it is only that which has
been slain which *can* rise again.

To the west, at every second, the sky shuddered in a blue
convulsion. My head was burning and pounding. I sat up thus
all through the night and did not fall asleep till about seven
in the morning, when the darkness had already drawn into
itself, beginning to turn green, and the roofs strewn with
birds had become visible.

I awoke: it was already ten (evidently there had been no
rising bell today). There was a glass of water on the table—

left standing there since yesterday. I gulped the water avidly
and dashed out: I had to go through with all this quickly, as
quickly as possible.

The sky was a desert, a blue desert gnawed clean by the
windstorm. The angles of the shadows prickly; everything
was in silhouette, cut out of the blue autumnal air, and so
fine that one feared to touch it lest it screek and scatter into
glass dust. And this kept going through my mind: You
ought not think, you must not think—you must not think,
otherwise———

And I did not think; probably I did not even see, actually,
but merely registered them. There, on the pavement: branches
from somewhere or other; the leaves upon them were green,
amber-toned, mulberry-hued. There, above: birds and aeros
darting about, their paths crossing. Over there: mouths gaping, hands waving branches. And all these were, most likely,
bawling, cawing, buzzing.

Next, streets as empty as if they had been swept by some
plague. I remember: I stumbled against something that was
unbearably soft, yielding and yet, for all that, motionless. I
bent over: it was a corpse. A male number. Sprawling on his
back, his bent legs apart, like a woman's. His face . . . I
recognized the thick Negro lips, that seemed to be splattering
laughter even then; I recognized his teeth. With his eyes
puckered tight he was laughing in my face. A second: I had
stepped over him and started running, because by that time I
could no longer bear anything; I had to go through with everything quickly, for otherwise (I felt) I would break, snap, like
an overloaded rail.

Fortunately, there were only twenty steps more; the gold-
lettered sign, *Bureau of Guardians,* was already in view.
I paused in the doorway, downed as big a gulp of air as I
could, and entered. Inside, in the corridor, holding sheets of
paper and thick notebooks, the numbers were standing in an
endless queue, the nose of one number almost up against the
nape of the neck of the number in front. Every now and then
they would move a step or two, at a snail's pace, and then
stop again. I began darting up and down the queue; my head
had fragmented and every fragment was hopping off on its

own; I kept plucking at the sleeves of the numbers, I implored them, as a sick man implores to be given as quickly as possible something that, in a second's most poignant torture, will sever everything at one swift blow, as if with an ax.

Some female number or other, tightly drawn in by a belt over her unif, had both of her gluteal hemispheres jutting out distinctly and was constantly rolling them from side to side, as though it was precisely there that her eyes were located; she snorted at me: "He's got a bellyache! Show him to the lavatory—over there, second door on the right!"

And they aimed their laughter at me, and because of that laughter something rose in my throat, and I would either have started screaming in a moment or else—or else————

Suddenly someone seized my elbow from behind. I turned around: translucent winged ears. Not their usual rosy hue, however, but crimson; his Adam's apple bobbing so restlessly that it seemed likely to rip through its thin dust-cover at any moment.

"What brings you here?" he asked, his eyes quickly drilling into me.

"Hurry—let's go into your office!" I simply clutched at him. "I must tell you everything, this very minute! This is splendid, my being able to tell everything precisely to you. It may be dreadful, that it should be precisely you—yet that's splendid, splendid————"

He, too, knew *her,* and that made the torture all the greater for me, yet it was possible that he, too, would shudder, and then we would do the killing together—I would not be alone during this, my last second on earth————

The door slammed to. A bit of paper was stuck to the bottom edge of the door, and it scraped over the floor as the door was closing, after which a certain peculiar, absolute-vacuum stillness fell upon the room, as if a bell glass had been put over it. If he had but uttered a single word—it did not matter what, the most trifling word—I would have come out with everything at one sweep. But he kept silent.

And so, straining all of myself so that my ears began to hum, I spoke (without looking at him): "It seems to me that I always hated her, from the very beginning. I struggled.

. . . However—no, no, don't believe me: I could have saved myself and did not want to be saved; I wanted to perish, a notion which was most precious of all to me—well, not to perish, exactly, but that she should——— And even right now—even right now, when I already know everything. . . . Do you know—do you know that The Benefactor summoned me?"

"Yes, I know."

"Well, the things He told me. . . . Do understand—it was precisely as if someone were to yank the floor out from under you this minute and you went tumbling together with everything that's on this desk, with the paper, the ink—the ink would splash out and you and everything else would turn into a single ink blot—"

"Go on, go on! And make it fast—there are others waiting out there."

And thereupon I, spluttering, getting all tangled up, told him everything that had happened, everything that is entered in these pages. About my real *I* and my shaggy *I,* and about what she had said at that time concerning my hands—yes, it was precisely with that that the whole thing had started; and how, at the time, I had not wanted to fulfill my duty, how I had kept deceiving myself, how she had secured forged certificates of ill health, how my morals had rusted from day to day, and about those subterranean corridors, and what had gone on there, beyond the Wall———

I got all this out of me in bizarre gobs, scraps; I spluttered, I ran short of words. The twisted, doubly curved lips with a mocking smile nudged the words I needed toward me; I would nod gratefully "Yes, yes—" And then (how had it come about?) he was already speaking for me, while I merely listened, except for an occasional "Yes, and then—" or "That's just how it happened—yes, yes!"

I felt a cold area forming about my collar, as if from ether, and I asked with difficulty: "But how is that possible? Why, you could not have learned that anywhere—"

His mocking smile (he was silent) was becoming more and more twisted. And then: "But, do you know, you intended to keep a thing or two back from me? There, you have enumerated all those whom you noticed on that occasion beyond the Wall, yet you have overlooked one. No, you say? But don't you remember catching a momentary, fleeting glimpse of . . . me? Yes, yes—me."

A pause. And suddenly, as if a bolt of lightning had gone through me from head to foot, it became shamelessly clear to me—he, he too, was one of them. And all of me, all of my agonies, all that I had brought here, swooning, exerting the last of my strength, as if I were performing a great deal—all this was merely laughable, like the anecdote the ancients had about their Abraham and Isaac. Abraham, all in a cold sweat, had just raised the knife over his son—over himself—when suddenly he heard a voice above his head, coming down from on high: "Don't bother! I was just playing a trick on you—"

Without tearing my eyes away from the mocking smile, which was constantly becoming more twisted, I propped my hands against the edge of the desk, slid away from it, chair and all, slowly, s-l-o-w-ly, then abruptly grabbed all of me by the scruff of my neck and rushed out helter-skelter—past shouts, stair steps, mouths.

I don't recall how I found myself down below, in one of the public lavatories in a subway station. There, aboveground, everything was perishing, the greatest and most rational civilization in all history was crashing, while here, through someone's irony, everything remained as it had been, in all the splendor of its beauty: the gleaming walls; the comforting murmur of water; the music, also like unto water, crystal-clear, its source unknown, lending beauty to digestion. And to think that all this was condemned, that all this would become overgrown with grass, that only *myths* about all this would remain—

I broke into loud groans. And at that moment I felt someone comfortingly pat my knee. It was my neighbor, enthroned to my left, his forehead an enormous bald parabola, with indecipherable yellow lines furrowing it. And those lines had to do with me. "I understand you, I understand you fully," said he. "But, just the same, calm yourself; no need of getting all worked up. All this will come around again—

it will, inevitably. The only thing that matters is for everybody
to learn about my discovery. You are the first I am telling it
to: I have worked it out—there is no infinity!"

I gave him a wild look.

"Yes, yes, I am telling you—there is no infinity. If the
universe is infinite then the mean density of its matter must
equal zero. But since it does not—we do know that much—
it follows that the universe is finite; it is spherical in form,
and the square of its radius, the square root of Y, equals
the mean density of its matter multiplied by . . . there, that
is all I have to do: calculate the numerical coefficient, and
then . . . You understand, everything is finite, everything is
simple, everything is calculable—and in that case we will gain
our victory in a manner befitting philosophers—you understand? But you, my esteemed sir, are hindering me from
finishing my computation by making all that noise—"

I don't know which shook me up more, his discovery or
his imperturbability at that apocalyptic hour: he was holding
(I noticed this only at that point) a notebook and a logarithmic dial. And it came to me then that, even if everything
were to perish, it was my duty to you, my unknown, my beloved readers, to leave these entries of mine in a finished
state.

I asked him for some paper and right then and there I
wrote these last lines—

I was just about to put down a period—just as the ancients
used to put a cross over one of those holes in the ground into
which they dumped their dead—when all of a sudden my
pencil began to jiggle and fell out of my fingers. . . .

"Listen!" I persistently yanked at my neighbor. "You've got
to listen, I tell you! You must answer me—you must: what
about the point where your finite universe ends? What's there
—what comes after it?"

He did not have time to answer. There was trampling up
above, then coming down the steps———

FORTIETH ENTRY: *Facts. The
Bell Glass. I Am Certain.*
Daylight. Clear. Barometer at
760.

Can it be that I, D-503, really wrote all these hundreds of

pages? Can it be that at one time I felt all this—or imagined that I had felt it?

The handwriting is mine. And what follows is in the very same handwriting—but, fortunately, only the handwriting is the same. There are no ravings whatsoever, no preposterous metaphors, no emotions whatsoever. Facts only. Because I am well; I am perfectly, absolutely well. I smile; I cannot help but smile: they have extracted some sort of a sliver out of my head; my head is light, empty. To be more exact: it is not empty, but there is nothing extraneous in it, nothing that would interfere with smiling (smiling is the normal state for a normal human).

Here are the facts. That evening my neighbor, who had discovered the finitude of the universe, and I, and all the others there with us, were seized for not having certifications of fantasiectomy and hauled off to the nearest auditorium (its number, 112, was for some reason familiar). There we were bound to the operating tables and subjected to the Grand Operation.

The next day I, D-503, appeared before The Benefactor and imparted to Him all I knew about the enemies of our happiness. Why could this possibly have seemed difficult to me? It is incomprehensible. The only explanation lies in my former malady, the soul sickness.

On the evening of the same day—seated with Him, The Benefactor, at the same table—I found myself for the first time in the famous Chamber of the Gas Bell Glass. That woman was brought in. She was to give her testimony in my presence. This woman remained contumaciously silent—and smiled. I noticed that her teeth were sharp and very white— and that this created a beautiful effect.

Then she was led in under the Gas Bell Glass. Her face became very white and, since her eyes were dark and large, this created an extremely beautiful effect. When they started pumping the air out of the Gas Bell Glass she threw her head back, half closing her eyes and compressing her lips: this reminded me of something. She kept looking at me as she gripped the arms of her seat—kept looking until her eyes closed altogether. Thereupon she was dragged out, quickly brought back to consciousness with the aid of electrodes, and was again made to sit under the Gas Bell Glass. This was gone through three times—and she still had not uttered a word. Others, who had been brought in with this woman, proved more honest: many of them started talking after the first treatment. Tomorrow all of them will mount the steps leading to the Machine of The Benefactor.

There can be no postponement, because the western districts of the city are still full of chaos, roaring, corpses, and —regrettably—a considerable body of numbers who have betrayed rationality.

We have, however, succeeded in constructing a temporary wall of high voltage waves on the transversal 40th Prospect.

And I hope that we will conquer. More than that: I am certain that we shall. For rationality must conquer.

1924; 1927; 1952

Valentin Petrovich KATAEV

[1897—]

Valentin Kataev was born in Odessa. As a student he volunteered for the army in 1915, was wounded twice and gassed. From 1918 to 1920 he had many adventurous experiences in the Ukraine during the civil war. He appeared in print prior to the October Revolution; worked on *Pravda* at the same time as Ilf and Petrov, whom he nicknamed his "plantation slaves," acting as their mentor and occasional collaborator; the team of humorists admitted that he was the "spiritual godfather" of *12 Chairs*. His most popular novel, *The Embezzlers* (1927), is still extremely amusing; he has many short stories to his credit, some of them as much imbued with grotesquerie and whimsicality as Greenevsky's; most of his plays were very successful. *Squaring the Circle* was, of course, given an anti-Soviet slant in its New York production, as if its main theme, a housing shortage, was a peculiarly Russian phenomenon.

Although primarily a satirist and humorist, Kataev's love of life and amazement before its beauty have enabled him to do "serious" work (but with a minimum of tendentiousness), such as *Onward, Time!* (1933); *Lone White Sail* (1936), a delightful juvenile; and *The Wife* (1944). However, *For the Soviet Power* (1949), although quite conforming to the formula of Psychological (Soviet) Realism, was found to be insufficiently seasoned with Beatification-of-Party-Workers' sauce, and the author obliged with a revised version in 1951.

THE IRON RING

Who's got some shag, fellows? Thanks! I must say they print our wall newspapers on rather atrocious stock—you can hardly roll a cigarette with it. Yes, I'll have another glass. Well, let's continue.

The Doctor had become fed up with the students, with the beer-drinking clubs, assignations, duels, and with the blue eyes of fair women—and so he set out with his poodle to wander the world over.

He followed the highroads as the Wandering Jew, sailed the seas as the Flying Dutchman, passed through cities as a traveler of noble birth. Many curious countries, peoples and places did the Doctor see.

He danced at a wedding in Barcelona, hunted elephants in India, in Nagasaki he became infatuated with geishas, while during his stay in Rome he penned an excellent novella in the spirit of the *Decameron*.

All these adventures of his he remembered excellently inasmuch as he was immortal; but, for that very reason, he was indifferent to all things.

For many years—and, perhaps, for ages—did the Doctor travel about in this manner. And his poodle kept trying to knock him off his feet, twisting and turning, putting its paws on his chest and barking viciously, at the same time thrusting out of its incandescent mouth a red tongue that looked like a child's snapdragon, the kind that whistles, or like the sting-tipped tongue of a heraldic lion.

Eternity: is it great or little? For brief human life, very great; for the avid human heart, far too little; but for the soul that has been definitely sold to the Devil a single year or all eternity equals exactly nothing.

Nothing could animate the Doctor.

On only one occasion did he smile.

This occurred on the wild Euxine littoral, at the hour of

the equinoctial tide, in the midst of spume, tiny shells and crags, where the Doctor encountered a certain poet who was absorbed in his reveries. The poet was deeply stirred as he stood there; his rufous hair was curly, he had on a coat with belled skirts and was brandishing the dismounted barrel of a hunting gun which, apparently, served him as a walking stick. His face, turned to the spume and the wind, wore an agitated expression, and his eyes, prominent and blue, glistened with the tears of inspiration.

"A thousand pardons, with all my soul," the Doctor spoke in irreproachable French, and doffed his hat. "A thousand pardons—since, without having been introduced to you, I have broken in on your solitude and have ventured to address you. For many years—and, perhaps, for ages—have I been wandering the world over. I have seen the faces of many people. Yet one as inspired, as glowing and deeply stirred as yours, I have not seen anywhere. Are you not, perchance, the possessor of the legendary talisman of happiness?"

"My dear sir," answered the poet, "I know not who you are nor what your destination is; I know not whether an evil or a kindly genius has brought you to our shores. However, your face is familiar to me; I will not venture to state definitely where I may have met you—in a dream or awake or in some book—yet no matter who you may be I greet you, a wanderer and a dreamer. Who knows what happiness is? Some deem gold happiness, some suppose it to lie in youth and love, there are certain madmen who consider that immortality and glory constitute happiness! Yet, my dear sir, am I happy? If this wind and the surf, and the light and shade and the voices of the waves be happiness, if the nature of human passions be happiness, if all the things that fill to overflowing the poor life of man be happiness—O, then am I happy, and I thank heaven for this imperfect, bitter, splendidly beautiful, ordinary human happiness!"

"This is the first time that I have beheld a truly happy man!" the Doctor exclaimed. "But—who are you?"

"What matters my name?"

"You are right," the Doctor remarked thoughtfully. "At any rate, perhaps you would be able to tell me where I am

right now, and whether there is not some inn where I may
lodge for the night?"

"You are not far from the new town of Odessa. Go up on
that high cliff and you will see it. There you will find an eating place where you can get a glorious bottle of Kishinev
wine and a tolerable supper."

"Farewell, my dear sir."

The Doctor called his poodle and turned to go. The poet
followed him with his eyes, vainly trying to bring back to
memory this familiar face. Suddenly the Doctor stopped.

"My dear sir," said he in agitation, coming back to the
poet, "in all probability you and I will never meet again, but
our brief encounter has been the most pleasant in my life,
inasmuch as I have for the first time beheld a truly happy
man. Take this ring, then, as a memento of our brief meeting. It is wrought of crude iron and set with a chip of turquoise, of trifling cost. Yet upon the hand of a happy man it
acquires the miraculous power of making all the surroundings
happy and splendidly beautiful. Take it. I feel that from you
it will pass on to someone else worthy of it. Farewell."

Thereupon the Doctor vanished, and the poet saw upon his
finger an iron ring set with a turquoise.

And amid the mysterious darkness of that night as he bent
over a notebook and absent-mindedly sketched a tiny feminine foot on its margins, the poet saw how the turquoise set
into the iron became suffused with an extraordinary pale-
blue light. This same pale blue filled with Mediterranean
water his nocturnal, semicircular window. And the golden
blades of the candles wavered lightly and purely, surrounded
with an aura of azure. The verses he wrote that night were
splendidly beautiful.

The following day Mme. Riznich was leaving for Italy. The
poet, in a high hat and close-fitting frock, was waiting on the
quai for the beauty. There was a strong wind. The sea was
restless, spumy, yet alluring. Turkish feluccas creaked near
the quai, swaying the metronomes of their masts. Sailors
of different nationalities were playing cards on coils of rope.
Flunkies were loading the traveling trunks and portmanteaus
of M. and Mme. Riznich upon launches. The ship was rock-

ing in the roadstead. Suddenly a carriage appeared. A horseman was cantering alongside it. The carriage halted. Its door flew open and a tiny foot stockinged in gray silk was thrust out, seeking a step. Flunkies dashed toward the carriage and Mme. Riznich, holding the skirt of her traveling dress, sprang out on the sand. Her stout husband clambered out after her. The horseman leapt off his horse and, after tossing the reins to the flunkies, approached the poet.

"She is going away—that is dreadful," said he.

"She is leaving," the poet repeated like an automaton. "She is leaving—"

"Happy man, you are loved," the other remarked with bitterness.

"Envy me not, friend Tumansky. She will sail away from us the now and we shall be on an equal footing—and, perhaps, my pain will be greater than yours."

Mme. Riznich and her husband walked up to the two friends.

"Oh, the guile of men!" she exclaimed, much too gaily. "I haven't had time to embark yet but you are already wearing a new talisman upon your hand. Can one believe friends who prate of their fidelity?"

M. Riznich smiled politely, and only the poet's cursory glance of love and bitter regret, intercepted by just such a glance from the beauty, remained as a tender memento of this worldly farewell.

The poet, overcoming his tears, brought the ship close to his eye through the rounded lenses of a spyglass. With her husband at her side she was standing by the ship's rail and waving a tiny handkerchief. Absorbed in her alone, the poet did not see the stranger with his poodle leaning against the cordage, surrounded by crates and red-sealed kegs. The wind was fluttering his cape and twisting his beard.

Careening from the wind that was buffeting its side, the ship was slanting off into the distance. In a short while it all but disappeared from view.

"Let us go, old friend. She is far away by now. The chess players have probably gathered already in the coffee house of the mustachioed Kapitanake, and the languorous Iphigenia is dispensing *rahat lokoum* and tonka-bean coffee from her tin tray. Come, then, and I will tell you an amusing story about a certain eccentric traveler who looks like Faust and who made me a present of this iron ring set with turquoise. Dry your tears; there are long-stemmed pipes awaiting us. Let us go then."

And they climbed over the new road, cut in the fresh clay of the cliff.

Much time has since passed, but the sky over the city then was of the same humid, pale-blue color as now, and the plums in the market place that August were covered with the same amazing turquoise dust. Therefore the iron ring must even to this day be in the possession of someone among the local citizenry. Practically none had ever seen this ring, and besides it is hardly likely that many know of its existence. It may well have happened that the poet, as he was leaving for the north, had put it on one of Iphigenia's tiny fingers as a memento of a fleeting passion; it may have found its way into the wrought-iron coffer of the legendary Maid of Athens who on a time had exchanged kisses with Byron, or passed through the long years from generation to generation, until it became lost amid the smoke of Interventionist landings and during the zealously executed requisitions of 1920.

They say that a certain privy councilor connected with a department having to do with printed matter had seen such a ring in the nineties of the last century upon the finger of a *bon vivant* whom he did not know, as the latter had stood counting his change at the box-office window under the arches of a municipal theatre. This official had a clear recollection of the gentleman's elegant Inverness cape, his roomy checked trousers, chestnut-hued side-whiskers, spectacles and collapsible opera hat. The gas jets were crackling with their pliant, firm flame-fans over the reticulated frame holding a poster printed in bold, huge chocolate-colored letters. The privy councilor had darted toward this gentleman but happened to step on an orange peel, slipping and all but falling, and by the time he had recovered his balance the stranger was no longer there, and all one could see in the plate glass of the slammed door was swaying constellations. A brief item concerning this incident was printed in the local *Telegraph,* and there the matter had ended.

The arts continued to flourish in the city, while the city itself, including its inhabitants, kept changing. In the summer it would be cluttered with mountains of building materials, beams, rails, bolts, kegs of Portland cement, of tar and clay. Ever new sailing ships, packet boats and ocean liners put in at its port.

One day a youngish bearded fellow in a beret and a Scotch plaid, carrying a Baedeker and accompanied by a poodle, happened to be walking from the harbor to the railroad depot. He was deafened by the silky swish of grain running into holds, by the pistol-like noise of falling iron beams, by trolley bells and curses, and blinded by the haze of quicklime, the sun, and the extraordinary vividness of the sky.

Still feeling underfoot the swaying of a deck, he walked through side streets and lanes in the delectable shade of grape-green acacias and squat, affable houses. A young woman was standing on the threshold of a Greek coffee house under whose coarse canvas awning clerks in unbuttoned white jackets, who were assistants to assistants, and merchants in fezzes were playing checkers. She was leaning against the sun-warmed jamb of the door and, with eyelashes lowered, was hovering between sleep and waking. The etched, oblique shadows of acacias stirred up and down her linen dress, her cap of black lace and the slender fingers crossed upon her breast.

"Mein Gott!" cried out the stranger, after one look at her.

The Greek woman straightened up and opened her dewy eyes.

"Iphigenia!" a woman's voice called her from within.

She adjusted her cap and quickly went in. The stranger halted, but the poodle dashed toward him, threw its front paws on his shoulders, fixed its pink evil eyes on his face and, letting its heraldic tongue loll all the way out, set up a venomous barking. The checker players turned around indolently. A mustachioed Greek was standing in the doorway of the coffee house. The stranger shifted his Baedeker from one hand to the other, sighed and, still seeking the shade, went on at a leisurely pace past small general stores and soda-water kiosks.

And again a certain time passed, after which there occurred a multitude of events that now seem utterly improbable yet are fully authenticated, and it would be odd even to talk about them, inasmuch as all of us have taken part therein, in one way or another.

All of us have witnessed a fair number of miracles in our time. But, my dear comrades, I swear to you by the classic form of the ballad that not a one of you has witnessed what I have. Just the other day, in the flea market, in a long row of field-officers' widows and washed-out countesses selling the last of their faded flummery, I saw a yellow-skinned Greek woman, no longer young, in a cap of black lace and an old silk dress. Her eyes were swollen from tears and dusted with atrocious face powder. In addition to that she was avidly inhaling on a stinking cigarette of shag, rolled from a scrap of newspaper, baring teeth that were amber-hued or down-right black. She was smiling imploringly and despairingly. I became curious: what could she be selling, this quondam exotic beauty? I drew near, elbowing my way through the soldier boys and the sailor lads, and had a look at the small rug spread out before her. Lying thereon were gray checked trousers, a collapsible opera hat, a spyglass and a diminutive handkerchief. "The Devil take it," I grumbled, "the only thing lacking here is an iron ring set with turquoise and a pair of chestnut-hued side whiskers; then, as likely as not, I would take the whole lot wholesale. For an old hand at romantic tales it might come in handy!"

And what do you think? The old witch, catching my mumbling, simply blossomed out, took to nodding and quickly lifted the tiny handkerchief. Lying under it was a pair of superb, luxuriant and curly chestnut-hued side whiskers, tied together with a bit of tape. And right then and there, upon one of the bony fingers of this mummy, I spied an iron ring, set with a chip of turquoise. But I did not get a chance to utter a word, for at that moment the regular rag-fair dragnet began. The throngs of traders and buyers darted off in all directions, colliding in their fright and dropping cakes and shoes. The desperate whistles of the military police came from everywhere, and the mounted men from a squadron of the internal guard of the Republic were caracoling like knights in a chess game over the squares of overturned trays and stands. Naturally, I had no intention of lingering and, as behooves an old hardened deserter, I lost no time disappearing, even though the cerulean perspective of coming into possession of the iron ring had smiled upon me. However, I am of the opinion that, after all, I had not lost much. Am I right? We are happy, young, poor as church mice—therefore there will always be a humid, lofty azure over us in these iron days of youth, and the plums in the market place will always be covered with a turquoise dust. However, to the Devil with this turquoise dust! As long as the plums are there and one can, with a certain deftness, always steal them.

"Why, you are in the vein today, old man, even though you are not exact about your historical facts! Well done, you pirate!"

"Citizens," the proprietor whispered in fright, appearing in the doorway, "quiet down, for God's sake. You're probably after having me executed by a firing squad. There, go ahead and trust the word of decent folk—and yet they call themselves poets. This isn't right. Finish your wine and go, I beg of you!"

"Take it easy, Dad. We'll clear out of here right away. Friends, today four bottles of excellent port have fallen to the lot of the three of us. In our beggarly days that is a rare occasion. Three bottles have been drunk. One more remains. Let us drink to Doctor Faust! Get your glasses ready."

"Thank you, gentlemen. Your health!" said a man in a plaid and a beret; raising his glass high, he drained it without stopping for breath, then tossed an iron ring on the table and disappeared. The ring rolled along the wet table, tinkling against the glasses.

"Where is he? Grab him! After him!" we started shouting and tumbled out into the street.

The cutting green light of spring twilight and the yellow streak of the evening glow slashed across our tipsy eyes like a razor. The street was deserted. The blue silhouette of a cathedral stood out sharply and somberly against the evening glow. The fresh smell of the sea was in the air. Somewhere shop shutters were being lowered with sinister rattling. And amid the advancing night, amid the stars emerging like milk teeth, the man with the plaid and the poodle went floating past us.

"Hey, fellows—there he is!"

The man with the poodle ducked to one side and started off at a run over the deserted street, past the beggarly, looted, shut-up shops.

"Stop yelling, fellows. You've drunk a copper's worth but are making enough noise for a bank note. There, now, all together!"

And we all sang out in chorus: "Bon voyage to you, Doctor, till we mee-eet again!"

The echo went rolling down the street.

"But where's the ring?"

We looked at one another in silence. The ring was not anywhere.

"Well, my friends, there is nothing we can do about it. Come over to my hideout. I have enough oil in my lamp for three hours more. And Stevenson is a splendid writer to read at one's leisure. I want to read "A Lodging for a Night" to you. It is a remarkable story about a certain cutpurse by the name of François Villon. And so, follow me!"

All this took place during the third year of our Republic.

1922

Ilya Grigorievich ERENBURG

[1891—]

This many-sided writer began as a poet, influenced by the Symbolists, the Decadents and the Futurists; the ultimate tags are Aesthete and Mystic. He was arrested, at fourteen, during the Revolution of 1905; in 1909 he went to Paris, but returned to Russia during the Revolution of 1917, getting more than a taste of the civil war in the Ukraine; shortly thereafter he was fulminating against the Bolsheviks and went abroad again; in 1924 he was permitted to return to Russia; he has traveled a great deal; was a correspondent during the Spanish Civil War and World War II, and in 1945 visited the U.S.A. at the invitation of our State Department.

His *The Extraordinary Adventures of Julio Jurenito* (1919) made him an international literary figure and showed him as a truer master of paradox than Shaw and a sardonic satirist equally adept with quarterstaff, poniard and vitriol; his superjournalistic exposés, factual or semifictional, are fascinating and lethal (*Trust D E* describes the conquest of Europe by American capital, with the deadline of 1940; *Factory of Dreams* pulverizes Hollywood; *10 Horse Power: Chronicles of Our Time* deals primarily with the automobile industry in Europe; *The United Front* tells the story of Ivar Kreuger, the Match King). *The Fall of Paris* (winner of the Stalin Prize in 1942) shows the betrayal of France by her depraved and rapacious bourgeoisie. As a propagandist during World War II, Erenburg was extremely effective—so effective, in fact, that the Soviets asked him to ease up when their allies switched from Vansittartism to the rehumanizing of the Germans.

At present Erenburg is the dean of Soviet letters, Russia's

365

only surviving *prosateur* of any stature—and the one Soviet Writer Most Likely to Die of Unexpedited Old Age.

THE MASTER'S PROPHECY CONCERNING THE DESTINIES OF THE TRIBE OF JUDAEANS

One wonderful evening in April we had gathered anew in the Paris atelier of the Master, on the seventh floor of one of the new houses in the Grenelle quarter. We stood for long at the great windows, admiring the beloved city with its unique, seemingly imponderable, illusory twilight. Herr Schmidt, too, was among us, but it was in vain that I strove to impart to him the beauty of the dove-gray houses, of the stony groves of the Gothic churches, of the leaden-hued reflected light on the slow-flowing Seine, of the chestnut trees in blossom, of the first lights in the distance and of the touching song of some hoarse codger standing with a hurdy-gurdy under our windows. He told me, did Herr Schmidt, that all this was no more than a resplendent museum, but that he had not been able to stand museums ever since his childhood years, but that there *was* one thing which did charm him— the Eiffel Tower, to be precise: light, graceful, bending before the wind like a reed and looking, against the soft blue of the April evening, like an unyielding, steely bride of other times.

Peacefully conversing in this manner we waited for the coming of the Master, who was out dining with some rather important military commissioner. The Master arrived shortly and, having put away in a small safe a heap of documents that had lost some of their crispness in his pocket, spoke to us gaily: "I have labored to very good effect this day. The affair is going well. Now we can rest and chat awhile. But before we do so I mustn't forget to prepare the copy of the announcements—and you, Alexei Spiridonovich, can deliver it tomorrow to the Union Printery."

Five minutes later he showed us the layout:

COMING! COMING!! COMING!!!
In the Near Future :::: To Be Presented
a t
BUDAPEST KIEV JAFFA ALGIERS
and
Many Other Localities
GALA PERFORMANCES
of the
DESTRUCTION
of the
TRIBE OF JUDAEANS
The
☞ Program ☜
Will Include in Addition
to the
Traditional
☞ POGROMS ☜
(So *Popular* and *Beloved* a *Feature*
with the Esteemed Public)
Certain OLD FAVORITES, Streamlined
to Conform with the SPIRIT of
OUR EPOCH
viz
Autos-da-fé of the Judaeans, BURIALS
of the Said Judaeans ALIVE, the
Aspersion of Sundry Fields with Judaean
BLOOD
and
As Extra Added
ATTRACTIONS
Such Recently Introduced
NOVELTIES
a s
!MASS EXPULSIONS!
!!Purges of Suspected Elements!!
Concentration Camps ! ! ! ! Crematoria
!GENUINE GENOCIDE!
etc etc etc etc etc etc etc etc etc
All Cardinals, Bishops, Archimandrites,
Dalai Lamas, Bonzes, Shamans, Ju Ju and Gri Gri
Men, British Lords, Roman Patricians, Polish Aris-
tocrats, Russian Liberals, French Journalists, Mem-
bers of the Hohenzollern Family and Others of
the Herrenvolk, All Greeks without Any Discrimination
as to Their Callings, as well as All Persons Desirous
of
Witnessing
These SPECTACLES
ARE CORDIALLY INVITED ::: FREE ADMISSION
Particulars Concerning Time & Place to Be Announced Later

"Master!" Alexei Spiridonovich cried out in horror. "This is unthinkable. The twentieth century—and such abominations! Finally, how can I bring this to the Union Printery—I, who have read Merejkowsky?"

"There is no use in your thinking that there is any incompatibility here. Very soon, in two short years, perhaps, you will be convinced to the contrary. The twentieth century will turn out to be a truly gay and frivolous century, without any prejudices whatsoever, while the readers of Merejkowsky will prove the most ardent attendants at these spectacles. You see, the ills of mankind are not childish measles but old, chronic attacks of gout, and mankind has certain habits as to the treatment thereof. You can hardly expect an old dog to unlearn its old tricks!

"In Egypt, whenever the Nile went on a strike and a drought began, the sages would recall the existence of the Hebrews, the said Hebrews were asked to drop in, were slaughtered with appropriate prayers and the soil would be aspersed with steaming-fresh Hebrew blood: 'May Famine pass us by!' Of course, this could replace neither rain nor the Nile in flood, but just the same it did furnish a modicum of satisfaction. However, even at that time there were men of caution, of humane views, who said that, as a matter of course, it could do no harm to slaughter a few Hebrews, but that the soil oughtn't to be aspersed with their blood, since that blood was venomous and brought up henbane instead of grain.

"In Spain, whenever any ills befell—the Black Death, say, or a run of head colds—the holy padres solemnly forgave the 'enemies of Christ and humankind' and, drenched in tears—not so copious, however, as to put out the fires—burned a couple of thousand Hebrews to a crisp: 'May Pestilence pass us by!' The local humanitarians, apprehensive of the high temperature engendered by the fires and of the ashes thereof, which the wind spread all around, whispered cautiously, in their neighbor's very ear, lest some stray Inquisitor overhear them: 'It might be best of all simply to starve them to death!'

"In southern Italy, whenever earthquakes occurred, the

people first of all fled north; then, in a cautious Indian file, came back on tippety-toe to see if their beloved soil was still quaking. The Hebrews likewise fled—even ahead of all the others, and also came back home—after all the others. Well, naturally, the earth was still quaking—either because they, the Judaeans, wanted the earth to do so, or because the earth no longer wanted anything to do with the Judaeans. In either case it was a good idea to bury alive some individual representatives of that tribe, which was done without any delay. And what were the leading citizens doing? Ah, yes, they were most apprehensive—that those who had been buried alive would finish the job and shake the earth all to pieces.

"There, my friends, you have a short excursus into history. And since mankind is slated for famine, and pestilence, and a fair number of earthquakes, I am merely evincing an understandable foresight in ordering these announcements beforehand."

"But, Master," Alexei Spiridonovich objected, "aren't the Jews human beings, even as you and I?" All the while that Julio Jurenito had been presenting his "excursus" this Slavic disciple of his had been heaving prolonged sighs and dabbing his eyes with his handkerchief but, just to be on the safe side, he had taken a seat as far away from me as possible.

"For is a football one and the same thing as a bomb? Or do you believe that a tree and an ax can be brethren? The Judaeans can be loved or hated, they can be looked upon with horror as incendiaries or with hope as saviors—but their blood is not yours and their affairs are none of yours. You don't understand? You don't want to believe? Very well, I'll try to explain things to you with greater clarity. The evening is calm and it is cooler now; I'll amuse you a little, over a glass of this light Vouvray, with a children's game. Tell me, my friends: suppose you were asked to retain but one word in all of human speech, your choice being limited to just one out of two, either *yes* or *no,* and all the others to be done away with. Which would you prefer? Let's begin with those of you who are older. What about you, Mr. Cool?" the Master turned to his American disciple.

"Of course it would be *yes*—affirmation and fundamentality are contained in that word. I'm not fond of *no*—it is immoral and criminal. Even when talking to a fired employee who is begging me to take him on again, I never use this *no*, which hardens the heart, but say instead: 'Wait a little, my friend—you'll be rewarded in the other world for your "suffering." ' Whenever I show a handful of dollar bills everybody says *yes* to me. Do away with whatever words you please, but leave me the dollars and that trifling *yes*, and I will undertake to make mankind whole again!"

"In my opinion both *yes* and *no* are extremes," said Monsieur Dellet, "whereas I like moderation in everything, something sort of middle-of-the-roadish. Oh, well, if one must make a choice I would say—let it be *yes*. *Yes* stands for joy, impulse and what not besides . . . everything! 'Madame, your poor husband has passed away. You desire a Class Four funeral—am I right?'—'*Oui!*'—'*Garçon*, Dubonnet!'—'*Oui*, M'sieu'!'—'Are you ready, Zizi?'—'*Oui, oui!*' "

Alexei Spiridonovich, still shaken by the previous discussion, could not collect his thoughts; he mooed, kept jumping up from his seat and sitting down again, and finally vociferated: "*Da!* I believe, O Lord! Give me the sacrament! Give me *yes*, the holy 'Yes!' of a pure Turgenev maiden! O Liza! 'Come, my dove, my undefiled!' "

Succinctly, and in a businesslike tone, as one who found this whole game preposterous, Herr Schmidt declared that the lexicon really ought to be re-examined, getting rid of a succession of archaisms, such as *spirit, sanctitude, angel* and the like, but as for *nein* and *ja*, they must of necessity be kept, since they were serious words. However, if it had been necessary for him to have made the choice yesterday, he would have preferred *yes* as something of a constructive nature and that could be likened to well-made holdfasts.

"*Sì!*" spoke up Ercole, the Italian disciple. "On all of life's pleasant occasions people say *yes*—it is only when they're kicking you out that they yell '*No!*' "

Aisha, that child of Africa, likewise preferred *Yes!* Whenever Aisha implored Krupto (his latest god) to be kind, Krupto said "Yes!" Whenever Aisha begged the Master to give him two sous for a bar of chocolate, the Master said "Yes," and gave him the money.

"But why are you keeping silent?" the Master asked me.

I had not responded before, apprehensive of vexing and upsetting him and my other friends.

"Master, I shan't lie to you—I would keep *no*. You see, to speak frankly, it is very much to my liking when something doesn't come off, when it ends in ruin. I'm very fond of Mr. Cool, but it would give me pleasure if he were suddenly to lose his dollars—just simply lose them, every last one, the way you lose a button. Or if M'sieu' Dellet's clients were to ball up the Classes. If the star performer in a Class Sixteen funeral—Full Care of Grave for Three Years—were to stand up in his coffin and yell out: 'Bring on those perfumed hankies—I want that Super Extra Funeral, which hasn't any Class number!' If the purest of virgins, one of those who hold up their little skirts daintily as they rush lugging their purity through this defiled world—if such a one were to come up against some determined vagabond in a grove on the outskirts of a town—well, that wouldn't be bad, either. And when a *garçon* slips and drops a bottle of Dubonnet it's simply glorious! Of course, as my great-great-grandfather, Solomon the clever, put it: There is a time to gather stones and a time to cast stones away. But I am a simple person: I have but one face and not two. Chances are somebody will have to gather those stones—it may well be Schmidt. But in the meanwhile I must say, not out of any desire to flaunt my originality but with a clear conscience: Destroy *yes*, destroy everything in the world, and it follows of itself that *no* alone will remain!"

While I was speaking all those who had been sitting on the divan with me shifted to another corner of the room. I was left by myself.

"Now you see that I was right," the Master turned to Alexei Spiridonovich. "A natural division has taken place. Our Judaean is left a solitary. You can destroy all the ghettos, do away with all pales of settlement, raze all frontiers, yet there is nothing with which to fill these twelve feet which divide you from him. We are Robinson Crusoes, all of us, or, if you like, all prisoners in solitary confinement—beyond that it is all a matter of character. One fellow may tame a spider, busy himself with learning Sanskrit and lovingly sweep the floor of his cell. Another beats his head against the wall; a bump rises; another bang, another bump, and so on: the man wants to find out which is harder, his head or the wall.

"Came the Greeks; they looked about them: Perhaps there are quarters better than these, without physical afflictions, without death, without agonies—there's Olympus, for instance! However, there's no help for it; we must needs make ourselves at home in this place. And in order to be in a cheerful frame of mind it will be best of all to declare all these inconveniences, including death, the greatest of blessings—there's no changing these inconveniences, anyway.

"Then the Judaeans came—and right off went *bang!* with their heads against the wall. 'Why is everything arranged the way it is? Here are two men—they ought to be equal. But, no: Jacob is in favor, while Isaac is out in the cold.' Machinations begin against earth and heaven, Jehovah and the Caesars, Babylon and Rome. Ebionites, ragtag and bobtail, to whom temple steps are lodgings, fall to toiling and moiling; they compound, even as an explosive is compounded in vats, a new religion of justice and beggary. Now, *now* indestructible Rome is bound to come tumbling down! And the beggars, the ignorami, the stolid sectarians go forth against the magnificence, against the wisdom of the world of antiquity. Rome trembles. Paul the Judaean has overcome Marcus Aurelius! However, ordinary folk, who prefer a snug little house to dynamite, start making the new faith livable; they get down to settling in this bare wickiup in a *nice,* homey fashion. Christianity is no longer a battering ram to break down walls with—no, it is a new stronghold. Human, convenient, gutta-percha compassion has been fobbed off in place of frightful, naked, destructive justice. Rome—the world—has remained standing.

"But, upon beholding this, the tribe of Judaea has repudiated its offspring and begun its machinations all over again. Perhaps somewhere in Melbourne someone is sitting right now and, not in deeds but in his thoughts, is doing a sapper's

work. And, once more, something is being compounded in
vats, and a new faith, a new truth, is being readied. And thus,
a few score years ago the Gardens of Versailles felt the first
attacks of an ague, every whit as the palace gardens of
Hadrian once did. And Rome flaunts its wisdom; Senecas
write their books; the brave cohorts are alerted. It is trembling
all over again, this *indestructible* Rome!

"Israel has brought forth a new infant. You shall yet be-
hold his wild eyes, his fine auburn hair, and his tiny hands
as strong as steel. Having given birth to this Messiah, this
people is ready to die. A heroic gesture: 'There are no more
nations; I, as a tribe, no longer am, but all of us are *we!*'
O, naïve, incorrigible sectarians! Your infant will be taken,
bathed, didied and dolled up, and those who do all this will
be altogether like Schmidt! Once more they will mouth 'Justice!' but will fob off Expediency in lieu thereof. And again
will ye depart, to hate and wait, to break the wall with your
heads and to moan: 'How long, O Lord, how long?'"

"I will answer: 'To the days of your madness and theirs,
to the days of infancy, to the days that are far off.' But in the
meantime this tribe will be bathed in its own blood even as
a woman in travail, giving birth, upon the squares of the cities
of Europe to yet one more child that will betray it.

"Yet how can I do aught but love this mattock in the hands
of the millennia? Graves are dug therewith—yet is it not therewith that the soil of a field is turned?

"Judaean blood will be spilt, the invited spectators will
applaud but, according to the ancient whisperings, it will
envenom the earth with still greater bitterness. The great
medicament of the Universe!"

And, approaching me, the Master kissed me hard on the
forehead.

1922

Yuri Carlovich OLESHA

[1899—]

Olesha is, by upbringing, an Odessite. After his service in the Red Army he became a Fellow Traveler. He began his literary career with humorous verse; he has written for children (*Three Fat Men* [1928], a rather Hoffmannesque tale which was also dramatized); short stories (*The Cherry Stone* [1930]); *List of Benefits,* a play, was produced in 1931, and he has done other literary work. With the publication (in 1927) of *Envy,* a short novel (later dramatized as *A Conspiracy of Emotions*), he not only became one of the leading Soviet writers but won the acclaim of émigré critics. The main theme of Olesha's works is the inability of the petty-bourgeois intellectual, the "lonely personality," to find a place amid the new (socialist) actuality. He is an apt satirist; the labels of Romantic and Realist could also be applied. He is a vivid, colorful artist and a master of form.

LEEOMPA

The boy Alexander was whittling panels out in the kitchen. The cuts on his fingers were getting covered over with gold-tinged crusts that looked edible.

The kitchen led out into the yard; it was spring; the doors were kept open; grass grew near the threshold; water gleamed where it had been spilled on a stone. A rat showed up from time to time in the rubbish bin. Potatoes, cut small, were frying in the kitchen. A small kerosene stove was being lit. The

375

life of this stove had a sumptuous beginning: as a torch that flamed up to the ceiling. The stove was dying as a very low flame. Eggs were bobbing in boiling water. One of the tenants was cooking crayfish. He would pick up a live crayfish by its middle, between thumb and forefinger. The crayfish were of the greenish hue of water in conduits. Two or three drops would suddenly spurt out of the water tap all by themselves. The tap would softly blow its nose. After that the water pipes on the floor above would start talking in several voices. Thereupon the twilight would immediately become definite. A drinking glass was the only object that remained standing on the window sill. It was receiving, through a wicket, the last rays of the sun. The water tap was talkative. Multiplex stirring and crackling were beginning about the cooking range.

The twilight was splendidly beautiful. People were nibbling pollyseeds; there was a sound of singing; the yellow light of indoors fell on the sidewalk; the provision shop was all lit up.

Ponomarev, who was critically ill, was lying in a room next to the kitchen. He was lying alone in the room; a candle was burning there; a vial of medicine had been placed above his head; the prescription tag attached to the vial trailed away from it like the train of a dress.

When acquaintances came to see him, Ponomarev would say: "Congratulate me; I'm dying."

Toward evening his delirium would begin. The vial of medicine eyed him. The prescription tag trailed away like the train of a dress. The vial was a marrying duchess. The vial was called Name Day. The sick man was delirious. He wanted to write a treatise. He was holding a conversation with the blanket.

"There, now," he whispered, "how is it you're not ashamed?"

The blanket sat alongside him; it lay down by his side; it left him now and then; it told him the news.

The things around the sick man were not many: the medicine, a spoon, the light, the wallpaper. The other things had gone off. When he had grasped that he had become gravely ill and that he was dying, he had also grasped how great and diversified the world of things was and how few of them remained in his power. With every day the quantity of things decreased. A thing so close to hand as a railroad ticket had by now become irretrievably distant for him. At first the quantity of things decreased at the periphery, far away from him; then this decrease began at an ever accelerating tempo to draw toward the center, toward him, toward his heart—penetrating into the courtyard, into the house, into the hallway, into the room.

At first the vanishment of things did not evoke melancholy in the sick man.

Various countries, America, the possibility of being handsome or rich, of having a family (he was single)—they all vanished. . . . His illness had no relation whatsoever to the vanishment of these things: in slipping away they kept pace with his increasing years; no, the real ache came only when it became clear to him that even those things which had constantly kept abreast of him were also beginning to recede from him. Thus, one day, he was abandoned by: his street, his work, his mail, horses. And at that point the vanishment became impetuous, taking place at his side, at his very elbow: the hallway had already eluded his authority—and in his room itself, before his very eyes, the significance of his overcoat, of the door bolt, of his shoes, came to an end. He knew: death, on its way to him, was annihilating the things. Out of all their enormous and futile quantity, death had left him only a few, and those were things which, if it lay in his power, he would never have admitted into his economy. He had been the recipient of a sneaky blow. He had been the recipient of the fearful visits and scrutinies of those who knew him. He had come to understand that he had not the strength to defend himself against the intrusion of these unasked for and unnecessary things, as they had always seemed to him. But now they were unique and absolute. He had lost the right to choose things.

The boy Alexander was making a model airplane.

The boy was far more complex and serious than all those others about him thought him to be. He cut his fingers; blood spurted out of him; he made a litter with his shavings; he soiled things with glue; he begged for silk, cried, had his head cuffed. The grownups considered themselves absolutely in the right. Yet the boy was acting in a perfectly grown-up manner;

more than that—he was acting as only a certain number of grownups can act: he was acting in full accord with science. The model was being constructed in accordance with a design, calculations were made—the boy knew the laws involved. He could have opposed the attacks of the grownups with an explanation of those laws, with a demonstration of experiments, but he kept silent because he did not consider that he had the right to show himself as more serious than the grownups.

The boy was surrounded by rubber bands, wire, panels, silk, the light tea-colored weave of silk, the smell of glue. The sky was glittering. Insects stalked over a stone. Within the stone a cockleshell had petrified.

Another boy, little more than a baby, naked except for blue bathing trunks, kept approaching the boy who was working. He touched things and got in the way. Alexander shooed him off. The naked, rubbery boy went all through the house; he went through the hallway, where the bicycle was. (The bicycle stood leaning with one of its pedals against the wall. The pedal had made a scratch against the wallpaper. It was this scratch that seemed to enable the bicycle to hold on to the wall.)

The little boy kept dropping in on Ponomarev. The youngster's head loomed dimly over the side of the bed. The sick man's temples were pale, like those of a blind man. The boy would walk right up to the head and look it over closely. He thought that that was how things were in this world, and had always been: a bearded man lying in a room, on a bed. The boy had just entered into cognition of things. He was not yet able to distinguish the time differences of their existence.

He turned around, and took to walking about the room. He saw the parquet squares, the dust under the plinth, the cracks in the plastering. Bodies were living, lines were combining and disposing themselves about him. The result would be a sudden focus of light—the boy hastened toward it, but he hardly had time to take a step when the change in distance annihilated the focus—and the boy looked about him, looked up and down, looked behind the stove, seeking, and spread his arms in bewilderment, failing to find anything. Each second created some new thing for him. The spider was astonishing. The spider fled at the boy's mere thought of putting his hand on the spider.

The things in their departure left only their names to the dying man.

In this universe there was an apple. It gleamed amid the leafage, it turned with the utmost lightness, it seized and turned with it chunks of the day, the azure out in the garden, the transom over the window. The law of gravitation was lying in wait for it under the tree, on the black earth, on the mounds of earth. Beadlike ants were running between the mounds. Newton was sitting in the garden. A multitude of causes, capable of evoking a still greater multitude of effects, was lurking within the apple. Not a one of these causes, however, was foreordained for Ponomarev. The apple had become an abstraction for him. And the fact that the substance of a thing was vanishing from him, while the abstraction remained, was for him excruciating.

"I thought that the outward universe did not exist," he pondered. "I thought that my eye and my hearing were directing things; I thought that the universe would cease to exist when I would cease to exist. But there . . . I can see how everybody is turning away from the still-living me. For I still exist! Why, then, don't the things exist? I thought that my brain had given them form, weight and color—but there, they have gone from me, and their names alone (useless names that have lost their masters) are swarming in my brain. And what do I derive from these names?"

With despondence Ponomarev regarded the child. The child was walking about. Things rushed to meet him. He was smiling to them, without knowing a single name. He would turn to leave, and a grandiose train of things surged in his wake.

"Listen," the sick man called to the child. "Listen. . . . You know, when I die nothing will remain. Neither courtyard, nor tree, nor Papa nor Mamma. I shall take everything along with me."

The rat made its way into the kitchen.

Ponomarev was listening: the rat was busying itself with household tasks, clattering dishes, opening the water tap, swishing something about in a pail.

"Aha—she's a dishwasher," Ponomarev reflected.

At the very same instant a disquieting thought entered his head: that the rat might have a name all its own that people did not know. He began thinking up a name of that sort. He was in delirium. As he kept thinking up this name he was being gripped harder and harder by fear. He understood that he had to stop, at no matter what cost, and not think of what name the rat had, yet at the same time he went on, knowing that at the very instant that this unique, meaningless and frightening name would come to his mind he would die.

"Leeompa!" he cried out suddenly in a dreadful voice.

The house was asleep. It was early morning, going on six. The boy Alexander was not sleeping. The kitchen door was open on the courtyard. The sun was still somewhere down below.

The dying man was walking through the kitchen, bent in at the belly, his hands, dangling at the wrists, extended. He was on his way to take the things with him.

The boy Alexander was running through the yard. The model airplane was flying ahead of him. This was the last thing Ponomarev caught sight of.

He did not take it with him. It flew away.

During the day a coffin—blue, with yellow decorations— appeared in the kitchen. The rubbery little boy had been peeping out of the hallway, his hands behind him. It became necessary to turn the coffin every which way, and for a long time, in order to get it through the door. Those who were carrying it caught it against a shelf, against a cooking pot; the plastering came down in a shower. The boy Alexander clambered up on the kitchen range and helped, holding up the bottom of the box. When the coffin penetrated into the hallway at last, instantly turning black, the rubbery little boy, his sandals flapping, ran ahead of it.

"Grandfather! Grandfather!" he started shouting. "They have brought you your coffin."

1935

Ivan Vassilievich EVDOKIMOV

[1887—]

Evdokimov was born at Kronstadt, studied history and philology at the University of St. Petersburg, and worked for a time as a telegraph operator. After the October Revolution he was a librarian, teacher, school superintendent and editor. His short stories began to appear in provincial papers in 1915 and 1916. In 1925 he published *Siverko,* a novella, followed by *Bells,* a full-length novel; these two works made the author a notable figure among the Fellow Travelers. *Bells* proved popular, and showed its author as a talented Realist.

His genres deal with the poorer folks, in village, small town or suburb; he deals with the folkways of working-class quarters and factory life; he is a master in depicting the revolutionary underground of 1905 and all its operations. However, *Clear Ponds* (1927) and *Beyond the Lake* (1928), although admittedly well-written novels, have been labeled as "light literature" by official Soviet criticism.

His own outlook on life is perhaps given best in the following excerpt from the author's preface to *Ravines,* the volume of short stories which includes "Train Ride": "The stories . . . deal with things funny and touching, with things tragic and curious. The renewal of our life, evoked by the October Revolution, could not help but stir up the muddiness of the old mores. The author attempts to depict in a satirical but unmalicious setting that which is undesirable, believing that a timely warning signal is always useful. The best that the Revolution has brought with it is making headway through all the pores of our Republic of Soviets; it will vanquish, will overwhelm; yet often, among the young grain, wormwood

381

still lifts its curly head. It must be plucked forth, huge root and all."

TRAIN RIDE

The mouzhik, holding above his head a long hamper woven of lathes, pushed his way through the crowd on the platform and into the car and perched himself on the very edge of a seat. He put the hamper on his lap, covered it over with a sack and took his stiff-brimmed cap off his dripping forehead. Something was stirring in that hamper, and then that something began squealing, ever so softly, then *oink*ing, and finally thrusting hard against the lathes.

"What have you got there?" a lady passenger raised her voice. She had just moved over on the seat to make room for the mouzhik, having felt sorry for him.

"A young pig, dear citizeness!" the mouzhik answered willingly and readily, and, peeping under the sack, he began to rumble caressingly: "There, piggy, piggy, what are you cutting up for? Keep still, keep still awhile, you potbelly!"

"What kind of disgrace is this!" the woman raised her voice again and leaned over toward her other neighbor, squeezing him against the window. "Citizens, they're carrying pigs in the same car with regular passengers!"

Her neighbor, the one whom she had crushed against the window, spread out his elbows and nodded knowingly to the woman: "Why don't you lie down right on top of me while you're at it, comrade? Move over, I'm telling you—what are you hugging me for? Well, now, if it was nighttime it would be a different matter—but in broad daylight it's kind of embarrassing."

The whole car snickered.

"How da-are you!" the lady passenger turned red. "You're being very impudent!"

"That's a fine how-d'you-do! She's squeezing me up against the wall, but it's me that's at fault!"

"But where am I to go?" the woman seethed. "I've got a pig on one side of me and you on the other—"

"Well, whoever told you to let this comrade with the pig sit down next to you? The seat is just for two—you and me—but now there's four of us."

The hamper was squirming on the mouzhik's lap.

"Why, there's nothing to be afraid of, citizeness dear," he hastily began. "It's only a little one—it won't start up with you. It's only the full-grown boars that ain't been fixed that might do so; they got a certain thing, now, that's cut out—same as there's castrates amongst human beings. They never even heard tell what females is for! And they don't start up, even if they do know. And pigs don't give off no odor. Not if you just don't feed them, so's they won't. So's they won't make no mess in front of folks, I figure. You know how animals are! They got no sense. Just keep on grunting. It oughtn't to be grunting, yet grunt it does. You just set your mind at rest, darling! It ain't going to jump out. Don't never be afraid of no domestic animal; it loves peace more than any human being does—more than its own master."

The lady passenger grew more and more insistently and malevolently indignant: "What gives you the notion I'm afraid? Anyway, this is an outrage! Pigs and passengers—passengers and pigs!"

"You are ab-solutely right!" a little ancient in the seat opposite came to her support. "Ab-solutely cor-rect! It is sheer unbridled mischief!"

"But how is a pig worse than a dog?" someone was shouting at the other end of the car.

"Or a cat?" someone else seconded him. "There are three dogs and a cat in this car!"

"On a farm all the animals share quarters with their masters. In the villages they walk about in the huts and do their business right on the floor."

"They show all they got, the bourzhuis!"

The car was filled with noise and shouting.

"You just carry your pigs, mouzhik, and the hell with them!"—"You listen to every fine-feathered bird and there won't be any living for the laboring proletariat!"—"It smells

and stinks, does it? Well, maybe their own bourzhui blubber
knocks us over worse than any pigs!"—"I'm a sick man, I
am. My feet give off a smell worse than any dead man's.
You wouldn't let me into a car, either? Deprive me of trans-
portation? Just fancy notions and airs left over from the old
regime!"

"There, dear citizeness, little citizeness," the mouzhik was
busy placating the lady passenger. "In just what way is my
little pig bothering you? If it was parading around on the
floor it might be another matter. It might go sniffing at your
pretty dress with its tiny snout, or at your little shoes, or
rooting at the packages of lunch, but as it is it's all under
cover, out of sight. The only thing is, it's grunting. Us, we
say things in words, whilst it just grunts those same words—"

"Conductor! Conductor!" the woman was straining her
lungs. "He doesn't understand—it's beyond him to understand!"

"A pig is livestock," the inevitable angelic passenger was
admonishing the mouzhik, "whereas we are human beings.
You, dear man, are a fool. You don't know the difference
between a pig and a man."

"Even Christ cursed the pig!"

"Hey, there, you dead hand of the church! Christ has long
since been blackballed!"

"Unanimously! With a reprimand!"

"Don't you listen to them, mouzhik—don't give in! They're
after buying that pig off of you dirt-cheap!"

"Pig is forbid—it is Devil," a caftaned Tatar put in.

"Come, now, is it my fault?" the mouzhik was justifying
himself. "I took over pig raising from my father. I got me
forty pigs—or just a few shy of that. Thoroughbred pigs,
that's what I got. The Soviet authorities themselves accept
them for breeding. I raise boars that weigh as much as six
hundred and fifty pounds!"

Squeals, and a deafening sound very like weeping issued
from the hamper, which had slipped off his lap.

"What's it to us—it's no skin off our noses," the hard-
pressed passenger next to the window broke into laughter.
"Get shut of her, mouzhik—I'm all in a sweat from the

squeezing this plump citizeness is giving me. I'm steaming like a kettle, or something—my shirt's sopping wet."

"Conductor! Conductor!"

The dogs started barking and were straining to get at the mouzhik. The car was now a free-for-all of voices and shouts; the passengers were swinging their arms, threatening one another, tossing things from rack to rack and laughing boisterously.

The mouzhik could not hold out. He put the hamper on top of his head once more: "You ain't been put on earth for nothing, little citizeness," he began to mumble at the woman amicably. "Not for nothing! You're only making trouble for your own self. Guess I'll go and put this in the baggage car. Keep an eye on that there little sack and my place!"

The mouzhik put the sack on the edge of his seat. The woman edged away from it squeamishly.

Shortly after a stop the mouzhik came back and sat down quietly, examining his baggage-car check. The woman was watching him out of the corners of her eyes with satisfaction.

"You've put me to expense, little citizeness," said the mouzhik. "And there's only a few stations left to where I'm bound. I might have carried that hamper for nothing. But as it is I'm only ten stations ahead, because you had to go and get all het up."

"Your little pig must be dreadfully lonesome," the lady passenger needled him.

"No, it ain't," and, in his turn, he smiled slyly, covering his mouth with a broad hand. "That there hamper had two pigs in it."

1929

Alexander Stepanovich GREENEVSKY
("A. Green")

[1880-1932]

An utter exotic not only in Soviet literature, but in Russian literature as a whole, Greenevsky began writing in 1906; his first book, *The Cap of Invisibility,* published in 1908, consisted of stories that showed the influence of sentimental, romantic but hardly unrealistic Kuprin; yet shortly, falling under the American's influence, Greenevsky aspired to be called the Russian Poe—and actually was (although it would be much more accurate to style him the Russian Dunsany, an author whom, in all likelihood, he had never read). He has also been described as "not merely a dreamer but a militant dreamer." And: "A cunning engraver of pipe-smoke visions." This refugee from reality created his own "cabined world of phantasms," fantastic cities of his own ("There is no city more harum-scarum, more marvelous than Lissé—unless it be Zurbaghan"), with magic ships sailing into their ensorcelled harbors, or setting forth from them, crewed by adventurers who had witnessed "touching and ever astonishing events" ashore.

His life was, unquestionably, a checquered one. As a youth he had been a sort of Gorkian vagabond, a gold-seeker, a sailor—although he made but one foreign cruise: to Alexandria. He knew no greater delight than knocking about some port, or looking out to sea for hours at a time; in 1924 he left Leningrad for Theodosia, having found life out of earshot of the surf unbearable. He could not write except in winter; summer was made for such medieval pastimes as archery and falconry. When young he had been a revolutionary and had earned a two-year imprisonment in Sebastopol; yet he lived through a decade and a half of blood-spurting history without giving any indication of having been even remotely aware of the Revolution other than the extremely inferential ones in his inimitable "The Ratcatcher." * He wrote *Red Veils, On the Slope of the Hill, The Golden Chain* and three other novels, as well as over three hundred stories, varying from very short to very long, but all symbolic, fantastic, whimsical, and he was the admitted master of Olesha, Kataev, Shaghinian, Fadeyev; yet the twenty-fifth year of his literary activity went unmarked. And when he died the next year (from cancer) his death, too, was almost unnoticed, except by a very few of his hardly innumerable friends.

Oddest quirk of all: the *Soviet Literary Encyclopaedia,* the scholarship of which is anything but sciolistic, can find no tag, no label, no pigeonhole for, or the least theological stricture against, this absolute phantast. The editor therefore ventures, most diffidently, to propose the as yet not dishonorable designation of storyteller.

THE GARRULOUS HOBGOBLIN

> *Standing by the window, I was*
> *humming a little song about Anna.*
> H. HORNUNG

I

A hobgoblin with a toothache: isn't that a libel on a being who has at his disposal so many witches and wizards that he can devour sugar by the barrel with impunity? But that's how it was, it really did happen: the tiny, melancholy hob-

* In *New Russian Stories;* New Directions, New York, 1953.—To the best of the present writer's knowledge this story, and the one given here, are the only two items of this author available in English.—*Ed.-Trans.*

goblin was squatting near a cold kitchen range which had long since forgotten what a fire was like. With his unkempt head rhythmically swaying he was holding on to his swathed cheek, mewling as piteously as a baby, and suffering pulsed in his turbid reddened eyes.

It was pouring. I had stepped into this neglected house to wait for the foul weather to improve and had caught sight of him, since he had forgotten that evanishment was in order.

"It doesn't matter now," said he in a voice that reminded one of the voice of a parrot when the bird is really having a talking streak. "It doesn't matter, because nobody will believe you if you claim that you saw me."

Performing the *jettatura* (i.e., extending the index and little fingers of my right hand), just to be on the safe side, I answered: "Don't be afraid. I'm not going to fire a bullet molded out of a silver coin at you, nor subject you to any involved incantation. However, the house is vacant."

The tiny hobgoblin sighed, before retorting: "But in spite of that it's so hard to get away from here. You just listen, now. I'll tell you all about it, after all, since I do have a toothache. It lets up when one is talking. Considerably so— *ouch!* My dear man, it was a matter of just one hour, yet because of that I got stuck here. You see, you must know what sort of thing this was, and why. My fellows, now—my fellows"—he sighed tearfully—"my fellows—well, to make it short, our sort has been getting the burrs out of horses' tails on the other side of the mountains for a long while by now, after leaving here; but I can't leave, since I've got to understand the thing.

"Look about you—there are holes in the ceiling and walls. But now imagine that the place is all glowing from copper utensils scoured as clean as clean can be, that there are gauzy white curtains on the windows, while there are as many flowers inside the house as there are in the forest all around it; the floor is brightly waxed, while the cold kitchen range, on which you are now sitting as on a gravestone, is glowing red with fire, and the dinner burbling in the pots on the range is emitting billows of mouth-watering steam.

"There was a quarry—a granite quarry—nearby. The man

and wife living here were a couple such as one rarely meets. The husband was called Philip, and the wife Annie. She was twenty and he was twenty-five. Here, if you please, is exactly what she was like"—here the goblin plucked a small wild flower which had sprung up from the soil that had accumulated through the years in a crack in the window sill, and offered it to me demonstratively. "I loved the husband too, but I had a greater liking for her; she wasn't merely the housewife— we hobgoblins find a certain charm in that which makes human creatures akin to us. She attempted to catch the fish in the stream with her hands; she used to tap on the great boulder at the crossing of the roads, listening to how long it took to cease from its ringing, and she would laugh when she saw a spot of sunlight like a yellow bunny on the wall. Don't be surprised; there is a magic about this, a great knowledge of a splendidly beautiful soul—but only we aegipeds can distinguish these signs: humans are not perceptive.

"'Annie!' the husband would call out gaily on coming home for dinner from the quarry, where he clerked in the office. 'I'm not alone—my Ralph is with me.' But this jest was repeated so often that Annie, not at all confused, merely smiled and went right on setting places for only two. And when they met it was as if they were finding each other for the first time: she would run to him and he would carry her into the house in his arms.

"Evenings he would take out Ralph's letters—the letters of his friend, with whom he had passed part of his life before marrying, and would reread them aloud, while Annie, with her head propped on her hands, listened attentively to the long-familiar words about the sea and the bright light of wondrous rays on the other side of our enormous earth, about volcanoes and pearls, about tempests and about battles fought in the shadow of enormous forests. And every word held a stone for her: a stone like the singing stone at the crossing of the roads, upon tapping which you heard a prolonged ringing.

"'He'll be coming soon,' Philip used to say. 'He'll come to us when his three-masted *Sindbad* gets to Gress. It's only an hour from there by railroad, and an hour from the railroad station to our place.'

"Occasionally Annie would become interested in some point of Ralph's life; thereupon Philip would launch enthusiastically into tales of his friend's derring-do, quirks, magnanimity, and instances of a destiny that made one think of a fairy tale: poverty, auriferous sands, the purchase of a ship, and a very lacework of clamorous legends, woven of ship riggings, sea foam, perils and windfalls. Eternal play. Eternal excitement. Eternal music of seashore and sea.

"I never heard them quarreling—and yet I hear everything. I did not see them exchange cold looks—no, not once —and yet I see everything. 'I feel sleepy,' Annie would say of an evening, and he would carry her to her bed, make her comfortable and tuck her in, as if she were a child. As she was falling asleep she would say: 'Phil, who's that whispering on the treetops? Who's that walking over the roof? Whose face do I keep seeing in the stream side by side with mine?'

"He would answer her uneasily, peering into her half-closed eyes: 'There's a crow walking over the roof; it's the wind that is soughing in the trees; what you saw in the stream was the gleam of stones. Go to sleep, and don't walk about barefoot.'

"After that he would sit down to the table to finish his most urgent paper work, then wash up, get the firewood ready, and go to bed; he fell asleep at once and always forgot whatever dreams he might have had. And he never tapped on the singing stone at the crossing of the roads, where fays weave remarkable rugs out of dust and moonbeams.

II

"Well, now, listen. There isn't much left for me to wind up the story of the three people who confounded a hobgoblin. It was a sunny day, with the earth in full bloom, as Philip, notebook in hand, checked off the piles of granite, while Annie, on her way back from the railway station where she had been making purchases, had stopped at her stone and, as always, had made it sing by striking it with a key. It was a piece broken off a crag, and about half your height. If you struck it it rang for a long while, more and more softly, but if you thought it had stopped ringing for good, all you had to do was to put your ear to it and you would then make out a barely audible voice within the boulder.

"Our forest roads are really gardens. Their beauty makes one's heart contract; the flowers and branches overhead are studying the sun through their fingers, a sun that keeps changing its light, since the eyes get tired of it and wander aimlessly; a yellow light, and a chalky one, and a dark-green are reflected on the white sand. Cold water on a day such as that is the best of all things.

"Annie stopped, listening to the forest singing within her very breast, and began to tap the stone, smiling whenever a new wave of ringing overcame the half-silenced sound. Thus did she amuse herself, thinking that no one saw her, but a man came around a turn in the road and approached her. His footfalls became quieter and quieter; finally he halted. Still smiling, she looked at him—without being startled, without stepping back, as though he had always been there, standing thus.

"He was swarthy—very swarthy, and the sea had left the keenness of the running wave upon his face. Yet it was splendidly beautiful, since it reflected a raging and tender soul. His dark eyes, growing still more vividly dark, were regarding Annie, while the radiant eyes of the woman gleamed meekly.

"You will be correct in concluding that I was keeping close to her heels since there are serpents in a forest.

"The boulder had long since fallen silent, but they were still looking at each other, smiling without words, without a sound; then he held out his hand, and she—slowly—held out hers, and the hands united them. He took her head cautiously, so cautiously that I was afraid to breathe, and kissed her lips. Her eyes closed.

"Then they separated—and the boulder was between them, as before. On seeing Philip coming toward them Annie hurried to meet him: " 'Here is Ralph; he has arrived.'

" 'Yes; so he has.' Because of his joy Philip could not even shout at first but, at last, he tossed his hat up in the air and shouted as he embraced the new arrival. 'You have already seen Annie, Ralph. Here she is.' His kind, firm face was flaming from the excitement of the meeting. 'You'll stay awhile with us, Ralph; we'll show you everything. And we'll talk to our hearts' content. Here is my wife, my friend—she, too, has been expecting you.'

"Annie put her hand on her husband's shoulder, then looked at him with that look of hers, the greatest, warmest and purest of looks, then shifted that look upon the newcomer without changing her expression, as if both were equally close to her.

" 'I'll be back,' said Ralph. 'I became all mixed up about your address and was thinking that I wasn't on the right road. That's why I didn't take my baggage along. And I'm going to get it right now.'

"They settled all the details and parted. There, that's all I know about it. And I don't understand it. Perhaps you will explain it to me."

"Did Ralph come back?"

"They were expecting him, but he sent a note from the railway station that he had met a man he knew who had suggested a deal that promised quick profits."

"And what about the others?"

"They died—they died long since, some thirty years ago. Cold water on a hot day. It was just a cold with her, at first. He was half gray as he followed her coffin. Then he vanished; the way they told it, he had locked himself in a room with a brazier full of charcoal. But what had happened before that? My teeth ache and I can't understand—"

"Let it go at that," I told him politely, shaking in farewell his shaggy, unwashed paw. "It is only we, the five-fingered ones, who can decipher the signs of the heart; hobgoblins are unperceptive."

1925

ILF and PETROV

(Ilya Arnoldovich ILF [1897-1937])
(Eugene Petrovich KATAEV [1907-1942])

Shchedrin-Saltykov took a Hannibal's oath against all the
deadly, pseudo-human aspects of czarism. The main target
of Ilf and Petrov was the practically indestructible Russian
bourzhui masquerading as the New Soviet Man (*12 Chairs,
The Golden Calf*—picaresque novels that have become classics
by now), but their pet *bête noire* was *haltura*. When the Russians have a word for something (they very seldom haven't)
it is apt to be more caustic, sweeping and puissant than any
approximation that even the Greeks may find in their lexicon.
The niggardly dictionary definition of *haltura* is *potboiling*.
Haltura should be taken over into English, for this one Russian word denotes and connotes, in the arts, not only potboiling but *bunkum, hokum, humbug, gimmick, corn* (mil-
dewed), *schmaltz* (rancid), *ham* (moldy), *pinchbeck, brum-
magem, strass, gold brick, French ivory, German silver,
Manchurian wolf, fake, sham, bogus, mock, ersatz* and much,
much besides. If one had to settle for a single word, it would
be the Gaelic *fainné* (a gold ring of the finest brass), which
has in its turn taken on a pseudo-American form of *phony*.
These two satirists attacked halturing, halturishness and halturniks at every point of the Haltura Sector (the most extensive, best protected and most favored on the Russian Arts
Front): cinema, circus, conversation, painting, theatre, literature—even furniture design. The two selections given here are
more devastating than all the rabid writings of all the
Eastmans and Struves.

Both Ilf ("tall, gaunt, stoop-shouldered, shy, not at all

talkative") and Petrov ("well-fleshed, broad-shouldered, noisy, talkative") were native Odessites.

Ilf, born into a poor Jewish family, worked as a machine-shop assembler, bookkeeper and stable manager; at eighteen he was a journalist in Odessa. He was one of the comparatively few Russian humorists who began as such, breaking into the humorous periodicals in 1919, at the height of the civil war. Not too long afterward he joined the staff of the *Train Whistle,* in Moscow, forming his partnership with Petrov, another staff member. Still another staff member was Petrov's brother, the famous Valentin Kataev, who acted as their preceptor and mentor and, in the beginning, formed a trio with them. Subsequently Ilf and Petrov joined *Pravda,* winning an audience of millions for their extremely popular satires directed against bureaucratism and bourzhui-ism written under the pen names of Tolstoievsky and the Chill Philosopher.

Ilf's health was sapped by the two-month, ten-thousand-mile automobile tour which the team made in 1936 to collect material for *One Story High America.* An item in the *New York Times* (July 6, 1942) states that Ilf drowned while swimming; actually he died of tuberculosis on April 13, 1937, in Moscow, where his body was cremated.

Petrov's article (both poignant and humorous), written after Ilf's death and explaining how the two literary collaborators and platform partners worked, conveys the impression that Ilf was extremely sensitive but not at all a melancholic; Ilf's own *Notebooks,* published posthumously, indicate that he might well have developed into a serious writer of importance.

Petrov edited several humorous periodicals, as well as the very popular *Little Flame,* a weekly which did a great deal to make the U.S.A. and Great Britain better understood by the Russians. He also had a reputation as a writer of film scenarios; the one for *The Circus* was done in collaboration with Ilf and his brother Valentin.

After Ilf's death Petrov continued writing sketches, stories, scenarios and comedies. Like so many leading Soviet writers during World War II, he was a correspondent at the front, with the rank of lieutenant-colonel, writing for the Soviet

Information Bureau and the North American Newspaper Alliance, his dispatches appearing in the *New York Times*. He was killed at his post on July 25, 1942, during the defense of Sebastopol, which he had covered for many months. His *Diary at the Front* was published posthumously.

12 Chairs and *The Golden Calf* were promptly seized and used as Big Berthas by the anti-Soviet industry. However, the most painstaking research shows no indication that these two satirists ever received as much as a slap on the wrist throughout their careers. And their *Feuilletons and Stories* were republished in a popular edition, in a first printing of 150,000 copies, as recently as June, 1957.

HOW THE SOVIET ROBINSON WAS CREATED

A paucity of literary material capable of riveting the youthful reader's attention made itself felt in the editorial office of *Adventure Industry,* a publication that came out every third week.

Some material, of a sort, there was, but none of it filled the bill. There was far too much drooling seriousness about it. Truth to tell, it cast gloom over the soul of the youthful reader; it didn't rivet him worth a hoot. And yet riveting him was precisely what the editor was after.

The upshot was that it was decided to commission a serial.

The fastest messenger at the editor's disposal was rushed off with a note to Moldovantzev, a writer, and the very next day found Moldovantzev perched on the merchantly couch in the editor's office.

"You understand"—the editor was dinning it into him—"this thing must be engrossing, fresh, chock-full of adventures. It must, on the whole, turn out to be the Soviet Robinson Crusoe. Done in such a manner that the reader won't be able to tear himself away."

"Robinson. Can do," the writer agreed laconically.

"Not just any old Robinson, however, but a Soviet Robinson."

"How else! Not a Rumanian one!" The writer wasn't the talkative sort. You could tell right off he was a businessman. And, sure enough, the novel was ready by the deadline. Moldovantzev hadn't departed too much from the great original. If it was Robinson they wanted, Robinson they would get.

A Soviet youth suffers a shipwreck. A wave casts him up on an uninhabited island. He is all by his lonesome, defenseless, face to face with the mighty forces of nature. He is surrounded by dangers: wild beasts, lianas, the rainy season looming ahead. But the Soviet Robinson Crusoe, simply brimming over with energy, surmounts all the seemingly insurmountable obstacles. And, three years later, a Soviet expedition finds him—finds him in the full flowering of all his forces. He has conquered nature, has built himself a little house, has ringed the little house with whole truck gardens of green growing things, has successfully gone in for breeding rabbits, sewn a blouse for himself (the kind Leo Tolstoi used to wear) out of monkey tails, and trained a parrot to wake him each morning with the words: "Attention! Off with that blanket—off with that blanket! We're starting the morning workout!"

"Very good!" commented the editor. "And that bit about the rabbits—it's simply magnificent. Quite in keeping with the times. But, do you know, the basic idea of the work is not quite clear to me."

"Man's struggle against Nature," Moldovantzev informed him with his usual terseness.

"Yes, but there's nothing Soviet about the novel."

"How's about the parrot? Why, I've made it take the place of a radio. An experienced broadcaster."

"That parrot is good. And that ring of truck gardens is good. Yet one doesn't have any feeling of the obligations of Soviet society. Where, for instance, is the Mestkom, the Local Trade Union Committee? Where is the leading role of the trade union?"

Moldovantzev suddenly became agitated. The instant he

felt that his novel might not be accepted his taciturnity vanished. He became eloquent.

"Where would the Mestkom come from? The island is uninhabited, isn't it?"

"Yes, you're prefectly right—it's uninhabited. But the Mestkom is a must. I'm not an artist of the word, but if I were in your place I would bring in the Mestkom. As a Soviet element."

"But then, the whole story is built on the island's being uninhabited—" At this point Moldovantzev chanced to look into the editor's eyes and stopped short. Those eyes were so vernal, one felt such March bleakness and watered-milk azure there, that the writer decided to compromise. "However, come to think of it," said he, holding up an index finger, "you're right. Of course. How come I didn't figure the thing out right off? *Two* people are saved from the ship-wreck: our Robinson and the Chairman of the Mestkom."

"And two other members who have been fired from the Mestkom," said the editor in a chilly tone.

"Oi!" squeaked Moldovantzev.

"Never mind *oi*'ing. Two fired members—and, while you're at it, one very active member, a woman—she'll collect the dues."

"What do you want a dues collector for? Whom is she going to collect dues from?"

"Why, from Robinson."

"The Chairman can collect from Robinson. It won't hurt the Chairman any."

"That's where you're mistaken, Comrade Moldovantzev. That's absolutely inadmissible. The Chairman of the Mestkom can't make himself small like that and run after Robinson to collect his dues. That's something we're putting up a fight against. He must busy himself with serious work which re-quires leadership."

"In that case we can save the female dues collector as well," Moldovantzev gave in. "It's all to the good, in fact. She can marry the Chairman, or Robinson himself. It'll make for livelier reading, at that."

"It's not worth while. Don't sink to the paperback level,

to unwholesome eroticism. Let her stick to collecting those
union dues and putting them away in the fireproof safe—"

Moldovantzev started fidgeting on the couch: "Just a
moment! You can't have a fireproof safe on a desert island!"

The editor cogitated awhile.

"Hold on, hold on!" he said at last. "You have a wonderful spot for that in the first chapter. Along with Robinson
and the members of the Mestkom, the wave casts various
things up on shore—"

"An ax, a carbine, a container of creosol, a keg of rum
and a bottle of an antiscorbutic," the writer solemnly recited
the list.

"Cross off the rum," the editor put in quickly. "Then
too, what's that bottle of antiscorbutic stuff doing there?
Who needs it? Better make that a bottle of ink! And a fireproof safe—that's a must."

"You sure are hipped on that safe! The membership dues
can damn well be kept in the hollow trunk of a baobab.
Who's going to steal them from there?"

"What do you mean, who? What about Robinson? And
the Chairman of the Mestkom? And the fired members? And
the General Store Commission?"

"It, too, was saved from the sea?" Moldovantzev asked
timorously.

"It was."

A silence ensued.

"Was a conference table also cast up by that same wave,
by any chance?" the author asked with crafty malice.

"Ab-so-lute-ly! After all, it is necessary to create con-
ditions under which people can work. Well, now, you've got
to have a water bottle, a hand bell, a cover for that conference
table. The wave can cast up any tablecover it has a mind
to: it can be red, it can be green—I'm not one to cramp a
creative artist's style. But, my dear fellow, here's what you
must do first and foremost. You must show us the masses.
The broad strata of the toilers."

"The wave can't cast up any masses," Moldovantzev turned
mulish. "That goes against the story line. Just think of it!

A single wave all of a sudden casts up tens of thousands of people! It's enough to make a cat laugh—"

"Incidentally, a modicum of wholesome, hearty, life-loving laughter," the editor put in, "can never hurt."

"No! No wave can do all that."

"Why a wave?" the editor was suddenly puzzled.

"Come, how else would the masses get on the island? For that island is uninhabited, isn't it?"

"Who told you it's uninhabited? You're mixing me all up, somehow. It's all plain. You have an island—it would be even better if it were a peninsula: less trouble that way. And a string of engrossing, fresh, interesting adventures takes place there. And the trade unions carry on their work there—none too arduously, at times. The girl, who is an active political worker, uncovers a series of irregularities—well, in the area of dues collections, let's say. She is helped along by the broad strata of the toilers. And by the repentant Chairman of the Mestkom. Toward the end you can stage a general meeting. That will prove most effective, precisely from the artistic point of view. Well, that about ties it up."

"But what about Robinson?" babbled Moldovantzev.

"Yes. Good thing you reminded me. This Robinson confuses me. Chuck him out on his ear. An incongruous, utterly unjustified figure of a chronic bellyacher."

"I get it all now," said Moldovantzev in a sepulchral voice. "I'll have it ready tomorrow."

"There, that's the lot. Go ahead and create. By the way, you have a shipwreck at the beginning of your novel. You know, you really don't need any shipwreck. Let the thing go without a shipwreck. It'll be more engrossing that way. Right? There, that's great! Keep well!"

Left alone, the editor broke into joyous laughter.

"At last," he soliloquized, "I'm going to have some real adventure stuff—and a thoroughly artistic work at the same time."

1933

ICH BIN FROM HEAD TO FEET

The stupidity that had been actually perpetrated bordered on dunderheadism—plus.

A German attraction had been imported for the circus program: Intrepid Captain Masuccio and His Talking Dog Brunhild. (*NB* All circus captains are always intrepid.)

The dog act had been imported by the Business Manager of the circus, a coarse, insensitive character impervious to the currents of contemporaneity. And public opinion in the circus world had been asleep at the switch insofar as this lamentable fact is concerned. Those involved woke up only when Captain Masuccio landed at the Bielorussko-Baltic depot.

The porter carried off on his hand cart the cage with the black poodle, clipped *à la* Louis XIV, and the suitcase containing the captain's cape, lined with white satin-liberté, as well as the captain's glossy gibus.

That same day the Artistic Soviet [or Council] of the circus auditioned the dog during the rehearsal. The Intrepid Captain kept doffing his glossy collapsible opera hat and bowing, playing straight man to the animal.

"*Wie viel*—how much?" he asked.

"*Tausend*—a thousand," the dog answered intrepidly.

The captain patted the poodle's coat of natural black caracul and sighed approvingly: "Oh, *mein* goot dog!"

The dog next pronounced, with considerable pauses between the words, *aber, unser, Bruder*—but, our, brother. Then she collapsed sideways on the sanded arena, meditated a long while, and at last said: "*Ich sterbe*—I'm dying."

It must be noted that usually applause broke out at this point. The dog had become accustomed to the plaudits and would take bows with her master. The Artistic Council, however, sat austerely on its hands. And Captain Masuccio, looking about him uneasily, got ready for the concluding—

and most ticklish—part of his turn. He picked up a fiddle. Brunhild sat up on her hind legs and, after waiting for a few beats, broke into timorous, loud, and none too articulate song:

"Ich bin von Kopf bis Fuss auf Liebe eingestellt—"

"What's—what's this *Ich bin* business?" asked the Chairman of the Artistic Council.

"Ich bin von Kopf bis Fuss—" mumbled the Business Manager.

"Translate it."

" 'From head to feet I am made for love.' "

" 'For love'?" the Chairman echoed, turning pale. "A dog like that ought to be slapped on the wrist. This number can't be allowed to appear."

Now it was the Business Manager's turn to turn pale.

"For what reason? Why slap the dog's wrist? A Famous Talking Dog Presenting Her Repertoire. European Success. What's so bad about the act?"

"What's so bad is precisely the repertoire she's presenting, which is arch-bourgeois, lower middle class, devoid of any educational values."

"Yes, but we've already shelled out foreign currency. And on top of that this dog and her Boccaccio are staying at the Metropole and she stuffs her guts with caviar. The Captain says she can't perform without caviar. That, too, is costing the government."

"I will make it brief," said the Chairman, clipping each word; "the act can't be passed in its present form. The dog must be furnished with our sort of material—consistent, summoning somewhere or inspiring to something or other, and not this . . . this demoralizing routine. Just stop and think! *Ich sterbe, ich liebe*—why, that is nothing but the problem of love and death! Art for art's sake! Humanism! From that it's only a step to an uncritical acceptance of our classical heritage. No, no—this number must be radically reworked."

"I, as a business manager," the Business Manager uttered sadly, "am not going to touch upon matters of ideology.

But, as an old idea-man on the arts-of-the-circus front, I'm telling you this: don't liquidate the fowl that fulfills its quota of golden eggs."

However, the proposition of writing new material for the dog was already being put to the vote. It was unanimously resolved to award the commission for an appropriate repertoire to a crack local brigade specializing in minor literary forms, consisting of Ussyshkin-Werther and his three brothers —Ussyshkin-Vagranka, Ussyshkin-Ovich and Grandpa Murzilka Ussyshkin. The Intrepid Captain, who hadn't understood a thing, was led off to the Metropole and advised to rest for the time being.

The crack literary brigade wasn't in the least fazed by the order to turn out a repertoire for a dog. The brothers started nodding in perfect time and did not as much as exchange looks. And all the while they had the air of having spent their entire lives writing for dogs, cats and trained cockroaches. On the whole, they had been tempered in literary battles and knew how to write in accordance with the ideology of the circus—the strictest, the most puritanical of ideologies.

The industrious clan of Ussyshkins buckled down to work without any shilly-shallying.

"Maybe we can use the bit we wrote for the Spider Woman?" Grandpa Murzilka suggested. "There was an attraction like that in Saratov, which had to be whipped into shape to fit in with the plan of the politicization of the circus. Remember? The Spider Woman personified High Finance, penetrating into colonies and dominion status countries. That was a swell number."

"No; you must have heard what the Artistic Council people said. They don't want any low comedy. The problem of this dog must be solved on the plane of the heroic elements of today!" Ovich objected. "First of all, we must write in verse."

"But does she know how to put verse over?"

"What's that got to do with us? Let her get reconstructed. She's got all of a week to do it in."

"It's got to be in verse, posolutely. Heroic couplets, on this and that topic of the day. As for the chorus, that doesn't have to be too difficult, tailor-made for a dog with a humorous bent. F'r instance . . . coming up, coming up . . . *ta-ra, ta-ra, ta-ra* . . . aha, got it!

> "A few more rows to each plow—
>   Bow-wow,
>   Bow-wow,
>   Bow-wow!"

"You're a fool, Buka!" Werther shouted. "There, I can just see the Artistic Council allowing you to have the dog say 'Bow-wow!' They're dead set against that. You mustn't overlook the living human being within the dog!"

"Gotta do it over . . . *too-roo, too-roo, too-roo.* . . . So. Here she is:

> "A few more rows to each plow—
>   Hurrah! All hail to Nav-Moscow!"

"But isn't that kind of shallow for a dog?"

"That's a dopey remark. Nav-Moscow is an organization for naval rescues. Where it's too shallow they don't bother."

"Tell you what: let's drop verse, on general principles. Verse always impels one to make mistakes, to go in for vulgarization. You're cramped by the beat, by meter. The minute you want to say the correct thing a cæsura gets in the way, or you can't find a rhyme—"

"Maybe we ought to give that dog a conversational format? A monologue? A topical skit?"

"It isn't worth while. There are dangers lurking there as well. You won't reflect this, you won't deflect that. Gotta do the whole thing differently."

The repertoire for Brunhild the Talking Dog was handed in on the date set. All those concerned gathered under the dusky cupola of the circus: every member of the Artistic Council, and Masuccio, whose somewhat bloated state might be ascribed to inordinate indulgence in caviar, and Brunhild herself, utterly demagnetized by her layoff.

Ussyshkin-Werther was conducting the run-through; he was also verbally setting the stage:

"The ringmaster announces the entrance of the Talking Dog. A small table is brought on and covered with a cloth.

The table is set with a water bottle and a hand bell. Brunhild comes on. She isn't wearing any of those bourgeois fripperies, of course, like jingle-bells, ribbons, long curls—away with them! She has on an unassuming long blouse, the kind Leo Tolstoi used to wear, and is carrying a brief case—not a leather one, however, but one made of canvas. The outfit of a rank-and-file member of society. Then Brunhild proceeds to read a brief, creative document of twelve typewritten pages—"

And Werther had already opened his rosy yap to declaim Brunhild's speech when Captain Masuccio suddenly stepped forward.

"Wie viel?" he asked. "How many pages?"

"Twelve pages—typewritten," Grandpa Murzilka informed him.

"Aber," said the captain, *"Ich sterbe*—I am dying. After all, this no more than a dog is. *Ein Hund,* one dog, so to say. She cannot twelve typewriter pages speak. I complain shall."

"What's all this, now—are we getting something in the nature of self-criticism?" the Chairman of the Artistic Council asked with a sneer. "No, I can now clearly perceive that this dog ought to have its wrist slapped. And slapped hard."

"Bruder," Masuccio said imploringly, "this is still a young *Hund.* She yet everything does not know. She wants to. But she still cannot."

"I'm busy, I'm busy," the Chairman delivered his ultimatum. "We'll do without the dog. There'll be one number less. *Nolens volens,* you have my condolence, but I'm letting you out."

At this point even the Intrepid Captain paled. He called Brunhild to him and walked out of the circus, waving his arms and muttering: "This only *ein Hund* is, after all. She cannot everything at once master."

All traces of the Talking Dog vanished.

There are some who maintain that the dog went to pieces, forgot how to say her *unser, Bruder,* and *aber,* that she turned into an ordinary mutt and that they call her Polkan now.

However, those who maintain these things are just solitary bellyachers, nothing but parlor skeptics.

Some say otherwise. They maintain that their information is as recent as can be, that Brunhild is in good health, that she is performing and is a hit. They even say that, in addition to the old words, she has acquired several new ones. Of course that's not the same as memorizing twelve typewritten pages, *aber* it is something, after all.

1933

Ruvim Isaievich FRAERMAN

Something like fifteen years ago, in connection with another story by Fraerman, the editor had to admit his failure in unearthing any biographical data concerning this author. Further research at this point has met with no better success. One can merely surmise from his stories that, at the time they were written (about twenty years ago) he was a young man, and that he wrote of Siberia from first-hand knowledge, most probably that of a native, although the possibility of an involuntary residence there is not ruled out.

THE DEATH OF YUN FA-FU

1

Yun Fa-Fu had spent all the forty years of his life by the side of a river. And although this river was not a broad one, its voice was nevertheless loud, and it sounded constantly before the house of Yun Fa-Fu. Day and night it flowed down from the mountain into the dale, which was called the Dale of Yellow Earth. And the water in the river was also yellow. But, like water everywhere, during the day it glittered in the sun and, at night, was dark.

Yun Fa-Fu was a simple man, with coarse face and coarse hands. He could, however, do so many things with those same hands: turn a comb from the jasper he found in the mountains, or hammer out a bowl of copper in no way inferior to those bowls that are sold in Yu-Tai, the town near which Buddha used to discourse. But above all else Yun Fa-Fu loved to sow wheat and rice. And if there were not land enough for him on the river bank he would build a raft out on the water and strew clay over it: yellow silt which Yun carried over in a basket. And his house, too, was a dugout of this silt. Nor should anyone get the idea that Yun Fa-Fu ever felt uneasy in this house. It was cool inside in summer and warm in winter, and at the entrance to this cave, supporting its arches, stood carved pillars hewn out of mulberry trees. As for the walls, Yun Fa-Fu sprinkled them with water from the river every day and covered them with glaze.

Yun Fa-Fu began to feel uneasy in his house only from the day the enemy—the Japanese—arrived in Shan-si, his native land.

They showed no mercy for anyone. On the other side of the river and on this, villages were burned down, while Yun Fa-Fu's two sons and his father were killed. Thereupon Yun Fa-Fu went off to join the partisans in the mountains, taking his gun along. And, although the gun was not much better than the first one ever made in this world by man, Yun Fa-Fu soon became a terror to the foe.

"Yun Fa-Fu," the leader of the partisans told him, "cover your tracks, conceal your body, and go back to the bank the enemy has occupied. You know this region well. As for your gun, leave it here with us for the time being."

And so Yun Fa-Fu became a scout. He covered his tracks, concealed his body, even stopped meeting his friends. But, to make up for that, his name soon became an object of hatred to the enemy. Not a day passed without the foe suffering a disaster: trains crashed down slopes and every movement of the enemy's troops became known to the partisans. The enemy was forced to give ground in defending his lines of communication. He abandoned one side of the river so that he might at least retain the other. But there, too, Yun Fa-Fu gave him no rest.

Thereupon a reward was offered for Yun's head. For a long time, however, no one showed up to put in a claim for it. But one day the soldiers brought someone to Major Tasimara—it was not Yun Fa-Fu, of course, but a neighbor of his, a rich Korean miller called Tsoi Nam-guy.

"Pay heed to my poverty and hearken to my wretchedness,"

said the miller, after making low obeisance. "Last year Yun Fa-Fu cut down a mulberry tree growing on the boundary of my field. And today I heard that about nightfall he will have to swim across the river here, near these reeds. But I know nothing concerning Yun Fa-Fu. Yet if there be any reward forthcoming for this information I may have earned it."

"And that is all you have come to tell me concerning Yun Fa-Fu?" asked the major.

"That is all," answered the miller.

"In that case you have told me nothing, yet you would like to receive the reward. For Yun has swum across this river many times. But probably he must swim like an eel, since we are not able to catch him. Just the same, I shall reward you if you will tell me the things Yun Fa-Fu liked to do when he was living in his house."

"That I can tell you," the miller made haste to answer. "Very early, when the shadow of my mill was lying still at a slant on the water, he loved to loosen the clods of his field with a mattock. He loved the morning rain, and the rain at evening. He loved to lift children up off the ground and to perch them on his shoulders, and took even my son in his arms, although I had strictly forbidden this."

"There, now, you see? Yet you said you knew nothing of Yun Fa-Fu. You know a very great deal about him," said the major with a faint smile. "Go, tell the soldiers to bring your son to me."

"What do you want my son for?" asked Tsoi Nam-guy in fright—since who could tell what Major Tasimara might have in mind with that faint smile of his?

But the major made no answer. And, since the major's teeth were crooked and long, like a polecat's, Tsoi Nam-guy naturally stepped back, without putting any more questions, and made still lower obeisance.

2

Yun Fa-Fu had been sitting a long while, lurking in the reeds by the river, with the river on all sides of him.

The warm water embraced his chest, his body, while coolness was fanning his face, since nightfall was nearing by now.

And so quietly did Yun Fa-Fu sit that tiny birds, yellow as hornets, sank down on the sedges close to him. And time went on, without any intervals. Only rarely did he put his head out and peer at the opposite bank, occupied by the enemy. By this time, however, there was not a single white-putteed soldier to be seen there. And this gladdened Yun Fa-Fu. He was waiting only for the fog to settle on the water and for the mountain magpies to fly to their nests for the night. Then, in the darkness, he would swim across the river without a sound. But for the time being he remained without stirring and watched a tall crane that stood among the reeds, just as unstirring as he. It was a sacred bird of the hue of lead and ashes, and slender white plumes that looked like strands of an ancient's hair drooped from its head. And Yun Fa-Fu, recalling his aged father who had been killed by the enemy, burst into tears, since (I repeat) he was a simple man and held that one must weep for the dead but love the living.

And at this point he caught a low sound that came to him from the river: it was either the voice of a woman or the faint plash of oars—one could not tell which. He parted the thick river grass that screened him like a curtain and looked out over the river.

Borne along by the current, floating down the very middle of the river, was a fisherman's boat. It was swirling upon the water like a leaf fallen off a willow. The woman standing up in the boat was managing it but poorly. Holding an oar with one hand she was clutching a child to her with the other.

"Why, she will drown!" Yun Fa-Fu reflected and looked ahead to see if anyone were hastening to her aid. But no matter where he looked, no one else was in sight.

Meanwhile the boat had begun to fill with water, and the woman was clutching the child still closer, defending it against death. And the child was whimpering.

"Is that not the voice of the son of Tsoi Nam-guy, the miller?" Yun Fa-Fu wondered.

And, suddenly, the boat careened and the woman and child fell into the river.

What Yun Fa-Fu did then was to follow the involuntary prompting of his heart. With his shoulder he clove the water, thrust it back hard with his foot, and ten strokes of his arms brought him alongside the boat. He seized the child and held it high out of the water upon his broad palm. And he called out to the woman: "Hold on tight to me!"

She swam up to him, still hanging on to the boat with one hand. And at that very instant Yun Fa-Fu felt a fearful blow from a short sword.

The cry of the child, who had again fallen into the water, rang out over the yellow river—and another cry, just as loud, came in answer to it from the river bank. It was the cry of Tsoi Nam-guy the miller, who had witnessed the death of his son.

As for Yun Fa-Fu, the thought came to him as the water filled his lungs and he was losing blood and consciousness: "That was no woman. They have caught me, even as birds are caught in snares."

And, in a short while, Yun Fa-Fu, still alive, was brought before Major Tasimara.

"Is this he?" Major Tasimara asked Tsoi Nam-guy, the miller.

"Yes, it is he," answered the miller, weeping for his son.

"There, now you may receive your reward," said the major, with a faint smile.

And, even before the mountain magpies started flying to their nests for the night, Yun Fa-Fu was executed against the wall of his house. Also, as the execution was in progress, Major Tasimara was saying to his friends: "Our day is our day—and not the day of our fathers. I have caught him merely because one must know the value and measure of all things."

In the meantime Yun Fa-Fu, with his throat slashed, was lying flat on his back upon the yellow silt out of which he had built his house and from which he used to wrest his bread, and the palms of his hands, accustomed to grasping a mattock, were turned to the earth, while his face was turned up to the sky, the profundity of which was immeasurable.

In the morning the soldiers cast Yun Fa-Fu's corpse into the river. And the wind from the mountains of Iin-Shaniu, gently, without raising any waves, drove it down the current.

Yet word of the death of Yun Fa-Fu floated down ahead of the wind.

The fishermen from the village of San-Chihoi came out in boats to intercept his body, and bore it over a flinty road up into the mountains, whither more and more recruits from the river folk were flocking to the partisans.

And here, near a quiet mountain temple, amid the blossoms of peach and cherry trees, they buried Yun Fa-Fu, and upon the lid of his coffin they drew in india ink the radiant ideographs of manship:

To His Glorious Name None Is Indifferent

1938

Boris Leonidovich PASTERNAK

[1890—]

*One of his poems is called "The Urals for the
First Time"; all his books might be called
"The Universe for the First Time."* . . .
*Of course, Bunin is more comprehensible—
and it is also easier to obtain fire by
striking safety matches than to strike
it from flint. But hearts catch fire from
flint sparks; matches are for cigarettes.*
ILYA ERENBURG (1920)

Pasternak is a native of Moscow; his father was an illustrator
and his mother a pianist. He studied law (University of Moscow), music (under Scriabin), and philosophy (Moscow and
Marburg, under Herman Cohen); visited Italy briefly; returned to Russia shortly before the Great Revolution. During
World War I, he worked in a factory in the Urals; after the
Revolution he was a librarian. In 1912 he started writing ex-
perimental poetry, but did not become well known until after
the Revolution. (*Doctor Zhivago* is by no means his first
unwilling participation in the far from amusing game of
Russian literary musical chairs.) In 1935 he was, in effect,
condemned to what is considered (at least in the American
area of the Free World) a Fate Worse Than Death: he hit the
literary skid-row of translation. However, neither the Russian
readers nor Verlaine, Goethe, Shelley, the poets of Georgia
and Armenia and, above all, that rude-mechanics-and-ground-
lings-hating bourzhui Shakespeare, have lost by the deal. His
translations, even by the admittedly high Russian standards,
are superb.

His stature as a great and exquisite poet is one point which needs no abiding of judgment. Russia, once so generously rewarded by God with poets (to quote Gogol), can (but does not) boast of the two (just two) surviving today. Pasternak is Russia's only living male poet of stature and authenticity, and the very last of Russia's intellectuals.

He is pre-eminent, however, only as a poet and a translator of poets. Even with the very long *Doctor Zhivago* his prose output is, perhaps not unfortunately, rather meager. Unfortunately, most of it has been more or less available in English, of a sort, for the last fifteen years, and Pasternak, even before the *succès fou* of his only novel, had become primarily a caviar-cult for M.A.'teur cognoscenti and thick-ankled priestesses of Culture.

"A District in the Rear" has the virtues of being thoroughly characteristic and of being just about the only piece of his prose which, as of the present, has not yet appeared anywhere else in English. Regrettably, it has not the added advantage of having been suppressed. It is considered, by non-Soviet critics, as either an attempt at a continuation of "The Childhood of Luvers" or a preliminary study for a chapter in *Doctor Zhivago*.

MARCH*

The sun is hotter than the top ledge in a steam bath;
The ravine, crazed, is rampaging below.
Spring—that corn-fed, husky milkmaid—
Is busy at her chores with never a letup.

* The poetical selections are from *The Poems of Yurii Zhivago,* translated by Bernard Guilbert Guerney and constituting the concluding part of *Doctor Zhivago,* by Boris Pasternak, published (and copyright, 1958) by Pantheon Books, Inc., New York. The editor hereby gratefully acknowledges his indebtedness to Pantheon Books, Inc., for permission to include these selections in this anthology.

The snow is wasting (pernicious anemia—
See those branching veinlets of impotent blue?)
Yet in the cowbarn life is burbling, steaming,
And the tines of pitchforks simply glow with health.

These days—these days, and the nights also!
With eavesdrop thrumming its tattoos at noon,
With icicles (cachectic!) hanging on to gables,
And with chattering of rills that never sleep!

All doors are flung open—in stable and in cowbarn;
Pigeons peck at oats fallen in the snow;
And the culprit of all this and its life begetter—
The pile of manure—is pungent with ozone.

1957

WIND

I have died, but you are still among the living.
And the wind, keening and complaining,
Makes the country house and the forest rock—
Not each pine by itself
But all the trees as one,
Together with the illimitable distance;
It makes them rock as the hulls of sailboats
Rock on the mirrorous waters of a boat basin.
And this the wind does not out of bravado
Or in a senseless rage,
But so that in its desolation
It may find words to fashion a lullaby for you.

1957

STAR OF THE NATIVITY

It was wintertime.
The wind blew from the plain
And the Infant was cold
In the cave on the slope of a knoll.

The breath of an ox served to warm Him.
The cattle were huddling
Within the cave.
Warmth hovered in a mist over the manger.

Up on a cliff shepherds shook from their sheepskins
The straws from their pallets
And stray grains of millet
And sleepily stared into the midnight distance.

Far off were fields covered over with snow,
And a graveyard, and gravestones and fences,
A cart with its shafts deep in a snowdrift
And, over the graveyard, a star-studded sky.

And seemingly near yet unseen until then,
Its light more timorous than that of a tallow dip
Set in the window of some watchman's hut,
A star glimmered over the road to Bethlehem.

Now it looked like a hayrick blazing
Off to one side from heaven and God;
Like the reflection of an arsonous fire,
Like a farmstead in flames or a threshing floor burning.

It reared in the sky like a fiery stack
Of straw, of hay,
In the midst of a Creation startled, astounded
By this new Star.

An increasing redness that was like a portent
Was glowing above it.

And three stargazers heeded, and hasted
To answer the call of these unwonted lights.

Gift-laden camels plodded behind them,
And caparisoned asses, each one smaller and smaller,
Were daintily, cautiously descending a hill.

And all of the things that were to come after
Sprang up in the distance as a strange prevision:
All the thoughts of the ages, all the dreams, all the worlds,
All the future of galleries and museums,
All the pranks of goblins, all the works of the workers of
        miracles,
All the yule trees on earth, all the dreams of small children,
All the warm glow of tremulous candles, all chains,
All the magnificence of brightly hued tinsel. . . .
(Ever more cruel, more raging, the wind blew from the plain.)
. . . All rosy-cheeked apples, all the blown-glass gold globes.

Part of the pond was screened by alders
But, beyond rook nests among the treetops,
Part could be seen clearly from the brink of the cliff.
The shepherds could mark well the camels and asses
Threading their way at the edge of the milldam.
"Let us go with all the others and worship the miracle,"
Said they, and muffled their sheepskins about them.

Plowing through snow made their bodies feel warm.
Tracks of bare feet, glinting like mica,
Led over the bright plain and beyond the inn's hut,
And the dogs sighting these tracks by the Star's light
Growled at them as if at a candle-end's flame.

The frosty night was like a fairy tale,
And some beings from the snow-crushed mountain ridge
Were mingling constantly, unseen, with all the others.
The dogs were wavering, looking back in terror,
And, in dire foreboding, cringed close to a young shepherd.

Through the same countryside, over the same highway
Some angels walked among the throng of mortals.
Their incorporeality made them invisible
Yet each step they took left the print of a foot.

Day was breaking. The trunks of the cedars stood out.
A horde of men milled by the stone at the cave's mouth.
"Who are you?" Mary asked them.
"We are from a shepherd tribe, and envoys of heaven.
We have come to sing praises to both of you."
"You cannot all enter. Bide awhile here."

In the gloom before dawn, gray as cold ashes,
The drovers and shepherds stamped to keep warm.
Those come on foot bickered with those who came mounted.
Near the hollowed-out log that served as a water trough
The camels bellowed, the gray asses kicked out.

Day was breaking. Dawn swept the last of the stars
Off heaven's vault as if they were ash motes.
And Mary, out of all the countless multitude, allowed
Only the Magi to enter the cleft in the crag.

He slept, all refulgent, in the manger of oakwood,
Like a moonbeam within a deep-hollowed tree.
In lieu of sheepskins His body was warmed
By the lips of an ass and the nostrils of an ox.

The Magi stood in shadow (the byre seemed in twilight);
They spoke in whispers, groping for words.
Suddenly one, in deeper shadow, touched another
To move him aside from the manger, a little to the left.
The other turned: like a guest about to enter,
The Star of the Nativity was gazing upon the Maid.

1957

A DISTRICT IN THE REAR

I

I remember that evening as if I were confronted with it right
now. Everything happened at my father-in-law's mill. I had
gone to town on horseback that day to attend to some of his
business matters.

I had started out early. Tonia and Shura were still asleep when I tiptoed out of their rooms into the glimmer of the night that was coming to its end. All around the birches were standing knee-deep in grass and in the whining of mosquitoes, peering intently at some point whence autumn was nearing. I was heading in the same direction.

There, beyond a ravine, stood a house with a yard; we had been living there but had moved to a forester's hut a short while before to make the place available for a summer resident. She was expected from day to day. Among the other matters I had to attend to in town, I would have to call on her.

I had on new boots, as yet not broken in. As I bent over to adjust the right heel something heavy flew noisily high above me. I raised my head. Two squirrels were playing tag, flying through the leafage with the speed of bullets. Here and there the trees came to life, tossing them with a long swing from treetop to treetop. Although the chase and pursuit were broken by frequent flights through the air, the latter were done with such smoothness that they left the impression of some sort of a scamper over the level stretch of the predawn sky. And there, beyond the ravine, Demid our farmhand was thundering with a water pail, opening the stable door and saddling Magpie.

The last time I had been to town was the middle of July. Three weeks had passed since then and during that time many changes for the worse had taken place. Truth to tell, I found it difficult to form any judgment about them. Alexander Alexandrovich had gone through with his insane purchase at the very beginning of the war. On the first day of our arrival from Moscow at the mill, as the local people called his forested acquisition for old times' sake, the Ural face of Uriatin was already obscured by refugees, Austrian prisoners of war and a multitude of military personnel and civilians, tossed up here from both capitals by the necessities of wartime, which were becoming ever more complicated. The town no longer represented anything by itself and merely reflected, as in a mirror, the changes taking place in the country and at the front.

The waves of evacuation had surged as far as this even before. But when, from the railroad crossing beyond the

Skobniaki, I beheld the mountains of equipment from the pre-
Baltic region dumped along the ways of the freight station
under the open sky, the thought came to me that years would
pass before someone happened to recall these alcohol stoves,
these rolled-steel tubes from Ravel, and so on, and that it
would not be we but these very mounds of rust which would
at some time bear witness as to how all this would end.

Despite the early hour, activity at the quarters of the military
commander was at its peak. Out in the yard the headman
of a crowd of Tatars and Votiaks was explaining that his
village was weaving baskets for sulphuric acid carboys for
the temporarily merged Maloyashvinsky and Nizhnevarynsky
plants engaged in defense work. In such cases the peasants of
entire districts were allowed to remain in their localities upon
the simple declarations of the plants. The mistake this group
had made consisted of their having shown signs of life and
allowing somebody to catch sight of them. Their dossier had
been lost in the shuffle and now, since those who had lost it
did not want to be burdened with a boring search for it, they
were being driven to the front. Even though their arguments
were acknowledged in the pleasantly warm office, out in the
yard no one would listen to them.

My papers proved to be in order, and the statute of exemp-
tions for hernias and ruptures, which allowed Demid to rove
in freedom, was also not disputed.

Around the corner from the military office, on the Hay-
market opposite the cathedral, was an inn, and there I stabled
Magpie, who was a hindrance in town where I had no great
distances to cover. It was Assumption, a fast day. For more
than a year no spirits had been sold in the government stores.
But because of its quiet and somberness the inn was exceptional
even amid the general sobering-up. A bootleg trade in fer-
mented mares' milk was carried on under its broad roof. If
one did not count the host, the place was a realm of women.
One of the landlord's daughters-in-law took the horse from
me.

"You haven't been thinking of selling?" the host asked me
from somewhere above, leaning out of a window and propping

his head on his hand. I did not at first grasp what his query referred to.

"No, we're not getting ready to sell," I answered. Evidently rumors of our forest lands had reached town and had become a byword on all tongues.

The street blinded me after the murkiness of the inn yard. Finding myself on foot after being in the saddle, I felt the coming of morning for a second time, as it were. Carts filled with cabbages and carrots were crawling along to market later than usual. They never got beyond Dvoryanskaya Street. By now they were being stopped at every step as if they were some very rarely seen phenomena, and their contents were bought up while they were still on their way to market. The peasant women who had raised the vegetables stood up in the carts and, as if they were haranguing from a public rostrum, vowed to serve everybody, but this failed to mollify the crowd, which was more noisy and quarrelsome than provincial crowds usually are and which kept increasing around the carts.

On my way to the town office of the Ustkrymzhensky plants, as I was going up a staircase painted to look like marble, I caught up with a gray-bearded townsman of Uriatin; he was wearing a short overcoat of Siberian cut with pleats that bestowed something feminine to his waist at the back. He was slowly clambering ahead of me and, on entering the office, blew his nose into a red bandanna, put on silver-rimmed spectacles and fell to studying the announcements in motley display on the wall to the left of the entrance. Beside the printed advertisements and prospectuses, in black and white and in color, which had been covering the wall for a long time, there showed whitely upon it several columns of slips of paper, typewritten and in longhand, and it was precisely these which attracted his attention.

Here were notices about the purchase of timber, standing and cut; requests for bids on contracts for all sorts of carting; a notice to workers and clerical help about a single bonus, amounting to three months' pay, due to the high cost of living; calls to reserve militiamen of the second category to report to the personnel desk. There was also an order about issuing to the workers and clerical help of food supplies from the company stores at a fixed monthly quantity and at prices approximating those charged before the war.

" 'Thirty-three and three-quarter pounds of rye flour, at the rate of one rouble thirty-five kopecks for thirty pounds; two pints of sunflower-seed oil at—' " the Uriatin burgher was reading aloud, a syllable at a time. Later on I found him in front of one of the counters, making inquiries as to whether the management would agree to settle for the advertised contracts not in bank notes but in card systems (that was precisely what he said), according to the specimen card on display. For a long while the clerks could not grasp what he was after, but when they did understand they told him that he was in an office and not a flour depot. I did not hear how the misunderstanding ended. My interest was diverted by Vyahrishchev.

The accounting department was partitioned in two by grilled counters; Vyahrishchev had planted himself in the middle of the room, thus compelling the young men in bellying jackets who were dashing with armfuls of paper out of the door of the managers' offices to veer; he was telling anecdotes to everybody in the place and choking on hot tea which he took, glass after glass, without finishing a single one, from the tray of a woman cook who came several times to distribute the tea in the office.

He was a military man from St. Petersburg, with the rank of captain, clean-shaven and sarcastic, and was in charge of receiving matériel at the war plants for the Chief Artillery Procurement Administration. These plants were about twenty miles to the south of Uriatin, i.e., in the opposite direction from our place. This was a long trip and had to be made on horses. Occasionally, when we were sent for, we went there as guests; this, however, has nothing to do with Vyahrishchev. The story of what sustained his constant wit deserves to be told.

II

I set out to see Istomina.

There was a story or two concerning this woman. She was a native of these parts—from Perm, apparently—and her destiny was somehow complicated and ill-starred. Her father, who had the un-Russian name of Luvers, had been ruined by the fall of certain stocks and had shot himself when she was still a child. The children and their mother had moved to Moscow. Then, when the daughter married, she had somehow found herself once more in her native region. The stories current about her had to do with the most recent period and will not take up much of our time.

Although instructors in institutions of learning were not subject to mobilization, her husband, Vladimir Vassilievich Istomin, who taught physics and mathematics in the Uriatin *gymnasia*, had volunteered for the front. For two years now there had been neither word nor sign from him. He was thought to be one of those killed in action, and his wife would by turns suddenly feel certain about her unconfirmed widowhood or have doubts about it.

I went to her official living quarters in the new *gymnasia* building, running up the back-stairs of several long flights in a very cramped stairwell, which consequently seemed crooked. The staircase reminded me of something.

The same feeling of familiarity overcame me at the threshold of her apartment. Several packing boxes, waiting to be wrapped, were standing in the foyer; through it one could see a corner of the dark drawing room taken up by a bookcase, empty and moved from its place, and a mirror which had been taken down. Through the windows, which probably faced north, one could see the school garden, its greenery ablaze from the light behind it. There was an unseasonable odor of naphthalene.

On the floor in the drawing room a pretty little girl of six was packing her dolls and their household effects and tying the bundle with a strip of soiled surgical gauze. I coughed. The girl raised her head. Istomina looked in from the room beyond; she was carrying an armful of gaily colored kerchiefs, the bottom ones trailing the floor while she held the top ones down with her chin. She was challengingly good-looking—almost offensively so. The restraint of her movements was very becoming to her and, perhaps, calculated.

"There, I have made up my mind at last," said she, without letting go of the armful of kerchiefs. "I've been leading you by the nose for a rather long while." A traveling hamper was standing open in the middle of the drawing room. She tossed the kerchiefs into it, adjusted her dress, smoothed down her hair and approached me. We exchanged greetings.

"The villa is furnished," I reminded her. "Why would you need your furniture there?" The thoroughness of her preparations made me uneasy.

"Why, that is really so, come to think of it!" she became agitated. "What am I to do now? The drays have been promised for three o'clock. Dunya, what time is it on your kitchen clock? Oh—why, I myself sent her to the janitor's. Katia, stop getting underfoot, for Christ's sake!"

"It's twelve," I told her. "The thing to do is to dismiss the extra moving men and retain just one. You still have a lot of time."

"Oh, but that isn't really what matters."

This was said almost with despair. I could not grasp what she was referring to. Suddenly I began getting an inkling of things. Probably she would no longer be permitted to stay in the official living quarters and she was hoping to find a permanent haven in our place. This would explain her belated removal. It would be necessary to warn her that we spent the winters in Moscow, the summer villa being boarded up when we left.

At this point the rumble of voices reached us from the staircase. Soon it filled the entry as well. In the doorway appeared a maid carrying several rolls of new matting, then the janitor came in with two boxes which he noisily lowered to the floor. Apprehensive of a preliminary delay I began saying good-bye.

"Well, now," I said, "I extend my best wishes, Eugenia Vikentievna. Hope to see you again soon. The roads have dried; it will be sheer pleasure to travel now."

Out in the street I recalled that I would not be starting

directly for home after leaving the inn but would have to drop in at the office for a small parcel which had been left for Alexander Alexandrovich. However, before going to the Hay-market I decided to stop at the railway depot for a bite: the buffet there was famous for its low prices and the excellence of its kitchen. On the way my thoughts reverted to Istomina.

Before this interview I had seen her two or three times, and at each encounter I had been haunted by a feeling that I had already seen her on some previous occasion. For a long while I considered this feeling deceptive and did not seek any explanation for it. Istomina herself contributed to that feeling. She was bound to remind everyone of something; she herself often resembled a recollection because of a certain vagueness about her mannerisms.

At the railway depot everything was in the wildest confusion. I immediately grasped that I would not fare any too well. Starting out as streams from the ticket windows, the churning throngs shortly filled all parts of the depot, with hardly room to turn in. The patrons in the buffet consisted for the most part of the military. Half of them could not find places at the tables and they milled about the diners, strolling in the aisles, smoking (despite the *No Smoking* signs posted everywhere), and perched on window sills. Some sort of a military man was constantly trying to spring up from his seat at one end of the main table; he was being restrained by his fellow officers. Amid the general hubbub one could not hear what was going on there but, to judge by the gesticulations of the waiter, who was trying to make excuses, it was he who was being shouted at. The manager of the buffet, a fat fellow who seemed to have been inflated to his unnatural proportions by the clattering of dishes in the place and by the proximity of the platform for arriving trains, was traversing the hall as he headed toward the disturbance.

I, too, attempted to go out on the platform so as to by-pass the crush and make my way to town along the tracks, but the doorman would not let me through. What struck the eye as one looked through the panes of the exit door was the unusual emptiness of the platform for arriving trains. The porters standing there were looking in the direction of an open platform

situated far along the tracks and serving as a continuation of
the covered platforms. The station master passed by on his
way there, accompanied by two gendarmes. People were saying
that there had been some fuss there during the recent en-
trainment of a regiment for the front, but no one rightly knew
just what it had been about.

I recalled all this toward the end of my return ride over
a road through a forest belonging to the Rynvensky official
villa, where Magpie, just as if she had become infected by
my fatigue, settled down to a walk, tossing her head, her
sides heaving. At this spot the same sort of thing was happening to the forest that had happened to my horse and to myself.
The road cut through the forest; it was little used and overgrown with grass. It seemed as if it had not been man who
had laid it out, but as if the forest itself, crushed by its own
unencompassableness, had stepped aside of its own volition at
this point to think things over at leisure. The vista seemed to
be its soul.

At its other end a rectangle of white, fenced in with rough
palings, wedged itself forward like a cape. It consisted of the
Yassyr-owned fields of summer corn. A little further on a
poverty stricken hamlet showed itself. The forest which framed
it against the horizon closed in a new wall still further on.
The Yassyrs and their oats were left behind as an insignificant
islet. Probably, just as in neighboring Pyatibratsk, the peasants
rented part of their land from the allotments.

I was riding at a walk and, as I slapped at the mosquitoes
on my hands, on my forehead and neck, was thinking about
my people, about my wife and son to whom I was returning.

I was thinking of them, catching myself in the thought that
I would arrive soon, and once more they would never learn
how I had been thinking of them as I rode over this road, and
it would seem to them that I loved them insufficiently, as if
I loved, in the way they wanted to be loved, some other and
remote thing, something that was similar to solitariness and
the pacing of a horse, something that was similar to a book.
Yet I simply had not the strength to explain to them that these
very things were nothing else save themselves and that their
dissatisfaction would be a torment to me.

It was astonishing how much justice there was on their side. All these things were signs of the times. They were perceived by the artless intuition of one's intimates. Something less known and more remote than all these predilections was already looming beyond the forest and was bound to sweep in a whirlwind over human destinies. And they had a presage of the coming partings and changes.

There was something odd about that autumn. Just as if nature, before drinking down the sea and having the sky as a bite after it, had gotten the notion of catching her breath, and that breath had been cut short. The cuckoo did not cuckoo rightly; the ripened air of the afternoon did not show rightly white and flattened out; certain herbs did not grow and redden rightly. And one man who did not know of anything more precious to him than his family was not returning rightly to that family.

After a while the forest thinned out. Beyond a shallow dell, which bordered on the forest and into which the road dipped only to rise again shortly, a foothill appeared with several structures on it. The grove in which the estate was situated served it as a substitute for an enclosure. The grove was so neglected that it might well have envied the woodpiles the foresters had prepared against the winter and which were to be found in various parts of the adjoining forest. Of all the follies committed by Alexander Alexandrovich this one was perhaps the most unforgivable. An old schoolfellow of his who was active in the local industries had sought out this witches' haunt for him. Alexander Alexandrovich, without as much as a look, gave his written consent to the deal instead of acquiring meadowlands somewhere in Central Russia, where his stores of knowledge concerning animal husbandry would have proved of great benefit to him. But benefits were something this educated and at that time still young man gave the least thought to. He, too, devoted his thoughts to that which was remote and abstract. For it was not by mere chance that I had been brought up in his house on an equal footing with Tonia, his daughter. Be that as it may, the situation was no longer something to joke about. What it called for was the sale of his treasure trove as soon as possible for firewood, for which there fortunately was a demand. Factories were changing over from mineral fuels to wood; there was more talk about this in town than about anything else.

The raspberry-colored roof of the wing of the house came into view. Magpie broke into a gallop. From a hill I caught sight of Tonia and Shura, laughing as they came running toward me from the direction of the ravine. The stable had been left wide open ever since morning. No sooner had I set foot to ground than the horse, tearing the reins out of my hand, made a dash into the stable for the feed and rest it offered and which the animal found too tantalizing to its eyes and nose. Shura began to jump and clap his hands, as though this performance had been gone through especially for his entertainment.

"Let's go in to supper," said Tonia. "How is it you're limping?"

"I simply can't step on this foot—it's gone to sleep. Never mind, it'll pass as soon as I stretch my legs a little."

Demid came out from around a corner of a shed and, after making a most depressing bow, went off to unsaddle and groom Magpie.

"By the way, there's an offering for Papa strapped on behind the saddle. It ought to be unstrapped and carried in. Where is he, incidentally?"

"Papa has left until Tuesday. Some people came from the plants today. Today is the ninth; some Maria or other is having a birthday there. And what is this package?"

"An allotment of provisions. If he's at Krymzha, so much the better. He'll get a second allotment."

"Are you angry, perhaps?"

"Judge for yourself—this is becoming systematic. We are neither loafers nor holy innocents, and as for your papa he is simply fine. Yet at the same time during my childhood I was living at the expense of all of you, Papa was living at the expense of his kindred, his kindred at the expense of somebody or other, and so on, *ad infinitum*. Yet we could live without being parasites. How many times did I offer to sum up what we know and what we can do—"

"Well, what about it?"

"That's just it—it's too late now. This thing has spread and has become a universal evil. In town they're dreaming all the time of latching on to some payroll where the pickings are better. This is a reversion to the times of demoniacal possession —do you realize just what that is? Take anybody you like—he or she is attached fast to something or other and does not even realize how many hands he or she passes through in this process of bestowal and entrustment. The source of independent existence has run dry. You must agree that there isn't much in this to rejoice about."

"Oh, all that is old stuff and tiresome! Look at what you're doing—there's the effect of your monologues."

The boy was crying.

After supper and a reconciliation I went to the steep slope that broke off sharply at the back of the grove, over the river. Odd, how up to now I have said nothing about this demon of the place, mentioned in songs and marked on all maps, whatever their scale may be.

This was the Rynva in its upper reaches. It emerged from the north at a single burst, as if in full awareness of its riverine name, and right there at its place of emergence, less than half a mile above our cliff, dallied in indecision, as if it were running its eyes over the sites subject to its occupation. Each of its hesitancies spread out in a curve. Its contemplation created creeks. The broadest of these ran below our place. At this point it could easily have been taken for a forest lake. On its further bank another district began.

I had lain down on the grass. I had been lying in it, stretched out, but instead of contemplating the river was senselessly wriggling the tips of the tight boots, studying them from the height of a propped elbow. In order to see the river it was necessary to raise the eyes just the least trifle. I had been getting ready all this while to do this and had been constantly putting it off.

Everything had worked out not the way I had wanted it to, but it had not worked out contrary to my wishes and, consequently, it had not worked out for anybody. There was no insistence about my wishes. My compliance did not originate in kindness. It was frightful to think that there was hardly anything which I was not ready to renounce. My kindred would have been better off without me; I was spoiling their lives.

By degrees I fell into a round of thoughts which during those years all the people on earth were accustomed to and which varied only with the situation and personal makeup of each, as well as with the different aspects of the period in which they occurred: alarming in the year of 'fourteen, still more indeterminate in 'fifteen, and without a single glimmer of light in that year of 'sixteen, in the fall of which these events were taking place.

It again occurred to me that perhaps it would have been better if, despite repeated rejections because of physical defects, I might still have sniffed gunpowder smoke. I knew that these regrets weren't worth a copper; it would be better if I were doing something about it.

But my previous regrets on this score had been based upon love of life. I regretted because a lacuna would remain in it if at an hour so memorable to my native land I was not sharing in the military exploits of my coevals. Now I was regretful because of repugnance. I felt regret because nonparticipation in the war was preserving my life, which by now bore so little resemblance to itself that one wanted to part with it before it abandoned one of its own self. And parting with it with the greatest dignity and the utmost benefit was possible only at the front.

In the meantime our bank of the river had become shadowed over. Near the opposite bank the water lay like a piece of a cracked mirror. The bank was reflected in it with sinister vividness that was in keeping with the spirit of this ill omen. The riverbank was low. The reflections were sucked in under the grassy eyebrow of a meadow. The reflections were contracting and diminishing.

The sun set shortly. It set behind my back. The river became dusty; it had grown bristles, had become greasy. Suddenly its warty expanse began to send up wisps of smoke in several places at once, just as though it had been set on fire both from above and below.

In Pyatibratsk the dogs started barking; one could hardly

hear them at this distance, but they were barking for some patent cause. Their barking was caught up in a zone very close to me; these dogs were barking loudly but without any cause. The grass under me had become noticeably damp. The first stars kindled upon it, looking like forest berries of delirious vividness.

In a short while the distant barking was renewed, but the dogs had exchanged their roles in space. Now it was those nearest to me who were barking for cause, while those in the distance were acting as a low-voiced howling chorus. The clatter of wheels reached me from the forest road. The uneven sounds of an even flow of talk, such as one usually hears during a trip, came to my ears. The speakers were jouncing in their tarantass. Getting up from the wet grass I set out to meet our summer resident.

1938

A QUOTA OF SOVIET SAWS
AND SAYINGS

> *It is from such living thoughts that I learned*
> *to think and write. . . . In general, proverbs*
> *and sayings are exemplary formulations of the*
> *entire vital, social-historical experience*
> *of the working people, and for the writer*
> *it is absolutely necessary to familiarize*
> *himself with this material, which will*
> *teach him how to clench words as fingers*
> *are clenched into a fist, and to loosen words*
> *that have been clenched by others.*
>
> GORKI

To name the writing Russians who have loved and cherished the proverbs and sayings of their land would be to call the entire illustrious roster. In Russian statecraft, also, the value and usefulness of these nuggets of diversified folk wisdom have always been fully appreciated. Certain sayings of Peter the Great are in daily use; Catherine the Great not only collected but created them—and many of hers are still green and thriving; Lenin applied them with lethal impact in his writings and speeches, and the extreme efficacy with which Khrushchev uses them is testified to by the newspaper reports that our present Vice President had boned up on homely wit before venturing to Moscow, so as to be able to cite proverbs to his own purpose.

The Russian Revolution has, understandably, relegated certain categories of the proverb to the archives; the Soviet Ivan Ivanovich Ivanov no longer gives a belch in a gale of wind about Czar and Orthodoxy, nor does he equate law with injustice, as he once so unerringly did. Comments on marriage

435

are apparently fewer though still as pungent as they ever were, but the status of woman in Russia seems to have improved vastly: proverbs concerning this extremely interesting creature have lost a great deal of their coarseness and almost all their brutality (I am not disregarding the probable bowdlerizing efforts of *halturish* editors and compilers). The bewildered and exasperated Russian may still mutter *"Babië!"* ("Dames!") but I doubt, even if he is a Ukrainian, that he will come up with: "A woman has a trick in stock for every tick of the clock," or: "Love your wife as you love your soul, but shake her like a pear-tree bole."

Also, there should be very little startlingly new about the irreligious proverbs. Slavic mystics and mysticism were never taken seriously anywhere but in the Western world, and to most of the writers and other intellectuals of Russia the Mysterious Slavic Soul was never anything but a hearty joke. "According to you," Belinsky wrote a century and a decade ago in his famous letter to Gogol, "the Russian folk is the most religious in the world—which is a lie! . . . Look a little more closely and you will see that this is a profoundly atheistic folk. There is still a great deal of superstition in it, but there is not even a trace of religiousness. Superstition passes with the advances of civilization, but religiousness often contrives to live side by side with those advances. . . . The Russian folk is not like that: mystic exaltation is not in its nature; it has too much common sense and clarity and positiveness of mind for that, and therein, it may be, lies the enormous scope of its historic destinies in the future. . . . It is a sin to accuse the Russian folk of religious intolerance and fanaticism; it is rather to be praised for its exemplary indifference to this faith business."

Many of the selections here given (culled for the most part from a compendium published in Moscow in 1958) are, of course, not of Soviet coinage but of Soviet currency, such as the fighting maxims, so successfully revived during World War II, of Suvorov (1730-1800), military genius, grandee and eccentric, and of that other popular commander, Kutuzov (1745-1813), General Field Marshal and Grand Duke of Smolensk. Other perennials are universal maxims, but with a Slavic touch; some are of literary origin; all, I think, attest that the Russians, even without the benefit of Czar and/or God, are still human, all too human. Obviously, the proverb, too, has not escaped the ubiquitous *halturnik,* whose efforts have all the unalloyed sincerity of a singing commercial; fortunately, the redolence alone of such things as *Meela i bogata kolkhoznaya hata* (Darling and rich is the collective farm hut) is enough to betray their nonfolk origin. In short, currency has been the touchstone, and where I have at all doubted my own judgment I have not hesitated to check with those Soviet visitors (of late quite many) who have been lured into my bookshop by a quotation from Pushkin in the window.

This is the third thimbleful I have dipped up from the Pacific of the Russian proverb. If the saltiness of the contents should arouse in the reader a thirst for more—well, in the words of a justly popular American song, "Why not?"

They have their proverb,
we have ours.

AVIATION

He who is born to creep cannot fly. *Gorki*

We are all born with wings.

Even the North is a kind mother to our airmen.

You fly all right, but where will you alight?

It's a blessed day: from Moscow to America is just across the way.

People have many ways to reach one another, but the way through the air is the widest of all.

BUREAUCRACY

A lot of protocol, but nothing done at all.

Paper is patient—it never blushes for shame.

He reported but did not finish his report; he started to finish his report—and the report was his finish.

One *today* is better than two *tomorrows*.

CHARACTERIZATIONS

Even a tractor has character.

In words a pipe organ, in deeds a kopeck whistle.

A kopeck's ammunition but a rouble's ambition.

A *koulak's* spite endures till his death or yours.

Now and then there's a Jake who's never made a mistake.

As keen as an ax to criticize; as deaf as an ax handle to criticism.

Done for, like a Swede at Poltava.

If you have a Pole for a friend you don't need an enemy.

Not a man, but an armful of mistakes.

Spit in his face and he'll say it's dew from heaven.

See how clever the Americans are—they even invented monkeys! *

DRINK

The overseer isn't worth a pin if he's fond of gin.

One day's spree, two days sick, and you've lost the whole week.

* Before the Revolution this was said of the Germans; the clincher (as noted by Leskov) is still the same, however: Only they [the monkeys] couldn't squat but kept jumping all the while, until a Moscow furrier sewed tails on to them—and they had to squat.

Nothing like a spree to clean your pockets out.

He's got a hole in his throat.

The drunkard talks big, but the morning after fears a pig.

He's a surveyor on the Hard Drink Tract.

Many would drink but few know how.

FIGHTING   *Don't fear—and don't boast, either.*

If the foe does not yield he is destroyed. *Gorki*

A frightened foe is a beaten foe.

Don't trust the foe's laughter.

To think that a disarmed foe cannot kill you is to think that a spark cannot start a conflagration.

Don't spare the rod and spoil the enemy.

Don't spare the foe—that's all you have to know.

What matters the strain if the foe is slain?

If the fighter uses his head his foe will be dead.

If strength is of no avail, skill may prevail.

Use horse sense in war and the foe is done for.

A gun will kill, but so will skill.

The better you know your enemy the easier he is to conquer.

A soldier who's smart can make a hand grenade even out of his mitten.

A clever foe can be of benefit, but a stupid friend can harm you.

What's not managed right is the foe's delight.

Don't figure the foe for a sheep but a wolf.

Turn into a sheep—there will be wolves aplenty.

You don't discuss an order—you carry it out.

Let a spy slip through and you lose face.

If the picket isn't wide awake, the enemy is.

Learn courage from a scout, caution from a sapper.

Look with both eyes; see as if you had three.

A careless scout is worse than an enemy.

If you don't want the enemy to hear something, don't tell it to a friend.

It's a poor soldier who doesn't hope to be a general.

You'll never get to be a general warming your arse around a stove.

You won't take a town just by looking at it.

If you're afraid of the enemy don't be a frontier guard.

If you would live, fight to the death.

The eyes frighten but the hands act.

A hero is someone who hasn't met somebody stronger.

There's a slew of brave lads—once the fight is over.

Either your chest in medals or your head rolling in the bushes.

Even a mouse plays the hero in its hole—but let's see one that won't break into a cold sweat at the sight of a tomcat.

If you would see the enemy's back don't show him yours.

The foe can't put out the sun or put us on the run.

Cure the coward with danger. *Suvorov*

Where two are afraid, send one.

What's rain to a soldier who's been under a hail of lead?

It behooves a soldier to be healthy, brave, firm, resolute, truthful. *Suvorov*

Where a goat got through, a soldier will, too. *Suvorov*

Not every bullet hits a bone—now and then one lands in the bush. (*Ne vsyakaya pulya po kosti, inaya i po kustu.*)

Don't fear the bullet in flight but the one in the gun.

Don't fear the bullet you can hear.

Every bullet bears a threat, but not each one carries death.

A bullet is like a bee: run and it will sting you.

A bullet pays no heed to rank.

The bullet is a she-fool; the bayonet is a fine lad. *Suvorov*

The bullet is a she-fool but it will find the guilty man.

The bullet is pointed, and yet she's no sister to the bayonet.

A bullet will deceive, but a bayonet will not betray.

He dodged a bullet, but got lodged on a bayonet.

A bullet can catch up with you, for it's fleet, but a bayonet will knock you off your feet.

You can't get at a man behind a rock with a bullet, but you can dig him up out of the ground with a bayonet.

A bayonet is no steed—it won't ask for feed; yet it'll carry you far in need.

If the bayonet is not enough we'll throw in the gunstock.

If the bayonet breaks, use the gunstock; if the gunstock fails, use your fists; if your fists give out, use your teeth.

A Russian soldier knows no obstacles.

Even one fighter all alone on the battlefield is an army—if he's a Soviet fighter. (Very widely current during World War II; based on a very old proverb: A man all alone on the battlefield is no warrior.)

We knew whom we had taken on; that's why we won.

An *artel* is a good thing even to beat the enemy with.

Today a tractor driver in the field; tomorrow a tank driver at the front.

FOOLS   *Russia brags of her fools.*

The fool found a pastime: cracking nuts with his forehead.

His head has been sparingly seeded.

A lad as big as a cart, but his mind isn't worth a fart.

Teaching a fool is like pouring water into a barrel without a bottom, like carrying water in a sieve, like throwing peas against a wall.

He'd be quite intelligent if he weren't such a fool.

Where two fools are fighting, there's always a third watching.

You can tell an ass by his ears and his hee-haws, a bear by his claws, and a fool by the way he wags his jaws.

Watch out for a goat from the front, a horse from behind, but a fool from all sides. (*Priest* is also used in place of *fool*.)

You can send an ass to Paris but his coat will still be a rusty red when he gets back.

An ass won't be a steed even in Kiev.

The ass was invited to the wedding—to haul water and firewood.

No matter how big the ass, he still won't turn into an elephant.

You can shower him with medals, but the ass will still an ass remain. *Krylov*

The wise man silence maintains when a fool complains.

The old man tells you what he used to do; the young man tells you what he will do; the fool tells you what he is doing.

We put all our hopes on a fool, but the fool, now, he went and got wise.

Every man has his own sort of folly in his head.

We don't have to go overseas for fools; we've got untapped mother lodes of them right to home.

KNAVES

He's cut out of a knave and lined with a swindler.

He'll top any knave by a yard.

Sew a tail on him and you can't tell him from a dog.

He sure is a trader: he sells wind in summer, leaves in the fall, snow in winter and colds in the spring.

He clipped the ends and left nothing in the middle.

He'll hatch a live chick out of a baked egg.

He gets honey from dead bees.

He dips up soup with an awl—and even at that, let's a little dribble back.

Don't let a thief near a cart, nor a *koulak* near a collective farm.

Even a wolf has a fur coat, only it's sewn on to him.

"A joke is a joke," said the wolf to the trap, "but let go of my paw, now." *Krylov*

Every knave has his own bookkeeping system.

He'll meet you with a pie, and heave a brick for good-bye.

LEARNING

Love the book—source of all knowledge. *Gorki*

There's no shame in not knowing—the shame lies in not learning.

It's difficult to teach what we ourselves don't know.

There's no such thing as old age when it comes to study.

A kindhearted simpleton is better than an ill-tempered scholar.

Even a bear is taught to dance.

Without instruction you can't weave even a bast sandal.

Don't teach the lame man how to limp.

Don't teach a fish to swim.

It isn't up to the eggs to teach the hen.

Don't teach a goat—it will snatch hay off a cart all by itself.

For all that is good in me I am indebted to books. *Gorki*

LIARS AND LYING   *Lies pay no duty.*

Lie, but in moderation.

Lie, but remember.

Stand without swaying, walk without stumbling, speak without
    stuttering, lie without getting all tangled up in your lying.

He can lie without batting an eye.

If you lie you won't die, but folks will stop believing you by
    and by.

He gets so tangled up in his lies he can't go home to sleep.

He lied through dinner but had enough left for supper.

A liar is easier to catch than a lame man.

Lying isn't tiring—as long as folks believe you.

He lies so hard that the sleigh has to groan.

If one knew it all, one wouldn't lie at all.

LUCK: GOOD—

Our happiness is like water in a dragnet: as long as you pull
    the net it bulges, but get it ashore—and there's nothing in it.
    L. Tolstoi

Luck without sense is a wallet full of vents.

Luck is no horse: it won't carry you along a straight path; it won't obey the reins.

Luck is good, even when hunting for mushrooms.

Luck and ill luck ride in the same sleigh.

Some folks are born wearing shirts.

In the USSR he who likes to work has the best luck.

His cow walks around in slippers.

—AND BAD

Some folks can shave with an awl, but with us even a razor won't shave at all.

Don't go looking for hard luck—it will find you all by itself.

Woe rides on woe and uses woe for a whip.

Fire is woe and water also; yet there's no worse woe than having neither fire nor water.

Trouble is bearable with laughter; it is unbearable with tears.

Even a hen will jeer at misfortune.

Even an unloaded gun will fire at misfortune.

He gets along from button to buttonhole.

He'll tackle everything, but doesn't succeed at anything.

First pancake lumpy; last pancake full of scrapings.

I struggled, I fought, but came home with naught.

He went for wool, but came home sheared.

I earned a copper—and that one rolled away.

MAN

Man—that has a proud sound. *Gorki*

The lynx has its markings on the outside; but man, inside.

All men are people, but not all people are men.

Even an evil man will live out his lifetime.

From pole to pole there is no man that's whole.

Strangers are an impenetrable forest.

You may get to know a man after you've eaten seven potfuls of cabbage soup with him.

Water overpowers all things, but man overpowers water.

To the fish, water; to the fowl, air; but to man, all the earth.

RELIGION   *The Russian utters the name of God*
                            even as he scratches himself. BELINSKI

He who lies a lot swears by God a lot.

What rotgut is to the belly, religion is to the spirit. (*Chto sivukha dlya briukha, to religiya dlya dukha.*)

Once we had church and likker, now we have the club and flickers.

Dropping in at the club beats the priest's flubdub.

Icons and masses are strictly for asses.

The crop doesn't come by God's grace but from the sweat on your face.

Never mind Elijah and St. Nick: the reaper and tractor will turn the trick.

You can't knead dough with an amen.

God won't help you but science will.

If you're friendly with science you need in God place no reliance.

Don't teach the priest—that's the devil's business.

Folks' superstition is the priest's nutrition.

Where saints are found, devils abound.

You ought to take the dear little God by His dear little leg and smash Him against the floor. (An extremely old saying.)

God's all right in his way, but don't sell yourself too cheap.

Without God as a rider the road's a lot wider.

RUSSIA AND THE RUSSIANS *Be jealous of our example.*
M. LOMONOSSOV

Those who are lucky are born under the Soviet star.

There is no power that can our Union overpower.

He who advances against the land of Russia will stumble.

Russia was too cold for the French but too hot for the Germans.

The land of others we don't crave, but we won't give up the land we have.

He who loves his native land will fight the foe to the end.

The fuller our ears of grain, the stronger our voice.

Life was dark and full of tears; it has become radiant during the Collective years.

Trouble and care are at an end; we live and serve our Soviet native land.

Live a long life and all life long serve our native land.

If it's to serve the people, you can manage to live even at the North Pole.

The Soviet village is one big family.

If all the people were to let out one breath at the same time, there would be a mighty wind.

The sea will never run dry and the people will not go astray.

Where the people have the power, victory and freedom are their dower.

The first man in a soviet is the first one to be held responsible.

Buckwheat grits are our mother, rye bread is our father.

There's lots of mushrooms overseas, too, but they ain't for our basket.

And life is good, and it is good to live. *Mayakovsky*

Moscow does not believe tears.

The Soviet people always looks ahead.

The Soviet beacon light shines far through the night.

SKEPTICISM

Oh, yes—when the crawfish will whistle.

—when the German will be human.

—when the Pole will turn honest.

That happened in the reign of Czar Codpease and Czaritza Carrottop.

Old stuff, from 'way back.

Make friends with the wolf but hold on to your ax.

"Still pounding water?"—"I am."—"But is any dust rising?"—"No."—"Keep on pounding."

Our little hen calfed and our shoat laid an egg.

The man says he caught a rabbit with a creel and a pike in a wolf trap.

SLUGGARDS

They live without reaping grain, but they eat the bread.

A shirker in a *kolhoz* fares like a wolf in a hard frost.

Don't let a goat into a cabbage patch and keep a lazy man out of a *kolhoz* barn.

When the Cossack isn't swilling vodka he's killing lice—but you'll never catch him loafing.

He can sleep sitting up, but he always lies down on the job.

His belly has dislocated his kneecaps.

He doesn't mind swallowing, but chewing is too much like work.

Lazy Andy always has an excuse handy.

He has a green thumb: work grows moldy in his hands.

His hut is roofed over with the sky; his field is fenced in with space.

White hands love work—if it's done by others.

Ever since childhood I have grown to hate those who are fat.
  Mayakovsky

A slacker in a factory is the same as a deserter at the front.

Drones have Sunday even on Monday.

He who doesn't work doesn't know what rest means.

TRAITORS

Those in error are corrected; those who are traitors are destroyed.

To kill one traitor is to save a thousand men.

The snake changes its skin once a year, but a traitor changes his every day.

For a dog on the make, an aspen stake. (A stake of aspen **is** considered an infallible quietus for a vampire.)

Even a forest will not stand if it is not thinned out.

WORK—   *Unity is a giant.*

During harvest time every man is a soldier at the front.

The bees and the ants live in an *artel;* they work fast and well.

One bee won't bring in a lot of honey.

A man all on his own will perish even at a pot of porridge.

At a Collective table the food is tastier.

A tractor in the *kolhoz*—grain on the cart.

Like tractor driver, like tractor.

We reaped rye with our hands before—now we have combines galore.

A brigadier* on the lea is like the captain at sea.

If his rye grows right, the brigadier's bright.

Where the brigadier is a dame, the men don't get to stop for a smoke.

Live and don't worry—there are no field boundaries now.

One *kolhoznik* can tell another by the way he works.

No need to fear the frost if the *kolhoz* is behind you.

The crop doesn't come so much from heavenly dew as from the sweating you do.

He who discipline does not shirk, always comes in time for work.

You won't grow rich working for a *koulak,* but you sure will grow a hump on your back.

Hired out, sold out.

A factory's glory is not in its plan but in its fulfilled (or exceeded) quota.

* A *brigadier* is a head worker, foreman, or overseer.

We have conquered in the war; we will conquer in peace.

—AND BOTCH WORK *Don't look at the work—look at the workmanship.*

Slap, dash—and throw it in the trash.

Work quickly done must be undone and redone.

Situation normal: the sleigh is in Kazan, the harness in Ryazan, and the driver in Astrakhan.

It's done in good season but without rhyme or reason.

A bit of trash with a little dust on it.

WORLDLY WISDOM

Water from a friend is better than mead from an enemy.

A good brood hen keeps one eye on the feed and the other on the hawk.

Be trustful but keep your eyes peeled.

Remember three things to do: eat, learn, work.

To be without a fur coat in winter is no disgrace, but it sure is cold.

Ask in a voice of thunder and you will be answered with a cloudburst.

Don't whisper to the deaf, don't wink at the blind.

The wolf was fooling around with a horse, and he carried off his teeth in his paws.

The mare went to law against the wolf—all that was left of her was her tail, mane, and one hoof.

I want is half of *I can.*

To promise is human; not to carry out a promise is devilish.

Today is yesterday's pupil.

The best jest is at one's own expense.

A life on one's knees is worse than death.

> *These ain't meant for you*
> *and me, but some queer*
> *folk far far be-*
> *yond the*
> *sea*
>
> .

Interior by Melanie Kahane, A. I. D.

No modern library is complete
without THE AMERICAN
COLLEGE DICTIONARY

1472 pages • **7″ x 10″** • large, clear type, Buckram binding, thumb-indexed **$6.00**
Buckram binding, without index, **$5.00** • Special red Fabrikoid binding, in handsome gift box, **$7.50** • De luxe red leather binding, gold edges, gift box, **$15.00**